'Merely for Money'?

Business Culture
in the British Atlantic, 1750–1815

EIGHTEENTH-CENTURY WORLDS

SERIES EDITORS:
Professor Eve Rosenhaft (Liverpool) and Dr Mark Towsey (Liverpool)

Eighteenth-Century Worlds promotes innovative new research in the political, social, economic, intellectual and cultural life of the 'long' eighteenth century (c.1650–c.1850), from a variety of historical, theoretical and critical perspectives. Monographs published in the series adopt international, comparative and/or interdisciplinary approaches to the global eighteenth century, in volumes that make the results of specialist research accessible to an informed, but not discipline-specific, audience.

'Merely for Money'?

Business Culture in the British Atlantic,
1750–1815

Sheryllynne Haggerty

LIVERPOOL UNIVERSITY PRESS

First published 2012 by
Liverpool University Press
4 Cambridge Street
Liverpool
L69 7ZU

This paperback edition published 2014

Copyright © 2012, 2014 Liverpool University Press

British Library Cataloguing-in-Publication data
A British Library CIP record is available

ISBN 978-1-84631-817-7 *cased*
      978-1-78138-010-9 *paperback*

Typeset in Caslon by Carnegie Book Production, Lancaster
Printed and bound by the CPI Group (UK) Ltd, Croydon CR0 4YY

Life is a roller coaster
My thanks to John for sharing the ride

Contents

List of Tables

List of Figures

Acknowledgements

T HE IDEA FOR THIS BOOK came to me whilst writing my first monograph. Having argued for a varied trading community that had a common culture, it made sense to investigate exactly what the nature of that culture was. The research conducted in order to illuminate that culture has been funded by a variety of sources. In the first instance the pilot project 'Business Culture and Community: Liverpool in the 18th Century British Atlantic' was funded by the ESRC (2004–5) (RES-000-22-070). Important in accessing sources in the United States was the Caird North American Research Fellowship (2006), jointly funded by the National Maritime Museum (UK) and the John Carter Brown Library (Rhode Island, USA). Research at the National Archives was supported by the Historic Society of Lancashire and Cheshire (2010). Some of the data used here was collected whilst I was post-doctoral fellow on a Leverhulme-funded research project entitled 'Merchants and Merchandising: Kingston, Jamaica in the Eighteenth Century'. My thanks must therefore go to the grantholders Ken Morgan and Trevor Burnard for their generosity in being able to use this material. My special thanks must go to the School of History and the Dean of Arts' Fund at the University of Nottingham for funding my sabbatical 2009–10 which gave me the time to write this book.

I would also like to thank Martin Brett for his generous access to his ancestor's records (the letter book and autobiography of Curtis Brett), Mark Casson and John J. McCusker for letting me use unpublished material, and Julian Hoppit for allowing me early sight of a part of what became his 'Compulsion, Compensation and Property Rights in Britain, 1688–1833',

Past and Present, 210 (Feb. 2011), 93–128. Ben Dew was also very helpful in providing early access to his edited volume in *Tea and the Tea Table in Eighteenth-Century England* (London: Pickering and Chatto, 2010), Vol. IV, *Tea and Politics*. Manuel Llorca-Jaña was very kind in searching his records and providing information on merchants trading to Latin America, as were Nick Draper and Rachel Lang of the Legacies of British Slave Ownership project in providing information on mercantile links with the compensation claims. I would also like to extend my thanks to Barclays Group Archives for permission to use material from their Arthur Heywood & Sons collection. All of the staff at the Liverpool Record Office were extremely helpful, especially Paul Webster who freely extended his help and provided jovial conversation. I was also very appreciative of the temporary home and help given by all the staff and the fellows in residence at the John Carter Brown Library during the summer of 2006. John Haggerty provided technical guidance for using Pajek in constructing the network diagrams produced in chapter six.

Discussions with my third-year seminar groups on 'Early Entrepreneurs' and with Emily Buchnea and Katie McDade have proved extremely useful. Many people were kind enough to read and provide feedback on various chapters. For their time and valuable comments my thanks go to: Hannah Barker, Richard Gaunt, Marsha Hamilton, Mina Ishizu, Ken Morgan, David Ryden, Susanne Seymour, Liudmyla Sharipova, Sue Townsend, Tony Webster and John Wilson. I would also like to thank Andrew Popp for discussions on social capital and for his general enthusiasm. For their forbearance in reading drafts of the whole manuscript, and for their insightful comments, words cannot express my gratitude to John Haggerty and Graeme Milne. I would also like to thank three anonymous reviewers who provided thoughtful and constructive feedback. All remaining errors, are of course, mine alone. Last but not least, I would like to thank Liverpool University Press, especially Anthony Cond and Alison Welsby for believing in this book and Rachel Clarke and Laura Tristram at Carnegie Publishing for their patience and painstaking work in copyediting the manuscript.

On a more personal note I am grateful to Liudmyla Sharipova, Sue Townsend and Mathilde Von Bülow for their friendship and laughter. Koshka and Jemima gave me joy and helped me de-stress. Of course, the largest thanks has to go to my husband John for putting up with rants and ravings, lows and highs, and for his unswerving support. Mostly I would like to thank him for always enjoying the stories of the characters in this book with me. In this he helped me bring them to life.

Note on textual conventions

A FEW TECHNICAL POINTS should be noted. In order to distinguish between individuals and merchant 'houses' the ampersand has been used to designate a mercantile 'house' or 'firm'. Prices are given in sterling except where noted. Quotations are given verbatim, except that square brackets are used where contractions have been extended or explanations added and ellipses where quotations have been contracted. In order to avoid repetition, frequent cross-references are given.

Abbreviations

AJL	Alexander Johnston Letterbook
AJS	*American Journal of Sociology*
APS	American Philosophical Society
AQ	African Questions
BFBR	Brown Family Business Records
BH	*Business History*
BHR	*Business History Review*
BMP	Kenneth Morgan, ed., *The Bright-Meyler Papers: A Bristol West India Connection, 1732–1837* (Oxford: Oxford University Press for the British Academy, 2007).
BoT	Board of Trade
CBL	Curtis Brett Letterbook
CBP	Cadwalader Bond Papers
CFC	Cropper Family Collection
CRA	Company of Royal Adventurers of England Trading to Africa and Successors
CWU	Claude W. Unger Collection
DCL	Daniel Clark Letterbook
DTP	David Tuohy Papers
EC	Earle Collection
EcHR	*Economic History Review*
HCPP	House of Commons Parliamentary Papers
HCSP	Shiela Lambert, ed., House of Commons Sessional Papers of the Eighteenth Century (Wilmington, Delaware: Scholarly Resources, 1975).

HLP	George C. Rogers Jr., ed., *The Papers of Henry Laurens*, Vols IV, V, VI, VII (Columbia, SC: Published for the South Carolina Historical Society by the University of South Carolina Press, 1974).
HSP	Historical Society of Pennsylvania
JJL	Joshua Johnson Letterbook
LCP	Library Company of Philadelphia
LivRO	Liverpool Record Office
LP	Liverpool Papers
MMMA	Merseyside Maritime Museum Archives
NAS	National Archives of Scotland
MHS	Massachusetts Historical Society
NLJ	National Library of Jamaica
NLS	National Library of Scotland
PEC	Papers of Edward Chaffers
PP	Parker Papers
RBL	Robert Bostock Letterbook
RP	Roscoe Papers
SGC	Simon Gratz Collection
SJLP	Semple, Jamieson, Lawson Papers
TLL	Thomas Leyland Letterbook
TNA	The Public Record Office at The National Archives (UK)
WDP	William Davenport Papers
WMQ	*William and Mary Quarterly*
WPL	William Pollard Letterbook

Introduction
Merely For Money?

To Trade: To traffick, to deal, to hold commerce;
to act merely for money; having a trading wind.[1]

THOMAS SHERIDAN'S COMMENT, insinuating that traders acted 'merely for money', encapsulates the premise of this book – or rather, the mirror of it. That is, this book argues that the business culture of the British Atlantic was one which was socially embedded and did not allow for pure profit maximising, at least in the short term – hence the question mark. In fact, Sheridan is more likely commenting on the idea that traders did not produce anything *per se*, but worked for profit from trade.[2] Indeed, many merchants were successful in making money and were well respected for doing so. By the second half of the eighteenth century a merchant was someone who 'trafficks to remote countries', a man of 'genius', noble and independent, who employed the poor and encouraged the industrious.[3] Their importance

---

1 Thomas Sheridan, *A General Dictionary of the English Language* [1780] (Menston: Scolar Press Limited, 1967).

2 The negative connotation of not producing anything was usually reserved for brokers, and especially stock brokers, who were seen as 'pests' who moved the stock of others around without risking their own capital. Huw W. Bowen, '"The Pests of Human Society": Stockbrokers, Jobbers and Speculators in Mid-Eighteenth-Century Britain', *History*, 78:252 (Feb. 1993), 38–53.

3 Sheridan, *A General Dictionary*; Joshua Montefiore, *The Trader's and Manufacturer's Compendium; Containing the Laws, Customs, and Regulations, Relative to Trade; Intended for the use of Wholesale and Retail Dealers*, 2 vols, Vol. I (London: Printed for the author, 1804), p. 284; *The Tradesman: Or, Commercial Magazine* (London: Sherwood, Neely & Jones, 1808), p. 66; William Gordon, *The Universal Accountant and Complete Merchant. In Two Volumes* (Edinburgh: Printed for the Author, and A. Donaldson, and sold by Donaldson at Edinburgh & Strand, London, 1763), Vol. I, p. 1.

to the economic well being of the country led the political œconomist Malachy Postlethwayt to consider the merchant 'the most useful Member of the Society in which he lives'.[4] Contemporaries clearly held merchants in high regard. Importantly, they enjoyed this approbation because the business culture that facilitated their success was informed, framed and shaped by the wider social, economic, political and cultural milieu in which these merchants operated. Therefore, they were not atomised, profit-maximising, rational economic men. Through self-enforcing behavioural patterns as a community, which were internalized and emotionalized to a large extent, their business culture formed a private-order institution that facilitated trade around the Atlantic during the turbulent period 1750–1815.[5] There was no way they could act 'merely for money'.

Moreover, these men were extremely sophisticated in their understanding of commerce. Their detailed and nuanced conception of their role demands a more complex approach if we are to understand their motivations for, approach to, and management of, their businesses. This book therefore takes an interdisciplinary approach. Whilst Sheridan's comment mirrors the premise behind this book, the cover image, a bill of exchange, represents the 'institutional elements' of their business culture, as informed by socio-economic literature.[6] The bill of exchange represents first, the risk merchants took in extending the credit that facilitated international commerce, including with people they never met, in new and faraway markets across the Atlantic ocean; second, it represents the personal trust that the debtor would pay, the assurance that laws would enforce payment if not, and confidence in the wider trading system; third, both the debtor and creditor were trusting to the reputation of the acceptor on whom the bill was drawn to honour the payment; fourth, there was an obligation for the drawee or acceptor to pay, but also for the remitter or drawer to give advance notice to, and to have the necessary credit with, the drawee;[7] fifth, this was all reliant on knowing

---

4 Malachy Postlethwayt, *Great Britain's True System* [1757] (New York: Augustus M. Kelley, 1968), Letter I, 'Of Increasing the Supplies, by Increasing the Public Debts, Considered', pp. 1–24, p. 21.

5 This was true even in non-repeat trade. Jean-Phillipe Platteau, 'Behind the Market Stage Where Real Societies Exist – Part 1: The Role of Public and Private Order Institutions', *Journal of Development Studies*, 30:3 (Apr. 1994), 533–77, p. 557.

6 Avner Greif uses the term 'institutional element' in arguing that reputational mechanisms were the main institutional elements of the Maghrabi business culture, *Institutions and the Path to the Modern Economy: Lessons from Medieval Trade* (Cambridge: Cambridge University Press, 2006).

7 Ephraim Chambers, *Cyclopædia: Or, Universal Dictionary of the Arts and Sciences. With A Supplement and Modern Improvements Incorporated in one Alphabet* (London: Printed

people with whom to take risks and whom to trust, gaining information on reputation and the social pressure to fulfil obligations – the merchants' networks. A bill of exchange was usually as small as around fifteen by ten centimetres and written on a flimsy bit of paper; it therefore also represents the fragile, illusive and emotive nature of the business culture, as well as its strength and versatility.

This book aims to understand these merchants and their business culture within the framework of the British-Atlantic world, or more precisely, the English-speaking Atlantic, and the areas with which those people traded. It is therefore Atlantic history as well as economic or business history.[8] Whilst the Atlantic was far from being the only sphere of expansion in the early-modern period, it was the dominant one for European powers and one which linked the four continents of Europe, Africa, North America and South America together. This was especially true of trade. Commerce was a major way in which these continents and their peoples and cultures were brought together, and economic history has been especially influential in the historiography of the British Atlantic.[9] Moreover, because merchants did not always adhere to geo-political constructs, whatever the wishes of their government,

---

for J. F. and C. Rivington, A. Hamilton, T. Payne and Son, W. Owen, B. White and Son (and 24 others in London), 1786–88), pp. 30–1, 470–1.

8 To some extent Atlantic history has been an Anglo-American enterprise, developing out of post-war discussions. See for example, Bernard Bailyn, *Atlantic History: Concepts and Contours* (Cambridge, MA and London: Harvard University Press, 2005); William O'Reilly, 'Genealogies of Atlantic History', *Atlantic Studies*, 1:1 (2004), 66–95. It is therefore an approach that does not always allow for other Atlantics or empires to fit in so easily, for example, the French or Amerindian. Bill Marshall, *The French Atlantic: Travels in Culture and History* (Liverpool: Liverpool University Press, 2009), pp. 3–5; Paul Cohen, 'Was there an Amerindian Atlantic? Reflections on the Limits of a Historiographical Concept', *History of European Ideas*, 34 (2008), 388–410.

9 Ian K. Steele, *The English Atlantic 1675–1740: An Exploration of Communication and Community* (New York: Oxford University Press, 1986); Kenneth Morgan, *Bristol and the Atlantic Trade in the Eighteenth Century* (Cambridge: Cambridge University Press, 1993); David Hancock, *Citizens of the World: London Merchants and the Integration of the British Atlantic Community, 1735–1785* (Cambridge: Cambridge University Press, 1995); John J. McCusker and Kenneth Morgan, eds., *The Early Modern Atlantic Economy* (Cambridge: Cambridge University Press, 2000); Douglas J. Hamilton, *Scotland, the Caribbean and the Atlantic World, 1750–1820* (Manchester: Manchester University Press, 2005); Simon D. Smith, *Slavery, Family, and Gentry Capitalism in the British Atlantic: The World of the Lascelles, 1648–1834* (Cambridge: Cambridge University Press, 2006); David Beck Ryden, *West Indian Slavery and British Abolition, 1783–1807* (Cambridge: Cambridge University Press, 2009); Nuala Zahediah, *The Capital and the Colonies: London and the Atlantic Economy* (Cambridge: Cambridge University Press, 2010).

a history of the merchant community also helps to alleviate potential issues of any perceived boundaries of Atlantic worlds or accusations of academic myopia.[10]

Therefore, whilst clearly centred on the British Atlantic, this book is not constrained by it. The focus is on trade between Great Britain, mainland northern America and the British Caribbean, but also includes the Western Coast of Africa and occasionally the French and Spanish territories around the Atlantic littoral where the British traded (legally and illegally). The time period, 1750–1815, has been chosen because it was one of long-term structural change punctuated by periods of short-term crises. In the long term it arguably covers two high points of the 'first' British Empire. What constituted that empire, and indeed the time-frame of it, is contested, but if we think in terms of a 'mercantilist', maritime trading empire we have a useful framework that is not too constrictive.[11] The Seven Years' War left Britain dominant in the Atlantic, and by the end of the French Wars Britain was also a major European and world imperial power.[12] This time period also covers three low points of the first empire: the 'loss' of the thirteen continental colonies, the decline (if not demise) of the mercantilist system, and another conflict with its former colonists in the Anglo-American War. In the short term, there were many credit crises (particularly in 1772, 1793 and 1810), wars during 1756–1763, 1775–1783 and 1793–1815, and many periods of political tension. This period is therefore excellent for examining how a British-Atlantic business culture functioned and coped, both in the long and short term.

In order to make manageable the vast array of sources available to such an undertaking, Liverpool is used as the axis for analysis. Liverpool was

---

10 See the discussions for example in David Eltis, 'Atlantic History in Global Perspective', *Itinerario*, 23:2 (1999), 141–61; Jack P. Greene, 'Comparing Early Modern Worlds: Some Reflections on the Promise of a Hemispheric Perspective', *History Compass*, 1 (Aug. 2003), 1–10; Peter A. Coclanis, 'Atlantic World or Atlantic/World?', *WMQ*, 63:4 (Oct. 2006), 725–42; Paul W. Mapp, 'Atlantic History from Imperial, Continental, and Pacific Perspectives', *WMQ*, 63:4 (Oct. 2006), 713–24; Aaron Spencer Fogelman, 'The Transformation of the Atlantic World, 1776–1867', *Atlantic Studies*, 6:1 (Apr. 2009), 5–28; Cohen, 'Was there an Amerindian Atlantic?'.

11 The term 'mercantilism' is of course also contested. See the further discussion below, p. 17. On notions of empire and especially of the sea, see David Armitage, *The Ideological Origins of the British Empire* (Cambridge: Cambridge University Press, 2000), esp. chapter four.

12 Lawrence Stone, 'Introduction', in Lawrence Stone, ed., *An Imperial State at War: Britain From 1689–1815* (London and New York: Routledge, 1994), pp. 1–32, p. 20; Christopher A. Bayly, *The Birth of the Modern World, 1780–1914: Global Connections and Comparisons* (Malden, MA: Blackwell Publishing Limited, 2004), p. 128.

the leading outport in the British Atlantic at this point, perhaps the most important in the Atlantic trade, and was the 'second seaport of the realm'.[13] It therefore represents a good case study. This also means that this book is slightly biased towards the experience of Britain, especially as both it, and its chronology, progresses. However, sources have been consulted in Britain, the United States and Jamaica in order to facilitate the analysis of a business culture which existed between merchants in Liverpool and their associates in Halifax (Nova Scotia), Providence (Rhode Island), Boston, New York, Philadelphia, Charleston, Baltimore, Norfolk (Virginia), Kingston (Jamaica), many other ports in the West Indies and the west coast of Africa, as well as other ports in Britain including Glasgow, Bristol and London. The United States is included as part of the British Atlantic as trade between the two areas remained economically interdependent despite the political break of 1783. Discretionary 'artistic licence' has occasionally meant the use of manuscripts not only of the associates of Liverpool merchants, but their associates in turn where it was clear that they were part of related wider networks and the same business culture. These sources include mercantile letters and accounts, House of Commons Sessional and Parliamentary Papers, records of the Board of Trade, Exchequer, Chancery, Colonial Office, Admiralty, Treasury, Privy Council and State Papers Foreign, newspapers, trade directories, formal and informal associational membership, merchant petitions and memorials, tracts on political economy and advice literature. Large collections regarding well-known individual merchants have been eschewed on the whole, except where those collections are available as printed editions or where expansion by geographical spread was required. This has facilitated the inclusion of as many merchants of varying degrees of prosperity as possible, rather than only the most successful. Moreover, using a variety of sources other than manuscripts shows the merchants in different arenas and has highlighted connections between them not necessarily obvious by using a few major collections. This is in accordance with the approach taken by Miles Ogborn in *Global Lives*, David Lambert and Alan Lester's 'Imperial Spaces, Imperial Subjects', and Margo Finn's call to 'personalise the process' and to 'link the micro with the macro'.[14] It has of course to be recognised, however, that in

---

13 Montefiore, *Trader's and Manufacturer's Compendium*, p. 476. One contemporary thought the United States 'infinitely more connected with the port of Liverpool than London', John Perhouse to James Perhouse, 4 Apr. 1806, John Perhouse Journal 1800–1838, APS; J. K. McDowell claimed the position of second city of empire for Glasgow in 1899. Quoted in John MacKenzie, '"The Second City of Empire": Glasgow – Imperial Municipality', in Felix Driver and David Gilbert, eds., *Imperial Cities* (Oxford: Oxford University Press, 1999), pp. 215–37, p. 215.

14 Miles Ogborn, *Global Lives: Britain and the World, 1500–1800*, Cambridge Studies

order to elucidate these stories it has still been necessary, by the very nature of the extant sources, to concentrate on a minority of the trading community, and an even smaller proportion of the wider population. For example, the trading community as a whole usually represented only about 2.5 to 3.5 per cent of the whole population of any port, and the merchants less than half of that.[15] Indeed, many of the merchants presented here were successful men, but not all were so, and in using this wider frame of reference it is hoped that the sources consulted are more representative of the generality of mercantile experience around the Atlantic. As Julian Hoppit has shown, investigating failure is illuminating in itself.[16] Some merchants had strong personalities or stories which clearly shone through in their records, and they are often given prominence. Many were pragmatic, some were enthusiastic, others were worriers and a few downright unpleasant. Hopefully, they will come to life through their own words and experiences.

As mentioned above, in order to elucidate the business culture of these men, socio-economic theory has been consciously and explicitly employed.[17] This is important for two reasons. First, as John Smail has noted, the economy and culture are two aspects of the same phenomenon.[18] Second, using socio-economic theory has facilitated a far more nuanced understanding

---

in Historical Geography, 41 (Cambridge: Cambridge University Press, 2008); David Lambert and Alan Lester 'Imperial Spaces, Imperial Subjects', in David Lambert and Alan Lester, eds., Colonial Lives Across the British Empire: Imperial Careering in the Long Nineteenth Century (Cambridge: Cambridge University Press, 2006), pp. 1–31; Margot Finn, 'Anglo-Indian Lives in the Later Eighteenth and Nineteenth Centuries', Journal for Eighteenth-Century Studies, 33:1 (Mar. 2010), 49–65, p. 52.

15 Sheryllynne Haggerty, The British-Atlantic Trading Community 1760–1810: Men, Women, and the Distribution of Goods (Leiden: Brill Press, 2006), pp. 67, 75, 77. In Boston the number of merchants ran at somewhere between those of Liverpool and Philadelphia in the 1760, 1770s and 1780s. John W. Tyler, 'Persistence and Change within the Boston Business Community, 1775–1790', in Conrad Edick Wright and Kathryn P. Viens, eds., Entrepreneurs: The Boston Business Community, 1700–1850 (Boston: Massachusetts Historical Society, 1997), pp. 97–119, pp. 101–2. The figure was higher in unrepresentative London where merchants accounted for around ten per cent of all householders. Zahediah, The Capital and the Colonies, p. 23.

16 Julian Hoppit, Risk and Failure in English Business 1700–1800 (Cambridge: Cambridge University Press, 1987).

17 This study has also confined itself to this literature because scholars in other disciplines such as Finance and Management or Geography conceptualise ideas such as risk in different ways. See for example, G. Dickinson, 'Enterprise Risk Management: Its Origins and Conceptual Foundation', The Geneva Papers on Risk and Insurance, 26:3 (2001), 360–66; Noel Castree, Nature (London and New York: Routledge, 2005).

18 John Smail, 'The Culture of Credit in Eighteenth-Century Commerce', Enterprise & Society, 4:2 (2003), 299–325, p. 301.

of the merchants' attitudes, motivations, and business management. Other historians have taken an interdisciplinary approach to great effect. These include Craig Muldrew on obligation, Avner Greif on reputational mechanisms, Dario Gaggio on social capital, and Francesca Trivellato on diasporas and institutions.[19] This book adds to that literature by taking risk, trust, reputation, obligation and networks to *all* be inter-related institutional elements of the business culture of the early-modern British Atlantic. In doing so it uses socio-economic theorists already well known to historians such as Robert Putnam, Francis Fukuyama, Mark Granovetter, Alejandro Portes and Mark Casson. However, it also uses the works of many other excellent (if less well known to historians) sociologists and economists. This has facilitated a sophisticated and nuanced analysis of the 'institutional elements', which in turn stresses the highly sophisticated nature of business culture in this period. For example, merchants clearly perceived and managed different types of risks appropriately. They were painfully aware of the need for personal trust, especially because they had to work in a system where institutional and general levels of trust were constantly in flux. Merchants also carefully constructed and managed their personal reputations, and used community reputations to their advantage. They tried their hardest to fulfil their obligations but found that the more successful they were, the more obligations were placed upon them. They used their networks in an instrumental manner, but found that networks were often abused as well as useful. These elements all came together to form a business culture which was both flexible and durable. Importantly, many aspects of this business culture were socially embedded. Therefore, whilst on many occasions these men were clearly conscious of acting out a role, many of their beliefs and norms were truly internalised and emotions often ran high. Using these theories explicitly has facilitated an engagement with primary sources in a new way. In doing so it is hoped that this book is not only academically rigorous, but accessible.

The next chapter provides the context for this business culture in terms of space, place and people. That is, the wider Atlantic world, the ports

---

19 Craig Muldrew, *The Economy of Obligation: The Culture of Credit and Social Relations in Early Modern England* (Basingstoke and New York: Palgrave, 1998); Greif, *Institutions and the Path to the Modern Economy*; Dario Gaggio, *In Gold we Trust: Social Capital and Economic Change in the Italian Jewellery Towns* (Princeton and Oxford: Princeton University Press, 2007); Francesca Trivellato, *The Familiarity of Strangers: The Sephardic Diaspora, Livorno, and Cross Cultural Trade in the Early Modern Period* (New Haven and London: Yale University Press, 2009). Xabier Lamikiz positively eschews theory, but still finds the concept of trust extremely useful in *Trade and Trust in the Eighteenth-Century Atlantic: Spanish Merchants and Their Overseas Networks* (Woodbridge, Suffolk and Rochester, New York: Boydell Press for the Royal Historical Society, 2010).

and commodities in which these merchants traded and some of the major personalities involved. The book then comprises three sets of linking chapters. First: risk and trust. The chapter on risk investigates how merchants conceived and managed various kinds of risks, whether natural, moral or technical, and argues that merchants perceived and managed these in different ways. The following chapter investigates how personal, institutional and general levels of trust were constructed, and the relationship between them. Of course risk and trust are closely interrelated, and this relationship is also explored. The second set of chapters focuses on reputation and obligation. These obviously link with risk and trust, but to a greater extent with each other, because only by fulfilling obligations could merchants retain their reputation. Therefore how personal reputations were constructed is investigated, but also how they were deconstructed through both gossip and the inability to fulfil obligations of various kinds. Furthermore, these two chapters also touch on the importance of reputation at the community and national level, and the concomitant obligations that attended success. The third set of chapters is designed to test the former. In particular, the chapter on networks sets out to demonstrate the dynamic but problematic nature of networks, and their use and function within business. In contrast to the cautionary tone regarding the use, abuse and success of networks, the chapter on crises provides a positive analysis of how the business culture in the British Atlantic dealt with the turbulent times the merchants experienced, and considers how three major events subtly changed aspects of that business culture over time. The conclusion picks up on a theme that runs throughout, the role of the British state, and argues that it was important in providing the context for successful British commerce in this period. However, more important was the business culture of the merchants which provided a socially-embedded, private-order institution. This allowed them to not only trade, but to regulate themselves in a period of immense change and thereby cope, manage, and even thrive, despite all the challenges they faced.

I

Space, Place and People

may your sales still increase and the elbows of your coat
be worn out in weighing the Jon. Pistoles.[1]

W HILST THE BUSINESS CULTURE of the merchants was shaped by the
wider economic, social, and cultural milieu in which they functioned,
Joshua Johnson's riposte in 1772 demonstrates that the long-term goal was to
make a profit. As Isaac Wikoff noted two years later, 'The Design of Trade
is to make a profit in the End. I am sure I would have Quit a business
immediately in which no Evident profit should arise.'[2] Johnson's reference to
weighing the pistoles and the 'Johannes' or 'Joe' conjures a wonderful image
of an avaricious merchant, but it also underscores the wider Atlantic context
in which these merchants interacted with the Spanish and Portuguese, and
indeed, other empires.[3] This chapter therefore sets the wider context for this
study. It first outlines the Atlantic world, and in particular, Britain's approach
to the Atlantic economy viz-à-viz that of Portugal, Spain, the Netherlands
and France. It then outlines the institutional framework in which British
merchants traded, and the major ports and commodities involved. Lastly, it
outlines some of the major characters that appear in this book. Some of these
men did not earn enough to wear out the elbows of their coats in counting
their profits, but most did come into contact with pistoles at one time or
another.

---

1 Joshua Johnson to Wallace & Davidson, 18 Feb. 1772, JJL.
2 Isaac Wikoff to Peter Ewer, 4 May 1774, Folder Isaac Wikoff to Peter Ewer, CBP.
3 The pistole was a contemporary term for the Spanish doblon, and the 'Johannes' or
'Joe' for the Portuguese dobra de quarto escudos, or peça. John J. McCusker, *Money
and Exchange in Europe and America 1600–1775: A Handbook* (London and Basingstoke,
MacMillan, 1978), pp. 5–6.

Space: The European Atlantic Economies

THE ATLANTIC OCEAN is a huge expanse of water. The north Atlantic touches Britain, Spain, France and Portugal, the north west coast of Africa, and from Greenland, by Nova Scotia, down the eastern seaboard of the United States to the West Indies. The southern Atlantic stretches along western Africa, down the coast of Brazil, Uruguay and Argentina to the Falkland Islands. Some would argue that the Atlantic world does not end there, so ensconced in Atlantic trade was the silver from Potosí (present-day Bolivia) for example.[4] The Atlantic ocean itself encompasses 26 per cent of the world's surface – over 36,000,000 square miles – and its depth ranges from just over 4,000 metres to more than 10,000.[5] Despite this vast expanse, it was already a space in which everything was on the move by the early-modern era, whether this was people, ideas or commodities. Vast numbers of people traversed this ocean, some by choice, many more by force. Between 1500 and 1820 2.5 million Europeans left for the 'New World', and more than 8.5 million Africans made the infamous 'middle passage'.[6] Notions about what the Atlantic ocean was, or could be used for, differed between Europeans, Africans and Amerindians, and frontiers and borders were changing all the time.[7] The making of the 'Atlantic world' was therefore a contested process, as indeed it has been in its historiography.[8] Both Europeans and Africans

---

4 See the discussion above, p. 3.

5 *Philip's World Atlas and Gazeteer* (9th edn), in Association with The Royal Geographical Society with the Institute of British Geographers (London: George Philip, 2001), p. 8.

6 James Horn and Philip D. Morgan, 'Settlers and Slaves: European and African Migrations to Early Modern British America', in Elizabeth Mancke and Carole Shammas, eds., *The Creation of the British Atlantic World* (Baltimore and London: Johns Hopkins University Press, 2005), pp. 19–44, p. 20.

7 James Taylor Carson, 'When Is An Ocean Not An Ocean? Geographies of the Atlantic World', *Southern Quarterly*, 43 (2006), 16–46.

8 For example, there are many 'Atlantics' posited such as the Portuguese, Dutch, French, Spanish or Amerindian, but also the white, green and black Atlantics, the latter dominating much of the literature. For the Portuguese, Spanish, Dutch and French Atlantics see below, pp. 12–15. See also Cohen, 'Was there an Amerindian Atlantic?'; Kevin Whelan, 'The Green Atlantic: Radical Reciprocities between Ireland and America in the Long Eighteenth Century', in Kathleen Wilson, ed., *A New Imperial History: Culture, Identity and Modernity in Britain and the Empire, 1660–1840* (Cambridge: Cambridge University Press, 2004), pp. 216–38; Allan Greer and Kenneth Mills, 'A Catholic Atlantic', in Jorge Cañizares-Esguerra and Erik Seeman, eds., *The Atlantic in Global History* (Upper Saddle, NJ and London: Pearson Education, 2006), pp. 3–19; Deborah Gray White, 'Yes, There is a Black Atlantic', *Itinerario*, 23:2 (1999), 127–40; Paul Gilroy, *The Black Atlantic: Modernity and Double Consciousness* (Cambridge, MA: Harvard University Press, 1993).

took too much cultural baggage with them to the Americas for it to be easily discarded; yet 'New Spain was clearly not old Spain, nor was New England old England.'[9] In the American South and the West Indies, African 'survivals' also led to syncretism rather than acculturation.[10] Despite the fact that Europeans chose to categorise the members of the various societies they encountered in the Americas simply as 'Indians', they differed at least as much as the various peoples of Europe. These various peoples, their ideas and their commodities, all served not only as 'a connecting element between European, North American, Caribbean, Latin American and West African History', but to transform their political, social and material cultures.[11]

Whilst a few of the first Europeans to cross the Atlantic may have been truly driven by a spirit of adventure, the majority were driven by greed and/or ambition.[12] Those ambitions were backed, and sometimes exceeded by, the various states to which those individuals belonged.[13] Whilst the most

---

9 J. H. Elliott, *Empires of the Atlantic World: Britain and Spain in America, 1492–1830* (New Haven, Connecticut and London: Yale University Press, 2006), pp. xiii–xiv. On English migration to America see Alison Games, *Migration and the Origins of the English Atlantic World* (Cambridge, MA and London: Harvard University Press, 1999).

10 See for example, Orlando L. Patterson, 'Slavery, Acculturation and Social Change: The Jamaican Case', *British Journal of Sociology*, 17 (1966), 151–64; Eugene D. Genovese, *Roll, Jordan, Roll: The World the Slaves Made* (New York: Vintage Books, 1972). On the transference of ideas, identities and notions of the other see Colin Kidd, *British Identities before Nationalism: Ethnicity and Nationhood in the Atlantic World, 1600–1800* (Cambridge: Cambridge University Press, 1999); Wim Klooster, *Revolutions in the Atlantic World: A Comparative History* (New York: New York University Press, 2009); John Thornton, *Africa and Africans in the Making of the Atlantic World* (Cambridge: Cambridge University Press, 1998); Tim Fulford, *Romantic Indians: Native Americans: British Literature, and TransAtlantic Culture, 1756–1830* (Oxford: Oxford University Press, 2006).

11 Horst Pietschmann, 'Introduction: Atlantic History – History between European History and Global History', in Horst Pietschmann, ed., *Atlantic History: History of the Atlantic System 1580–1830* (Göttingen: Vandenhoeck and Ruprecht, 2002), pp. 11–54, p. 36; James Taylor Carson, *Making An Atlantic World: Circles, Paths, and Stories from the Colonial South* (Knoxville, TN: The University of Tennessee Press, 2007).

12 Pietschmann posits four phases for this European expansion: first, the thirteenth to the mid-fifteenth century – dominated by the Reconquista; second, 1460–1580 which was the high point of Iberian expansion; third, 1580–1702/1714 with the rise of the French, Dutch and English empires; and last, 1714–1830, during which there was a rise in European conflicts over trading rights and acquisition of territory often formerly referred to as the 'Age of Discovery' or 'Age of Conquest' in much of the historiography. Pietschmann, 'Introduction', pp. 19, 12–13.

13 Bayly argues that much British imperial expansion was set in motion by the state for

infamous 'commodity' transported across the Atlantic was enslaved Africans, it was gold that first lured Europeans into the Atlantic, precious metals being an important part of the 'mercantilist' framework. The Portuguese were the first to venture into this ocean, by way of Africa. They captured Ceuta – on the northern tip of Africa – from the Moors in 1415, which gave them access to the upper Niger and Senegal, and thereby gold. Once Álvares Cabral's fleet found what was to become Brazil in April 1550, the experience of the Portuguese in Africa encouraged them to engage more in the slave trade for labour to grow sugar, with convenient religious sanction from various Papal Bulls.[14] In the sixteenth century Portugal's Atlantic expansion was challenged only by pirates from France, Holland and England.[15] However, the crown imposed such heavy duties on sugar that the benefits of empire accrued only to the Portuguese monarchy and the city of Lisbon. Finding gold in the late seventeenth century, and diamonds in the early eighteenth century (both in Menas Gerais), briefly rescued the Portuguese, but both commodities were again subject to heavy duties and so economic growth remained constrained.[16] Furthermore, the Portuguese empire's trade networks came under attack as a result of the persecution of Portuguese merchants in both Iberia and America for being 'crypto jews'. Therefore, despite the Pombaline reforms of the later eighteenth century, Portugal's Atlantic empire fell into decline.[17]

Spanish incursion into the Atlantic began in 1492 when Ferdinand and Isabella sponsored Columbus, a rare example of direct financial participation by the Spanish crown. Like Portugal, they had the backing of, and legitimisation from, the Alexandrine Bulls. It is far from clear that the motivations behind the Spanish Atlantic were of conquest rather than commerce, but the discovery of silver mines at Potosí in the high Andes in 1545 and in Zacatecas in northern Mexico a year later, was important in shaping how Spain perceived and controlled its Atlantic economy.[18] First, the safe shipment of silver back to Spain was given primary importance, with

example. Christopher A. Bayly, *Imperial Meridian: The British Empire and the World, 1780–1830* (Harlow: Longman, 1989), p. 102. He later says however, that 'government in all these great states was often something of a trick of the light'. Bayly, *The Birth of the Modern World*, p. 31.

14 Charles R. Boxer, *The Portuguese Seaborne Empire 1415–1825* (London: Hutchinson, 1969), chapters one and four.

15 Paul Butel, *The Atlantic*, tr. Iain Hamilton Grant (London and New York: Routledge, 1999), p. 130.

16 Boxer, *The Portuguese Seaborne Empire*, chapter seven.

17 Lamikiz, *Trade and Trust*, p. 6; Boxer, *The Portuguese Seaborne Empire*, pp. 191–94.

18 James Lang, *Conquest and Commerce: Spain and England in the Americas* (New York and London: Academic Press, 1975), p. 7.

all other commodities relegated to a lesser status. Second, the influx of that silver encouraged the Spanish crown and Castillians to live a lavish lifestyle that could not be supported in the long term. Third, the need to protect this cargo and for the state to siphon taxes from it, led to a monopoly system based in Seville on the *Carrera de Indias* and the *Casa de la Contración*.[19] In consequence, despite the desires and successes of conquistadores such as Hernán Cortès, commentators in Spain began to question the over-reliance on imports of metals as early as the 1580s, and by 1600 there was already talk of the 'decline' of the Spanish empire.[20] By the eighteenth century their role in Atlantic commerce was marginal.[21] The Bourbon reforms of the eighteenth century provided a new emphasis on trade, but by then it was clear that the British model was the one to emulate.[22]

Early Dutch Atlantic expansion is difficult to pinpoint, but attempts were made to colonise an area on the northern coast of South America as early as 1580, and a trading post in the Paramibo region, on the Suriname river, was established in 1613. Further north, the Dutch colony of New Netherland was formally established in 1614 but controlled by the Dutch West India Company from 1623 (established in 1621). The Dutch were also involved in the carrying trade for the Portuguese to Brazil, and for the English tobacco trade in the Chesapeake.[23] The disastrous year of 1672 during which they were at war with England and subject to invasions by French and German troops, is often seen as a watershed moment. Indeed, the Dutch chartered a new West India Company (1674), but their ambitions were smaller. Despite their misfortunes, the Atlantic trade continued to be lucrative for the Dutch, and they continued to be a major supplier of slaves to the French and Spanish to St. Eustatius and Curaçao respectively, and traded with North America, especially to North Carolina for rice.[24] However, the wars in Europe and the Atlantic of the late seventeenth and early eighteenth centuries – during which it subjugated its Atlantic interests in order to defend its interests at

---

19 Elliott, *Empires of the Atlantic World*, pp. 22–25, 406, 408, 110, 49. The *Casa de la Contración* supervised the American trade for the crown. For the failure of the *Carrera de Indias* see Lamikiz, *Trade and Trust*, chapter three.

20 Elliott, *Empires of the Atlantic World*, p. 26.

21 Lamikiz, *Trade and Trust*, p. 2.

22 Lamikiz, *Trade and Trust*, p. 14.

23 Victor Enthoven, 'Early Dutch Expansion in the Atlantic Region, 1585–1621', in Johannes Postma and Victor Enthoven, eds., *Riches from Atlantic Commerce: Dutch Transatlantic Trade and Shipping 1585–1817* (Leiden and Boston: Brill Press, 2003), pp. 17–47. Pietschmann argues that they lost their colony in Brazil as much to rebels as to the Portuguese, 'Introduction', p. 41.

24 Wim Klooster, 'An Overview of Dutch Trade with the Americas', in Postma and Enthoven, *Riches from Atlantic Commerce*, pp. 365–83, pp. 375–79.

home – forced the Dutch to withdraw from the competition for empire in the Atlantic.[25]

The French first entered the Atlantic by fishing for cod off the coast of Newfoundland, where by 1580 they arguably had the largest fleet in the Atlantic.[26] There were also some abortive attempts to create settlements in Brazil and Florida in the 1550s and 1560s, but it was not until 1608, with the foundation of Quebec, that they entered a more formal or colonial phase of expansion.[27] The French were also heavily involved in the slave trade. They were the third largest carrier after Portugal and Great Britain, and were often in competition with the British on the West African coast, especially in the later eighteenth century.[28] By the mid-eighteenth century 'France challenged British ambitions to control world trade.'[29] France's obsession with its sugar islands following the 'sugar revolution' in the Caribbean meant that they were large producers of sugar which brought them vast amounts of wealth; the French also dominated coffee production. However, the 'unashamed wealth' of St. Domingue meant that France abandoned any real attempt at a continental empire, especially after its navy was destroyed during the Seven Years' War, and its American empire became rather insular.[30] Despite this loss, France's Atlantic trade was at its height in the third quarter of the century.[31]

25 Butel, *The Atlantic*, p. 131; Jan de Vries, 'The Dutch Atlantic Economies', in Peter A. Coclanis, ed., *The Atlantic Economy during the Seventeenth and Eighteenth Centuries: Organization, Operation, Practice, and Personnel* (Columbia, SC: University of South Carolina Press, 2005), pp. 1–29, p. 9.

26 Laurier Turgeon, 'Codfish, Consumption and Colonization: The Creation of the French Atlantic World during the Sixteenth Century', in Caroline A. Williams, ed., *Bridging the Early Modern Atlantic: People, Products and Practices on the Move* (Aldershot: Ashgate, 2009), pp. 33–56, pp. 34–37.

27 Marshall, *The French Atlantic*, pp. 65 and 2; see also Butel, *The Atlantic*, pp. 113–15.

28 David Eltis, 'The Volume and Structure of the Transatlantic Slave Trade: A Reassessment', *WMQ*, 3rd ser., 58:1, New Perspectives on the Transatlantic Slave Trade (Jan. 2001), 17–46, p. 43; Marshall, *The French Atlantic*, p. 46. The number of French vessels engaged in the slave trade more than doubled between 1764 and 1789. Pierre H. Boulle and D. Gillian Thompson, 'France Overseas', in William Doyle, ed., *Old Regime France 1648–1788* (Oxford: Oxford University Press, 2001), pp. 105–38, p. 134. See the discussions regarding French competition below, pp. 127, 157–58, 219–20.

29 Boulle and Thompson, 'France Overseas', p. 105.

30 Jack Greene, John J. Tepaske, Edward L. Cox, Kenneth R. Maxwell and Anne Perotin-Dumon, 'The Atlantic Empires in the Eighteenth Century', *International History Review*, 6:4 (Nov. 1984), 507–69, pp. 555–56; Butel, *The Atlantic*, pp. 122, 153; William Doyle, 'Introduction', in Doyle, *Old Regime France*, pp. 1–6, p. 5. On the so-called sugar revolution see B. W. Higman, 'The Sugar Revolution', *EcHR*, 53:2 (2000), 213–36.

31 Boulle and Thompson, 'France Overseas', pp. 130–34.

However, it was a fragile economy, and a series of crises spelt the end of the old regime by 1788, reducing the French Atlantic to a few island outposts.[32]

The English arrived late on the Atlantic scene. No doubt lured by stories of Spanish success, John Cabot was authorised to conquer and possess any territory in the north Atlantic in 1496. However, a number of religious and succession issues dominated policy at home, and it was only around 1580 that Atlantic exploration was taken seriously by the English. In 1584 Walter Raleigh led his abortive attempt to set up a colony and privateering base at Roanoke Island, off the coast of what was later to become North Carolina.[33] A successful plantation did not occur until the charter of the Virginia Company in 1606 to settle the Chesapeake Bay, and even that was heavily reliant upon the kindness of the native population - for which they received little thanks.[34] Following this, other plantations were conceived, mostly along the model of chartered companies. This expansion included Cromwell's 'Western Design', which was unsuccessful in emulating the Spanish by finding gold, but gained the English riches from sugar.[35] The English did not find gold or silver, but being forced to literally 'plant' their colonies not only with people but with staple crops, provided a more profitable and sustainable empire in the long run. Importantly, in contrast to the overly controlling hand of the Portuguese and Spanish, the Dutch who were distracted by events in mainland Europe, and the French who over concentrated on sugar, the English sustained a relatively less interventionist economic policy towards their involvement in the Atlantic world.[36] Alongside a determination to back up their commercial empire with their navy as part of a 'Blue Water Policy', this left the British dominant in the

---

32 Joël Felix, 'The Economy', in Doyle, *Old Regime France*, pp. 7–41, p. 39; Greene et al., 'The Atlantic Empires', p. 556.

33 Elliott, *Empires of the Atlantic World*, pp. 5–7. See also Karen Ordahl Kupperman, *Roanoke: The Abandoned Colony*, 2nd edn (Lanham, MD and Plymouth: Rowman & Littlefield Publishers, 2007).

34 James Horn, *A Land as God Made It: Jamestown and the Birth of America* (New York: Basic Books, 2005), esp. pp. 50–59. Those at Roanoke were equally ungrateful. See Kupperman, *Roanoke*, chapter five.

35 Karen Ordahl Kupperman, 'Errand to the Indies: Puritan Colonization from Providence Island through the Western Design', *WMQ*, 3rd ser. 45:1 (1988), 70–99.

36 Elliott, *Empires of the Atlantic World*, p. 16. Patrick O'Brien argues that the ability of the British government to tax was important to the success of the British economy, but he gives little attention to the role of overseas trade and customs and excise, 'The Nature and Historical Evolution of an Exceptional Fiscal State and its Possible Significance for the Precocious Commercialization and Industrialization of the British Economy from Cromwell to Nelson', *EcHR*, 64:2 (May 2011), 408–46.

Atlantic at the end of the Seven Years' War.[37] Even following the loss of the thirteen continental colonies, the British still had an informal economic empire in the Atlantic.

The success of the British model meant that it became the one to emulate, but there were in fact many similarities between the various empires. For example, both England and Spain had been proto-colonisers before they set off around the Atlantic more widely: England in Ireland, Scotland and Wales, and Spain with the *Reconquista*.[38] Nor can we say that the Spanish, Portuguese or English empires were simply ones of conquest or commerce. They all used religion to legitimise the taking of land and the subjugation of native peoples: the Spanish and the Portuguese via their Papal concessions and the English as defenders of the faith.[39] The French, Spanish, Dutch and English all had monopolistic trading companies through which the crown controlled their interests to a lesser or greater extent, and both France and England set up ports as entrepôts through which to conduct their colonial trade with customs advantages for re-exporting merchants.[40] Furthermore, the early-modern Atlantic world was 'entangled';[41] Portuguese and Dutch merchants had settled and were active in Nantes, there were many Spanish merchants in London and most ports hosted merchant 'nations' of various types.[42] The English and Scots sold their American tobacco to the French Royal Tobacco monopoly.[43] Dutch and British merchants traded with one another despite the regulations their governments put in place, and French officials in Martinique and Spanish officials in Cuba were involved in condoning smuggling with English and Dutch merchants.[44] It is clear that

---

37 Daniel A. Baugh, 'Britain's Blue Water Policy, 1689–1815', *International History Review*, 10:1 (Feb. 1988), 33–58.

38 Elliott, *Empires of the Atlantic World*, p. 17.

39 Elliott, *Empires of the Atlantic World*, p. 10.

40 Butel, *The Atlantic*, p. 131.

41 Elijah H. Gould, 'Entangled Histories, Entangled Worlds: The English-Speaking Atlantic as a Spanish Periphery', *American Historical Review*, 112:3 (Jun. 2007), 764–86.

42 For example, the English and Dutch in Bilbao, and the Jews in Livorno. Lamikiz, *Trade and Trust*, chapter one, Trivellato, *The Familiarity of Strangers*. See also Philip D. Curtin, *Cross-Cultural Trade in World History* (Cambridge: Cambridge University Press, 1984).

43 The French monopoly sales were important for liquidity because they bought in cash and short bills, but expected a low price in return. Jacob M. Price, 'Buchanan & Simson 1759–1763: A Different Kind of Firm Trading to the Chesapeake', *WMQ*, 41:1 (1983), 3–41, pp. 36–38. See the case study on James Lawson below, pp. 170–79.

44 Claudia Schnurmann, 'Atlantic Trade and American Identities: The Correlations of Supranational Commerce, Political Opposition, and Colonial Regionalism', in Coclanis, ed., *The Atlantic Economy* pp. 186–204; Kenneth J. Banks, 'Official Duplicity: The Illicit Slave Trade of Martinique, 1713–1763', in Coclanis, ed., *The*

European merchants around the Atlantic found enough common ground to put their differences aside, to 'see beyond ethnicity'.[45] The Atlantic was therefore in many respects an 'uncontrolled space' in which 'people collaborated in trade, mediation and other exchange processes without regard to language, culture, religion or colour'.[46]

PLACE: THE BRITISH ATLANTIC

WHILST MANY MERCHANTS of the European nations were therefore 'cross-cultural brokers', the British (as a nation) were dominant economically by the second half of the eighteenth century.[47] Whether this was due to a coherent strategy or 'mercantilist' policy has been much debated.[48] Indeed, there have been discussions as to who drove this 'policy' – the state or the merchant body.[49] Some have argued that there was no policy at all, John Seeley famously suggesting that the empire was gained in 'a fit of absence of mind'.[50] However, the term mercantilism is used here to be representative of a body of thought, not exclusive to Britain of course, which encompassed belief in zero-sum economics and intervention by the state – even though it was ironically a relative lack of intervention that made Britain successful. The Navigation Acts, chartered companies, a supportive customs and excise system and wars fought over trading rights as well as formal empire all formed part of the institutional framework in which eighteenth-century British merchants functioned. Table 1:1 shows clearly that this framework

---

Atlantic Economy, pp. 229–51; Laura Náter, 'The Spanish Empire and Cuban Tobacco during the Seventeenth and Eighteenth Centuries', in Coclanis, ed., *The Atlantic Economy*, pp. 252–76.

45 April Lee Hatfield, 'Dutch and New Netherland Merchants in the Seventeenth-Century English Chesapeake', in Coclanis, ed., *The Atlantic Economy*, pp. 205–28, p. 209.

46 Pietschmann, 'Introduction', pp. 41, 33.

47 Curtin, *Cross-Cultural Trade*, p. 2.

48 See for example, Eli F. Heckscher, 'Mercantilism', *EcHR*, 7:1 (1936–37), 44–54; D. C. Coleman, ed., *Revisions in Mercantilism* (London: Methuen, 1969); D. C. Coleman, 'Mercantilism Revisited', *Historical Journal*, 23:4 (1980), 773–91.

49 Michael J. Braddick, 'The English Government: War, Trade, and Settlement, 1625–1688', in Nicholas Canny, ed., *The Oxford History of the British Empire: Vol. I, The Origins of Empire* (Oxford and New York: Oxford University Press, 1998), pp. 286–308, p. 301; Gijs Rommelse, 'The Role of Mercantilism in Anglo-Dutch Political Relations, 1650–74', *EcHR*, new ser., 63:3 (Aug. 2010), 591–611.

50 John Robert Seeley, *The Expansion of England: Two Courses of Lectures* (London: MacMillan & Co., 1883), p. 8.

supported the growth of trade between Britain and the British West Indies and the thirteen colonies/United States over the period 1760 to 1810. It is also worth noting the balance of payments differentials for both the British trade with the British West Indies, and with the thirteen colonies/United States and British North America. This was largely offset by a thriving coastal trade between the British West Indies and ports such as Charleston, Philadelphia, Boston and New York. The North Americans earned much of the freight in this trade and so earned invisible income which allowed them to balance their payments with Britain.[51] It is clear however, that despite the dip in trade due to the non-importation Acts and (an incomplete) cessation during the American War of Independence, trade expanded impressively over the whole period. This was especially the case in British exports. As a share of total overseas trade, exports to British North America, the thirteen colonies/ United States, the British West Indies and Africa increased from 18.41 per cent in 1750, to 35.36 per cent in 1810.[52]

The growth experienced in British Atlantic trade is particularly impressive given the number of credit crises and wars over this period. This was at least partly attributable to a number of assurance structures.[53] Chartered companies were important, at least in the seventeenth century. They had been used since the Muscovy Company was established in 1448 to find a passage to the East.[54] They were convenient because individuals (rather than the Crown) undertook the financial risk in exchange for monopoly rights. The most famous of course were the East India Company (1600) and the South Sea Company (1611), but there were many others.[55] These

---

51 James F. Shepherd and Gary M. Walton, *Shipping, Trade, and the Economic Development of Colonial North America* (London and New York: Cambridge University Press, 1972), p. 138.

52 The share of imports for the same area was 33.95 per cent for 1750 and 33.22 per cent in 1810. Calculated from B. R. Mitchell and Phyllis Deane, *Abstract of British Historical Statistics* (London: Cambridge University Press, 1962), pp. 310–11.

53 On assurance, see chapter three, pp. 84–93.

54 This paragraph based on Elizabeth Mancke, 'Chartered Enterprises and the Evolution of the British Atlantic World', in Elizabeth Mancke and Carole Shammas, eds., *The Creation of the British Atlantic World* (Baltimore and London: Johns Hopkins University Press, 2005), pp. 237–62. For a fuller outline of the various British Chartered Companies see P. J. Griffiths, *A Licence to Trade: The History of English Chartered Companies* (London: E. Benn, 1974).

55 On the relationship between the East India Company and empire see Huw V. Bowen, *The Business of Empire: The East India Company and Imperial Britain, 1756–1833* (Cambridge: Cambridge University Press, 2006). On the South Sea Bubble see John Carswell, *The South Sea Bubble* (London: Cresset Press, 1960), p. 132. The South Sea 'bubble' story has centred around blind speculation, social mobility and consequent economic dislocation. However, the term was not used until around 1771, and it

TABLE 1:1   ATLANTIC TRADE WITH GREAT BRITAIN 1760–1810
(IN '000S).

	British North America		Colonies/United States		British West Indies	
	Imports	Exports	Imports	Exports	Imports	Exports
1760	36	179	832	2713	1907	1300
1765	94	345	1160	1973	2302	1072
1770	106	374	1095	1955	3342	1339
1775	136	659	1953	197	3628	1717
1780	120	837	20	829	2606	1752
1785	209	691	894	2308	4354	1236
1790	202	841	1191	3432	3891	1986
1795	315	1000	1352	5254	4099	2461
1800	393	976	2358	7886	7369	4087
1805	294	865	1767	7147	6720	3832
1810	885	1845	2614	7813	8258	4790

Source: Compiled from B. R. Mitchell and Phyllis Deane, *Abstract of British Historical Statistics* (Cambridge: Cambridge University Press, 1962), pp. 309–10.

included the Virginia Company (1606), Newfoundland Company (1610), Massachusetts Bay Company (1619) and the Hudson's Bay Company (1670). The early companies were set up to challenge the Iberians' claims in the Americas, but the success of the early colonies increased the tendency of the British to use chartered companies. Connecticut (1662), Rhode Island (1663), Carolina (1663), New York (1664), the Bahamas (1670) and Pennsylvania (1681) all received company charters.[56] The Royal African Company (1663) and its predecessors were established to take advantage of the West African

was known originally as the South Sea Scheme. See Julian Hoppit, 'The Myths of the South Sea Bubble', *Transactions of the Royal Historical Society*, 6th ser., 12 (2002), 141–65, 163. Peter Garber argues that linking the bubble with terms such as 'irrational exuberance' and 'herding' is misleading, and that the South Sea Bubble, the Tulip Mania and the Mississippi Bubble reflected normal pricing behaviour in a market economy and all involved 'financial manipulations, monetary creation, and government connivance on a scale that was not matched again until this century, but which have now become commonplace'. Peter M. Garber, *Famous First Bubbles: The Fundamentals of Early Manias* (Cambridge, MA: MIT Press, 2000), pp. 2–6, 13–14.

56 New York was taken over formally from the Dutch in 1664. See Cathy Matson,

gold trade and then the slave trade, although by the late 1690s 'interlopers' were a serious problem. From 1712 the company licensed private traders and by the 1730s its forts were in decay.[57] The charter for Massachusetts of 1691 marked a change towards 'royal' colonies by which the Crown took more control over land and its people via a governor. The East India Company's renewed charters moved along the same lines.[58] On the whole, however, the East India Company and Hudson's Bay Company excepted, the chartered companies were in decline during the eighteenth century, roughly mirroring the increasing influence of metropolitan government. However, the legacy of those chartered companies set the framework for much of the early Atlantic.

Whereas chartered companies were often designed to take or keep land from the Spanish and French, the Navigation Acts were designed to engross the carrying trade across the Atlantic – especially from the Dutch – and to encourage English shipping.[59] The Merchant Navy was therefore a crucial instrument of English commercial policy from the Interregnum and Restoration periods onwards.[60] The Navigation Acts of 1650 and 1651 forbade the importation into England of all goods except in English ships or ships owned by the producing country, which eliminated third party carriers. Foreign ships were barred from trading in the colonies. A second major act was passed in 1660. It also forbade the importing into, or exporting from, the English colonies of any goods except in English or colonial ships (with ¾ of the crew English) and it forbade certain colonial articles – such as sugar, tobacco, wool and cotton – from being shipped to any country except England or an English plantation, in order to keep them from competitors. Another act along similar lines was passed in 1663, and they were all codified in 1696. These acts were mostly successful in taking the trade from the Dutch, despite the fact that they were largely ignored or circumvented. Merchants in Britain no doubt benefitted from the enforced increase in the pattern of shipping, but whether

Merchants and Empire: Trading in Colonial New York (Baltimore and London: Johns Hopkins University Press, 1998), esp. chapters one and two.

57 For example, 'Charter to Senegal Adventurers' (1588); 'Governor and Company of Adventurers trading to Gynney and Bynney' [Guinea and Benin] (1618); and 'Royal Adventurers into Africa' (1660), in K. G. Davies, *The Royal African Company* (London: Longmans, Green and Co., 1957), pp. 39–43, 101, 152.

58 Anthony Webster, *The Twilight of the East India Company: The Evolution of Anglo-Asian Commerce and Politics, 1790–1860* (Woodbridge, Suffolk: Boydell Press, 2009), chapter two.

59 Braddick, 'The English Government'.

60 William J. Ashworth, *Customs and Excise: Trade, Production and Consumption in England, 1640–1845* (Oxford: Oxford University Press, 2003), p. 35.

they were economically beneficial for merchants in the colonies has been much debated.[61]

Customs were of course an important source of income for the state, and protectionism may have been a pragmatic approach to revenue in negotiation with various interest groups, rather than a clear (mercantilist) policy, but it was successfully and systematically pursued.[62] Customs and excise were an important part of the 'fiscal-military' state, at its height in the later eighteenth and early nineteenth centuries.[63] Within this system, import and export duties were used alongside the Navigation Acts to stem foreign competition and to promote domestic manufacture such as wool, and later fustians, which were not subject to excise.[64] This was of course at the expense of the colonists, in preference for English merchants. There was also a drawback system, which was a return payment of import duties when goods were subsequently exported. This helped to promote Britain as an entrepôt, especially in colonial and Asian goods, and importantly, viz-à-viz the Dutch. Consumption was also taxed, particularly on those goods which were perceived as luxuries. Thus the professional excise (introduced in 1643) eventually came to be seen as the 'easiest' and 'equallest' form of taxation.[65] On the whole this system enjoyed a large approval rating over a range of orders of people. Merchants in particular were relatively content to help pay for the fleets that protected them from enemy ships and privateers in convoys and controlled smuggling.[66] This is not to say that certain interest groups always simply acquiesced with the state. The West-India interest fought its corner and frequently lobbied for changes in taxation on the important commodity of sugar, for example.[67]

---

61 See for example, Robert Paul Thomas, 'A Quantitative Approach to the Study of the Effects of British Imperial Policy in Colonial Warfare', *Journal of Economic History*, 25 (Dec. 1965), 323–43; Larry Sawyers, 'The Navigation Acts Revisited', *EcHR*, new ser., 45:2 (May 1992), 262–84.

62 This section is based on Ashworth, *Customs and Excise*, chapter two, except where noted.

63 Andrew Thompson, 'Empire and the State', in Sarah Stockwell, ed., *The British Empire: Themes and Perspectives* (Malden, MA and Oxford: Blackwell Publishing, 2008), pp. 39–61, p. 39.

64 Fustians came to replace calico imported from India. Ashworth, *Customs and Excise*, p. 38.

65 Cited in Michael J. Braddick. *The Nerves of State: Taxation and the Financing of the English State, 1558–1714* (Manchester: Manchester University Press, 1996), p. 99.

66 Patrick O'Brien, 'Inseparable Connections: Trade, Economy, Fiscal State, and the Expansion of Empire, 1688–1815', in P. J. Marshall, ed., *The Oxford History of the British Empire: Vol. II, The Eighteenth Century* (Oxford: Oxford University Press, 1998), pp. 53–77, esp. pp. 70–71.

67 Ryden, *West Indian Slavery*, chapter five.

Overall, however, the system worked to the benefit of the merchants, as well as the state.

There was also a close relationship between the state and merchants when it came to war. The Navigation Acts unsurprisingly caused wars with the Dutch in 1652–54, 1665–67, 1672–74 and 1694–99. Importantly, however, the relationship between the state and a financial elite 'provided much of the capital and resources to support the state and private enterprise at home and abroad'.[68] Merchants often provided finance for wars by investing in bonds and government consuls and later through institutions such as the Bank of England, and in return they expected the state to provide convoys to protect their shipping in wartime. They also expected the state to negotiate treaties at the end of wars that realised more than simply formal 'imperial' ambition. The Treaty of Utrecht in 1713 was a good example of this, which secured the *Asiento* (contract to deliver slaves to the Spanish colonies) for the British. Using Royal African Company ships, the South Sea Company delivered slaves to Vera Cruz, Cartagena, Panama, Havana and various South American ports.[69] There was also much 'island swapping' during the French Wars, but the British usually managed to negotiate for the most profitable ones in terms of trade, thus confirming this reciprocal relationship.[70]

Despite changes to these institutions over time, the British state, whether by default or design, retained a reasonably balanced and consistent approach to the Atlantic economy in the long term. Certainly the British state and its merchants had a particular understanding which promoted economic growth and allowed the mercantile community to deal with, react to, and even benefit from, the difficult economic environment in which it worked. Whilst this book will argue that the business culture of the merchants was central to their success, their relationship with the British state was an important factor in this culture, and in facilitating British economic dominance in the Atlantic.

This special relationship notwithstanding, Britain's commercial empire was larger than its formal empire because British merchants were rarely fully constrained by the regulations set in place by the British state or by

---

68 Huw V. Bowen, *Elites, Enterprise and the Making of the British Overseas Empire 1688–1775* (Basingstoke, London and New York: MacMillan Press, 1996), p. 47.

69 The *Asiento* was granted for thirty years but it effectively ceased in 1739 with the outbreak of the War of Jenkins' Ear. Apart from the trade in slaves it incorporated the right to send a trading vessel annually to Spanish-America which was seen as a means for contraband as well as legal trade. Adrian Pearce, *British Trade with Spanish America, 1763–1808* (Liverpool: Liverpool University Press, 2007), pp. 18–20.

70 This did not always secure the planters from international competition however. Ryden, *West Indian Slavery*, pp. 234–44.

geo-political borders. They not only traded with merchants in the United States after 1783, but also with merchants in the colonies of other European nations; those of the French and Spanish in particular.[71] This allowed them to trade in an enormous variety of goods, to a very large number of ports. As noted above, this book uses Liverpool as its axis, the leading outport in the period covered by this study. Despite the fact that Liverpool is renowned for its role in the slave trade, and was dominant *in* it from 1750 onwards, it was never dominated *by* it.[72] Slaves were of course one of the most important 'commodities' distributed around the Atlantic, and brought Liverpool merchants into contact with the west coast of Africa, the British West Indies (and many ports of the French and Spanish colonies), and the southern colonies of continental America.[73] However, Liverpool, like Glasgow and Bristol, was engaged in a wide variety of trades which brought it into contact with all the major commodities of the Atlantic economy and with the ports and mercantile communities through which they were distributed.[74] Many goods came from farther afield than the Atlantic, such as timber from the Baltic, and tea, spices, calicoes and silks from China, much of which (excepting the timber) was exported around the Atlantic world.[75] Of these, tea was the most important, which was imported to the value of

---

71 This section is based on Jacob M. Price, 'The Imperial Economy, 1770–1776', in Marshall, *The Eighteenth Century*, pp. 78–104, except where noted.

72 D. P. Lamb, 'Volume and Tonnage of the Liverpool Slave Trade 1772–1807', in Roger Anstey and Paul E. Hair, eds., *Liverpool, the African Slave Trade, and Abolition* (Liverpool: Historic Society of Lancashire and Cheshire, Occasional Series, Vol. 2, 1976), pp. 91–112, p. 91. It is likely that the slave trade was 'pervasive' rather than dominant, as Draper has recently argued for London. Nick Draper, 'The City of London and Slavery: Evidence from the First Dock Companies, 1795–1800', *EcHR*, 61:2 (2008), 432–66. See also Sheryllynne Haggerty, 'Liverpool, the Slave Trade and Empire', in Sheryllynne Haggerty, Anthony Webster and Nicholas J. White, eds., *The Empire in One City? Liverpool's Inconvenient Imperial Past* (Manchester: Manchester University Press, 2008), pp. 17–34.

73 The slave trade to continental America declined after the 1730s when the slave population of areas such as Maryland and Virginia was growing rapidly through natural increase. Lorena S. Walsh, 'Liverpool's Slave Trade to the Colonial Chesapeake: Slaving on the Periphery', in David Richardson, Suzanne Schwarz and Anthony Tibbles, eds., *Liverpool and Transatlantic Slavery* (Liverpool: Liverpool University Press, 2007), pp. 98–117, p. 101.

74 It is of course impossible to cover all the commodities and ports in the Atlantic here. Only the major ports included in this study are mentioned.

75 Tea of course was purchased predominantly from the East India Company for re-export. The East India Company (in its various forms) exported silver to pay for Chinese tea, which under the mercantilist system was of course very unpopular. Webster, *Twilight of the East India Company*, pp. 28–29.

£484,000 in 1750 and £2,560,000 in 1815.[76] In terms of Atlantic commodities, sugar from West Indian ports such as Kingston (Jamaica) and Bridgetown (Barbados) was by far the most significant. This also saw impressive growth; imports rose from a value of £1,270,000 in 1750 to £5,440,000 in 1815. Tobacco imported from the Chesapeake colonies (Maryland and Virginia), particularly through Norfolk, was also significant, about 85 per cent of which was re-exported to Europe by 1775, especially to France. However, tobacco experienced mixed fortunes in terms of value, if not volume. Imports of tobacco were worth £481,000 in 1750 but only £416,000 in 1815. Over 30 per cent of all British tobacco imports arrived via Scotland, particularly Glasgow, in the mid-eighteenth century.[77] About 65 per cent of rice from Charleston (South Carolina) and Savannah (Georgia) was imported into Britain (much of which was re-exported), with the rest going direct to the West Indies and southern Europe.[78] Coffee had been an important re-export commodity from the East in the early eighteenth century, but by the mid-eighteenth century, it was being grown in Jamaica and other West Indian islands, with about 94 per cent of imports being re-exported to the Low Countries, Germany and northern Europe where it was even more popular than in Britain. It was imported to a value of £75,000 in 1750, but had risen impressively to £5,340,000 by 1815. Also important were dyestuffs, used in domestic textile manufacture. These were imported to the value of £506,000 during 1772–1774 and £1,413,000 by 1815.[79] The northern ports, including Halifax, Nova Scotia and Boston, Massachusetts, were important suppliers of beaver skins used for felt and hats, naval stores such as timber, deals, pitch and tar for shipbuilding, but also staves for barrels and pot ash and pearl ash for soapmaking and glassmaking. The seas around Nova Scotia also provided much fish. Before 1600, iron came from the Baltic, but by the eighteenth century it was also being imported from Philadelphia in Pennsylvania, Baltimore in Maryland, and from Port Tobacco and Norfolk in Virginia, where it was useful as ballast for tobacco. Cotton was originally imported from the West Indies, but by the first decade of the nineteenth century, imports of raw cotton came from the

---

76 Figures for imports taken from Mitchell and Deane, *Abstract*, pp. 286–90. For the consumption of these exotic products see James Walvin, *Fruits of Empire: Exotic Produce and British Taste, 1660–1800* (New York: New York University Press, 1997).

77 T. M. Devine, 'The Golden Age of Tobacco', in T. M. Devine and Gordon Jackson, eds., *Glasgow, Vol. I: Beginnings to 1830* (Manchester and New York: Manchester University Press, 1995), pp. 139–83, p. 143.

78 Licences were given in order to export rice from the colonies direct to Europe. Price, 'The Imperial Economy', p. 85.

79 Figures for 1772–74 from Price, 'The Imperial Economy'. Figure for 1815 includes dyewoods and dyestuffs. Mitchell and Deane, *Abstract*, p. 290.

United States, just in time for the boom in cotton-goods production of the nineteenth century.

Growth in total exports and re-exports from Britain were equally spectacular. In 1750 they amounted to £12,699,000 but had risen to £68.4 million by 1815.[80] Within this, exports to America and Africa outweighed trade to the East.[81] The dominant commodities going through ports such as Liverpool, Glasgow, and Bristol were textiles: wool from Yorkshire, and then linen. Total exports of textile yarn and manufactures were valued at nearly £6 million in 1750 and at nearly £32 million in 1815.[82] There was also a wide variety of hardware typical of the 'industrial revolution' exported – such as Birmingham 'toys', Sheffield metalware (including tools for farming and shackles for slaves) and guns. Total exports of metals and metal manufactures increased from a value of £489,000 in 1750 to £871,000 in 1815.[83] There were also a wide variety of other goods such as pottery and various miscellaneous commodities such as clocks, books, beer, cheese, shoes, bridles, salt, coal, furniture and even pianos. Basically, anything the relatively dependent societies in the Americas needed to survive, or which Africans were prepared to accept in exchange for their slaves. Merchants in the colonies were increasingly providing capital for shipping, especially those in northern ports such as Boston, New York and Philadelphia, and were becoming increasingly dominant in the coastal trade along the eastern seaboard.[84] Commodities trans-shipped in this way included livestock and forest products from Massachusetts to the West Indian islands, wheat from Pennsylvania, Maryland and Virginia to Massachusetts and New Hampshire, and iron from Pennsylvania and Maryland. Bread and flour, dried fish, rice, wood products, pine boards and barrel staves were also sent from North America to the West Indies, which exported rum, molasses and coffee in return. Therefore, an extremely wide range of commodities were transported around the Atlantic, both produced within it and brought in from the East.

---

80 Mitchell and Deane, *Abstract*, pp. 280, 282. All figures for 1750 are for England and Wales, and for Great Britain in 1815.

81 Price, 'The Imperial Economy', p. 102.

82 Includes cotton, woollen, linen and silk yarn and manufactures. Mitchell and Deane, *Abstract*, pp. 294–95.

83 Figure for 1750 is for non-ferrous metals and manufactures and for 1815 hardware and cutlery. Mitchell and Deane, *Abstract*, pp. 294–95.

84 John J. McCusker, 'The Shipowners of British America before 1775', Paper given at the International Symposium on 'The Shipowner in History' at the National Maritime Museum, UK (Sep. 1984), p. 18; id., 'Sources of Investment Capital in the Colonial Philadelphia Shipping Industry', in John J. McCusker, *Essays in the Economic History of the Atlantic World* (London and New York: Routledge, 1997), pp. 245–57.

PEOPLE: THE MERCHANTS

MERCHANTS AROUND the British Atlantic therefore traded in a wide variety of goods over four continents, but who were the men that distributed these commodities around the Atlantic, and sometimes, literally traversed the ocean themselves? Mostly they were merchants, the elite of the trading community.[85] Such men were clearly importers and exporters, and the prestige that went with the nomenclature meant that many more men called themselves merchants than truly were.[86] Indeed, the reputation of the merchant was on the rise during the eighteenth century. This was no doubt due to the perception of the increasing importance of international commerce to the wealth of Britain. As Elliott notes, 'The insistence of Hakluyt and his friends on an empire based on the exchange of commodities rather than the acquisition of precious metals played its part in helping to give merchants and their values a new prominence in the English national consciousness.'[87] This was clearly an eighteenth-century phenomenon. *The Tradesman* commented in 1808 that 'it is only within the last century that the mercantile interest has been especially regarded'.[88] As was noted in the introduction, the merchant came to be seen as a man of industry, foresight and œconomy, a man of 'extensive genius', who encouraged trade, the arts and society.[89] He was a man of skill, with knowledge of the commodities in which he dealt, of the customs, languages and currencies of the countries to which he traded, of weights and measures, and of geography and navigation.[90] Such men 'came to occupy an unprecedented place in the national esteem' as the 'cult of commerce became an increasingly important part of being British'.[91]

This book will argue that one reason for the success of these merchants was a relatively homogenous, commonly understood and conformed-to business culture. However, this does not mean that these merchants were a homogenous group of men, or of a certain 'typology'. Obviously they

85 For who was part of the wider trading community see Haggerty, *The British-Atlantic Trading Community.*

86 Haggerty, *The British-Atlantic Trading Community*, pp. 74–75.

87 Elliott, *Empires of the Atlantic World*, p. 26.

88 *The Tradesman*, p. 67.

89 Gordon, *The Universal Accountant*, Vol. II, p. 1; Gordon, *The Universal Accountant*, Vol. I, p. 1; Robert Campbell, *The London Tradesman*, 3rd edn (London: Printed by T. Gardner, 1757). pp. 284, 292.

90 Campbell, *The London Tradesman*, p. 293.

91 David Ormrod, *The Rise of Commercial Empires: England and the Netherlands in the Age of Mercantilism, 1657–1770* (Cambridge: Cambridge University Press, 2003), p. 1; Linda Colley, *Britons: Forging the Nation 1707–1837* (New Haven and London: Yale University Press, 1992), p. 56.

were individuals with strong personalities who learned to behave in certain ways. Their letters and actions reveal their underlying personas, and the ways in which as individuals, they coped with, and reacted to, events that affected them commercially. It is therefore worth briefly introducing here the main characters and some of their correspondents. As mentioned in the introduction, these were not necessarily the most elite or successful merchants – though some were – but those whose stories and actions shone through due to their distinctive characters, good fortune, or indeed, misfortune.

The Earles were a prominent Liverpool merchant family, and two generations were active during the period covered by this book. The first consisted of Ralph (1715–90), Thomas (1719–81) and William Earle (1721–88) who were in various partnerships between themselves and with others.[92] Ralph was chiefly engaged in the timber trade with the Baltic, William in the slave trade and general North American trade, and Thomas ran a sister house in Livorno with the backing of Thomas Hodgson, another Liverpool worthy. They had good contacts in Liverpool through the Town Council, the Committee of the African Company of Merchants Trading to Africa from Liverpool, and the drinking club the Mock Corporation of Sephton.[93] They also had other investments with Thomas Hodgson and with William Davenport, a leading slave trader. As a family they were important investors in the slave trade, especially to Old Calabar, but also had good links with the Norfolk, Virginia, firm of Sparling & Bolden, trading in tobacco, and with Henry Laurens (see below) of Charleston, South Carolina, for rice. The business eventually went into the hands of William's sons, Thomas (1754–1822) and William (1760–1839), who traded as T. & W. Earle & Co. They traded in wine, oil, silk and sugar, and continued the Livorno firm until 1808. Thomas and William were also active in privateering during the American War of Independence, and continued to be involved in the slave trade. The Earles were a well-connected and wealthy family, eventually purchasing properties on the outskirts of town. The Earles also had interests in the Caribbean that lasted well beyond the period dealt with here, including in British Guiana.[94] Thomas and William Earle died with estates valued at £70,000 and £45,000

---

92 This section is based on Dawn Littler, 'The Earle Collection: Records of a Liverpool Family of Merchants and Shipowners', *Transactions of the Historical Society of Lancashire and Cheshire*, 146 (1997), 93–106, except where noted.

93 Minutes of the Town Council, MIN COU I, LivRO; Committee Book of the African Company of Merchants trading from Liverpool, 352/MD1, LivRO; Mock Corporation of Sephton, 367 SEF, LivRO.

94 Legacies of British Slave Ownership Project, http://www.ucl.ac.uk/lbs/, accessed 15 Sep. 2011. Including, but not restricted to, Claim: British Guiana 477.

respectively.[95] Clearly the family as a whole were risk takers with diverse trading interests. Their success gave them political power, but they also appeared to become part of an isolated and elitist group centred on the Town Council at the end of the eighteenth century.[96]

The Rathbones were another successful Liverpool family.[97] Six generations were called William, the second having come to Liverpool around 1725. The most active during the second half of the eighteenth century was William Rathbone IV (1757–1809). He was a well-respected member of the Quaker community until 1805 when he was expelled after having criticised the Society's actions in Ireland.[98] William IV served his apprenticeship in his father's house, as did his son in turn from 1805. He was a major player in the commission trade to continental America for people such as Andrew Clow (see below). He imported rice, wheat, flour, tar and barrel staves from the colonies/states, and exported the archetypal industrial revolution manufactures of textiles, pottery and metalware from the Liverpool hinterland. As a Quaker he was against the slave trade, but clearly was not averse to trading with slave societies. In 1790 he went into business with his sister's husband Robert Benson, and a former clerk, James Cropper, but this partnership was dissolved in 1795 when Benson became ill. In 1796 Rathbone IV went into business with William Hughes and William Duncan (Rathbone, Hughes & Duncan) – the firm with which this book is mostly concerned – at which point, he became a sleeping partner. At his death, the firm changed its name to Hughes & Duncan. Both firms traded with the Brown family of Providence, Rhode Island (see below). Rathbone IV and his partners were all well-respected and well-known merchants who dealt with many houses in continental America.

---

95 David Pope, 'The Wealth and Social Aspirations of Liverpool's Slave Merchants of the Second Half of the Eighteenth Century', in Richardson et al., *Liverpool and Transatlantic Slavery*, pp. 164–226, p. 210.

96 For more on the institutional networks in Liverpool at this time see John Haggerty and Sheryllynne Haggerty, 'The Rise and Fall of a Metropolitan Business Network: Liverpool 1750–1810', *Explorations in Economic History*, 48:2 (2011), 189–206.

97 For the early Rathbone family see Lucie Nottingham, *Rathbone Brothers: From Merchant to Banker, 1742–1792* (London: Rathbone Brothers PLC, 1992), and for a case study of William Rathbone IV see Haggerty, *The British-Atlantic Trading Community*, pp. 230–34. See also Eleanor A. Rathbone, *William Rathbone: A Memoir* (London: MacMillan, 1908).

98 Eddowes to Roscoe, 23 May 1805, 920 ROS 1343, RP. The tracts were William Rathbone, *A Narrative of Events That Have Lately Taken Place in Ireland Among the Society Called Quakers, With Corresponding Documents and Occasional Observations* (Liverpool: Printed by M'Creery, 1804); William Rathbone, *A Memoir of the Proceedings of the Society Called Quakers, Belonging to the Monthly Meeting of Hardshaw, in Lancashire* (Liverpool: Printed by M'Creery, 1805).

As a Quaker he could not serve on the Town Council, but he was a member of the Liverpool American Chamber of Commerce established in 1801. He also gave evidence to Parliamentary enquiries on various issues demonstrating that his opinion was valued. However, he always worked on commission and as ship's husband. Rathbone never owned shares in any ships, and very rarely imported or exported commodities at his own risk, and then in only small amounts.[99] This, and his correspondence, demonstrates that he was a reliable merchant, but not a risk taker. However, he still was successful enough to leave £20,000 in real property alone when he died.

Henry Laurens (1724–1792) was also a well-known and well-respected merchant, planter, and latterly, revolutionary war statesman.[100] Born in Charleston, South Carolina, he set up his business there following a three year apprenticeship in London (1744 to 1747). He was in a couple of partnerships before finally setting up on his own in 1762, having married Eleanor Ball in 1750.[101] He and his various partners exported Carolina rice, indigo, deerskin and naval stores to Britain, continental Europe and West Indian ports, and imported wine and spirits, textiles, sugar and slaves, although he disengaged from the slave trade in 1763.[102] However, it is with this latter trade that he came into contact with Liverpool merchants John Knight, John Mears, John Tarleton and Joseph Manesty, and so it is this trade that is focussed on here. He was extremely successful, and became one of the wealthiest and most respected merchants in Charleston, eventually serving on the Council and as President of the Continental Congress from November 1777 to December 1778. Laurens was clearly ambitious, and despite his success was not averse to 'puffing' his own abilities to his correspondents, nor to advising them of what obligations they were under. At the same time he was a pragmatic man and used the phrase, 'whatever is, is right' in order to explain changes regarding trade, political or personal opinions. Judging by the tone of his letters he was an affable character, with whom people got on easily, at least until he retired from trade around 1770.

Andrew Clow (?–1793) was an ambitious, driven man.[103] Brought up in manufacturing textiles in Manchester, England, he moved to Philadelphia

---

99 No Rathbone is listed in the Liverpool Ship Registry between 1786 and 1808. R. Craig and R. Jarvis, *Liverpool Registry of Merchant Ships* (Manchester: Printed for the Chetham Society, 1967).

100 This section based on C. James Taylor, 'Henry Laurens', in John A. Garraty and Mark C. Carnes, eds., *American National Biography* (Oxford: Oxford University Press, 1999).

101 First with George Austin alone, and then with Austin and George Appleby.

102 He was later reported to have said that he abhorred the slave trade, but he owned 298 slaves in 1790.

103 See the case study on Andrew Clow below, pp. 188–96.

circa 1784 to take advantage of the opportunities offered by the end of the American War of Independence. He set up on his own at first, but then went into business with his friend and former bankrupt, David Cay. Early on the house exported wheat, flour and timber, and imported textiles and hardware from England.[104] Clow used one of the few people he trusted, William Rathbone IV, as his main shipping agent in England. Despite his lack of trust in people, or perhaps because of it, Clow was extremely active in building his networks, and increased his correspondents around the Mediterranean in addition to his wide networks around the Atlantic. Over time he therefore added to his commodity portfolio, including Caribbean rum and sugar, Spanish lemons, Indian textiles and gauze from Cyprus. He also invested in shipping and in various government securities. In 1790 $61,123.57 went through his bank account, whilst competitors Joshua Gilpin and Stephen Girard had $49,133.23 and $19,229.33 go through their accounts respectively, in the same year.[105] He had clearly cornered a significant portion of the Philadelphia trade in a short time. No proof was found that Clow was married, despite having a child, this may be attributed to the fact that he was extremely active and mobile, literally traversing the Atlantic himself every year from 1785 until 1793, when he and Cay both died in the yellow fever epidemic. Clow was a risk taker, and extremely ambitious. He was a controlling character, and not an easy person to get on with. However, it would seem that being a good businessman meant that people were prepared to conduct business with him despite his irascible character.

The Browns of Providence were a leading mercantile family throughout the period covered by this book and were involved in a number of partnerships.[106] This study is concerned with four of them, Obadiah Brown & Co. (?–1762), Brown & Benson (1783–1794), Brown, Benson & Ives (1792–1796) and Brown & Ives (1796–?). In the early period the family was mostly concerned with importing molasses from the West Indies for distillation into rum for the slave trade. They were occasionally involved in the slave trade itself, in which Providence was a major continental player, but they withdrew from the trade in 1765 following a large loss. By the 1760s they had diversified into producing spermaceti candles and cordage at their ropeworks, and in 1765 established an iron foundry. During the American War of Independence the family, having initiated trade with France and Holland, supplied the

---

104 I have been unable to track down the exact relationship between these two men which might explain why Clow continued to tolerate Cay who was clearly inept.

105 Bank of North America Personal Ledgers, 1542/36B-C/Vol. 6, HSP.

106 This section is based on James B. Hedges, *The Browns of Providence Plantation*, 2 vols (Providence: Brown University Press, 1952, 1968); Robert P. Emlen, 'Nicholas Brown', in Garraty and Carnes, *American National Biography*.

continental army with canon, anchors, English manufactured goods and cloth, and were also involved in privateering. On Independence, the family became more involved in trade to the East, including China and Java as well as the Baltic. However, in the period running up to the Anglo-American war they were more involved in exporting American produce to Europe, particularly via Liverpool, where they traded with Rathbone & Benson, and had correspondence with Martin, Hope & Thornely amongst others. The Browns were therefore involved in a wide variety of Atlantic trades and also in manufactures and other investments. When Nicholas Brown died in 1796 he left over $200,000 in public securities alone, having become one of the wealthiest men in the state. The Browns were therefore a successful and respectable family business, though they were clearly willing to take risks and to invest in new ventures whenever the opportunity arose or circumstances changed, including privateering and circumventing trade embargoes.[107]

The Parker family represents the archetypal firm that used intermarriage to develop and secure their networks around the Atlantic, which stretched from Glasgow and Liverpool to Virginia, Grenada and Demerara.[108] As with the Browns, the longevity of the family business meant that they were engaged in various partnerships. James Parker (1729–1815) was born in Scotland but worked in Virginia between 1745 and 1750, as a factor for Alexander Spiers, a leading merchant in Glasgow.[109] In 1758 he went into partnership with William Aitchison (n/k), another Scot in Norfolk, Virginia. Together they exported the local staple tobacco, mostly to Glasgow and Liverpool, and imported general merchandise via Glasgow and Liverpool using the store system. Indeed, they had a variety of stores as well as a ropeworks. James Parker returned to Glasgow with the onset of the American War of Independence and thereby lost all of his land in Virginia. His son Patrick Parker returned to Norfolk in May 1783 after his education. In 1789 James Parker promoted a new strand of his trade by sending his other son, Charles Stewart Parker (1771–1828), to Grenada as an apprentice to George Robertson (n/k). In 1792 a new firm was set up involving Charles Stewart Parker, George Robertson, James McInroy (n/k) and Samuel Sandbach (1769–1851) (a former clerk). Robertson and Parker ran the firm in Grenada and Sandbach and McInroy in Demerara. From these islands they exported cotton and coffee, importing English manufactures in return. Charles Stewart Parker returned

---

107 See the discussion below, pp. 226–30.

108 This section is based on the guide to the Parker Papers at LivRO. Samuel Sandbach later set up the firm Sandbach, Tinne & Co., the records of which are held at MMMA.

109 J. H. Soltow, 'Scottish Traders in Virginia, 1750–1775', *EcHR*, new ser., 12:1 (1959), 83–98, p. 87.

to Scotland in 1794 and in 1803 Sandbach went back to Liverpool to control their operations in that port. The firm was bound by intermarriage; Charles Stewart Parker married a niece of George Robertson, and Samuel Sandbach's daughter married Charles Stewart Parker's eldest son. This strategy, though not successful for everyone, worked for the Parkers by reducing transaction costs and facilitating trust. They were therefore involved in most of the major trades in the Atlantic, but not heavily in the slave trade (except for the slaves they imported for their plantations). As a family they had a wide range of interests in the Caribbean, especially in British Guiana.[110] They were also a mobile network, prepared to take advantage of new opportunities and were therefore risk takers on the whole which served them well. Samuel Sandbach later joined the Liverpool East India Trade Committee and eventually became mayor of Liverpool 1831–32.[111]

James Lawson (n/k) was originally from Strathhaven in Lanarkshire but his business was based in Glasgow where he lived with his wife.[112] His brother-in-law and business partner, John Semple (d.1773), was based in Port Tobacco, Maryland. Active in the later 1750s and early 1760s, it was a medium sized firm, which imported tobacco and pig and bar iron into Glasgow and Liverpool, and exported dry goods in return. In 1760 they imported 762 hogsheads of tobacco into Glasgow, compared to the largest firm which imported 4,945 hogsheads. There were seven other firms which imported over 500 hogsheads, but still less than Lawson. Lawson had good contacts with other Glasgow firms such as Buchanan & Simson, and with Liverpool merchants James Gildart and Haliday & Dunbar. However, the majority of his business dealings were tied up with his family, which eventually became a huge problem for him. By 1774, despite being a reputable merchant with good contacts, he had lost at least £10,000 and was being harassed by his creditors, mainly due to the activities of his brother-in-law who kept acting against his advice. In contrast to his reckless brother-in-law Lawson was risk averse, a habitual worrier, and seemed a naturally gentle person. One wonders whether, given his disposition, he was in the right profession at all.

Samuel Rainford left his large and troublesome family behind in Liverpool in order to try his fortunes in Kingston, Jamaica.[113] He had established himself as a merchant there by 1774 and used his Liverpool networks for access to credit. He later set up in partnership with his brother Robert and

110 Legacies of British Slave Ownership Project. Including, but not restricted to, Claims: British Guiana 1848, 1081, 1296, 546, 668.
111 East India Trade Committee Minute Book 1812–1833, 352 MIN/COU I 2/8, LivRO.
112 See the case study on James Lawson below, pp. 170–79.
113 See the case study on Samuel Rainford below, pp. 179–88.

the son of his financial backer, Jonathon Blundell junior, in 1779 as Rainford, Blundell & Rainford. They imported dry goods, food and largely engaged in the slave trade, exporting goods such as sugar and pimento in return. Initially successful, he and his backer, Jonathon Blundell senior, had a serious disagreement and parted ways which eventually led to the disintegration of Rainford, Blundell & Rainford. Given that Blundell was his main link to the slave trade investment groups via the Council and African Committee in Liverpool, this hurt Rainford's reputation in that port to some extent. However, he built up his networks and reputation around the Atlantic in other trades and invested unsuccessfully in a cotton estate as well. He died in 1798 possessed of about £15,700 sterling, some land and houses. However, seeing as Blundell had at one point advanced him around £16,000, this was not a sizeable balance. Samuel was clearly a risk taker, having migrated to Kingston in the first place, but his letters make it clear that he was also a kind, thoughtful man who supported his errant family in Liverpool and kept up a long-term remote friendship with Liverpool merchant Edward Chaffers.

These mini biographies have served as an introduction to some of the main characters in this book, but they are also meant to provide an insight into the different personalities, circumstances and motivations of individual merchants. Many others are mentioned later in the text. These include Thomas Leyland, David Tuohy, Peter Holme, Robert Bostock and John Leigh of Liverpool, the Brights and Meylers of Bristol, Joshua Johnson, Peter Clement and Joseph Hadfield in London, Alexander Johnston in New York, William Pollard, William Sitgreaves, Issac and Peter Wikoff and Daniel Clark in Philadelphia, Nathaniel Phillips and Curtis Brett in Jamaica, and Richard Miles in Cape Coast Castle, on the slave coast of Africa. Many others are also mentioned in passing, as they came into the orbit of the main characters. Despite their very different personalities, these men were all part of the merchant community and (mostly) conformed to the business culture which this book hopes to illuminate. It is now time to investigate their varying attitudes towards, and management of, risk.

2

Risk

Misfortunes may be sure to happen that human prudence cannot
forsee or guard against, but many there are that might be prevented
by prudence and proper attention.[1]

MISFORTUNES may be sure to happen! Merchants such as James
Clemens understood that risk was an everyday part of their work;
it was frequent and pervasive. More importantly, they realised that some
risks could not be guarded against, but that prudence and attention to detail
could help to manage others. Benjamin Franklin noted in 1760 that whilst
the needs of life were fixed and determined, 'The *Variety of Losses* a Trader
is liable to, by Trusting at Land, and Adventuring by Sea, by perishable
commodities, and Perils from Thieves and Fire, make it manifest, that
he is set in the midst of Contingencies' [emphasis in original].[2] Franklin
clearly perceived that risks were of different types: trusting at land we can
understand to be the moral hazard of other people; the risk of the sea and
fire we can take to be natural hazards; and in perishable commodities we can
think of technical hazard or knowledge aspects of the market.[3] Moreover, the

---

1 James Clemens & Co. to Capt Speers, 3 Jun. 1767, Ships' Papers, 380 TUO 4/2, DTP,
   LivRO. James Clemens joined the Liverpool town council in 1767 and was mayor
   in 1775, Liverpool Town Books. He was involved in at least ten slave trade voyages:
   26027; 82204; 90408; 90613; 90684; 90685; 90786; 90767; 90768; 90841. http://www.
   slavevoyages.org/tast/database/search.faces, accessed 8 Sep. 2011.
2 Benjamin Franklin, *The Way to be Wise and Wealthy: Recommended to All; Applied,
   more particularly, and accommodated to the several Conditions and Circumstances of
   the Gentleman. The Scholar, the Soldier, the Tradesman, the Sailor, the Artificer, the
   Husbandman*, by a Merchant, 4th edn (London: Printed for L. Davis and C. Reymers,
   1760), p. 40.
3 Peter Mathias also uses this terminology in his 'Risk, Credit and Kinship in early

ever-present nature of these risks caused constant anxiety. In another advice book of 1763 William Gordon noted that 'No profit is equal to the anxiety a man must be under, who hath perhaps as much at risk as he is worth in the world.'[4] Coping strategies varied: some merchants were risk averse, whilst others fully embraced risk, thriving in times of war, or being involved in the slave trade for example.[5] Risks, however, are socially constructed, and it is therefore important to place the perception and management of risk in historical context.

This chapter first considers the socio-cultural construction of risk before discussing risk and risk management in terms of natural, moral, and technical hazard. It will argue that although eighteenth-century merchants did not use terms such as natural, moral or technical hazard, they did perceive these types of risks separately and differently. Moreover, their nuanced understanding of these risks meant that they were mostly able to manage them extremely well.

THE SOCIO-CULTURAL CONSTRUCTION OF RISK

IT IS IMPORTANT to first consider what risk is, and in particular the difference between risk, hazard and uncertainty. Modern theorists clearly note the differences. James Short argues that 'Hazards are threats to people and what they value and risks are measures of those hazards.'[6] In contrast, uncertainty is where the probability of a hazard becoming a risk is inestimable or unknown. The hazard is the independent variable, whilst it is peoples' assessment of the probability (uncertainty) of that hazard occurring that leads to it being assessed as a risk. Risk is therefore the product of the probability, and consequences of any given hazard, or 'the potential for realization of unwanted, negative consequences of an event'.[7] In eighteenth-century terms, for example, we might think of the probability of the hazard of storms at sea

Modern Enterprise', in John J. McCusker and Kenneth Morgan, eds., *The Early-Modern Atlantic Economy* (Cambridge: Cambridge University Press, 2000), pp. 15–35.

4 Gordon, *The Universal Accountant*, Vol. II, p. 9.

5 Risks were higher and often of a different kind in the slave trade. See Sheryllynne Haggerty, 'Risk and Risk Management in the Liverpool Slave Trade', *BH*, 51:6 (Nov. 2009), 817–34.

6 James F. Short, 'Defining, Explaining, and Managing Risks', in James F. Short Jr. and Lee Clark, eds., *Organisation, Uncertainties and Risk* (Boulder, San Francisco and London: Westview Press, 1992), pp. 3–23, p. 5.

7 Deborah Lupton, *Risk* (London and New York: Routledge, 1999), pp. 7–9; Rowe quoted in Kathleen J. Tierney, 'Toward a Critical Sociology of Risk', *Sociological Forum*, 14:2 (Jun. 1999), 215–42, p. 217.

sinking a merchant's vessel. Merchants in the eighteenth century did use all of these terms, although not so precisely as we might like for our convenience. For example, James Lawson of Glasgow was very concerned at the end of the Seven Years' War with rumours of conquered islands being given back to the French and Spanish. He wrote 'it is very uncertain what turn Peace will give Trade'.[8] We might class such uncertainty, or lack of information, as technical hazard. In 1786 Liverpool merchant Thomas Leyland realized that dealing with certain people – moral hazard – was problematic and judged that he 'would cheerfully allow them a few pounds right or wrong to get quite out of any further hazard'.[9] Clearly, not all risks were the same, and needed managing differently as James Clemens realised; nor were eighteenth-century merchants always clear in their use of these terms. However, given that Short argues that the distinction between risk and hazard is often blurred by modern analysts, we can perhaps forgive contemporary merchants for doing the same.[10]

Notwithstanding any possible blurring of concepts, the notion of risk management was already well understood as a concept by the mid-eighteenth century.[11] In fact the serious study of risk had begun during the Renaissance. By 1725 mathematicians were collating tables of life expectancy and mortality rates and marine insurance was thriving. In 1730 the bell curve and standard deviation were devised and theories of utility and probability followed fast. The growth of science and mathematics led people to believe that, to some extent, they could take control over the accidental. They also understood, like modern theorists, that there were two separate and distinct elements to risk management: the objective facts (as far as they could be known), and the subjective view on the desirability of the possible outcome. Of course not all outcomes are equal, or are judged to be equal by different individuals. Decisions about risk are therefore made as part of a psychological process somewhere between the two, in what Naomi Lamoreaux calls 'the gap'.[12] Decision making about risk is therefore both culturally constructed and a very individual and emotive process.

8 James Lawson to John Semple, 10 Sep 1762, Letterbook 1762–1766, f. 17, SJLP.

9 Thomas Leyland to George & Thomas Keogh, 15 Jun. 1786, TLL, f. 16, LivRO.

10 Short, 'Defining, Explaining, and Managing Risk', p. 5.

11 This paragraph heavily relies on Peter L. Bernstein, *Against the Gods: The Remarkable Story of Risk* (New York: Wiley & Sons, 1996), introduction and chapters six and seven; Lupton, *Risk*. See also Stephen Hilgartner, 'The Social Construction of Risk Objects; Or; How to Pry Open Networks of Risk', in Short and Clark, *Organisation, Uncertainties and Risk*, pp. 39–56.

12 Naomi Lamoreaux, 'Reframing the Past: Thoughts about Business Leadership and Decision Making under Uncertainty', *Enterprise & Society*, 2:4 (Dec. 2001), 639–59, pp. 362, 643.

Objects of risk have to be defined before they can be managed, and are shaped by public discourse (institutions, the government and large-scale events for example) and private discourse (including shared experience with colleagues and personal predilections). A good example is hurricanes. Hurricanes had always existed in the Caribbean, but were defined as a new risk by Europeans as trade and plantation economies in the West Indies grew during the seventeenth and eighteenth centuries.[13] How a person perceived the risk of the hurricane was further shaped by personal experience, for example if he had travelled to, or lived in, the Caribbean himself. If a merchant had nearly been bankrupted by the failure of a Jamaican planter due to hurricane damage, he may have been less likely to trust Jamaicans in the future; an example of what Hancock calls 'network memory'.[14] Culture more generally can also help construct risks by contributing to a communal notion of risk, and obligations and expectations further shape those notions. For example, newspaper reports and talk in the coffee house of the devastation caused in Jamaica by the hurricane of 1772 would have shaped communal understanding of risking financial investment in the Caribbean.[15] Of course, such a disaster would also highlight a certain risk and make it appear more 'real'.[16] However, having a family member as a factor in Jamaica would still oblige a merchant to send cargoes there. Such decisions may be further shaped by personal preferences (the gap). At what point for example, would a merchant think the likelihood of losing a vessel at a certain time of year to a hurricane so low that he thought the cost of insurance no longer worthwhile? This is what Ralph Keeney refers to as the 'lives versus dollars' problem.[17] Trusted, up-to-date information is also important in risk assessment, and this was a world of far from perfect information. For example, the choice of whether or not to take out insurance for a vessel travelling to the Caribbean may have been determined by current insurance rates. However, in 1808 Thomas Martin, a Liverpool merchant, felt that he

13 Matthew Mulcahy, 'Weathering the Storms: Hurricanes and Risk in the British Greater Caribbean', *BHR*, 78 (Winter 2004), 635–63.
14 Lee Clarke, 'Context Dependency and Risk Decision Making', in Short and Clarke, *Organisations, Uncertainties and Risk*, pp. 27–38, p. 32; David Hancock, 'The Trouble with Networks: Managing the Scots' Early-Modern Madeira Trade', *BHR*, 79, Special Edition on Networks in the Trade in Alcohol (Autumn 2005), 467–91.
15 This was aggravated the by the recent collapse of the Ayr Bank. Mulcahy, 'Weathering the Storms', p. 655.
16 Robert A. Stallings, 'Media Discourse and the Social Construction of Risk', *Social Problems*, 37:1 (Feb. 1990), 80–95, pp. 80–81.
17 Ralph L. Keeney, 'The Role of Values and Risk Management', *Annals of the American Academy of Political and Social Science*, 545, Challenges in Risk Assessment and Risk Management (May 1996), 126–34, p. 127.

could not comment on the rate of insurance to America because 'he had not had advice from Liverpool of the rate of insurance for some days'.[18] He was in a situation of uncertainty.

Perceptions of risk are also shaped by institutions. In this respect the legal climate and government intervention is also important, even if the law often lags behind cultural and economic shifts.[19] For example, the rise in bankruptcy laws, the various Debtor's Acts of George III and the development of law protecting property around the Atlantic, encouraged trade by reducing the risk of extending credit, even at a distance.[20] Another example would be the Free Ports Act of 1766 which legalised trade with the Spanish and French colonies. The trade would have continued with or without government sanction, but to some, being legal may have made it appear less risky.[21] Rhetoric from, and between, the government, institutions such as trade associations, lobby groups and the media, also shaped (and in some cases, manipulated) discourse over risk. Merchants from the outports sent many memorials to central government over issues such as the Corn Laws, taxation, the slave trade and the effects of war. In 1814 the merchants of Liverpool submitted a memorial regarding the risk from American cruisers.[22] In time of war, merchants expected the government to mitigate their risk by providing convoys as reciprocation for their investment in empire.[23] As will be discussed later, these relationships between the state and the mercantile community were very important.

At the same time, governments help to promote new risk construction. Seventeenth- and eighteenth-century expansion in the Atlantic world is a great example of this. By creating chartered companies, the English government not only promoted expansion, but shifted the risk to others, both financially and physically. Governments can therefore create what Tierney calls 'a political economy of space'.[24] This is where certain groups are disadvantaged so that risks are unequally imposed on society. For example,

---

18 Evidence of Thomas Martin, 22 Mar. 1808, HCPP, 1808 (119), p. 47.
19 Short, 'Defining, Explaining, and Managing Risk', pp. 7–9.
20 See the section below on institutional trust, pp. 84–93.
21 On the Free Port System see Frances Armytage, *The Free Port System in the British West Indies: A Study in Commercial Policy, 1766–1822* (London, New York, Toronto: Longmans, Green and Co., 1953).
22 Memorial of the Merchants, Ship Owners, Underwriters and others, interested in the Shipping and Commerce of the Port of Liverpool, 1 Sep. 1814, HCPP, 1814–15 (45) (60), p. 4.
23 See a further discussion of these relationships below in the chapters on obligation pp. 150–59 and crises, *passim*.
24 Tierney, 'Toward a Critical Sociology', esp. p. 232.

mercantilist laws prevented colonists from manufacturing certain goods and forced them to ship via England or English colonies. They also curtailed the use of metal and paper money in the colonies.[25] This put colonists on the American mainland and (potentially) the British West Indies at a serious disadvantage in terms of balance of payments. In 1764 Charles Stewart wrote from London to his Virginia partners that 'The Merchants here, it seems, won't let your paper money alone while there is a shill[g] of it in the country, except they are insured against imaginary losses and ill found apprehensions.'[26] The British government also promoted staple agriculture production in the colonies and prohibited secondary manufacture as part of its mercantilist policy. As the production of tobacco in the colonial south and sugar in the West Indies were far more vulnerable to natural crises than manufacture at home, this was a clear example of extra risk being placed on those with less power at the periphery. Print was also significant in shaping perceptions of risk. One example of this is the many printed price currents sent from Liverpool to America during the Anglo-American crisis, which highlight a sense of panic and speculation that fluctuated almost daily according to the news from America and the Continent.[27] Often such news was interpreted according to how trusted the information was, or what the receiver wanted to believe; especially because information was often out of date or based on rumours.[28] As Ogborn notes, all text has to be seen in context, and speech, word and print are put together and used in particular situations.[29] Merchants therefore made decisions about risk that were shaped by interpretive filters from communal and national socio-cultural constructs. Merchants were not atomised individuals, but worked in the context of their surroundings in which hazards were only assessed as risks through such processes.[30]

As noted above, risk taking is also a subjective process. Some people appear to be more likely to take risks than others, although this is also shaped

25 Claire Priest, 'Law and Commerce, 1580–1815', in Michael Grossberg and Christopher Tomlins, eds., *The Cambridge History of Law in America, Vol. I, Early America 1580–1815* (Cambridge: Cambridge University Press, 2008), pp. 400–46.

26 Charles Stewart to Aitchinson & Parker, 29 Jan. 1764, Folder 920 PAR I 27/5, PP.

27 William and Rathbone Papers and Hughes and Duncan Papers, *passim*, BFBR, John Carter Brown Library.

28 See for example, information on the gold rush. Richard T. Stillson, *Spreading the Word: A History of Information in the California Gold Rush* (Lincoln and London: University of Nebraska Press, 2006); Clarke, 'Context Dependency', p. 30.

29 Miles Ogborn, *Indian Ink: Script and Print in the Making of the English East India Company* (Chicago and London: University of Chicago Press, 2007), pp. 23, 25.

30 Clarke, 'Context Dependency', p. 36; Lupton, *Risk*, pp. 38–39.

by gender constructions, life cycle and personal predilections. However, we cannot say that all merchants were risk takers simply because they were involved in overseas trade. Many were managers rather than entrepreneurs, others took over their business from their fathers, and not all were good at assessing or managing risk in any case. Some advocate a gendered element in risk taking. For example, Stephen Lyng has argued that men are more socialised towards skill orientation and that they feel less responsible for the care of others. This means that men are more likely to have an illusory sense of control than women, which leads them to underestimate risks, both of which are important for high-risk decision making.[31] There is also an element of 'heroic life' in extreme risk taking, which is a 'profoundly gendered' concept.[32] It is argued that whereas men take pride and delight in taking risk, women are more likely to feel guilt or shame for having potentially put themselves or their family's finances in jeopardy. It is true that in Liverpool and Philadelphia during the period 1766 to 1805 women did not account for even one per cent of all merchants, but this was largely due to their socially-constructed gendered roles and legal restrictions on their access to capital and credit.[33] At the same time it is arguable that many female traders took risks, but were not able to do so at the top of the status tree of traders. There is no doubt however, that there was an element of the performance of masculinity in eighteenth-century trade. Becoming a respectable merchant was also to become a man, and slurs against that reputation were often seen as slurs against masculinity.[34]

Age may also be a factor. Deborah Lupton suggests that young people, especially young men, are more likely to take risks.[35] Certainly merchants were aware of higher risk at the start of someone's career. Henry Laurens introduced a Mr Hest (his former clerk) to John Knight of Liverpool saying that he expected he would establish a good house 'after struggling thro some difficulties that young Adventurers must expect to encounter'.[36]

---

31 Stephen Lyng, 'Edgework: A Social Psychological Analysis of Voluntary Risk Taking', *AJS*, 95:4 (Jan. 1990), 851–86, 873.

32 Lupton, *Risk*, p. 158.

33 Haggerty, *The British Atlantic Trading Community*, p. 77.

34 John Smail, 'Coming of Age in Trade: Masculinity and Commerce in Eighteenth-Century England', in Margaret C. Jacob and Catharine Secretan, eds., *The Self Perception of Early Modern Capitalists* (New York: Palgrave MacMillan, 2008), pp. 229–252; Toby L. Ditz, 'Shipwrecked; or, Masculinity Imperiled: Mercantile Representations of Failure and the Gendered Self in Eighteenth-Century Philadelphia', *Journal of American History*, 81:1 (Jun. 1994), 51–80.

35 Lupton, *Risk*, p. 157.

36 Henry Laurens to John Knight, 8 May 1764, *HLP*, Vol. IV.

Nathaniel Phillips was disappointed that a venture had gone wrong in 1761, saying that he confessed 'it is very discouraging to a young adventurer'.[37] Some of these difficulties may be attributed to lack of skills, judgment or track record, as well, of course, as risk taking itself. Whatever young men's propensity to risk, experienced merchants and advice literature encouraged them to be prudent, frugal and industrious. William Gordon, having commented that an imprudent step may ruin a merchant's fortune, would have agreed with Thomas Leyland's decision to refuse an extension of credit until a bill was paid.[38] Leyland wrote 'I have for some time past declined all money engagements which exceed the funds in my possession.'[39] Such prudence is often thought of as a precautionary savings model. That is, older people are less prepared to lose wealth already obtained. Therefore it is possible that caution, or risk aversion, may increase with age. In 1805 William Rathbone IV advised a young man trying to make his way in New York that 'Thou knowst that persons of age & experience are more timid than young people.'[40] Peter Clement wrote to Andrew Clow in 1790 that they [Clow and his partner Cay] would rather wait a while 'than put to hazard what we have lately Earned by much pains and toil'.[41] At the same time however, those who are extremely wealthy can afford to take risks, at least with part of their fortune.[42] Wealth therefore gives people a choice that others do not have the luxury of. For example, merchants often invested surplus capital in ship-owning, insurance or land development, and whilst this was often seen as diversification to spread risk, it could also be seen as accepting new or more varied risks. For some, the greater the risk, the greater the approbation – as long as the risk taking of course, was successful.[43]

This search for public acknowledgment is also an important part of extreme risk taking, or 'edgework'. This is not about giving up control,

37 Nathaniel Phillips to Hilton & Biscoe, 3 Feb. 1761, Mailhet & Phillips Letterbook, 1759–?, Phillips Papers, National Library of Wales.

38 Gordon, *The Universal Accountant*, Vol. II, p. 1; Franklin, *The Way to Be Wise and Wealthy*.

39 Thomas Leyland to John Cullimore, 3 Jun. 1786, TLL, ff. 28–29.

40 William Rathbone to Thomas Rutter, 14 Mar. 1805, William Rathbone IV Letterbook, RP II 1.169, Sydney Jones Library.

41 Peter Clement to Andrew Clow, 6 Sep. 1790, Folder P. Clement, Andrew Clow & Co., CWU, HSP.

42 Louis Eeckhoudt and Harris Schlesinger, 'Putting Risk it Its Proper Place', *American Economic Review*, 96:1 (Mar. 2006), 280–89, pp. 280–82.

43 Quoted in Cathy Matson, 'Introduction: The Ambiguities of Risk in the Early Republic', *BHR*, 78 (Winter 2004), 595–606, pp. 601, 606. Wealth can also mean that women are prepared to take risks. See the references to gambling in Amanda Foreman, *Georgiana, Duchess of Devonshire* (London: Harper Collins, 1998).

but rather proving you have the skills and mindset to control an extremely risky situation. Lyng has argued that it is an important search for self in an over-socialized world, especially if that person is not really subsumed well into the community. It is about the experience itself, and involves high self-belief and almost ritualistic planning.[44] There are contemporary examples of this behaviour. Andrew Clow was an extremely controlling person who only really trusted his own judgment. He traversed the Atlantic every year to personally choose his goods and meet with his contacts. Interestingly, Lyng argues that we cannot understand such risk taking purely as a personality trait, but that we must also think about the historical context. This is an argument also made by Julian Hoppit who sees rising bankruptcy in the eighteenth century as a reflection of increased risk taking that failed. This was because the economy was growing so quickly, that many felt they had a good, or at least an equal chance, within this environment.[45] The expansion of the colonies and trade within this period meant that there were lots of opportunities for risk taking, especially during periods of tension or war. Indeed, war provided an extra opportunity for profit and speculation for those not averse to it. Many were of this disposition. For example, Stephen Girard of Philadelphia was always keen to take advantage of such situations, saying, 'I shall always take the gamble.'[46] Conway & Davidson of Liverpool wrote to Brown & Ives in Providence in 1809 that the news that the 'Non Intercourse Act Was Again put in force' had increased the spirit of speculation to a 'Mercantile Fever' and that this had induced the speculators to work on a Sunday![47] The high rate of failure at these times however, also suggests that there was a good deal of misjudgement of those opportunities.

In contrast, it would appear that some people are naturally more risk averse, over and above the precautionary savings model. Liverpool merchants William Rathbone IV and Thomas Martin were two of many that did not ship goods at their own risk, but preferred to work on commission.[48]

---

44 Lyng, 'Edgework'. Lyng has borrowed the term from Hunter S. Thompson. Lyng is mostly concerned with high-risk sports such as sky diving, but many of the elements he talks about are linked with entrepreneurship, such as self-belief, control, narcissism, individualism, and under-estimating risks. See Mark C. Casson, *The Entrepreneur: An Economic Theory* (Oxford: Martin Robinson, 1982), pp. 30–31.

45 Hoppit, *Risk and Failure*, chapter one.

46 Quoted in Cathy Matson, 'Accounting for War and Revolution: Philadelphia Merchants and Commercial Risk, 1774–1811', in Jacob and Secretan, *The Self Perception of Early Modern Capitalists*, pp. 183–202, p. 187.

47 Conway & Davidson to Brown & Ives, 16 Sep. 1809, Folder Conway & Davidson, B.64, 20–22, BFBR.

48 Evidence of Thomas Martin, 22 Mar. 1808, HCPP, 1808 (119), p. 47.

Likewise, in 1769 Peter Wikoff of Philadelphia wrote to John Ewer in London that he wanted to get on 'a more Sure & Certain footing', and that he was going to do this by importing fewer goods in the future.[49] In some cases however, it is possible to think that people were simply in the wrong profession. When Nathaniel Phillips' partner died in 1760, he wrote regarding James Mailhet's rather small fortune from trading in Jamaica that, 'I must here observe to you that he was rather too Timorous a Trader to make a Fortune.'[50] James Lawson of Glasgow appeared constantly worried about his business, especially the tobacco trade. He wrote in 1763, 'I really tremble to think what will be the consequences of such a Trade.'[51]

At the same time there is no doubt that some people in certain circumstances will take more or higher risks than others, or see different opportunities.[52] As Peter Bernstein notes, this is a good thing because 'If everyone valued every risk in precisely the same way, many risky opportunities would be passed up.'[53] Some groups may be perceived as more risk averse, for example the Quakers. Fox & Sons of Falmouth commented regarding one firm that 'it appears they have Quaker fears of all foreign transactions' [emphasis in original].[54] Others, however, were prepared to take more risks if they felt the reward was potentially high. Clearly there is a link between risk and profit. In 1772 Joshua Johnson noted that, 'If the tea is low at the March sale, I propose to sport a little in that.'[55] In contrast, even contemporaries realised that, 'There are some who have naturally adventurous spirits, who are resolved to be all or nothing.'[56] However, 'edgeworkers' such as Andrew Clow and very timorous traders were the exception. Most merchants were prudent; they

49 Peter Wikoff to John Ewer, 20 Oct. 1769, Folder Peter Wikoff to John Ewer, CBP.
50 Nathaniel Phillips to Hilton & Biscoe, 10 Jun. 1760, Mailhet & Phillips Letterbook 1759–?.
51 James Lawson to John Semple, 9 May 1763, Letterbook 1762–1766, SJLP.
52 The ability to take risk is a key entrepreneurial characteristic. Mark C. Casson, *Entrepreneurship and Business Culture: Studies in the Economics of Trust* (Aldershot: Elgar, 1995), p. 95.
53 Bernstein, *Against the Gods*, p. 105.
54 Joseph Hadfield to Andrew Clow, 23 Sep. 1790, Folder Joseph, John & Thomas Hadfield 1785–88, Andrew Clow & Co., Box 12, CWU. This is of course a stereotype as many Quakers were involved in overseas trade as shown by the large numbers in the Philadelphia trading community. Thomas M. Doerflinger, *A Vigorous Spirit of Enterprise: Merchants and Economic Development in Revolutionary Philadelphia* (Williamsburg, VA: University of North Carolina Press, 1986).
55 Joshua Johnson to Wallace and Davidson, 25 Feb. 1772, JJL.
56 Gordon, *The Universal Accountant*, Vol. II, p. 9. Bernstein notes that risk comes from risicare which means to dare in Italian. 'In this sense, risk is a choice, rather than a fate.' *Against the Gods*, p. 8.

were prepared to take risk, but had a healthy respect for the challenges facing them, and did their best to manage them effectively.

There were of course situations which were put down to God, fate, bad luck or misfortune. These were usually when someone was unable to say what happened, or what went wrong, or where there was a large degree of uncertainty.[57] For example, William Earle was still able to write 'which goods please God come to hand' in 1760.[58] If not God, then fate or magic could be blamed. Curtis Brett wrote in 1767 following a particularly troublesome order, that 'I am now tempted to think there is some spell on this Article of shoes.'[59] As late as 1803, following the death of four managers at Pomeroon, a Demerara sugar estate, the owners wrote that, 'Particular ill luck seems to Attend us with our managers on that place.'[60] Note that they did not mention the debilitating climate. Luck, however, could be good as well as bad. Henry Laurens hoped that good luck would help him in a slave trade vessel which was due to arrive at a dangerous time on the coast. He hoped to make a great sale 'if every [thing] conspired in ones favour at the same time'.[61] Luck could also be relative. Clement Noble, on a slave trade voyage on the African Coast circa 1783, wrote to Richard Miles, the Governor of Cape Coast Castle, following a number of events against his favour:

> Bad luck you' say throughout the whole expedition; But not so bad as my neighbour Aspinall [a Liverpool captain], For the people [African traders] has run off with his boat altogether.[62]

There is a sense however, that even luck could be altered or shaped. Alexander Johnston, having travelled around the Atlantic, made the decision to settle in New York following the American War of Independence. He wrote to a colleague that he was 'determined to try my luck, and with the assistance of my friends endeavour to establish myself in business'.[63] He used his experience and knowledge to make the rather astute assessment that New York would soon take over from Philadelphia as the great port of the Eastern

---

57 Bernstein, *Against the Gods*, p. 121.
58 William Earle to Sparling & Bolden, 25 Mar. 1760, Letter Book of William Earle, EC/2/2, MMMA.
59 Curtis Brett to Francis Allwood, 24 Dec. 1767, CBL, in private hands.
60 McInroy, Sandbach & McBean to James McInroy, 7 Jun. 1803, Folder 920 PAR, IV 1/4, PP.
61 Henry Laurens to John & Thomas Tipping, 15 Dec. 1763, *HLP*, Vol. IV.
62 Clement Noble to Richard Miles, n.d. (c.1783), CRA, Part I, TNA; possibly James Aspinall, see voyage 82769, Eltis et al., eds., *The Trans-Atlantic Slave Trade Database*, http://www.slavevoyages.org/tast/database/search.faces, accessed 29 Nov. 2009.
63 Alexander Johnson to Thomas Gordon, 3 Dec. 1783, AJL, NLJ.

Seaboard.⁶⁴ We should not take these comments too literally individually, but collectively they demonstrate that merchants still allowed for luck, fate or other factors they could not control or understand. Mostly however, merchants in this period felt that much *was* in their control, and this is turn affected their attitudes towards risk and risk management. William Gordon noted that, 'Commerce is not a game of chance, but of science.'⁶⁵ Most merchants believed the truth was somewhere in between.

MANAGING RISK

I T WAS NOTED ABOVE that William Gordon realised that merchants faced a variety of hazards. We can group these, in modern categories, under three main headings: natural, moral, and technical. That is, hazards posed by the vagaries of nature and war, those posed by decisions made by other people, and those posed by technology, or, more precisely, the lack of it. Natural hazards of course include the sea, disease, hurricanes and other extreme conditions of nature. Also included here, because they were mostly out of the merchants' control, are hazards caused by war, including privateering. This is not to say that conversely, many merchants did not take advantage of these situations themselves. Moral hazard of course represents the risk of trading with other people. Changes in markets as places and markets as commodities, as well as knowledge about vessels and other trading expertise, are included in technical hazard, because they are all concerned with knowledge. As will become clear, these categories are not always distinctive, and often overlap, but for ease and clarity of discussion they have been grouped in this way.

Some elements of risk were handled at a different level, or collectively. For example, it is well known that most, though certainly not all, merchants reduced risk by going into partnerships (not necessarily the family firm) which gave access to finance, knowledge, expertise and skills.⁶⁶ Others shipped their goods to various people, using different vessels to the same location, in order to spread the risk of financial failure or the loss of vessels at sea. Merchants of course used a variety of risk-reduction or management strategies, and it is not possible to cover them all here. However, examples have been chosen in order to highlight the major elements of risk and their management.

---

64 *Ibid.* See also Doerflinger, *A Vigorous Spirit of Enterprise*, chapter eight.
65 Gordon, *The Universal Accountant*, Vol. I, p. 4.
66 See for example Hancock, *Citizens of the World*, pp. 104–14.

Natural Hazard

As Clarke and Short argue, 'few natural disasters are entirely unexpected'.[67] They tend to advance in stages: order, chaos and the reconstitution of order. Bad weather usually occurs in winter, people learned that hurricanes arrived in late summer and autumn, and privateers were expected in wartime. Natural hazards can also be exacerbated by human elements such as unreliable technology, not insuring a vessel, or human frailties. For example, who was at fault in the case of a drunken sailor who fell in a dock which did not have adequate barriers?[68] Natural hazard was also an area in which much of the actual risk was shifted onto the sailors and supercargoes, even if the merchant still carried most of the financial risk. If bad choices were made by the merchant – such as sending an unseaworthy vessel to sea – then the risk was also imposed unfairly. Importantly, merchants perceived natural hazards differently to other types of hazard. For example, William Earle was disappointed about the fine prospects of the *Francis* after it was lost off the coast of Fuerteventura in June 1760. However, although he had received 'the most shocking diasgreable Acc^{tt}' of its loss, there was no sense of blame towards the captain. Rather, the weather was blamed.[69] John Copland of Liverpool described the captain of a vessel as 'poor Nelson' after he and all his crew were supposed perished following the floundering of the vessel due to a gale in 1783.[70] Three years later Thomas Leyland appeared stoical about his vessel, the *Nelly*, running into a storm in which the decks were cleared and the hold filled with water. Such 'Acts of God' were apparently put down to bad luck.[71]

This did not mean that merchants could do nothing to mitigate natural hazards. Good planning and insurance went a long way to help manage these risks; therefore a level of blame was placed if ill-conceived decisions were made. For example, it was well known that the Delaware froze over during the winter and so Clement Biddle specifically asked for candles to arrive in

---

67 Lee Clarke and James F. Short, 'Social Organisation and Risk: Some Current Controversies', *Annual Review of Sociology*, 19 (1993), 375–99, p. 378.

68 Liverpool had a system to cope with this very scenario, and had long poles with hooks placed around the dock to drag people out. A guinea was given to the rescuer for someone pulled out alive, and half a guinea if they were dead. David Brazendale, ed., *Georgian Liverpool: A Guide to the City in 1797* (Lancaster: Palatine Books, 2007).

69 William Earle to John Humphreys, 3 Jun. 1760, Letterbook of William Earle 1760–1761, EC.

70 John Copland to Richard Miles, 22 Aug. 1783, CRA, Part I.

71 Thomas Leyland to Cahill & White, 22 Dec. 1786, TLL.

Philadelphia before the ice stopped navigation.[72] Likewise, in January 1792, William Wilson of Alexandria was unwilling to take more flour on board until the weather had broken.[73] However, competition to be the first to arrive at a market could encourage people to take unnecessary risks. The captain of the *Manchester* did not really want to leave Liverpool in July 1790 because of the contrary winds, but seeing another vessel also bound for Philadelphia departing, he felt compelled to sail.[74] As noted above, extreme weather conditions became more of a reality for Europeans over the seventeenth and eighteenth centuries, as those sailing to the southern states, and especially the West Indies, had to endure hurricanes. They were a constant concern for merchants even if people such as Henry Laurens had learned about the seasonality of the storms and the signs associated with them. Small steps such as taking down part of mills and fastening doors and windows with wood were taken to mitigate the threat from hurricanes, but to a large extent these risks were lived with rather than managed.[75]

The risk of sickness and death was also high in the American South and the Caribbean, but was also an ever-present reality for sailors, especially those involved in the slave trade.[76] Fevers and gastro-intestinal problems were the largest health issue for the crew as well as enslaved Africans. Merchants warned their captains not to stay on the African coast too long in order to protect their health, and to purchase only the fittest slaves at the start of the journey because they would have to be in the hold the longest. In 1751 William Earle instructed the captain of the *Chesterfield*, on its way to Calabar, not to 'Risqᵉ your own lives by such long detention'.[77] However, it was realised that deaths occurred regularly on such voyages and slave traders

---

72 Clement Biddle & Co. to Nicholas & John Brown, 28 Aug. 1768, Correspondence with Francis & Relfe, Folder 6, BFBR.

73 William Wilson to Andrew Clow, 16 Jan. 1792, Andrew Clow & Co., Letters Received, Baker Library.

74 Andrew Clow to David Cay, 29 Jul. 1790, Folder Admin 1789–90, Andrew Clow & Co. Correspondence, CWU.

75 Most storms develop in the eastern Atlantic Ocean off the African coast, although some originate in the Caribbean. They form during the summer and autumn months when the ocean water temperature is highest, and are carried by the trade winds. Hurricanes occasionally move up to the mid-Atlantic and New England states, but they are most common and destructive in the Caribbean basin. Mulcahy also mentions the additional risks of slave insurrections, drought and insects. They caused huge economic losses. Mulcahy, 'Weathering the Storms', pp. 653, 636, 652, 638, 639 and 649.

76 This paragraph is based on Haggerty, 'Risk and Risk Management'.

77 Letter of Instructions from the owners of the Chesterfield, 22 May 1751, D/Earle/1/1, EC.

such as Robert Bostock gave instructions as to who was to take over if the captain of a vessel died, and on down through the mates in turn.[78] Nor was it only on slave adventures that such precautions were stipulated. The owners of the brigantine *Juno*, with a cargo of mahogany, told the captain William Smith that in case of misfortune, his mate Samuel Bowen would take over.[79]

Piracy was on the decline in the eighteenth century, having been re-categorised by the state, but war and privateering were prevalent.[80] The choice to go to war was out of the hands of the merchants, the decision being made by the state. Merchants were usually against war because it interfered with trade, however, they were keen to lobby the state to get the best outcome once war was at hand.[81] The many wars of the eighteenth and early nineteenth centuries did mean that they were an almost constant threat. This not only made markets unpredictable (or even inaccessible), it also heightened the risk of being taken prisoner, of having goods confiscated and/or vessels lost through privateering. During the Seven Years' War Daniel Clark of Philadelphia felt that he could not risk ordering more goods from Haliday & Dunbar of Liverpool until peace came.[82] Such hazards were only too real throughout the period. In 1795 James McInroy captaining the *Union*, left Tobago and was met by a French privateer the day after he sailed. He and his crew managed to fight her off, but he wrote that the privateer had 'Crippled us so much, that We Were forced in here [Grenada] to refit'.[83]

A principal way in which the problems of shipping in wartime were managed was through the convoy system. This particular management of risk required the assistance of the state.[84] Of course convoys altered planning, as well as glutting markets by several vessels arriving at port at once. Liverpool-based captain Richard Woods found that he was forced to leave with a convoy from Jamaica during the American War of Independence because it was the last that year, and his frustration was evident. This meant that he had not had enough time to load the vessel properly. 'I fear the Ship won't be half

---

78 Robert Bostock to William Walker, 31 Mar. 1786, RBL, LivRO.
79 Owners of the Juno to William Smith, 4 Apr. 1804, Folder Maritime, Brig Juno, 3 Apr. 1804–30, May 1807, BFBR.
80 Ogborn, *Global Lives*, chapter seven. See also David J. Starkey, *British Privateering Enterprise in the Eighteenth Century* (Exeter: University of Exeter Press, 1990).
81 On the obligations between the mercantile community and the state, see below, pp. 150–59.
82 Daniel Clark to Haliday & Dunbar, 14 Nov. 1761, DCL, HSP.
83 James McInroy to James Parker, 1 Nov. 1795, 920 PAR I 50/4, PP.
84 Responses to many large-scale natural disasters can only be handled by large organizations. Tierney, 'Toward a Critical Sociology', p. 230. The British government also helped with loans to West Indian colonies following particularly bad hurricanes. See below, p. 203.

full ... this proves a Verrey [sic] Unfortunate Adventure When Men meet with Loss and Disapointment [sic] it Generally makes them very peevish and illnatur'd.'[85] Others found the convoy system very reassuring. Merchants often gave standing orders to their correspondents to insure vessels for them, but in 1760 Nathaniel Phillips of Jamaica felt that the risk of sailing with a convoy was so trifling that he wished his London correspondents had not fully insured the journey because it was expensive.[86] War of course raised the cost of insurance in the first place.[87] During the Seven Years' War Charles Stewart (of the Parker network), then in Norfolk, felt that '25 Guineas from hence to London is an excessive premium, much greater than the risk and which no trade can bear' (the lives versus dollars issue).[88] In contrast, David Tuohy found it impossible to get insurance for the *Tim* – most likely sailing from Liverpool to Ireland during the American War of Independence – because the underwriters felt the risk was too high.[89] In their own way, underwriters were both reconstructing and shaping responses to risk, just as their perceptions in turn were shaped by events during periods of war.[90] As many merchants were also insurance brokers, there could also have been a conflict of interest. For example, John Stanton and Thomas Case of Liverpool were both merchants involved in arranging insurance as part of their business portfolios.[91]

---

85 Richard Woods to David Tuohy, 6 Jun. 1781, Letters to David Tuohy, 380 TUO/1, DTP.

86 Nathaniel Phillips to James Hibbert & Son 16 Feb. 1760, Mailhet & Phillips Letterbook 1759–?, f. 5 (second sequence).

87 In 1724 the rate for London to Jamaica was 2.10 per cent, whilst in 1782 it was 12 per cent with convoy and 20 per cent without. Hugh Anthony Lewis Cockerell, *The British Insurance Business 1547–1970: An Introduction and Guide to Historical Records in the UK* (London: Heinemann Educational Books Ltd, 1976), p. 10; Raymond Flower and Michael Wynn Jones, *Lloyd's of London: An Illustrated History* (Newton Abbott: David & Charles, 1974), p. 63. In 1806–7, the rate of insurance from Liverpool to America rose from 3 to 5 per cent with the news of the Berlin Decree. Evidence of Thomas Martin, 22 Mar. 1808, HCPP, 1808 (119), p. 46.

88 Quoted in Glenn A. Crothers, 'Commercial Risk and Capital Formation in Early America: Virginia Merchants and the Rise of American Marine Insurance, 1750–1815', *BHR* (Winter 2004), 607–33, p. 63.

89 Joseph Bland to David Tuohy, 19 May 1779, 380 TUO 1/1, DTP. It was not possible to confirm the destination of the *Tim*, but David Tuohy was mostly involved in trade to Ireland and the West Indies.

90 Clarke and Short, 'Social Organisation and Risk', p. 381.

91 John Stanton was a ship's captain first, but worked his way up to eventually become involved in insurance and lending money to other merchants in Liverpool. See Insurance and Disbursement Book for the Molly, D157 M/3371 & M/3372; John Stanton Private Account Book. D157 M/T 3375, both Derbyshire Record Office; Haggerty, 'Liverpool, the Slave Trade', pp. 19–24.

Others of course embraced war as a financial opportunity and many were engaged in privateering.[92] Fortunatus Wright, William Boats and Ambrose Lace, all of Liverpool, applied for Letters of Marque in 1756 at the outbreak of the Seven Years' War.[93] On the 22 December 1757 George Hopkins left Porte Plate [St. Domingue] in the company of three New York privateers. They engaged a vessel for 'Seven Hours Pritty Warm.'[94] Hopkins ended up taking the other vessel and wrote to John Brown in Providence, apparently very pleased with himself. David Tuohy was involved in cruising off the Spanish Main during the American War of Independence, although without much luck. His captain, Richard Woods, wrote that 'I have comply^d with the Instructions, and if I Cant Meet With the Enemy its not my fault but Misfortune.'[95] This is an interesting example of misfortune being blamed for not being able to take a risk.[96]

Moral Hazard

The term moral hazard may not have been used before the mid-nineteenth century, but the concept was well understood, and there is no doubt that trading around the Atlantic world posed a huge agency problem for merchants.[97] William Gordon noted that 'unless a trader thoroughly knows his correspondent, and can absolutely depend on his honour and punctuality

---

92 For more on privateering see below, pp. 158–59, 203–4, 209–10.

93 Letters of Marque or Reprisals Against France from the 27 May 1756–16 Sep 1756, HCA26/5, TNA; see also Gomer Williams, *History of the Liverpool Privateers and Letters of Marque with An Account of the Liverpool Slave Trade 1744–1812* [1897] (Liverpool: Liverpool University Press, 2004).

94 George Hopkins to John Brown, [?] Jan. 1758, Correspondence with Francis & Relfe, Folder 8, BFBR.

95 Richard Woods to David Tuohy, 6 Jun. 1781, Letters to David Tuohy, 380 TUO/1, DTP.

96 Bernstein notes that for some, not taking a risk is considered more expensive that not 'playing' at all. *Against the Gods*, p. 108.

97 Robin Pearson, 'Moral Hazard and the Assessment of Insurance Risk in Eighteenth- and Early-Nineteenth-Century Britain', *BHR*, 76 (Spring 2002), 1–35, p. 6. For good précis of these issues see Norman Strong and Michael Waterson, 'Principals, Agents and Information', in Roger Clarke and Tony McGuinness, eds., *The Economics of the Firm* (New York and London: Basil Blackwell Ltd, 1987), pp. 18–41; Michael C. Jensen and William H. Meckling, 'Theory of the Firm: Managerial Behaviour and Ownership Structure', *Journal of Financial Economics*, 3 (1976), 305–60. Moral Hazard occurs where the principal and agent have the same information up to the point where the agent selects an action; adverse selection is where the principal does not have access to the same information as the agent, and the principal cannot know whether the agent's decision was the optimal one for the principal. Strong and Waterson, 'Principals, Agents and Information', p. 21.

in business, he runs greater hazards than every one is aware of'.[98] However, in the ever-growing and changing mercantile community of the Atlantic world, it was not always possible to know 'of', let alone personally 'know', all your correspondents. Most of these trading relationships were within non-negotiated exchanges; that is, not subject to formal contracts.[99] However, even within partnerships, it was not always possible to predict how the other person would react. In late 1802 John MackPherson dissolved his partnership in Demerara with Mr Greigh[?]. For the next six months MackPherson went around collecting the debts owed to the partnership, but in March 1803 he 'took an Irish leave of the colony ... in an American vessel'.[100] Presumably this was a reference to the poor reputation of the Irish, meaning that he had absconded from the island with the money.[101] An extreme case perhaps, but various mechanisms were used to manage distant relationships in order to reduce the potential for such occurrences. This of course incurred information costs, but reduced the risk.[102] Occasionally partnership agreements were drawn up between partners, and basic credit terms were usually set out in letters between the principal and the agent, but often these were not enforceable in practice, especially across the Atlantic. Such problems could be overcome by reputational mechanisms and monitoring, but other strategies such as repeated exchange, advance payment and vertical integration were also used.

Historians usually stress the importance of familial, ethnic or religious ties in ameliorating the moral hazard of networks.[103] Such networks were thought to provide trustworthy agents, secured by the 'implicit contract of family'.[104]

---

98 Gordon, *The Universal Accountant*, Vol. II, p. 6.

99 Linda D. Molm, Nobuyuki Takahashi and Gretchen Peterson, 'Risk and Trust in Social Exchange: An Experimental Test of a Classical Proposition', *AJS*, 105:5 (Mar. 2000), 1396–427, p. 1396.

100 McInroy, Sandbach, McBean & Co. to J. McInroy, 10 Apr. 1803, 920 PAR 1/2/2, PP.

101 For the reputation of the Irish see Hilary McD. Beckles, 'A "riotous and unruly Lot": Irish Indentured Servants and Freemen in the English West Indies, 1644–1713', *WMQ*, 3rd ser., 47 (1990), 503–22. For the reputation of various 'nations', see below, pp. 121–30.

102 Jensen and Meckling, 'Theory of the Firm', pp. 309, 327, 333.

103 For a fuller discussion of the issues covered in this paragraph, see the chapter six on networks.

104 See for example, Mary B. Rose, 'The Family Firm in British Business, 1780–1914', in Maurice W. Kirby and Mary B. Rose, eds., *Business Enterprise in Modern Britain from the Eighteenth to the Twentieth Century* (London: Routledge, 1994), pp. 61–87; Leonore Davidoff and Catharine Hall, *Family Fortunes: Men and Women of the English Middle Class 1780–1850* (London: Hutchinson, 1987), esp. chapter four; Mathias, 'Risk, Credit and Kinship'; Margaret Hunt, *The Middling Sort: Commerce, Gender, and the Family in England, 1680–1780* (Berkeley, Los Angeles and London: University of California Press, 1996); Yoram Ben-Porath, 'The F-Connection: Families, Friends, and Firms,

This of course did occur. The Rathbones of Liverpool passed their business from father to son in successive generations, and the Parker family dynasty which stretched between London, Glasgow, Liverpool, Virginia, Demerara and Grenada, was secured by family ties, strengthened by inter-marriage.[105] Ascribed trust based on ethnic and religious ties was also thought to be more secure.[106] However, family networks were far from always being reliable and obligations based on ascribed trust were not always fulfilled.[107] Therefore, whilst such networks were useful at the start of a merchant's career, if he wanted to expand his business, in terms of place or commodity markets or simply to gain a larger slice of an existing trade, he needed to go outside these limited, tight-knit relationships. Branching out gave wider access to skills, knowledge and finance, as well as information and people, through networks of weak ties.[108]

Merchants could at least know 'of' a potential correspondent by recommendation and letters of introduction. Taylor & Jackson of Manchester wrote to Andrew Clow in 1789 that their mutual friend Joseph Hadfield had recommended his house, and that they were sending two bales of textiles to try the market (and no doubt his house too).[109] Such recommendations did not always put people's minds at rest. Henry Laurens decided in 1764 that he did not know a Mr Head well enough and so was reluctant to go into business with him despite some handsome credentials from his Liverpool correspondent John Knight.[110] Andrew Clow wrote to his partner in 1790 regarding an order of goods which had been shipped on behalf of a particular individual:

> I presume you will consider the stability of the House before you dispose of the Goods, I am not anxious to go to great lengths with any individual [he

---

and the Organization of Exchange', *Population and Development Review*, 6:1 (Mar. 1980), 1–30, p. 1.

105 Nottingham, *Rathbone Brothers*; PP, *passim*.

106 Lynne G. Zucker 'Production of Trust: Institutional Sources of Economic Structure, 1840–1920', *Research in Organizational Behaviour*, 8 (1986), 53–111; Ann Prior and Maurice Kirby, 'The Society of Friends and the Family Firm', *BH*, 35:4 (1993), 66–85; James Walvin, *The Quakers: Money and Morals* (London: John Murray, 1997).

107 See discussion on obligation in chapter five, and a further discussion on networks in chapter six.

108 Hancock, *Citizens of the World*, pp. 104–14; Mark S. Granovetter, 'The Strength of Weak Ties', *AJS*, 78:6 (May 1973), 1360–80.

109 Taylor & Jackson to Andrew Clow & Co., 25 Jul. 1789, Folder Andrew Clow, 1786–1789, Andrew Clow & Co., CWU.

110 This particular case may have been as much about personality as risk. Henry Laurens to John Knight, 22 Dec. 1764, *HLP*, Vol. IV. John Knight had business interests in the Caribbean as well. See John Tomlinson's Account Current with John Knight, 380 MD 127, LivRO.

wanted to spread the risk around various correspondents], but I had this order executed on your very strong recommendation of his Solidity, which I hope you are well convinced of.[111]

Nor was it just in commodity dealing that such care was taken. Clow was also heavily involved in stock investments, and when he came to sell some he told his broker William Wilson to 'be careful to deal with none but those that can be depended upon'.[112] Such monitoring was continuous of course, because even a long standing, reputable house, could fall to misfortune.[113]

If it was not possible to get a recommendation or letter of introduction, one way of managing risk was through repeated exchange. That is, building up trust over time by taking small risks in the first instance. In 1761 Philadelphia merchant Daniel Clark made the acquaintance of a Manchester manufacturer, Mr Hyde, in consequence of which Clark sent him a small order for low-priced goods.[114] Quaker Owen Biddle of Philadelphia wrote a similar letter to John Ewer in 1771. He had 'taken the Liberty to send thee a small Order ... Should this Order be compleated [sic] to satisfaction it will induce a further & more extensive correspondence'.[115] Such small beginnings could prove useful in the long term by leading to co-investment and gift-giving.[116] Liverpool merchant Charles Angus wrote to Grenadian-based merchant Edward Stewart in 1799, trying to encourage him to buy slaves from Liverpool ships rather than those from Lancaster. He wrote that they could start small, but that if they got on they could invest in a ship together.[117] This is not to say that such reciprocal relationships were always successful; 'even in established relations, exploitation is always possible'.[118] Samuel Rainford moved to Kingston, Jamaica, and set up in business with leading Liverpool merchant Jonathon Blundell. However, even with an interest in the firm, Blundell did not fully support Rainford and the business ended extremely acrimoniously. In a similar manner the *Bright-Meyler Papers*

111 Andrew Clow to David Cay, 4 Oct. 1790, Andrew Clow Business Papers, Folder David Cay, CWU.

112 Andrew Clow to William Wilson & Co., 21 Jan. 1792, Andrew Clow & Co., Letters Received, Folder One, Baker Library. For reputation more generally see chapter four.

113 For more on monitoring see chapter four, *passim*.

114 Daniel Clark to Hyde & Hamilton, 20 Nov. 1761, DCL.

115 Owen Biddle to John Ewer, 11th Mon. 15, 1771, Folder Owen Biddle to John Ewer, CBP.

116 Molm et al., 'Risk and Trust in Social Exchange'. For more on staying, gift giving and co-investing see chapter three, pp. 75–77.

117 Charles Angus to Edward Stewart, 5 Mar. 1799, Charles Angus Letterbook, University of West Indies Archives, Mona, Jamaica.

118 Molm et al., 'Risk and Trust in Social Exchange', p. 1401.

show that even family relationships could not always be relied upon. Morgan describes Robert Bright as 'hapless' and noted that the fact that he did not go to Jamaica to assist his brother with his store was probably a good thing, as he 'frittered away money and had no experience of life or business'.[119]

If for some reason both personal recommendations and taking small risks would not answer, then an advance payment could always serve where trust was missing (though the advance payer had to trust the supplier to provide the goods of course). This did not happen very often, but was certainly another option. The Herculaneum Pottery in Liverpool apparently had an issue with its customers from Nova Scotia. Thomas Leonard in 1810–11 and John Allbro in 1814, both of Halifax, had to pay in advance for their pottery orders. Leonard got a slightly better deal as he received interest on his credit balance as well as a discount, but Allbro only received the discount.[120] Some went to great lengths to secure money for such advances for trade. In 1772 William Pollard of Philadelphia was acting as an intermediary and negotiating between Edward Barret based in Jamaica but at that time in Philadelphia, and Peter Holme of Liverpool.[121] Barret wanted Holme to advance him £2000 for which he would ship rum and sugar annually in return until the debt was paid off. Some of this debt was to go to Thomas & Clayton Case of Liverpool, but the remainder could be used for purchases.[122]

One very interesting example of collective risk management is the guarantee system devised for West Indian planters' purchases of slaves.[123] The West Indies had a poor reputation for payment and much of this was attributed to an adverse selection problem – that they would prefer to engage in conspicuous consumption and buy more slaves before they paid the outstanding debts.[124] During the seventeenth and early eighteenth centuries, payments had been made either in produce, bills of exchange, or less often, specie. Bills were preferred, but those from West Indian planters were far from reliable and so a system of guarantees was developed. In essence, English merchants would not sell slaves to planters in the West Indies unless

---

119 *BMP*, pp. 44, 37.
120 Herculaneum Potteries Ledger, ff. 131, 174, 198, LivRO.
121 Such intermediators need a reputation for integrity. Mark C. Casson, 'Institutional Economics and Business History: A Way Forward?', *BH*, Special issue on Institutions and the Evolution of Modern Business, 39:4 (1997), 151–71, esp. pp. 159–64. Barret was from Jamaica but was spending time with his family in Philadelphia. William Pollard to William Reynolds, 25 May 1772, WPL, HSP.
122 William Pollard to Peter Holme, 16 May 1772, WPL.
123 For more on the guarantee system see Kenneth Morgan, 'Remittance Procedures in the Eighteenth-Century British Slave Trade', *BHR*, 79 (Winter 2005), 715–49.
124 See chapter four for the reputation of mercantile communities, pp. 121–26.

the debt was underwritten by a merchant house in Britain, most often in London, it being the predominant capital market. These guarantees would be for a particular number of slaves, on a specific vessel, and via specific agents in the West Indies. Whilst to some extent this reduced choice, it made selling slaves in the West Indies a far less risky proposition. This institution was used by merchants all around the Atlantic and by 1779 the system was so integrated into business practice that William Davenport of Liverpool advised a potential trading partner that they must have a guarantee in England, or else it would be 'morally impossible' to fit-out ships for their consignments.[125]

Technical Hazard

William Gordon exhorted merchants to know the world and its markets because knowledge was central to managing risk, whether it was the vessel itself, or markets as places or commodities.[126] In many ways, technical and natural hazards are linked. The sea is a natural hazard, but the degree of risk is often dependent on the quality of the vessel, which in turn is determined by the present technology available, and by human decision making. Hurricanes and other severe weather caused changes in commodity markets. Constant changes in fashions caused frequent alterations in demand and supply. However, if 'the meaning [of a hazard] is in the response', that is, how it is managed, then contemporaries thought very differently about the hazards posed by markets and commodities and their carriage in vessels than about the hazards posed by the weather and other risks they could not control.[127] How such risks were managed was also important in reactions to merchants who suffered by such an event. For example, whilst one could not blame a particular person for a sea squall or an act of war (they might blame the relevant state for the latter), making a bad decision due to a lack of knowledge or expertise – or even worse, extreme risk taking – was frowned upon, and an element of blame came into play. Therefore, the use of improved navigational charts, better and faster vessels, more sophisticated maps, sheathing and arming of vessels, and the increased availability and use of printed price currents and newspapers and communications more generally, not only gave merchants the sense of a 'Demise of Distance' but also a sense of control.[128]

---

125 William Davenport to Vance, Caldwell & Vance, 28 Feb. 1779, Letterbook and Accounts, D/DAV/2/1, WDP, MMMA.

126 Gordon, *The Universal Accountant*, Vol. II, p. 3.

127 Clarke and Short, 'Social Organisation and Risk', pp. 376–77.

128 Crothers, 'Commercial Risk', pp. 608–9, 615. Steele, *The English Atlantic*, p. 273; John J. McCusker, 'The Demise of Distance: The Business Press and the Origins of the

There were therefore various ways to obtain information and knowledge to combat technical hazards. There was also a plethora of advice literature available.[129] These included one-off publications, annual yearbooks and monthly magazines such as *The Tradesman*. They covered a wide variety of information, for every level of experience. For example, *The Merchants Guide* of 1774 gave instructions on Custom House procedures, *The Merchant Freighter's and Captains of Ships Assistant* facilitated the calculation of freight rates, and William Gordon gave advice on copying letters, accounts and the calculation of bounties.[130] Such books were used around the Atlantic, for example, *The American Instructor; or, Young Man's Best Companion*.[131] Some were even locally produced such as *The Liverpool Memorandum* of 1753, although they contained much the same information as the national editions.[132] For those who wanted to acquire a wider perspective there was always Postlethwayt's 'dissertations' or Pelatiah Webster's 'essays' on trade, as well as Adam Smith's writings.[133] Educational publications remained important throughout a merchant's career, as evidenced by Samuel Rainford's library when he died in Jamaica in 1798. His inventory included Guthrie's *Grammar*, Blackstone's *Commentaries* and a Spanish-English dictionary.[134] On a more day-to-day basis there were newspapers, price currents, the coffee house and exchange.[135]

Information Revolution in the Early Modern Atlantic World', *American Historical Review*, 110:2 (Apr. 2005), 295–321.

129 On advice books see Daniel A. Rabuzzi, 'Eighteenth-Century Commercial Mentalities as Reflected and Projected in Business Handbooks', *Eighteenth Century Studies*, 29:2 (Winter 1995/96), 169–89.

130 *The Tradesman*; *The Merchant's Guide* (Liverpool: Printed by William Nevitt, 1774); James Boydell, *The Merchant Freighter's and Captains of Ships Assistant – Being Tables Calculated with the Greatest Accuracy* (Three King Court, Lombard Street, London: 1764); Gordon, *The Universal Accountant*, Vol. I.

131 G. Fisher, *The American Instructor; or, Young Man's Best Companion* (Philadelphia: Benjamin Franklin and D. Hall, 1748).

132 *The Liverpool Memorandum Book or, Gentleman's, Merchants & Tradesmen's Daily Pocket Journal, For the Year 1753* (Liverpool: Printed by R. Williamson and sold by C. Hitch and L. Hawes, London, 1752).

133 See for example, Postlethwayt, *Great Britain's True System*; Pelatiah Webster, *A Seventh Essay on Free Trade and Finance* (Philadelphia: Printed by Eleazer Oswald at the Coffee House, 1785); Adam Smith, *An Inquiry in the Nature of the Wealth of Nations* [1776] (Oxford: Oxford University Press, 1998).

134 Rainford's books covered a wide range of subjects as befitted his status. Inventory of All and Singular Goods and Chattels of Samuel Rainford, 19 Jan. 1799, 920 CHA 1/24, PEC, LivRO.

135 For more on the access to and importance of information see Sheryllynne Haggerty, 'Trade and the Trans-Shipment of Knowledge in the Late Eighteenth Century', in

Of course the most usual way to gain technical experience was through an apprenticeship as a merchant's clerk. Such training and monitoring encouraged a high level of responsibility and accountability, as well as helping individuals to manage risk effectively.[136] Apprenticeships were accessed via networks of family and friends, often accompanied by a fee of between £50 and £100.[137] A good apprenticeship would give formal training in accounting and letter writing, wharfside and Custom House procedures, as well as access to contacts which could be used for development in the future. Most would hope to get promotion through being used as a supercargo on a voyage or by working in a sister house or as a factor.[138] Some would receive a formal education at one of the new commercial schools such as the Warrington Academy. For example, David Tuohy sent his nephew to study navigation, arithmetic and bookkeeping, before sending him on a slave trade voyage as supercargo.[139] It is worth noting, of course, that such institutions had to be trusted themselves.[140]

Such knowledge and experience helped merchants to combat the technical hazards facing them, including the market place, the commodity, and even the vessel in which they were carried. For example, merchants thought of certain market 'places' as more risky than others, and knowledge of the market (or lack thereof) might deter them from embarking on a venture. David Tuohy, whilst still a captain, declined captaining a slave ship to Angola in 1772, partly because he had not sailed there for a while and the situation would have changed, and partly because of the strong competition there from French vessels.[141] Henry Twentyman advised Thomas Leyland

---

Yrjo Kaukiainen, ed., special issue on information, communications and knowledge of *International Journal of Maritime History*, 14:2 (2002), 157–72. See also Jacob M. Price, 'Directions for the Conduct of a Merchant's Counting House, 1766', *BH*, 28:3 (1986), 134–50.

136 Clarke and Short, 'Social Organisation and Risk', p. 389.

137 Campbell, *The London Tradesman*, p. 336.

138 Brian P. Luskey, '"What is My Prospects?": The Contours of Mercantile Apprenticeship, Ambition, and Advancement in the Early American Economy', *BHR*, 78 (Winter 2004), 665–702. Interestingly, Luskey suggests that many clerks opted to remain as such in the high-risk environment of the early nineteenth century, pp. 676–77.

139 Edward Tuohy to his father, 18 May 1772, Letters from David Tuohy, 380 TUO 2/7, DTP. The Warrington Academy relocated to Manchester in 1786 and was renamed the Manchester Academy, *BMP*, p. 57, fn. 237.

140 On institutional trust, see below, pp. 84–93.

141 David Tuohy to Mr Barker, 13 Jan. 1772, Letters from David Tuohy, DTP. Competition with the French was a common complaint, and was especially used by the pro-slavery lobby during the abolition movement. See the case study on abolition of the British slave trade in the chapter on crises, pp. 214–24.

of the state of the Antigua market in 1787, but Leyland replied that 'I never sent [sic] any Goods to the West Indies to sell for my own account, and I think I know such a business to [sic] well to ever embark on it.'[142] Breaking into a new market or commodity was a particularly risky proposition, whatever the stage of a merchant's career. In 1789, Charles Stewart Parker wrote to his brother in Virginia that he was very wary of re-shipping goods from Grenada to the Dutch, French and Spanish colonies because 'risquing Property in foreign Governments is always Dangerous'.[143] This was because the large number of conflicts and changes to the government of colonies meant that institutional trust, especially in other nations, was a constant concern.[144] Of course, some merchants relished the challenge of a new market. Despite being made bankrupt, on receipt of his certificate in 1803, John Leigh not only plunged himself into the British slave trade before its demise, but also 'laid out a ship for the Brazils' in 1808 once it ended.[145] He was even planning to build a new vessel specifically for the trade. When Brown & Ives wanted to start trade with Liverpool in 1804, they carefully considered what commodity they might send there and the reputation of the house they consigned the goods to. They chose well in Rathbone, Hughes & Duncan, a well-known risk-averse firm with plenty of knowledge and experience of the trade with America, and they chose the fashionable mahogany as a commodity.[146] The relationship with Rathbone, Hughes & Duncan (and its derivative firms) was to last into the 1820s, but unfortunately the mahogany market in Liverpool was well stocked and there was little demand, which goes to show that even established merchants could take bad risks on a new commodity without correct and up-to-date information.[147]

It was therefore very important to have knowledge of the commodities

142 Thomas Leyland to Henry Twentyman, 14 Jun. 1787, TLL.
143 Charles Parker to Patrick Parker, 3 Dec. 1789, 920 PAR I 50/1, PP.
144 On institutional trust see below, pp. 84–93.
145 John Leigh to A. & A. Hume, 4 Oct. 1803, John Leigh Letterbook, 1803–5; John Leigh to John Parker & Son, 18 May 1808, Letterbook of John Leigh & Co. 1808–9, TNA. John Leigh might be called a 'serial entrepreneur', as tolerance of failure is a key personal characteristic. See Donald K. Kuratko and Richard N. Hodgetts, *Entrepreneurship: Theory, Process and Practice* (Mason, Ohio: Thomson/South Western, 2004), chapter four, esp. p. 133.
146 This shipment came from St. Domingo, but due to wholesale woodcutting in the West Indies, much mahogany came from Central America by this point. See Jennifer L. Anderson, 'Nature's Currency: The Atlantic Mahogany Trade and Commodification of Nature in the Eighteenth Century', *Early American Studies*, 2:1 (Spring 2004), pp. 47–80.
147 William Holroyd, Brown & Ives, Samuel Ames … to Rathbone Hughes & Duncan, 7

in which you traded – in addition to the geographical markets – as many commodities were perceived as more risky than others. Whilst enslaved persons were justly assessed to be the most risky 'commodity', other commodities could also be seen as more problematic than others. For example, experience was essential in understanding the different grades of tobacco or textiles, even if, as John Perhouse of Philadelphia considered, his time at a manufacturing warehouse had been a 'stupid employment'.[148] In contrast, Andrew Clow made sure that everyone knew that he had been brought up in the manufacturing business in Manchester and so was acquainted with the principal manufacturers in England. He boasted that this meant that he could acquire and sell goods on terms better than many.[149] James Lawson wrote to his partner John Semple in Virginia during 1760 bemoaning the state of the tobacco market in Europe generally; there had been good harvests in America as well as in France, and so the market was overstocked.[150] Whilst he thought tobacco would become 'a Ruinous Trade', he also considered that 'It would be madness to plunge into a new Branch [of trade] in such precarious times as is at present.'[151] Jacob Samson, based in Jamaica in 1788, wrote that millinery was a 'hazardes' [sic] article.[152] Risk in commodities was clearly also time-sensitive – no doubt millinery was not such a high-risk article in Jamaica once the post-war glut had cleared.

Moreover, some commodities were at more risk of damage than others during transport. A slave cargo was the only one that presented a rebellion risk, but silks, sugar, tea, tobacco and spices also required special care, more than say, a cargo of metalware or timber. Employing a good cooper or stevedore was therefore essential, as was having an understanding of specialist packing. Hats and books were shipped in cases or boxes, cheeses were sewn in canvas and tarred to protect them from rats, air-tight barrels were required for sugar, and cheap mugs were sent across the Atlantic without handles to reduce breakage.[153] Moreover, the vessel itself should be appropriate for the

---

Apr. 1804; Rathbone, Hughes & Duncan to Owners of the Juno, 17 May 1804, Folder Maritime, Brig Juno 3 Apr. 1804–30 May 1807, BFBR.

148 John Perhouse to James Perhouse, 4 May 1804, John Perhouse Journal.

149 Lithgow and Harrison to Clow, 11 Feb. 1785, Folder 1785–1798, Andrew Clow & Co., CWU.

150 James Lawson to John Semple, 14 Jan. 1760; James Lawson to John Walker, 14 Jan. 1761; James Lawson Letterbook, 1758–1762, SJLP.

151 James Lawson to John Semple, 9 May 1763; 10 May 1762, James Lawson Letterbook, 1762–1766, SJLP.

152 Jacob Samson to Levy Cohen, 3 May 1788, Lowe v Cohen, C15/19, TNA.

153 Nuala Zahedieh, 'Credit, Risk and Reputation in Late-Seventeenth-Century

commodity in question. Perhaps it was a scarcity of shipping that induced experienced Liverpool merchant Joseph Manesty to engage the *Barter* in 1764, without a raft port for shipment of lumber from Charleston.[154] This, said Henry Laurens, and the inexperience of the captain, made the work go 'very heavily'.[155] The choice of vessel was therefore important, not only in terms of the safety of the crew, but in terms of having the correct vessel for each particular trade. This was also another instance where much of the risk was removed from the merchant onto the crew. The merchant still bore the financial risk, but whilst on the high seas, it was the crew as well as the commodity that suffered if the vessel was not seaworthy, even though the decision was out of their hands.[156] Henry Laurens was troubled by a Liverpool vessel, the *Hope*, in early 1764, when it hit the bar on the way in. Captain Dennison was extremely anxious to please his employers and this made him a little over zealous in loading the vessel. Although he had got the vessel repaired, the crew were anxious about the amount of rice being loaded and were threatening to desert: an interesting case in which moral and technical hazard were present without malicious intent. Laurens advised him to be cautious. He was glad to report that Dennison had got over the bar on 5 March 1764, and wished for him to arrive safely at John Knight's door 'where you will probably think of what is best to be done with such a crazy carcass'.[157]

Clearly the vessel itself also had to be in good order before others would

---

Colonial Trade', *Research in Maritime History*, 15, Merchant Organization and the Maritime Trade in the North Atlantic, 1660–1715, ed. Olaf Janzen (1993), 53–74, pp. 55–56; Richard B. Sheridan, *Sugar and Slavery: An Economic History of the British West Indies, 1623–1775* (Kingston, Jamaica: Canoe Press, 1974), pp. 112–18; Edwin Atlee Barber, *Anglo American Pottery: Old English China with American Views*, 2nd edn (Philadelphia: Patterson and White, 1901), p. 8. Tobacco had to be imported into Britain in hogsheads or chests by statute to reduce smuggling, though much was still imported in loose rolls. Ashworth, *Customs and Excise*, pp. 170–71.

154 A raft port is a square hole cut through the buttocks of a vessel to receive planks or pieces of timber which could not be received otherwise. Chambers, *Cyclopædia: Or, Universal Dictionary*.

155 The *Barter* had come from Barbados, arriving in Charleston in Jan. 1764; Henry Laurens to Joseph Manesty, 17 Jan. 1764; Henry Laurens to Joseph Manesty, 24 Feb. 1764; Henry Laurens to John Haslin, 15 Mar. 1764, *HLP*, Vol IV. The *Barter* was not a slave trade vessel however. Eltis et al., *The Trans-Atlantic Slave Trade Database*, accessed 20 Nov. 2009.

156 Tierney, 'Toward a Critical Sociology', p. 231. Clarke and Short argue that the issue of fairness is important in perceptions of the management of risk, 'Social Organisation and Risk', p. 384.

157 Henry Laurens to John Knight, 20 Jan. 1764; Henry Laurens to John Knight, 24 Feb. 1764; Henry Laurens to John Knight, 5 Mar. 1764, *HLP*, Vol. IV.

consign their goods in it. William Smith was the captain in charge of a shipment of mahogany, logwood and staves from Providence to Liverpool, but he was having trouble obtaining a return cargo because there were 'Ships here With So Much better Accommodations'.[158] He wrote that he had to ensure the vessel was caulked properly because 'This place is very pertikler ... What Situation vessels is in.'[159] In the end Smith sent a few crates of goods at his own risk so that the stowage would be more stable as the ship was not full, but not everyone was as lucky as Brown & Ives in having such a dedicated captain.[160] In the same year William McBean (of the Parker network) encountered related problems. He sent goods from Demerara to Liverpool on the *Bachus*. However, the cargo was delivered in very bad order, which McBean put down to the state of the vessel. He noted, 'I was fearful of it, nothing but the greatest scarcity of shipping at the time would induce people to ship in her.'[161]

The slave trade is a good, if extreme example, of where knowledge of the commodity, markets and the vessel all came together, especially because it was the riskiest of the Atlantic trades.[162] As Stephen Behrendt has noted, Liverpool's slave captains, and, it is arguable, its merchants, were well known to have good human capital in this trade, and even Bristol slave traders used Liverpool captains and vessels.[163] Good access to credit and manufactures through networks in the north west, experience of purchasing on the African coast and good factors or partners in the West Indies, were all essential for a successful slave voyage. The slave trade is also a good example of where definitions of risk shaped technology.[164] Liverpool merchants trumpeted the fact that they had specially designed vessels, with scuttles and gratings which

---

158 William Smith to Owners of the Brig Juno, 30 Jun. 1804, Folder Maritime, Brig Juno 3 Apr. 1804–31 Dec. 1804, BFBR.

159 William Smith to Owners of the Brig Juno, 13 Jun. 1804, Folder Maritime, Brig Juno 3 Apr. 1804–31 Dec. 1804, BFBR. Insurance policies often determined the quality of the vessel. For example, policies often stipulated that vessels in the slave trade had to be copper bottomed. Cockerell, *The British Insurance Business*, p. 14.

160 The ship's husband in Liverpool agreed that he would not have to pay freight on these goods. Rathbone, Hughes & Duncan to Brown & Ives, 25 Jun. 1804, Folder Maritime, Brig Juno 3 Apr. 1804–31 Dec. 1804, BFBR.

161 William McBean to Samuel Sandbach, 11 Apr. 1804, Folder 920 PAR IV 1/1/10, PP. The *Bachus* was not a slave trade vessel however. Eltis et al., *The Trans-Atlantic Slave Trade Database*, accessed 20 Nov. 2009.

162 For a more detailed version of this paragraph see Haggerty, 'Risk and Risk Management'.

163 Stephen D. Behrendt, 'Human Capital in the British Slave Trade', in Richardson et al., *Liverpool and Transatlantic Slavery*, pp. 66–98.

164 Hilgartner, 'The Social Construction of Risk Objects'.

encouraged airflow to protect their 'cargo'. They also regularly carried doctors on board, even before Dolben's Act made it compulsory. Slave vessels also had larger crews, were more heavily armed in order to prevent insurrection and had a gun wall or 'barracada' (from behind which sailors could safely fire on the slaves) and netting around the vessel in order to prevent slaves committing suicide.[165] It has been argued that they were the most important technology of the day.[166] This technical knowledge stood them in good stead against abolitionist pressure.[167]

VERTICAL INTEGRATION OR DIVERSIFICATION?

Most merchants engaged in a variety of trades and markets in this period in order to spread risk.[168] Some went further, and vertical integration, both backward and forward, could also be seen as a way to manage risk by keeping decision-making 'in-house' and by not being fully exposed to the market.[169] Conversely, it is also possible to frame the move into landownership, manufacturing or insurance and shipping, as taking extra risks, yet many successful merchants diversified their business portfolios in this way. Vertical integration might include purchasing sugar estates in the West Indies and/or investing in sugar houses to process the sugar. It might also involve investment in manufacturing.[170] For example, Samuel Holland of Liverpool,

---

165 Marcus Rediker, *The Slave Ship: A Human History* (London: John Murray, 2007), p. 51. For a description of the daily tasks in preparing a ship for slaves see Log of the Madampookata and Count de Nord and Agamemnon, 380 MD 52, LivRO.

166 Marcus Rediker, 'History from Below the Waterline: Sharks and the Atlantic Slave Trade', *Atlantic Studies*, 5:2 (Aug. 2008), 285–97, p. 285.

167 See below, pp. 218–19. It could be argued that such pressure was another technical hazard.

168 Ray B. Westerfield, *Middlemen in English Business: Particularly Between 1660 and 1760* (New Haven, CT: Yale University Press, 1915), p. 332; Haggerty, 'Liverpool, the Slave Trade'.

169 Backward integration might also be called upstream, and forward, downstream integration. Whilst investing in a sugar estate gave someone first access to the commodity, for example, it did not control the price as determined by demand and supply, it is not anti-competitive. Steve Davies, 'Vertical Integration', in Clarke and McGuinness, eds., *The Economics of the Firm*, pp. 83–106, pp. 84–85.

170 There is of course a huge debate about the extent to which profits from the slave trade were re-invested in manufacturing in Britain and helped drive the industrial revolution. Eric Williams, *Capitalism and Slavery* (Chapel Hill, NC: University of North Carolina Press, 1944); Joseph Inikori, *Africans and the Industrial Revolution in England: A Study in International Trade and Economic Development* (Cambridge: Cambridge University Press, 2002).

who was involved in exporting pottery to Philadelphia, was a proprietor and office holder of the Herculaneum Pottery, which he found advantageous in the extension of generous credit terms.[171] This allowed him to make extra profits from a product to which he had good access. Such diversification and vertical integration was normal practice. Hancock's 'associates' were involved in plantations in the West Indies and American south, the slave trade factory of Bance Island off the Sierra Leone river, and various forms of finance.[172] Merchants such as Andrew Clow in Philadelphia invested in securities, banking, and less successfully, manufacturing.[173] Merchants in Virginia invested in insurance when access and costs from London became problematic.[174] John Semple invested in iron founding in Maryland and Samuel Rainford ventured in cotton estates in Jamaica.[175]

However, as Simon Smith has shown, such vertical integration could be a double-edged sword, and much merchant 'investment' in the West Indies for example, was by default. Certainly it was not 'a sustained policy'.[176] The Parker network's positive investment in cotton estates in Demerara, one called Woodlands and another named Coffee Grove, was unusual.[177] At the same time, their partner in Liverpool, Samuel Sandbach, who had originally invested with them, was reticent by 1812 about extending his ownership of land there. He clearly felt that he was already in deep enough. He wrote to Parker that:

The more I look into the subject mentioned in your private letter of the 26th now before me, the more I dislike it. The most honest way for me to express myself

171 Herculaneum Pottery Ledgers 1806–1812, ff. 350, 357 and 420, 380 MD 48; *Billinge's Liverpool Advertiser and Marine Intelligencer*, 21 Nov. 1796; 24 Nov. 1806, Herculaneum Potteries Minute Book 1806–1822, LivRO; Alan Smith, *The Illustrated Guide to Liverpool Herculaneum Pottery 1796–1840* (London: Barrie and Jenkins, 1970), p. 21.

172 Hancock, *Citizens of the World*, chapters five to eight.

173 Richard G. Wilson, *Gentleman Merchants: The Merchant Community in Leeds 1700–1830* (Manchester: Manchester University Press, 1971), chapter seven; Doerflinger, *A Vigorous Spirit of Enterprise*, chapter seven; Robert E. Wright, 'Bank Ownership and Lending Patterns in New York and Pennsylvania, 1781–1831', *BHR*, 73:1 (1999), 40–60.

174 Crothers, 'Commercial Risk'.

175 See the case studies on Semple's partner James Lawson, and Samuel Rainford below, pp. 170–88.

176 Smith, *Slavery, Family and Gentry Capitalism*, p. 182.

177 See for example, Charles Stewart Parker to John Bolton, 14 Jun. 1798, 920 PAR III 25/12; William McBean to J. McInroy, 30 Nov. 1804, 920 PAR IV 1/2/4, PP. Their investments were not always successful. Other estates such as Pomeroon and Hyde Park did very badly. William McBean to Samuel Sandbach & Co., 25 Dec. 1803, 210 PAR IV 1/1/7, PP; William McBean to Samuel Sandbach, 4 Feb. 1804, 920 PAR IV 1/1/8, PP.

then is, that I shall be most happy to meet with you or M^r McInroy or both, on any other business, but not upon that, for I will enter into no negotiation which makes me an Owner of more Cotton Estates in Demerary.[178]

It was not just in the West Indies that such investments were problematic. John Semple, mentioned above, invested in iron manufacture in Maryland with disastrous results. His poor partner, the worrier James Lawson, had to travel to the colony himself in order to stave off his own bankruptcy.[179] Attempts to engage in manufacturing by Philadelphia merchants were not always successful and of course Robert Morris famously went bankrupt following land speculation.[180] Therefore, whilst vertical integration and diversification could be seen as a risk-spreading strategy, it was not always through choice, and could be problematic even when it was.

Conclusion

MERCHANTS WERE CLEARLY extremely sophisticated in their perceptions and management of risk. They perceived the hazards posed by the sea, people and markets in very different ways and managed them accordingly. Natural hazards were managed through knowledge of place and timing, whilst insurance and convoys helped to further mitigate those risks. Merchants used reputational mechanisms, repeated exchange, advance payments and institutional forms such as the guarantee system to manage moral hazards, whilst expertise in particular markets or commodities and even the vessels themselves all played an important part in the management of technical risks. Moreover, the state implicitly and explicitly both helped to construct, shift, and shape risk.

Merchants' attempts to minimise risk and transaction costs were not always successful, but as a community, their overall success in managing risk meant that they could negotiate the difficult world around them and continue in business. This is not to say that all merchants were natural risk takers. James Lawson for example, was a worrier, and edgeworkers such as Andrew Clow were rare. Perhaps merchants took more risks when they were younger, and others may have taken more risks during periods of high speculation. Choice of commodity or market, and the timing of being involved in them, was also a risk-management strategy to some extent. Many more were involved in dry goods than the slave trade or privateering. Most

---

178 Samuel Sandbach to Charles Stewart Parker, 28 Sep. 1812, 920 PAR III 17/1, PP.
179 See his heartrending letters in James Lawson Letterbook 1770–1776, SJLP.
180 Doerflinger, *A Vigorous Spirit of Enterprise*, p. 326.

merchants were neither high-risk takers or risk averse, but somewhere in between. As James Clemens realised, merchants could not foresee or guard against every risk, but most of them, if not all, aimed to be prudent, and to use their skills and knowledge in giving their business their proper attention. The ability to take and manage those risks was an essential element in the private-order institution of their business culture. However, in order to do so, it was essential for some form of trust to be in place, whether at the personal, institutional or general level.

3
Trust

as he *trusts others*, so he is *trusted* by others; and 'till the game is up,
and a Balance made, either by Death or some other conclusive Event ...
it cannot be known on which Side he stands with the World.[1]

Franklin's 'game' encapsulates the idea behind Robert Axelrod's famous book *The Evolution of Co-operation*, wherein the logic of co-operation is investigated through game theory. It is perhaps strange to see Benjamin Franklin using nearly the same terminology as a modern political scientist, but it reminds us of the always illusive nature of trust. As was demonstrated in the previous chapter, risk could be managed to some extent, but eventually trust had to come into play. Interestingly, Axelrod's 'tit-for-tat' game is not about punishment, as it might at first sound, but about being 'nice', never being the first to defect. Rather, to win the game in the long run, one needs to practise reciprocity. That is, someone has to take the risk to trust someone else, possibly without good reason. Indeed, Molm et al. argue that taking that 'risk is a necessary condition for the development of trust'.[2] Whilst cheating may look promising in the short term, 'the shadow of the future' means that co-operation should benefit everyone in the long term.[3] The longer the shadow, the more likely actors are to be trustworthy. Franklin realised both the elusive nature of trust, and its 'shadow' – in this case until death. Trust was also a complicated process in which personal, institutional and general levels of trust were interlinked.

Like risk, trust is also an emotive, socially-constructed process, because

---

1 Franklin, *The Way to be Wise and Wealthy*, p. 40. This comes from a discussion on credit, but the point is the same.
2 Molm et al., 'Risk and Trust in Social Exchange', p. 1422.
3 Robert Axelrod, *The Evolution of Co-operation* [1984] (London: Penguin Books, 1990).

uncertainty makes people anxious. George Robertson noted from Grenada in 1790, 'The business & Credit has now become to[o] Extensive to depend on a Single Life in case of Accident & in case of sickness without a partner on the Spot I must either sacrifice my Life or my Business.'[4] Therefore, the emotions produced by uncertainty mean that trust is 'always provisional and contested'; it is not absent or present, but rather 'routinely produced' as circumstances change, just as risk is constantly reframed.[5] This means that perceptions are important in creating conditions of trust or mistrust which can in turn develop into virtuous or vicious spirals, taking on a life of their own.[6] This chapter first considers the emotive nature of trust before discussing the distinction between personal trust, institutional trust (assurance) and general trust (confidence). It then goes on to consider how these levels of trust were built up and maintained, and the interconnections between them.

TRUST AS EMOTIVE, EMERGENT PROCESS

PEOPLE TRUST OTHERS as a result of the past, present and future. It is therefore temporal, and like risk, constantly produced and contested. It is also a 'process of constant imaginative anticipation of the reliability of the other party's actions'.[7] That is, trust is based on reputations, evaluations of present information, assumptions about the actions of others and belief in their morality and honesty. It is therefore an emotive process, and perhaps for some people, a challenging one. Joshua Johnson clearly did not have much faith in his fellow merchants in London. In 1772 he noted that, 'A man must always have his eyes open here. Indeed, if nature had been lavish enough to have given him a pair behind, he would have had use for them.'[8] However,

---

4 George Robertson to George Rainy, 15 Dec. 1790, Folder 920 PAR I 50/1, PP.

5 Gaggio, *In Gold We Trust*, p. 323; Zucker, 'Production of Trust', p. 59. Trust may also be present to varying extents in different societies. It is notably absent in countries that have suffered trauma from war or other huge upheavals, for example various parts of Africa and the ex-Soviet block where social norms and experiences are not present for generalised trust. John Humphrey and Hubert Schmitz, *Trust and Economic Development*, Institute of Development Discussion Paper, 355 (Aug. 1996), pp. 18–19; Jean-Phillipe Platteau, 'Behind the Market Stage Where Real Societies Exist – Part II: The Role of Moral Norms', *Journal of Development Studies*, 30:3 (Apr. 1994), 753–817, pp. 754–55.

6 Onora O'Neill, *A Question of Trust: The BBC Reith Lectures 2002* (Cambridge: Cambridge University Press, 2002), p. 25.

7 Dmitry Khodyakov, 'Trust as a Process: A Three Dimensional Approach', *Sociology*, 41:1 (Feb. 2007), 115–32, p. 126.

8 Joshua Johnson to Wallace & Davidson, 29 Aug. 1771, JJL.

emotions and attachments built through trade were often very strong and positive, and merchants who were good friends shared ribald stories alongside their trading news. Whilst Robert Bostock merely noted to his correspondent, 'The Friendship subsisting between you & me I make no doubt of your doing the Best you can for my Interest', Samuel Bean in Jamaica wrote to Robert Morris in Philadelphia telling him he had got 'infernally drunk' and teased Morris about losing a woman to a rival.[9] The problem with emotions of course, is that abuses of trust cause strong feelings of betrayal, a reflection of the antagonism between the market and social relations.[10] This is especially important where the very sources of trust also provide the means of abuse; for example, through family, ethnicity or religion.[11] Putting people into a market situation deeply affects the way that people feel for one another, and causes conflict even if, or – perhaps especially – when, such ties are present.[12] 'Trust can therefore be conducive to mischief.'[13] For example, the Bright-Meylers found that family members were exactly those abusing the trust placed in them, and Samuel Rainford in Jamaica, found that, to his detriment, family members were placed before other loyalties.[14] Having a brother-in-law as his partner did not help James Lawson either.

These emotions were of course exacerbated by the fact that our merchants were working in an environment of imperfect information.[15] Moreover,

---

9 Robert Bostock to J. Cleveland, 18 Oct. 1788, RBL; Samuel Bean to Robert Morris, 18 Oct. 1761, Folder Robert Morris, Willing, Morris & Co. Correspondence, Robert Morris Collection, Levis Collection, Box 1, HSP.

10 Dario Gaggio, 'Pyramids of Trust: Social Embeddedness and Political Culture in Two Italian Gold Jewelry Districts', *Enterprise & Society*, 7:1 (2006), 19–57, p. 29; Mick Moore, 'How Difficult is it to Construct Market Relations? A Commentary on Platteau', *Journal of Development Studies*, 30:3 (1994), 818–30, p. 826.

11 Mark S. Granovetter, 'Economic Action and Social Structure: The Problem of Embeddedness', *AJS*, 91:3 (Nov. 1985), 481–510, p. 491; Susan P. Shapiro explicitly builds on this problem in 'The Social Control of Impersonal Trust', *AJS*, 93:3 (Nov. 1987), 623–58.

12 In fact Greif argues that Europe had weak kin-based institutions in the late medieval and early-modern period, *Institutions and the Path to the Modern Economy*, p. 26.

13 This mischief might be between two or more individuals, or collectively through collaboration and price fixing. Humphrey and Schmitz, *Trust and Economic Development*, p. 3.

14 Morgan, *BMP*, passim; John Haggerty and Sheryllynne Haggerty, 'Visual Analytics of an Eighteenth-Century Business Network', *Enterprise & Society*, 11:1 (Mar. 2010), 1–25.

15 Platteau, 'The Role of Public and Private Order Institutions', pp. 540, 545. He also says that in a market economy people are not differentiated before entering the exchange, p. 539. I do not agree with this because judgments were constantly made about other actors.

people will often trust the information that corresponds to their current stock of knowledge, or what they want to be true.[16] Trust can therefore be engendered by affirming our own beliefs or wants, perhaps to our detriment. Emotions also mean that lack of knowledge, or conversely, past experience, fear, or ethnocentricity, cause mistrust, or at least complicate notions of trust. The stereotype of the miserly Jew is infamous, and yet their trust networks were renowned. Likewise Quaker merchants were thought to have a superior moral business culture in which Meeting House rules were transferred into the Counting House.[17] Mick Moore has argued that morality plays a role in the ability to trust people, but it also brings yet another element of emotion to the trust-building process.[18] Therefore in contrast to Quakers, Andrew Clow thought New England traders 'a designing faithless pack' and West Indian planters were thought unreliable payers.[19] With regard to West Indian bills John Leigh noted that 'we are Determined never to have any more cargoes sold for Planters bills which are so very uncertain of being accepted or paid'.[20] As Gaggio has observed, the spatial context was also important.[21] Immigrants found being trusted problematic, and so often moved in groups of families, such as the Huguenots to South Carolina or the Sephardim Jews to Livorno.[22] Of course meeting with 'others' of various kinds also caused problems of trust all around the Atlantic littoral. It is clear that emotions caused problems with trust as well as helping to build

---

16 Steven Shapin, *A Social History of Truth: Civility and Science in Seventeenth-Century England* (Chicago and London: University of Chicago Press, 1994), p. 4. The perceived creditability of sources can change with experience. Stillson, *Spreading the Word*.

17 James Coleman, 'Social Capital in the Creation of Human Capital', *AJS*, 94, Supplement: Organization and Institutions: Sociological and Economic Approaches to the Analysis of Social Structure (1988), 95–120, pp. 99–100; Walvin, *The Quakers*; Frederick B. Tolles, *Meeting House and Counting House: The Quaker Merchants of Colonial Philadelphia 1682–1783* [1948] (New York: The Norton Library, 1963). Shapiro might see the Quakers as an early form of gatekeeping by a 'professional' association. 'The Social Control of Impersonal Trust', pp. 639–41.

18 Moore, 'How Difficult is it to Construct Market Relations?'.

19 Andrew Clow to David Cay, 14 Apr. 1788, Folder Mar.–Apr. 1788, Andrew Clow & Co., SGC, HSP.

20 John Leigh to Isaac Barker, 16 Dec. 1806, John Leigh Letterbook 5 Jul. 1806–7 Mar. 1807.

21 Gaggio, *In Gold We Trust*, p. 39. For reputations by 'community', see below, pp. 121–30.

22 A single newcomer has no-one to cooperate with. Axelrod, *The Evolution of Co-operation*, p. 63; Bertrand Van Ruymbeke, 'The Huguenots of Proprietory South Carolina', in Jack P. Greene, Rosemary Brana-Shute, and Randy J. Sparks, eds., *Money, Trade, and Power: The Evolution of Colonial South Carolina's Plantation Society* (Columbia, SC: University of South Carolina Press, 2001), pp. 26–48; Trivellato, *The Familiarity of Strangers*.

it. Therefore, we need to consider other ways in which trust was constructed and maintained.[23]

TRUST, ASSURANCE, OR CONFIDENCE?

MOLM et al. define (personal) trust as 'expectations that an exchange partner will behave benignly, based on the attribution of positive dispositions and intentions to the partner in a situation of uncertainty and risk'.[24] Indeed, as noted above, risk and trust are interdependent. This is due to the fact that, as Oliver Williamson argues, because risk is impossible to calculate, we have to trust at some point, otherwise we would not be able to function.[25] Someone has to decide to trust, to open themselves up to opportunistic behaviour. When a Liverpool merchant sent dry goods to a Charleston factor he did not know, he exhibited trust by taking that risk. This does not mean however that such trust was placed without making informed choices.[26] 'Trust is not a matter of blind deference, but of placing – or refusing – trust with good judgement.'[27] The Liverpool merchant would certainly have used his contacts at the coffee house and exchange, and perhaps correspondents in Charleston, to gain information about the Charleston factor before sending the goods. He would have judged the information costs worthwhile. The fact that this is an informed choice leads Williamson to argue that using the term 'trust' in a commercial context is problematic because there are usually cost-effective safeguards (assurance structures). He argues that in commerce, it is calculative risk that is being taken, as opposed to trust being placed.[28] Certainly eighteenth-century merchants worked in a context of reputation mechanisms, trusted agents and institutional safeguards such as the law, but real (personal) trust does seem to have been placed. Trust is also constructed over time. As Axelrod argues, 'The foundation of cooperation is ... the durability of the relationship' even if the actors had never met.[29] Our Liverpool merchant and Charleston

---

23 Platteau, 'The Role of Public and Private Order Institutions', p. 533.
24 Molm et al., 'Risk and Trust in Social Exchange', p. 1402.
25 Oliver E. Williamson, 'Calculativeness, Trust and Economic Organisation', *Journal of Law and Economics*, 36:2 (1993), 453–86, p. 6.
26 Humphrey and Schmitz, *Trust and Economic Development*, pp. 4–6.
27 O'Neill, *A Question of Trust*, p. vii.
28 Williamson argues that terms such as 'calculative trust' are a contradiction in terms, and that 'real' personal trust should be reserved only for family, friends and lovers, 'Calculativeness, Trust and Economic Organisation', p. 484.
29 Axelrod, *The Evolution of Co-operation*, p. 182.

factor would have trusted each other a lot more after ten years of successful dealings than at the start of their relationship, and such trust may have been more difficult to shatter. Such long-term relationships did not mean that the uncertainty associated with risk was reduced or completely removed, but believing that others would behave benignly allowed actors to take risks in the first place.[30] Personal trust is therefore an expectation of benign behaviour based on inferences of traits and intentions. It is based on the idea that most people believe, like Adam Smith, that 'honesty is the best policy'.[31] There is consequently an emotional investment as well as a financial one.

In contrast, assurance (institutional trust) is where expectations are based on 'knowledge of an incentive structure that encourages such behaviour rather than exploitation'.[32] Eighteenth-century merchants faced many uncertainties such as wars and credit crises through which they had to trust. Such exogenous factors were obviously outside of their control and therefore it was not only benign behaviour that facilitated risk-taking. Humphrey and Schmitz argue that the 'main way that such uncertainty is resolved is through conventions, which are taken-for-granted rules and routines between the different partners … These constitute frameworks of economic action'.[33] The business culture of the eighteenth-century British Atlantic constitutes such a framework because it had an incentive structure which encouraged benign behaviour.[34] For example, a merchant with a cash-flow problem received help and encouragement if he owned up to his situation, whereas someone who tried to hide his poor financial situation might be forced into bankruptcy.[35] 'Candor and a full declaration of the State of your Affairs, will be the most likely means to induce the leinty [sic] of your Creditors', wrote William Sitgreaves in 1783.[36] The business culture of eighteenth-century merchants therefore worked as a private-order institution that provided an incentive structure, of which trust was a part. This business culture worked within and

---

30 Molm et al., 'Risk and Trust in Social Exchange', p. 1425.

31 Quoted in Jeremy Shearmur and Daniel B. Klein, 'Good Conduct in the Great Society: Adam Smith and the Role of Reputation', in Daniel B. Klein, ed., *Reputation: Studies in the Voluntary Elicitation of Good Conduct* (Ann Arbor: University of Michigan Press, 1997), pp. 29–46, p. 32.

32 Molm et al., 'Risk and Trust in Social Exchange', pp. 1396, 1403.

33 Humphrey and Schmitz, *Trust and Economic Development*, p. 8. For an example of this in history see S. R. H. Jones, 'Routines, Capabilities and the Growth of the Firm: Messrs. Ross & Glendinning, Dunedin, 1862–1900', *Australian Economic History Review*, 42:1 (Mar. 2002), 34–53.

34 Reputational mechanisms and obligation are dealt with in the following chapters.

35 Haggerty, *The British–Atlantic Trading Community*, pp. 172–82.

36 William Sitgreaves to Cornelius Terbush, 25 Jun. 1783, William and John Sitgreaves Letterbook, HSP.

alongside other assurance structures such as the law, chartered companies, trade associations and banks.[37]

At the widest level our merchants had to trust in the colonial, mercantilist framework in which they conducted their trade, but Humphrey and Schmitz argue that trust at this level, in the whole system of commerce, is actually confidence.[38] Confidence is distinguished from trust because it relies on a level of knowledge or predictability. Confidence allows you to feel as if you are in control; it is 'when you know what to expect in a situation; trust is what you need to maintain interaction if you do not'.[39] Some of this confidence came from the informal sanctions of the business community, but much came from formal institutions. This included laws which protected property and thereby facilitated credit, but also the wider system of regulation such as the Navigation Acts, convoys, trade treaties, etc. Therefore, assurance structures helped to provide confidence. It is clear that the different levels of trust overlapped, and were interdependent and complicated. As Niklas Luhmann notes 'the relation between trust and confidence is not a simple zero-sum game in which the more confidence is given the less trust is required and vice versa'.[40] Merchants were able to place personal trust because they assumed that the assurance structures would help them if it failed, and confidence in the wider system facilitated this. Whatever we call these levels of trust, as Steven Shapin argues, 'it is incorrect to say that we can ever have experience outside a nexus of trust of *some kind*' [emphasis in original].[41] However, assessing where one level of trust ends, and another starts, is not easy. We cannot say for example, when individual disappointment translates into a general lack of trust in the system. However, the fact that the market did not fall into chaos despite the various crises of the period, and that opportunities presented to abuse trust were in fact rarely seized, suggests that various levels or types of trust not only interacted with one another, but did so in a positive way.[42]

---

37 Platteau, 'The Role of Public and Private Order Institutions', p. 577.

38 Humphrey and Schmitz, *Trust and Economic Development*, p. 3.

39 Adam B. Seligman, 'Trust and Sociability: On the Limits of Confidence and Role Expectations', *American Journal of Economics and Sociology*, 57:4 (Oct. 1998), 391–404, p. 391.

40 Niklas Luhmann, 'Familiarity, Confidence and Trust: Problems and Alternatives', in Diego Gambetta, ed., *Trust: Making and Breaking Cooperative Relations* (New York and Oxford: Basil Blackwell Ltd, 1988), pp. 94–107, p. 99.

41 Shapin, *A Social History of Truth*, pp. 11–12, 21.

42 Platteau, 'The Role of Public and Private Order Institutions', p. 540; Shapiro, 'The Social Control of Impersonal Trust', p. 652.

MANAGING TRUST

SOCIOLOGISTS have described notions of trust in various ways, but it is possible to group these notions in order to make sense of them. This is shown in Table 3:1. We have already outlined personal trust, assurance and confidence, but sociologists further refine personal trust. Personal trust can also be distinguished between characteristic-based *ascribed* trust and *process-based* trust; *competency*, *goodwill*, and *contractual* trust; and *negotiated* and *non-negotiated* agreements.[43] Ascribed trust is placed where actors believe certain trustworthy characteristics to be inherent within the other person. Here we might include family, Quakers as fair traders, or the Scots trading networks around the Atlantic. Process-based trust is that which is built up over time, often starting with a very small risk at first, but which gradually increases. Competency trust is believing that the person has the correct skills; goodwill trust is where people perform over and above expectations; contractual trust is when you believe the person will perform their tasks, *as if* a contract were in place. Negotiated and non-negotiated trust has to do with contracts, and these are dealt with in turn below. As personal trust is so complicated, and the most relied upon by eighteenth-century merchants, more space is devoted to it in this chapter than the other levels or types of trust.

TABLE 3:1   LEVELS AND TYPES OF TRUST

Personal: Trust			Institutional (Hyphenated): Assurance	General: Confidence
Ascribed	Competency	Negotiated/	Laws & Courts,	Wider social,
Process based	Goodwill Contractual	Non- negotiated	Chartered Companies, Trade Associations, Banks, Business Culture	economic, political and cultural context

---

43 Mari Sako, *Prices, Quality and Trust: Inter-Firm Relations in Britain and Japan* (Cambridge: Cambridge University Press, 1992), pp. 37–38.

Personal Trust

The production of trust can rest on sharing a common base of knowledge which may have nothing to do with the exchange *per se*.[44] This means that much of the trust we produce at the personal level is ascribed, and there are many reasons why we choose to trust one person over another. Usually ascribed trust is given among groups with a strong common identity, such as family, ethnicity, religion, language, or nation. Historians have placed much emphasis on ascribed trust and the subject is more than adequately covered elsewhere.[45] However, whilst ascribed trust was important for merchants at the beginning of their careers – especially amongst immigrant or transient communities – it provided only a limited basis for transactions. Therefore this section concentrates on various forms of process-based trust, which facilitated the extension of networks far more widely.

Process-based trust, based on reciprocal exchange, was important around the distances of the Atlantic because the actors did not have to know one another personally either previous to, or even after, the exchange. The fact that this trust was 'impersonal' did not mean that 'affective commitment' was not created. Two merchants that began as strangers might end up putting considerable capital at risk together as their transactions increased over time, even if they never met.[46] Indeed, by eventually becoming predictable and reliable, the trading relationship became an object of value in itself.[47] Success in transactions built up positive emotions associated with the exchange so that actors attributed 'the positive emotions in part to their relationship with one another'.[48] Therefore, it is not so much the exchange itself and the

---

44 Zucker, 'Production of Trust', p. 93.

45 Much of the historiography is dominated by discussions of the Quakers. See for example Prior and Kirby, 'The Society of Friends'; Rose, 'The Family Firm'; Walvin, *The Quakers*, pp. 66–85; Mathias, 'Risk, Credit and Kinship'. On the importance of family see Davidoff and Hall, *Family Fortunes*; Hunt, *The Middling Sort*; Stana Nenadic, 'The Small Family Firm in Victorian Britain', *Business History*, 35:4 (1993), 86–114. Interpretations of networks are now being complicated. See for example Hancock, 'The Trouble with Networks'; Albane Forrestier, 'Risk, Kinship and Personal Relationships in Late Eighteenth-Century West Indian Trade: The Commercial Networks of Tobin & Pinney', *BH*, 52:6 (2010), 912–31; Trivellatto, *The Familiarity of Strangers*; see the essays in Andreas Gestrich and Margrit Schulte Beerbühl, eds., *Cosmopolitan Networks in Commerce and Society, 1660–1914* (London: Supplement no. 2 of German Historical Institute London Bulletin, 2011).

46 Shapiro, 'The Social Control of Impersonal Trust', esp. p. 635.

47 Molm et al., 'Risk and Trust in Social Exchange'.

48 Edward J. Lawler and Yeongkoo Yoon, 'Commitment in Exchange Relations: Test of a Theory of Relational Cohesion', *American Sociological Review*, 61:1 (Feb. 1996), 89–108, p. 94. The form of letter writing in such an exchange is also important, see below, pp. 110–11.

volume of exchange, but the success of the exchange that is important. Their exchanges became a shared event even when they had never met, through a process which Lawler and Yoon have termed 'relational cohesion'. The actors *'perceive* their relation to be a distinct unifying object' [emphasis in original].[49] It is clear that many merchants built up their trade through such reciprocal exchange throughout our period. This was also a risk management strategy as was noted in the previous chapter. Daniel Clark of Philadelphia met a partner of the firm Haliday & Dunbar of Liverpool in 1760, and in consequence sent a small order to the firm.[50] In 1766 Isaac Wikoff of Philadelphia wrote to John Ewer in London that the goods sent him in the spring had been on as good terms or better than had been imported by others, and this had led him to submit yet another order.[51] Brown, Benson & Ives of Providence, having met the son of a Widow Ruden, decided to send a 'merely introductory' order to her at Suriname in 1792. At the same time they asked for a cargo of molasses in return, flattering her with regard to her 'extensive connextions' [sic] which would allow her to help their captain.[52] Building up trust in this manner also occurred at the regional level. For example, Mifflin & Massey of Philadelphia gradually extended more credit and for longer periods of time as their customers became trusted.[53] Liverpool merchant William Earle also sent ivory to Owen Griffiths, writing that 'this first correspondence may bring on further dealings'.[54] Such transactions, if successful, led to a frequency of exchange which could produce pleasure and satisfaction. This in turn led to expectations of future financial rewards, and reduced uncertainty.[55]

Such relationships could be long term which led to trust being cemented by commitment behaviours such as staying, gift giving and contributing.[56] For example, Peter Wikoff became concerned that other merchants were receiving goods at lower prices than he was, and asked London-based John Ewer in April 1770 to try to get them lower as he 'would rather be Supplied by you than go else where'.[57] His loyalty must have paid off, because by

49 Lawler and Yoon, 'Commitment in Exchange Relations', p. 94.
50 Daniel Clark to Halliday & Dunbar, 26 Sep. 1760, DCL.
51 Isaac Wikoff to John Ewer, 1 Jun. 1766, Folder Isaac Wikoff to John Ewer, CBP.
52 Benson, Brown & Ives to Widow Ruden & Son, 5 Oct. 1792, Folder 4, West Indies Correspondents, BFBR.
53 Mifflin and Massey Ledger 1760–1763, HSP, passim.
54 William Earle to Owen Griffith, 22 May 1760; 24 May 1760, Letterbook of William Earle, D/Earle 2/2, EC.
55 Lawler and Yoon, 'Commitment in Exchange Relations', p. 95.
56 Lawler and Yoon, 'Commitment in Exchange Relations', p. 92.
57 Peter Wikoff to John Ewer, 14 Apr. 1770, Folder Peter Wikoff to John Ewer, CBP.

September 1770 he had received confirmation from Ewer that he would send the goods as cheaply as he could. In return Peter Wikoff noted that, 'it will put it in my power to remit you punctual, also encourage me to send you much larger orders'.[58] It also meant of course, that he may not have tried to see if he could get better or cheaper goods from someone else, and an opportunity cost was paid.[59] Punctuality was another reason for 'staying'. John Leigh of Liverpool thanked Isaac Barker of St. Vincent for his 'punctuality remitting for which we shall give your preference in sales of our cargoes of slaves that may arrive at your Island'.[60] Other behaviours associated with affective commitment or relational cohesion were gift-giving and contributing. For example, Samuel Rainford in Jamaica often sent small presents to his friend and colleague Edward Chaffers in Liverpool, such as in January 1794 when he sent six pots of sweetmeats to 'Present ... to Mrs Chaffers with my most Respectful complements.'[61] 'Contributing' such as investing together is dealt with below under formal contracts, but certainly meant a commitment over the long term, and often entailed large amounts of capital.[62] It is important to note however, that the choices associated with these behaviours were shaped by power relationships. A rich merchant with many connections not only suggested that he was trustworthy, it also meant that he was much freer to say no to a potential or failing relationship than a merchant at the beginning of his career. Isaac Wikoff (the brother of Peter, also in Philadelphia) wrote to John Ewer throughout 1771 and 1772 complaining about the quality of various textiles, but kept his tone intentionally polite and blamed the packers rather than Ewer.[63] Perhaps Isaac Wikoff had little choice of correspondents in London because the power relationship was confirmed in a letter sent to Ewer in 1774. Wikoff wrote to Ewer concerned about the debts he owed him, declaring that 'its true I am so much in your power'.[64] We saw in the previous chapter that those who had power could demand advance payments from those without the requisite reputation. With regard to trust too, the more dependent actor had less power and was more likely to make one-sided commitments, perhaps because they had no other choice.[65] Whereas Wikoff

---

58 Peter Wikoff to John Ewer, 25 Sep. 1770, Folder Peter Wikoff to John Ewer, CBP.

59 Molm et al., 'Risk and Trust in Social Exchange', p. 1406.

60 John Leigh to Isaac Barker, 16 Sep. 1806, John Leigh Letterbook, 5 Jul. 1806–7 Mar. 1807.

61 Samuel Rainford to Edward Chaffers, 21 Jan. 1794, 920 CHA/1/10, PEC.

62 See below pp. 79–81.

63 Isaac Wikoff to John Ewer, 1 May 1771; 12 Oct. 1771; 4 Feb. 1772, Folder Isaac Wikoff to John Ewer, CBP.

64 Isaac Wikoff to John Ewer, 4 May 1774, Folder Isaac Wikoff to John Ewer, CBP.

65 Molm et al., 'Risk and Trust in Social Exchange', pp. 1399, 1408.

seemingly had to stay with Ewer, Ewer probably had many correspondents to choose from along the Eastern sea-board.

Mari Sako further complicates the trust constructed through reciprocal exchange by categorising it into three types: competency trust which relies on technical knowledge and managerial expertise (the person has the requisite skills to complete the task entrusted); goodwill trust where commitment may be expressed as the willingness to do more for each other than is formally expected; and contractual trust where both trading partners uphold universal ethical standards, well-known norms, and/or keep written or oral promises (there is some confusion over to what extent contractual agreements are negotiated or non-negotiated).[66] Certainly such subtleties of trust were evident in the correspondence of eighteenth-century merchants. Thomas Leyland wrote to his correspondent in Hanley Green (one of the six towns of Stoke-on-Trent in central England) that 'I leave the quality & prices to your prudence & care.'[67] John Leigh wrote to John Gordon in Barbados that he was pleased with the sales from the *Narcissus*, knowing that he would do his best for his interest.[68] In contrast, Daniel Clark was worried that although he had done his best for Francis Dromgoole of Liverpool, the results were not very good. He hoped it would not deter Dromgoole from further adventures to Philadelphia. At the same time however, Clark hinted that Dromgoole's own competency was also in question, noting that 'Earthern ware at any Rate is not an article that a person Can deal in to this place from Liverpoole to any advantage for Captains of Vessels are able to Undersell Any importer.'[69] In fact, Daniel Clark had surpassed expectations, and had created goodwill trust by receiving the shipment in the absence of Dromgoole's brother, who was away from Philadelphia at the time. Expressions of gratitude were clear when merchants felt a correspondent had exceeded expectations. In 1764 Henry Laurens was 'exceedingly oblig'd' to John Knight for taking care over welcoming Mr Hest (his protégée) in Liverpool, as well as his kind intentions in introducing a Mr Head to him.[70] No doubt such goodwill actions contributed to the positive emotions produced by the exchange relationship over time, over and above the volume of transactions.

An important facet of trust built up through reciprocal exchange is that it is non-contractual. That is, many transactions are separately performed

---

66 Sako, *Prices, Quality and Trust*, pp. 37–38. Negotiated and non-negotiated agreements are dealt with below, pp. 77–81.
67 Thomas Leyland to John Mare, 14 Jun. 1786, TLL.
68 John Leigh to John Gordon, 5 Nov. 1806, John Leigh Letterbook 5 Jul. 1806–7 Mar. 1807.
69 Daniel Clark to Francis Dromgoole, 16 Oct. 1771, DCL.
70 Henry Laurens to John Knight, 22 Dec. 1764, *HLP*, Vol. IV.

and non-negotiated; one transaction may or may not lead to another, and the length of time over which reciprocation may occur is not known. This was mostly the case in our period, with people taking small risks at first, and increasing them over time as trust was constructed. Most merchants fulfilled their *implied* contracts thereby building up contractual trust. In contrast, negotiated exchanges are those explicitly bargained for within a one-off process. Ironically, a contract, which is designed to reduce risk, also reduces trust, because by making a binding agreement there is no shared risk, and therefore no trust is constructed. In these cases, assurance, through institutions to enforce that agreement, is even more necessary.[71] However, most transactions in our period were made in a context where the terms of business were generally understood and commission rates in various trades well known. At the same time, whilst formal agreements were few, correspondents would often spell out in letters what they understood the terms of trade to be, to avoid any misunderstandings which might lead to conflict. In 1759 Daniel Clark wrote to William Neale of London that:

> I understand your time of credit is Twelve Months. I do agree to allow you five PCt p Ann £ for what sum or sums may not be paid by that Time, upon this cargoe as well as Upon any future Order I may send you.[72]

Twenty-four years later William Sitgreaves did much the same. His old London correspondent having decided to withdraw from the American trade after the American War of Independence, Sitgreaves wrote to Thomas Powell in London to introduce his house (he was in partnership with his son John). Having dealt with London correspondents before he suggested the following terms:

> to have our goods shipped at 12 months Credit, for a Commission of 2½ percent, to be allowed 5 perCent per Ann: Interest for whatever Money we pay before that time; and if the Time of Payment should be prolonged, to allow you Interest at the same rate.[73]

All very normal terms, but the increasing use of civil courts for debt action, and the fact that such letterbooks were used as evidence, may have encouraged the writing of such 'procedural norms' into letters of trade.[74] At the same time, impersonal process-based 'contractual' trust was established

---

71 Molm et al., 'Risk and Trust in Social Exchange', pp. 1398–1402.
72 Daniel Clark to William Neal, 20 Dec. 1759, DCL.
73 William Sitgreaves to Thomas Powell, 24 Sep. 1783, William and John Sitgreaves Letterbook.
74 Bruce H. Mann, 'The Transformation of Law and Economy in Early America', in

without the need to resort to formal contracts, which were less likely to produce trust. Ten years later, Andrew Clow was supporting Samuel Brown in his endeavour to set up a house in Port au Prince, St. Domingue. Having set out the terms of business verbally 'at great length', he still felt compelled to instruct him to send good merchantable coffee, sugar of a good colour, to write frequently with the state of the market and to make sale to the best advantage, before wishing him to be 'sufficiently rewarded for your Labour' [to make a profit].[75] He clearly laid out the terms of the (non-negotiated) contract. William Earle, realising that credit times were lengthening in the West Indies in the 1760s, asked his captain to get bills at as short a date as possible and also that 'whoever you sell wth have ye agreement in writing'.[76] Such agreements were not true contracts as they were only confirming normal trading conditions. However, if the conditions were not met the debts could still be pursued through the assurance structures of reputational mechanisms, or the courts.[77]

In contrast, formal contracts were really only used for situations outside of normal trading activity. This might occur when there was large capital at stake in 'contribution' activities such as when setting up in partnership, involvement in joint ventures by way of vertical integration or another large concern. For example, John Bicknill and George Nicholson of Kingston, Jamaica, used a formal contract to set up their partnership in 1750. The partnership was to commence on the 20 May 1750 and to last for eight years and three months. The profits and debts were to be shared equally. Bicknill's capital was £679 Jamaica currency and George Nicholson gave Bicknill a half share in four parcels of land in Kingston, Jamaica, and the buildings, slaves and tools on those lands.[78] Presumably these properties were used for the business and were worth about the same amount of money as Bicknill's investment. This was not a large capital by the standards of the day, but if

---

Grossberg and Tomlins, eds., *The Cambridge History of Law in America*, pp. 365–99 esp. pp. 377–89.

75 Andrew Clow to Samuel Brown, 15 Jun. 1793, Folder Samuel Brown, Andrew Clow & Co., CWU.

76 William Earle to Captain Copland, 26 Apr. 1760, Letterbook of William Earle.

77 On reputational mechanisms see below, chapter four.

78 Articles of Agreement ... Between John Bicknill ... and George Nicholson, 20 May 1750, Jamaica Deeds, Widener Library. Colonies used sterling but valued silver (the official circulating medium of exchange – even though the British West Indies used gold in practice) differently which meant the exchange rate with Britain varied. The exchange rate for Jamaica currency was remarkably stable in the eighteenth century, being 140 per £100 sterling. The exchange rates of other colonies such as New York, Philadelphia and South and North Carolina fluctuated quite widely. See McCusker, *Money and Exchange*, pp. 234–35, 246–53, 164–65, 185–86, 223–24 and 218–19.

both had put in everything they owned they would have wanted to ensure their investment was safe. Robert Benson and James Cropper, both of Liverpool, also made a formal agreement when they went into business in 1799. They made this contract despite the fact that Cropper had previously been an apprentice to the Benson family, that they had known each other for at least nine years, and that they were both Quakers. Under the agreement Cropper received two thirds profit and Benson one third. The partnership was to last either until they had made £1200, to be split equally between them (possibly an 'incentivization' scheme), or until 1 January 1802. They were to put in an equal sum, so it is likely that Benson was to take a less active part, but in return gave Cropper access to his networks and reputation.[79] Some agreements were less formal. Mifflin & Massey of Philadelphia simply wrote their respective capitals in the first page of their ledger and updates in further pages as their partnership progressed.[80]

Other agreements were set up as part of investment in vertical integration or diversification. For example, Edward Chaffers, William Siddall, Ambrose Lace and Thomas Foxcroft drew up a formal agreement when they invested in a ropery together in Liverpool.[81] In 1766 Jonathon Blundell, Peter Holme, Ralph Earle, William Earle, Thomas Hodgson, Patrick Black, Thomas Lickbarrow and John Sparling set up a sugar refinery in Liverpool for which they drew up formal articles of partnership.[82] This latter investment was no doubt facilitated through associational membership.[83] Jonathon Blundell, Ralph and William Earle, Thomas Hodgson and John Sparling all served on the Committee of the African Company of Merchants trading from Liverpool. In 1776 Arthur Heywood also drew up articles of partnership for a bank along with his son Richard and the banker Joseph Denison in London. Every partner was to have free access to the books and was able to forbid any transactions deemed too risky.[84] Five per cent interest was to be

---

79 Agreement between James Cropper and Thomas Benson, 1 Sep. 1799, D/CR/2/2; Indenture between James Cropper … and William Rathbone and Robert Benson, 1 Aug. 1790, D/CR/2/2, Cropper Family Collection, MMMA. See also Nottingham, *Rathbone Brothers*, chapter four. James Cropper was later to become a leading abolitionist. Brian Howman, 'Abolitionism in Liverpool', in Richardson et al., *Liverpool and Transatlantic Slavery*, pp. 277–96.

80 Mifflin and Massey Ledger 1760–1763, ff.1, 20.

81 See 920 CHA 9, *passim*, PEC.

82 Articles of Partnership 31 Mar. 1766, D/EARLE/4/1, EC.

83 Committee Book of the African Company of Merchants trading from Liverpool.

84 The agreement was very particular about the nature of the business of the bank, which was essentially risk averse. Free access implied honest dealings. Toby Ditz, 'Secret Selves, Credible Personas: The Problematics of Trust and Public Display in the Writing of Eighteenth-Century Philadelphia Merchants', in Robert Blair St.

paid on any monies invested and the profits to be shared: Arthur one quarter, his son Richard one quarter, and Denison in London, one half.[85] The records do not show if Denison put in larger capital, or whether this was a premium for his London expertise and contacts. Larger one-off investments outside normal trading terms seemed to make a formal negotiated contract worthwhile.

Occasionally more formal contracts were made between merchant houses contributing together for a particular adventure.[86] Obadiah Brown & Co. of Providence set up a formal agreement with Francis & Relfe of Philadelphia in 1760 for a shipment of sugar to Lisbon. The reason for this contract may have been because some of the capital put up by Brown was in doubt and also that being a period of war, everyone was feeling slightly more risk-averse. Furthermore, the adventure was at the risk of Obadiah Brown & Co. only, which may have presented them with an adverse selection problem.[87] This was quite unusual however, and negotiated contracts were not usually made for day-to-day business.

As mentioned above, constructing trust at a personal level is an emotive process and naturally reactions to failures in personal trust were also emotional. Because 'actors in reciprocal exchange are more likely than those in negotiated exchanges to attribute the partner's behaviour to personal traits of the partner … rather than the assurance structures that surround the exchange', blame is placed on the individual when events go awry.[88] Therefore the failure of real personal trust could be devastating and perceived as a betrayal.[89] Worrier James Lawson's letters on the failure of his partnership are heartrending. When he eventually went to Virginia to sort out his affairs with his partner and brother-in-law, John Semple, he quite clearly felt betrayed. In 1773 he wrote 'He is the most unreasonable Man ever existed, I am truly to be pitied for ever having been so unlucky as being concerned

---

George, ed., *Possible Pasts: Becoming Colonial in Early America* (Ithaca and London: Cornell University Press, 2000), pp. 219–42, p. 223; Ditz, 'Shipwrecked'. Contrast the open book policy in Britain with concerns over confidentiality of Spanish merchants. Lamikiz, *Trade and Trust*, chapter six.

85 Articles of Partnership, 26 Aug. 1776, 0199–0060(2), Arthur Heywood & Sons, Barclays Archives.

86 Failure to write a contract enforceable at law could cause huge problems. See for example, Trivellato, *The Familiarity of Strangers*, chapter ten.

87 The questionable money was that still due from particularly named insurance policies. Francis & Relfe were to purchase the sugars and ship them to Lisbon. Memorandum of Agreement, 22 Oct. 1760, Folder Correspondence with Francis & Relfe 1746–1762, BFBR.

88 Molm et al., 'Risk and Trust in Social Exchange', pp. 1404–6.

89 Williamson, 'Calculativeness, Trust and Economic Organisation', p. 482.

with such a worthless Wretch.'[90] Nearly two years later he bemoaned the fact that he had lost £10,000 due to Semple's actions.[91] Andrew Clow's sometime partner David Cay also committed an unforgiveable crime. In financial difficulties, and seemingly too weak willed to face bankruptcy proceedings, he fled to Philadelphia at some point in 1784 or 1785. His friend Peter Clement wrote to him from London that 'Resentment & revenge against you and every one that avous [sic] your friendship for you seems to gather strength in Wood Street.'[92] Cay had compounded his problems by asserting that another merchant, Andrew Service, was not in financial difficulties. Clement continued, 'what infatuation possess'd you to say again & again that AS is in a thriving way & perfectly safe'.[93] Cay's folly was obviously notorious, and this may have been down to the fact that he had been in financial difficulties once before. In April 1788 a Mr R. Adams wrote to him that 'upon the Whole you may likely be better in any other part of the Globe than England'.[94] Curtis Brett was equally bitter concerning his ex-partner Francis Allwood. Although they had had a formal contract written up, Brett obviously felt that far more than a breach of (formal) contract had taken place. Allwood had lent money to a Mr Ogle in breach of their partnership articles. Brett wrote of Allwood, 'If he loses the Whole of it [his money], it is a proper Punishment for his not acting with Integrity towards me. I would as soon cut off my Right Hand, as be guilty of a similar Breach of Trust.'[95] Even negotiated exchanges were therefore not completely absent of 'real' trust, and goodwill trust was present side-by-side with negotiated agreements. Some of this language may have been posturing in order to preserve honour and reputation, and designed for public consumption at the exchange and coffee house. However, it is still clear that emotions truly ran high at such times.[96]

Failures of trust in newer relationships were still viewed harshly, if less emotionally. Robert Bostock was angry that a cargo of slaves had been

---

90 James Lawson to John Alston & James Morton, 31 Jan. 1773, James Lawson Letterbook 1770–1776, SJLP.

91 James Lawson to Thomas Phelps & Co., [?] Sep. 1774, James Lawson Letterbook 1770–1776.

92 Peter Clement to David Cay, 6 Dec. 1786, Folder Nov.–Dec. 1786, Andrew Clow & Co., and files 1784–1790 generally, SGC.

93 Peter Clement to David Cay, 6 Dec. 1786, Folder Nov.–Dec. 1786, Andrew Clow & Co., SGC.

94 R. Adams to David Cay, 6 May 1788, Folder Mar.–Apr. 1788, Andrew Clow & Co., SGC.

95 Curtis Brett to John Mead, 20 Jun. 1771, CBL.

96 Ditz, 'Secret Selves, Creditable Personas', p. 94; Ditz, 'Shipwrecked'.

detained for a long time in Antigua. He wrote his correspondents on the island that if it was the captain's fault he would turn him out.[97] Possibly Captain Fryer was a relatively new employee and their relationship had not yet been built up in terms of competency trust. A similar situation occurred when an adventure went wrong for Captain William Robinson. He held a quarter share of the *Grenada* with Christie & Christie, a merchant house in London. There was a lot of damage to goods meant for barter on the African coast, and a bill of exchange was lost, which was put down to Robinson's neglect or incompetency. Their differences could not be resolved, and the case went to court in the Exchequer.[98] Again, this was possibly a newer relationship in which competency trust had not had time to build up.[99] Conversely, being accused unfairly of a breach of trust was also a hurtful business. Andrew Clow was not an easy person to please and even his friends found him exasperating. Joseph Hadfield of London had long been a correspondent of Clow and David Cay in Philadelphia. Having found out that his arrangements for a vessel had not met with Clow's approbation he complained to Clow's house (for Cay's consumption) that 'I can only observe that in future I shall <u>literally</u> follow the orders – but I had imagined he [Clow] was too confident of my good wishes towards your House – to think that I should do anything without being fully justified and when I see him I will convince him that I acted directly in opposition to my own Interest.'[100] Hadfield obviously believed that he had built up goodwill trust with Clow, and the fact that his intentions were questioned was insulting.

Personal, non-negotiated trust became increasingly important when other factors made agreements less binding and negotiated exchanges less secure.[101] A good example of this is periods of war or conflict, when surrounding assurance structures such as the law were not always enforceable, or were changing rapidly. For example, the political conditions following the American War of Independence caused uncertainty, as did the fast changing trade conditions during the French Wars.[102] However, because affective commitment is stronger under reciprocal rather than negotiated exchange, it allowed many of the relationships around the Atlantic to continue even when institutional trust was weak and general trust or confidence low. At the same

---

97 Robert Bostock to Lightfoot, Mills & Co., 18 Aug. 1788, RBL.
98 Christie & Christie v Robinson, E 134/6Geo3/East4, TNA.
99 The trust placed in ships' captains was immense, and requires a study of its own.
100 Joseph Hadfield to Andrew Clow & Co., 4 Apr. 1792, Folder Joseph, John & Thomas Hadfield, Business Correspondence, Andrew Clow & Co., CWU.
101 Molm et al., 'Risk and Trust in Social Exchange', pp. 1398–402.
102 The way in which merchants dealt with these situations is covered in more detail in chapter seven.

time, personal trust did not always facilitate trade. Purchasers of slaves in Charleston were 'very cautious of binding themselves to strangers' and others were even sceptical of partners.[103] Dealing with those outside your 'world in common' could also be problematic, let alone with 'others' of various types. In such circumstances, where personal trust was not possible or sufficient, institutional trust could provide an assurance structure.[104]

Institutional (hyphenated) Trust: Assurance

Institutional-based (hyphenated) trust, or assurance, arises due to, or is required by, a number of factors. It is often present or required when the geographical distance covered by a market becomes too large for process-based trust alone to cope, when transactions cross group boundaries (especially of ethnicity or race), when there is a diversification of groups, firms or industries, and when the rules of the game are too few or too frequently violated. Certainly the latter was not true in the eighteenth century, when lapses in trust appear surprisingly few compared to the number of transactions. Institutions, and the regulations provided by them, usually increase as process-based trust declines.[105] There was certainly a rise in institutions during the period covered here, often created as a reaction to certain crises.[106] The causality of this relationship is uncertain however, because as Fukuyama and O'Neill have argued, over-reliance on institutions can lead to declining levels of personal and general trust.[107] The relationship between the various levels of trust is therefore problematic, but whilst institutionalised trust is not a substitute for generalised morality, it can help to generate exchange when levels of other types of trust are low. In some ways therefore, we institutionalise our *mis*trust by placing our trust in an agency instead. Therefore our trust is hyphenated.[108] Some have argued that this is not trust at all, but assurance. Institutions providing such assurance include social and political institutions which facilitate our knowing where to place trust, such as the government, laws and the court system, corporate or trade bodies such as chartered companies, chambers of commerce, trade associations and

---

103 Henry Laurens to John Knight, 12 Jun. 1764, *HLP*, Vol. IV; John Perhouse to James Perhouse, 4 Apr. 1806, John Perhouse Journal 1800–1838.

104 Williamson, 'Calculativeness, Trust and Economic Organisation', pp. 483–84.

105 Zucker, 'Production of Trust', pp. 85–90; Platteau, 'The Role of Public and Private Order Institutions', p. 564.

106 See the chapter seven on crises.

107 Francis Fukuyama, *Trust: The Social Virtues and the Creation of Prosperity* [1995] (New York: Free Press Paperbacks, 1996; O'Neill, *A Question of Trust*.

108 Humphrey and Schmitz, *Trust and Economic Development*, pp. 12–13; Williamson, 'Calculativeness, Trust and Economic Organisation', p. 474.

banks.[109] Importantly however, those institutions in turn must be credible. It is not possible to cover all the different types of hyphenated or institutional trust in the eighteenth century, but a few examples will make the point.

The law is significant because it assigns property rights, obviously of significance to a capitalist economy. Importantly however, those institutions must be credible, autonomous and able to enforce regulations that infuse trading confidence.[110] Anyone can write an IOU, but the acceptor has to trust the courts to enforce payment if the writer defaults.[111] During the eighteenth century important changes were made on both sides of the Atlantic which affected property rights associated with credit – the lynchpin of trade.[112] These included: changing attitudes towards usury which encouraged investment, the decreasing stigma of bankruptcy; a rise in the use of the civil courts for small debts claims; the Colonial Debts Act of 1732 which made land, houses and chattels (including enslaved people) liable for satisfying debts; and a rise in the use of bonded debts, especially in the slave trade.[113] Other examples include: the Debtors' laws brought in by George III; Jamaica's laws enforcing interest payments on bills of exchange after judgment in court in 1750 and 1755; and the formalising of the offsetting of mutual debts against one another in 1769.[114] Colonisation meant that English laws were diffused around the Atlantic but altered to deal with particular circumstances. For example, Connecticut, Pennsylvania, and Massachusetts refused to have a Court of Equity, North Carolina upheld property rights for women within its patriarchal framework, and the West Indies and other slave societies had laws particular to the control of their property in enslaved persons.[115]

---

109 O'Neill, *A Question of Trust*, p. vii; Moore, 'How Difficult is it to Construct Market Relations', p. 823.

110 Williamson, 'Calculativeness, Trust and Economic Organisation', p. 477.

111 Platteau, 'The Role of Public and Private Order Institutions', p. 544.

112 Interestingly Julian Hoppit has recently argued that some property rights were eroded after 1688, 'Compulsion, Compensation and Property Rights in Britain, 1688–1833', *Past and Present*, 210 (Feb. 2011), 93–128.

113 Eric Kerridge, *Trade and Banking in Early-Modern England* (Manchester: Manchester University Press, 1998), pp. 34–39; Hoppit, *Risk and Failure*, chapter two; Margot Finn, *The Character of Credit: Personal Debt in English Culture, 1740–1914* (Cambridge: Cambridge University Press, 2003), esp. chapters five and six; Bruce H. Mann, 'The Transformation of Law and Economy in Early America', in Grossberg and Tomlins, eds., *The Cambridge History of Law in America*, pp. 365–99; Mann, 'The Transformation of Law and Economy'; Morgan, 'Remittance Procedures', pp. 719–20.

114 Hoppit, *Risk and Failure*, chapter three; *Acts of Assembly, Passed in the Island of Jamaica, From the Year 1681 to the Year 1769 Inclusive: In Two Volumes* (Kingston, Jamaica: Printed by Alexander Aikman, 1787).

115 Courts of Equity were often disliked because they were seen as expensive, time consuming, relying upon the independent judgement of a Chancellor and their

Despite these differences, the laws regarding debts were designed to help creditors and were basically the same around the British-Atlantic world. Therefore, it was understood that the legal system in the colonised part of the British Atlantic would (generally speaking) enforce the collection of debts such as book credit, bonds and mortgages. Concerns soon ensued when those assurance structures were absent. Sparling & Bolden of Liverpool wrote to their sister house in Virginia in 1788 explaining that if the state assembly would not enforce the payments of debts to British subjects, then trade between them would soon cease.[116]

If the institution (rather than an individual) was to be trusted, the credit-ability of that institution was crucial. If it was found to be wanting, trust would not be constructed or could decline. For example, contemporary œconomist Malachy Postlethwayt bemoaned the fact that the British Government increased its debt and borrowed even more from the mercantile class. He argued that the government should pay interest on its old debts first, otherwise lending to the government would be 'uncertain and precarious' and people would be deterred from investing in government bonds.[117] Postlethwayt also argued that the Navigation Acts were not enforced properly, which allowed the Northern British colonies to continue an illegal commerce with the French and Dutch nations and their sugar islands.[118] Another example is the House of Assembly in Jamaica, which commented that a court of Chancery had not been held there between 3 December 1779 and 8 June 1780, agreeing that it should be held more regularly.[119] It was noted above that uncertainty over the legal system could cause worries. Similarly, reinterpretations of

association with the prerogative powers of the King. Pennsylvania had a Court of Equity for a short period only in the early eighteenth century. Maylynn Salmon, *Women and the Law of Property in Early America* (Chapel Hill: University of North Carolina Press, 1986), chapter five.

116 Sparling & Bolden to Sparling, Lawrence & Co., 29 Jan. 1788, Sparling & Bolden Letterbook 1788–1799, LivRO.

117 Postlethwayt, *Great Britain's True System*, 'Letter I: Of Raising the Supplies, by Increasing the Public Debts, Considered', pp. 1–24, p. 8. In fact such concerns had been voiced as early as the late seventeenth century. A thriving secondary market allowed those who no longer trusted the government to sell their investments on. Anne L. Murphy, *The Origins of English Financial Markets: Investment and Speculation before the South Sea Bubble* (Cambridge: Cambridge University Press, 2009), pp. 61–64. See also the controversy regarding the creditability of the English government during the South Sea Scheme. Hoppit, 'Compulsion, Compensation and Property Rights', pp. 103–8.

118 Malachy Postlethwayt, *Britain's Commercial Interest Explained and Improved* [1757] (New York: August M. Kelly, 1968), 'Dissertation XVIII: The Cause of the Present State of Our Affairs in America Farther Considered', pp. 483–99, esp. pp. 483–86.

119 Journals of the Assembly of Jamaica, Vol. 7, 19 Apr. 1780, p. 281.

the law could cause consternation, and it has of course been argued that it was changes in taxation law which caused the conflict leading up to the American War of Independence.[120] Changes to the Navigation Laws, such as by the various Orders in Council brought in by the British Government during the French Wars, changed the relationship not only with France, but importantly, with the United States as well, eventually leading to the Anglo-American War.[121]

Lapses in the law, whether through loopholes or lack of enforcement, were often taken advantage of by British merchants around the Atlantic. This was normal behaviour on the margins, also practised by the Dutch, French and Spanish, such was the 'entangled' world of the Atlantic.[122] Merchants in the British West Indies traded with the French and Spanish colonies both legally and illegally during our period, and for a long time before. The Free Ports Act of 1766 was brought in to legalise this trade.[123] Here too, changes in the interpretation of laws proved antagonistic with other countries, perhaps creating more bad feeling than when laws were absent. Following the American War of Independence, it would appear that the customs officers in Jamaica became less liberal in their interpretation of the Free Ports Act and 'a sudden change in the conduct of the Officers' had been noticed.[124]

---

120 For the causes of the American War of Independence see: Bernard Bailyn, *The Ideological Origins of the American Revolution* (Cambridge, MA: The Belknap Press of Harvard University Press, 1967); Gary B. Nash, *The Urban Crucible: The Northern Seaports and the Origins of the American Revolution*, Abridged edn (Cambridge, MA and London: Harvard University Press, 1979); Marc Egnal and Joseph Ernst, 'An Economic Interpretation of the American Revolution', *WMQ*, 3rd ser., 29:1 (1972), 3–32; Marc Egnal, *A Mighty Empire: The Origins of the American Revolution* (Ithaca and London: Cornell University Press, 1988); Gordon S. Wood, *The Radicalism of the American Revolution* (New York: A. A. Knopf, 1991). See also Andrew O'Shaughnessy, *An Empire Divided: The American Revolution and the British Caribbean* (Philadelphia: University of Pennsylvania Press, 2000).

121 G. W. Daniels, 'American Cotton Trade with Liverpool under the Embargo and Non-Intercourse Acts', *American Historical Review*, 21:2 (Jan. 1916), 276–87.

122 See Schnurmann, 'Atlantic Trade and American Identities'; Hatfield, 'Dutch and New Netherland Merchants'; Banks, 'Official Duplicity'; Náter, 'The Spanish Empire and Cuban Tobacco'; and Gould, 'Entangled Histories, Entangled Worlds'.

123 Armytage, *The Free Port System*, esp. chapter two. Armytage argues that this was an elaboration of protectionist policy because it only allowed in goods that were not in competition with the British planters and promoted the sales of manufactured goods through the British West Indies, p. 2. However, Pearce states that 'they represented the first significant attempt to launch an experiment in free trade and a portentous, if small, breach in the old imperial system', *British Trade with Spanish America*, p. 52.

124 The Memorial and Petition of the Merchants of Kingston, c. May 1786, BoT, WI, BT 6/75, f. 44, TNA.

The officers started enforcing the law very literally regarding the exact tonnage and number of decks of foreign vessels, and were seizing them if they did not comply. A Jamaican complained that 'Within Eight Days past such circumstances have happen'd as threaten a Total Loss of foreign Trade to this Island.'[125] A committee of merchants in Jamaica argued that to keep to the strict letter of the law without notice would 'destroy that Confidence and faith under which these unfortunate people have hitherto dealt with us'.[126] They argued that these measures were impolitic, and had forced the Spaniards to trade with places such as Philadelphia who were selling them exactly the same articles.[127] One contemporary noted that 'The Spanish traders had always been timorous and wary.'[128] Foreign traders, finding our institutions reinterpreted, had lost confidence, and were therefore going elsewhere.[129] Changing laws could sometimes be as dangerous as not having them in place at all.

Alongside the legal framework, chartered and joint stock companies were also extremely important institutions during the early-modern period.[130] Central to the planting and colonising mission, they removed much of the risk from the Crown to groups of individuals, and conveniently also allowed the Crown to place blame on them for any problems at appropriate moments of foreign policy making.[131] However, they could also be problematic, especially if they failed in their roles as 'gatekeepers'.[132] The East India Company's officers were accused of corruption, looting and bribing, and its 'nabobs' derided as nouveau riche and for trying to marry into old gentry families.[133] The Royal African Company was also problematic; unable to protect or engross British trade on the African coast it had been accused of being

---

125 Extract of a Letter Dated Kingston, Jamaica, 15 Feb. 1789, BoT, WI, BT 6/75, f. 31.
126 Copy of Memorial of the Merchants of Kingston, 22 May 1786, BoT, WI, BT 6/75, ff. 47–48.
127 Extract of a letter from John Whitaker, 12 Aug. 1789, BoT, WI, BT 6/75, f. 59.
128 Cited in Armytage, *The Free Port System*, pp. 47–48.
129 The reputation of the state is dealt with in the next chapter.
130 About one hundred joint stock companies were formed between 1685 and 1695. Murphy, *The Origins of English Financial Markets*, p. 1.
131 Mancke, 'Chartered Enterprises'. For an outline of the various British Chartered Companies see Griffiths, *A Licence to Trade*.
132 See the discussion below, pp. 107–8.
133 Nicholas B. Dirks, *The Scandal of Empire: India and the Creation of Imperial Britain* (Cambridge, MA: Harvard University Press, 2006). They also caused problems in terms of property rights, for example following the East India Company's move from a commercial concern to a territorial power in the 1760s. Chartered Companies declined along with the rise in influence of metropolitan government. Mancke, 'Chartered Enterprises', pp. 246–48.

corrupt and inefficient.[134] It may have been rehabilitated as an institution by the literature, but there is no doubt that some of its officers were corrupt.[135] Richard Miles, Governor of Cape Coast Castle, was involved in some slave trading on his own account along with John & Thomas Hodgson of Liverpool, against the restrictions of his office. Noticeably, the letter regarding this transaction was marked 'private'.[136]

Banks could also work as gatekeepers, and, it has been argued, were important for the evolution of modern Britain.[137] In 1764 the Bank of England had severely restricted the number of bills it was discounting due to the large amount of forged paper money circulating in England. According to Curtis Brett, then in London, this situation was exacerbated by the large credit given to the colonies which was causing great distress in the post-war dislocation.[138] The members of the Philadelphia Chamber of Commerce thought the Bank of the United States a very trusted institution for the development of the early United States. In a petition of 1810 supporting the continuance of its charter, they argued that the immense faith and confidence in the institution was demonstrated by the fact that a large amount of its capital was provided by widows, orphans and charitable institutions.[139] Moreover, several million dollars of stock in the bank were held by foreigners and people not resident in the United States. They noted that 'The establishment of the Bank [1791] may justly be regarded as the era which marks the rise of commercial credit, confidence and enterprise.'[140] Banks clearly played an important role in providing assurance.

Another group was the chambers of commerce. These were established in

---

134 K. G. Davies, *The Royal African Company* (London: Longmans, Green and Co., 1957)
135 It has been argued that the decline of the RAC was not due to monopoly inefficiency, but market conditions. Ann M. Carlos and Jamie Brown Kruse, 'The Decline of the Royal African Company: Fringe Firms and the Role of the Charter', *EcHR*, new ser., 49:2 (May 1996), 291–313.
136 John & Thomas Hodgson to Richard Miles, 25 Feb. 1783, CRA, Vol. II.
137 Murphy, *The Origins of English Financial Markets*, p. 2.
138 Curtis Brett to Francis Allwood, 23 Jan. 1764, CBL.
139 The Bank of England had a similarly wide customer base. Ann M. Carlos and Larry Neal, 'The Micro-Foundations of the Early London Capital Market: Bank of England Shareholders During and After the South Sea Bubble', *EcHR*, new ser., 59:3 (Aug. 2006), 498–538. Similar claims could be made for the East India Company. See Bowen, *The Business of Empire*, chapter four.
140 Memorial of the Members of the Chamber of Commerce of Philadelphia relative to the Bank of the United States, 1810, LCP. For the importance of the early Philadelphia banks in the economic development of the early United States see Robert E. Wright, *The First Wall Street, Chesnut Street, Philadelphia, and the Birth of American Finance* (Chicago and London: University of Chicago Press, 2005).

many trading cities during the latter half of the eighteenth century, including in London, Glasgow, Philadelphia and New York. A Liverpool Chamber of Commerce was established in June 1774. As there were many slave traders involved, its activities included petitioning the government regarding such issues as provisioning the West Indies, and prosecuting captains following bad practices on the coast of Africa, in addition to such issues as postal arrangements and the protection of the corn trade.[141] Philadelphia had its own Chamber of Commerce from 1801 of which only citizens of the United States and trading merchants could be members, and which dealt with such concerns as port duties and the arming of vessels.[142] Glasgow had its Chamber of Commerce from 1783, and New York from as early as 1768.[143] Many cities also had other trade associations such as London's 'Society of West India Planters and Merchants', Glasgow's 'West India Association' and Liverpool's 'African Committee' which defended the slave traders' interests.[144] These institutions were mostly concerned with defending the various trades of their cities, but they worked as gatekeepers, at least for their own areas of interest. They also confirmed the status and reputation of the city by their very existence.

Of course, where merchants were trading outside their community space, assurance structures or institutions were often absent. Europeans clearly felt themselves superior to those they encountered, and more technically advanced. For example they considered 'That the Trade on the Coast of Africa differs from the Trade of Civiliz'd Nations'.[145] However, it was found

---

141 'An Abstract of the Proceedings and Resolutions of the Several Committees of the Chamber of Commerce for the Port of Liverpool, From the First Establishment on the 24th June 1774 to the 24th June, 1777,' LCP; Liverpool also had an American Chamber of Commerce from 1801, Minutes of the Liverpool American Chamber of Commerce 1808–1908, LivRO.

142 Articles of Association and Rules of the Philadelphia Chamber of Commerce, 1801, p. 8; Memorial of the Philadelphia Chamber of Commerce, 1803; Representation of the Philadelphia Chamber of Commerce, 1804, LCP.

143 Chamber of Commerce and Manufacturers in the City of Glasgow, Vol. I, 1783–1788, Mitchell Library. The New York chamber immediately set up a Monthly Committee to arbitrate disputes. Priest, 'Law and Commerce', p. 412.

144 Ryden, *West Indian Slavery*; Glasgow West India Association Minutes 1807–1969, Mitchell Library; Committee Book of the African Company of Merchants trading from Liverpool, 1750–1820.

145 Europeans considered their representational technologies of the alphabet and printing press part of what made them superior to the 'natives' and helped the British to justify their empire. Ogborn, *Indian Ink*, p. 13 and chapter one generally; Memorial of the Merchants of Leverpoole trading to Africa desirs to have liberty to import from any parts of Europe East India Goods Rifles & Brandy for African Trade, 16 Mar. 1765, T1/447/349–350–351, TNA.

early on in the expansion around the Atlantic that present-giving, or gifting, might be useful. This had long been a strategy in traditional societies and helped to build emotional attachment.[146] Gift-giving was used in early exchange with the Amerindians for example.[147] Postlethwayt however, was against alcohol as a present because it intoxicated the native Americans, whereas he considered that the French had been more politic.[148] As trade developed – such as in South Carolina's trade with the native Americans – 'Indian Traders' were licensed, and fairness in dealing with the tribes was seen as a way to bind them to the British Empire.[149] The Hudson's Bay Company was also pragmatic in its approach to trade. The native Americans were demanding consumers – more interested in the quality and variety of goods than quantity – checking goods carefully for defects. Interestingly, the Company promoted the learning of Algonquian Cree (the local language) by its factors in order to promote trade and the loyalty of its customers.[150] The building up of such institutional trust promoted trade in the long term as well – on British terms at least. Therefore, the morality of trust could be differentiated, limited, or at least unequal.[151]

Another form of gifting was the practice of giving presents and hosting dinners on vessels on the African coast, sometimes known as to 'stroke the Capt[n] hand', which remained an important part of facilitating the slave trade into the late eighteenth century.[152] Process-based trust and gift-giving however, was not always enough on the African coast. As late as 1787 Robert Bostock, sending a vessel to Cape Mont [Sierra Leone] told his captain 'not to trust any goods to the nation there on Any Aco[t] whatsoever'.[153] This lack

---

146 Platteau, 'The Role of Public and Private Order Institutions', p. 550. Salutation [kūrnish] and gift giving [nazr] was also used in India. Ogborn, Indian Ink, p. 28.

147 Kupperman, Roanoke, pp. 68–71.

148 Postlethwayt, Britain's Commercial Interest Explained, 'Dissertation XVI: A Succinct View of the Constitution of the British Plantations in America …', pp. 421–59, pp. 428–29.

149 Eirlys M. Barker, 'Indian Traders, Charles Town and London's Vital Link to the Interior of North America, 1717–1755', in Greene et al., Money, Trade and Power, pp. 141–65.

150 Ann M. Carlos and Frank D. Lewis, 'Marketing in the Land of Hudson Bay: Indian Consumers and the Hudson's Bay Company, 1670–1770', Enterprise & Society, 3:2 (Jun. 2002), 285–317

151 Platteau, 'The Role of Moral Norms', p. 770.

152 Anon, West African Account, n.d. British Library; Christopher Fyfe, ed., Anna Maria Falconbridge, Narrative of Two Voyages to the River Sierra Leone with Alexander Falconbridge, An Account of the Slave Trade in Africa (Liverpool: Liverpool University Press, 2000), p. 198.

153 Robert Bostock to Captain Berne, 2 Jul. 1787, RBL.

of trust worked both ways. Slave captains did not always adhere to what was considered good practice and the role of Liverpool traders in the Old Calabar massacre of 1767 meant that the English, if not all Europeans, were not always trusted by African traders.[154] Not that the lessons of the past were always learned despite being part of the 'network memory'.[155] In 1777 it was reported that Captain Johnson of the snow *Patty* of Liverpool had forcibly carried off a number of canoemen from Badagry which had occasioned the total exclusion of the English from that port and was likely to have other disagreeable consequences.[156] Such behaviour meant that the Africans unsurprisingly preferred to use their own institutions in order to enforce debt collection and other terms of trade. For example, in the Bight of Biafra, the most popular destinations for Liverpool traders, African customs were adopted which helped to overcome the problem of trust between African and European traders. These included pawnship, fictive kinship and the Ekpe (Leopard society). Human pawns were used as 'hostages' in order to secure delivery of slaves, and this was reasonably effective as early as the 1760s. Fictive kinship was also engendered by some Africans visiting and being educated in Liverpool, and slave traders resident in Liverpool had usually been slave captains with years of experience trading on the coast.[157] Making barter arrangements in the form of a 'palaver' was also a convoluted and time-consuming business involving hosting by the Africans.[158] The problem of trusting a racial 'other' in West Central Africa was circumvented by Europeans trading with the Afro-Portuguese community.[159] Therefore,

---

154 Examination of Captain Hall, 22 Feb. 1788, BoT, AQ, I, ff. 62–63, BT 6/9, TNA; see also Williams, *History of the Liverpool Privateers*, Part II, chapter three.

155 Hancock, 'The Trouble with Networks', p. 479.

156 'An Abstract of the Proceedings and Resolutions … 1777'. A snow was a two-masted transport vessel. Alan McGowan, *The Ship: The Century before Steam, The Development of the Sailing Ship 1700–1820* (London: Her Majesty's Stationery Office for the National Maritime Museum, 1980), p. 18.

157 Paul E. Lovejoy and David Richardson, '"This Horrid Hole": Royal Authority, Commerce and Credit and Bonny, 1690–1840', *Journal of African History*, 45 (2004), 363–92; Paul E. Lovejoy and David Richardson, 'Trust, Pawnship and Atlantic History: The Institutional Foundations of the Old Calabar Slave Trade', *American Historical Review*, 104:2 (1999), 333–55; Paul E. Lovejoy and David Richardson, 'African Agency and the Liverpool Slave Trade', in Richardson et al., *Liverpool and Transatlantic Slavery*, pp. 43–65. Europeans also adopted the use of cowrie shells, beads and manilas as forms of payment for Africans, although they did not accept them in turn for payment of European goods. Marion Johnson, 'The Atlantic Slave Trade and the Economy of West Africa', in Anstey and Hair, *Liverpool, the African Slave Trade*, pp. 14–38.

158 See a good description in Fyfe, *Narrative of Two Voyages*, pp. 32–36.

159 Lovejoy and Richardson, 'Trust, Pawnship and Atlantic History'; Lovejoy and

when they really wanted to merchants managed to deal with problems of trust even with other cultures.

Assurance structures such as chambers of commerce and trading associations were constructed by the merchants themselves. They formed part of the private-order institution of a business culture which encouraged benign behaviour, even in non-repeat trade.[160] It is also clear however, that merchants were prepared to adopt the customs of 'others' in order to facilitate trade. Assurance structures such as the law and other institutions were therefore important in facilitating trade where other types or levels of trust were low, but it is important to understand that such institutions could cause mistrust as well.[161] Institutional agencies can therefore promote generalised trust only if they are trusted themselves.[162]

General Trust: Confidence

Humphrey and Schmitz argue that general trust in the wider system of exchange is in fact confidence.[163] The wider context in which our merchants worked was the colonial and mercantilist economy of the British-Atlantic world as shaped by the institutions discussed above. Merchants understood the basic rules of the game, and the assurance structures they provided. The trouble was that the circumstances in which those rules were played kept changing. Wars and credit crises shortened the shadow of the future, and without a sufficiently large shadow, cooperation was easily destabilised.[164] Although it is clear that personal, institutional and general levels of trust interacted with one another, it is difficult to establish exactly when general levels of trust came into being. It is therefore easier to examine general trust, or confidence, through failures in it. The many wars and conflicts of the eighteenth century periodically reduced general levels of confidence in the system and such ruptures in the economic order hurt process-based (personal) trust as well.[165] How these difficult situations were dealt with is considered in detail in the chapter on crises, but it is worth briefly considering them here.

Richardson, "'This Horrid Hole"'; Herbert S. Klein, *The Atlantic Slave Trade* (Cambridge: Cambridge University Press, 1999), pp. 65–69.

160 Platteau, 'The Role of Public and Private Order Institutions', p. 557.

161 Humphrey and Schmitz, *Trust and Economic Development*, p. 12; Zucker for example notes that after 1800 process-based trust broke down and so even more 'corporate actors' emerged which meant that standardization and regulation also increased. Zucker, 'Production of Trust', pp. 87–93.

162 Zucker, 'Production of Trust', p. 40; Shapiro, 'Social Control of Impersonal Trust', p. 641.

163 Humphrey and Schmitz, *Trust and Economic Development*, pp. 3, 11.

164 Axelrod, *The Evolution of Cooperation*, p. 174.

165 Humphrey and Schmitz, *Trust and Economic Development*, p. 20.

Wars, or even the threat of them, were one of the main reasons for a decline in confidence. In 1774 Liverpool merchants were worried about developments in the American mainland colonies, and wrote to various other trading towns to see what measures were being taken given the precarious nature of property (in debts) at that time.[166] A little over a year later, Owen Biddle of Philadelphia wrote that in the aftermath of Lexington and Concord the whole continent was in confusion, 'little business was being transacted, and Many people show an unwillingness to pay their Debts'.[167] Indeed, many people took advantage of this situation as was shown by the necessity of the Jay Treaty.[168] However, trade soon got underway after the war and by 1784 Alexander Johnston was able to write from New York that 'The prejudices of the minds of people begin to wear off by degrees, though you may readily conceive, that it will require a longer time to [...?] a conciliation in this place than any other on this Continent.'[169] In the run up to the Anglo-American war similar concerns were voiced.[170] Liverpool merchant Thomas Martin gave evidence to the House of Commons in 1808 regarding the Orders in Council of the previous year. He noted that 'many of the capitalists in the manufacturing towns, who were in the habit of purchasing goods and sending them for sale to the United States, are declining the business'.[171] A year later, the situation was still bad: 'Credit ... suffered much, and a distrust still operating.'[172]

The end of wars could just as easily be problematic because there were usually post-war booms followed by gluts and consequent busts. For example, in 1763 Charles Stewart wrote from London to his friends in Virginia that

166 'An Abstract of the Proceedings and Resolutions ... 1777', p. 4.

167 Owen Biddle to John Ewer, 2 May 1775, Folder Owen Biddle, CBP.

168 In 1795 the Jay Treaty arranged for the United States' government to pay $600,000 to the British government in full payment for outstanding debts, which was to distribute the money as it saw fit. This was estimated to represent a payment of only 2s. 6d. in the pound. M. M. Schofield, 'The Virginia Trade of the Firm of Sparling and Bolden of Liverpool 1788–99', *Transactions of the Historic Society of Lancashire and Cheshire*, 116 (1965), 117–65, p. 126.

169 Johnston was probably referring to the occupation of New York by the British forces. Alexander Johnston to Samuel Gardiner, 1 Feb. 1784, AJL. There remained in the United States a high level of dependency on British trade until the early nineteenth century. See Sheryllynne Haggerty, 'The Structure of the Philadelphia Trading Community on the Transition from Colony to State', *BH*, 48:2 (2006), 171–92.

170 Both the American War of Independence and the Anglo-American war are discussed in further detail in the chapter on crises.

171 This was putting many out of employment and the prices of goods were falling rapidly. Evidence of Thomas Martin, 1808 (119), p. 80, HCPP.

172 Printed circular of Morrall & Borland, 14 Nov. 1809, Folder Morrall & Borland, BFBR.

'A general diffidence prevails at present, as it is not known who can hold out in these trying times, and the Bank of England which used to give life and spirit to the trade of the Kingdom ... is now extremely cautious.'[173] The reduction in assurance by the bank was lessening confidence as a whole. The post-war gloom spread around the colonies as well. In 1764 Tench Francis wrote from Philadelphia that money had grown scarce and as 'People who us'd to buy on Credit are become so precarious ... we know not who safely to trust. I long to see old Times revive, Credit once more established, & Trade get on some solid Footing.'[174] A post-war boom followed by a glut was also evident following the American War of Independence and many traders in Philadelphia went bankrupt, including Clement Biddle.[175] Pragers, Liebaert & Co. of that city wrote to H. Cohen, their supplier in London, that they had sold little of his millinery. 'Trade in general is still continuing dull, and the daily failures produce an incredible mistrust.'[176] Indeed, wars often caused bankruptcies, but such individual failures were hardly ever personal events in the interconnected credit of this period. In 1810 Buchanan & Benn, again writing to Brown & Ives, informed them that business in Liverpool had been much interrupted by the failure of several banking and mercantile houses in London which had 'materially affected public confidence'.[177] A lack of confidence, whether promoted by wars or the financial crises that usually followed them, presented itself as mistrust.

CONCLUSION

IT IS CLEAR that the various levels and types of trust were interconnected, but, assessing the exact relationship between the different levels of trust is difficult. Platteau argues that 'The honesty equilibrium will rise when everyone believes everyone else will be honest'; but how this state of affairs is created and then maintained is uncertain.[178] During the period 1750–1815, there is no doubt that personal trust was extremely important, whether ascribed or process based. Institutions were in existence and growing in number, yet the frameworks and regulations which were constructed by them

---

173 Charles Stewart to Aitchinson & Parker, 15 Nov. 1763, Folder 920 PAR I 27, PP.

174 Tench Francis to Nicholas Brown & Co. 17 Apr. 1764, Correspondence with Francis & Relfe, Folder 13, BFBR.

175 At least 68 firms failed in Philadelphia during the 1780s. Doerflinger, *A Vigorous Spirit of Enterprise*, pp. 262–63.

176 Pragers, Liebaert & Co. to H. Cohen, 11 May 1785, Lowe v Cohen, C105/19.

177 Printed circular of Buchanan & Benn, 23 Aug. 1810, Folder Buchanan & Benn, BFBR.

178 Platteau, 'The Role of Moral Norms', p. 759.

were not always enforceable around the Atlantic, and they did not always act as trusted gatekeepers. Equally, whilst institutions can stand in for personal trust, especially when trade becomes too large for personal trust to cover all the options, Putnam and Fukuyama have shown that an over-reliance on them can result in a low-trust society.[179] There is a paradox here, as Shapiro notes: 'The more we control the institution of trust, the more dissatisfied we become with its offerings.'[180] At the same time, markets function best when there is at least a minimum level of general trust, or confidence, however that is produced.[181] Yet, even when confidence was dented by wars and credit crises and trust in institutions wavered, merchants around the Atlantic continued to do business. Personal trust took over when institutional and general levels of trust were low. Therefore, whilst all the levels of trust were important in facilitating risk, personal trust was more important in times of crisis. The institution of the business culture as a whole was also important. Straddling the boundaries of personal and institutional trust, it allowed the British-Atlantic trading community to keep functioning – albeit at reduced levels during periods of stress. We shall see the proof of this in the chapters on networks and crises. First however, we need to investigate the assurance structures of reputation and obligation, which were also essential elements of that business culture.

---

179 Fukuyama highlights the role of settling out of court in Japan. Fukuyama, *Trust*, chapter 16.
180 Shapiro, 'The Social Control of Impersonal Trust', p. 652.
181 Humphrey and Schmitz, 'Trust and Economic Development', p. 16.

4

Reputation

As to asking an Anticipation on a Cargo Not Arrived,
we would sooner have our Bills protested.[1]

I F THERE WAS ONE CLEAR signal to start asking questions about a
merchant's financial viability, it was one of their bills of exchange being
protested for non-payment. This usually meant that the payer did not have
enough funds with the drawee, and whilst this did not necessarily mean
the payer was insolvent, it certainly started rumours.[2] Joshua Johnson noted
in 1771 that Hanbury & Co. had protested Barnes & Ridgate's bills, which
had hurt their credit.[3] A merchant's ability to get credit was so tied up with
reputation, that it *was* his reputation, hence the term credibility. Credit was
an 'intensely *social* fact' [emphasis in original], but also an emotive one.[4] A
reputation could take years to construct, yet a small piece of gossip, a sniff
of scandal, a rumour of a bill protested, and the merchant's reputation could
be deconstructed in seconds. As William Gordon noted in 1763, 'a merchant
ought constantly to have in view, the support of his personal credit, which if
is but once blown upon, is not without great difficulty achieved'.[5]

---

1 Observations and Extracts on Affairs, 9 Jul. 1793, Folder Andrew Clow & Co., Legal,
   1793–99, Andrew Clow & Co., Letters Received, Baker Library.
2 Bills could be protested for non acceptance and for non payment (if not paid after
   acceptance). A bill might not be paid because the acceptor was in financial difficulties.
   For a contemporary and excellent introduction to bills of exchange see Timothy
   Cunningham, *The Merchant's Lawyer: Or, the Law of Trade in General ... To Which is
   Added a Complete Book of Rates*, Vol. II, 2nd edn (London, 1768).
3 Joshua Johnson to John Davidson, 27 Aug. 1771, JJL.
4 Muldrew, *The Economy of Obligation*, p. 174 and chapter six generally.
5 Gordon, *The Universal Accountant*, Part II, p. 7.

It is therefore very unlikely that William Wilson in the quotation above would *really* sooner have had his bills protested. His correspondent in Philadelphia, Arthur Jones, had asked him about the prospects of a cargo of wheat he was sending to Wilson at Alexandria (Virginia). Wilson was not prepared to comment in advance for fear that he would be wrong and his judgment subsequently questioned. Nor were 'the Creatures who are generally buyers of wheat' prepared to risk their reputation on speculating about possible prices and the market for wheat; they would 'freeze with terror to be asked the question'.[6] During another transaction in which it had taken a long time to sell some flour sent by Jones to Wilson, Jones had expressed his worries over his cash flow problems. Frustrated, and feeling that Wilson did not care about his predicament, he wrote:

> Really Gentlemen We are mortified to have expressed our Anxiety to you, we expected our flour would have been sold and converted into Bills ... we had much rather our flour had been sold at 4 dollars P Barrel than we should have been made to forfeit our plighted honor,

that is, his 'honor' being his reputation.[7]

This story shows that a variety of factors went into the construction of reputation, what Jeremy Shearmur and Daniel Klein call the 'reputational nexus'.[8] Financial creditability was the most important aspect, but knowledge, skills, judgment and integrity also helped to construct a merchant's reputation. Moreover, a good reputation helped merchants to 'make judgements about other people's honesty'.[9] Reputation mechanisms were therefore an important element in trusting others, and thereby taking risks. As such they were an important element in the British-Atlantic business culture. This chapter first outlines the importance and variety of reputational mechanisms and then looks at how direct and indirect reputation mechanisms were used to gain entry into the market. It next considers how reputations were then constructed and maintained through correct 'performance', before

---

6   Observations and Extracts on Affairs, 9 Jul. 1793, Folder Andrew Clow & Co., Legal, 1793–1799, Andrew Clow & Co., Letters Received, Baker Library.

7   Arthur Jones to William Wilson, 9 Jul. 1793, Folder Andrew Clow & Co., Legal, 1793–1799, Andrew Clow & Co., Letters Received, Baker Library. Anthony Pagden posits two contemporary understandings of honour; one private, where the man is his own legislator, and one public, which requires the honourable action to have a witness. Arthur Jones probably meant his honour in this public form – his reputation. Anthony Pagden, 'The Destruction of Trust and its Economic Consequences in the Case of Eighteenth-Century Naples', in Gambetta, *Trust*, pp. 127–41, p. 133.

8   Shearmur and Klein, 'Good Conduct in the Great Society', esp. pp. 38–39.

9   Muldrew, *The Economy of Obligation*, p. 148.

investigating how reputation was deconstructed through gossip and scandal. Lastly it briefly touches on the importance of reputation at the community level. People being what they are, merchants rarely commented on behaviour they considered 'normal' or 'good', and so this chapter often concentrates on 'bad' behaviour or non-performance. It also focuses on the financial aspects of reputation due to the importance of credit and creditability to the early-modern Atlantic economy.

REPUTATIONAL MECHANISMS

RECENTLY there have been many discussions concerning human and social capital, in addition to that of financial capital.[10] However, reputation is also a form of capital.[11] As we saw above, those without a good reputation were seen as more risky and could easily find that they had to put up collateral, pay in advance, or were turned away altogether.[12] A positive reputation is therefore a valuable asset which inspires trust and facilitates access to resources.[13] The desire to construct and maintain a good reputation also acts as a monitoring mechanism that forces self-interested persons to be honest. Reputational mechanisms are not a panacea, otherwise institutions would not be necessary, but they do perform an important role.[14] Furthermore, we

---

10 For a fuller discussion of this topic, see pp. 134–36.

11 Bourdieu first raised the issue of different types of capital. He included financial capital, cultural capital (similar to what we think of as human capital), and social capital. Pierre Bourdieu, 'The Forms of Capital', in Mark Granovetter and Richard Swedberg, eds., *The Sociology of Economic Life*, 2nd edn (Cambridge: Westview Press, 2001), pp. 96–111. Geographers also now discuss natural capital (a place's natural resources), including how social capital can help acquire access to them or muster defence against climate change. See for example, W. Neil Adger, 'Social Capital, Collective Action and Adaptation to Climate Change', *Economic Geography*, 79:4 (2003), 387–404.

12 Galassi and Newton found that those applying to the Sheffield Union without a good reference would have to produce larger collateral for their loans. Francesco L. Galassi and Lucy A. Newton, 'My Word is My Bond: Reputation as Collateral in Nineteenth-Century English Provincial Banking', http://www2.warwick.ac.uk/fac/soc/economics/research/workingpapers/publications/twerp599.pdf, accessed 20 Jan. 2010, p. 8.

13 John Doorley and Helio Garcia note that whilst modern executives agree with this, they rarely treat it as such, perhaps because it is still difficult to measure, *Reputation Management: The Key to Successful Public Relations and Corporate Communication* (New York and London: Routledge, 2007), p. 4.

14 See previous chapter for institutional trust. Platteau, 'The Role of Public and Private Order Institutions', pp. 543–49, 564; Galassi and Newton, 'My Word is My Bond',

do not know to what extent factors that went into a good reputation were internalized or simply acted out. In some ways, as Muldrew notes, this does not matter, because it is the perception that is important; but the angsting of merchants and other traders about their behaviour suggests that they were internalized to a large extent.[15] Individual reputations (including of those working within a partnership) can be based on a wide range of factors. Francesco Galassi and Lucy Newton found that personal wealth, leisure pursuits, membership of institutions and lifestyle were extremely important, if not unambiguous signals, in considering a person's reputation.[16] Other factors, such as letters of introduction, past behaviour and adherence to certain 'rules of engagement' also helped in the construction of a reputation. These factors were all important because, as Francesca Carnevali has noted, reputation is constructed within embedded relations.[17] Whilst there are disagreements over the relative importance of social relations, reputation effects and morality, eighteenth-century reputations were certainly 'shaped in congress with society'; they were culturally constructed.[18] This meant that merchants worked to construct and refine a portrait of their own reputation, or 'character', at least as seen through the lens of others.[19] Once this complicated character was constructed it was then carefully protected. As Adam Smith noted: 'A dealer is afraid of losing his character' because his self-interest meant that he wanted to continue trading; 'when a person makes perhaps 20 contracts in a day, he cannot gain so much by endeavouring to impose on his neighbours, as the very appearance of a cheat would make him lose.'[20] What we call reputation effects, or reputational mechanisms, Smith

---

p. 12. Greif argues that reputation mechanisms formed an economic institution in themselves for Maghribi traders in the eleventh century. Avner Greif, 'Reputation and Coalitions in Medieval Trade: Evidence of the Maghribi Traders', *Journal of Economic History*, 49:4 (Dec. 1989), 857–82.

15 Muldrew, *The Economy of Obligation*, p. 156; Jacob and Secretan, *The Self Perception*; Hannah Barker, 'Soul, Purse and Family: Middling and Lower-Class Masculinity in Eighteenth-Century Manchester', *Social History*, 33:1 (Feb. 2008), 12–35.

16 Galassi and Newton, 'My Word is My Bond', p. 11.

17 Francesca Carnevali, '"Crooks, Thieves, and Receivers": Transaction Costs in Nineteenth-Century Industrial Birmingham', *EcHR*, new ser., 57:3 (Aug. 2004), 533–50, p. 535.

18 Granovetter, 'Economic Action and Social Structure'; Moore, 'How Difficult is it to Construct Market Relations?'; Deborah Valenze, *The Social Life of Money in the English Past* (Cambridge: Cambridge University Press, 2006), p. 146.

19 Shearmur and Klein, 'Good Conduct in the Great Society'. pp. 38–39.

20 Adam Smith, 'Lecture on the Influence of Commerce on Manners', reproduced in Klein, *Reputation*, pp. 17–20, p. 17. Smith thought that a commercial society had negative effects such as neglecting education, and a decline in personality and morals.

described as 'the discipline of continuous dealings'.[21] He did not appear to distinguish between character and reputation. Nor did Daniel Defoe, who noted that if a merchant is slandered in his character, or reputation, 'he is immediately and unavoidably blasted and undone'.[22] This would suggest that these ideas were truly internalised to a large extent, even if there was still an element of 'performance'.[23]

The desire for Smith's continuous dealings (the shadow of the future) was a major motivation for constructing and maintaining a good reputation. However, there are other, related, motivations. Avner Offer argues that regard, or the good opinion of others, is a powerful incentive in itself. He posits that a certain satisfaction or positive emotion comes through receiving sympathy, approbation and the granting of attention.[24] For example, Henry Laurens apparently enjoyed dealing with other merchants of good reputation. He wrote to John Tarleton in September 1764 that 'it gives me great pleasure to serve, & I count it an honour to correspond with a gentleman of your integrity & generosity'.[25] No doubt a good deal of flattery was involved here, but both men probably felt some approbation by being involved with other elite merchants. Similarly, John Knight would no doubt have enjoyed the fact that he was listed by Henry Laurens alongside the Brights of Bristol and Mr Oswald of London as 'worthy friends and benefactors'.[26]

A sense of morality also pervaded eighteenth-century business culture. Merchants worked within a framework that they considered to be correct behaviour and were quick to highlight misbehaviour or transgressions which went deeper than simply not paying on time.[27] For example, James Clemens

---

21 Gordon Tullock, 'Adam Smith and the Prisoners' Dilemma', in Klein, *Reputation*, pp. 21–28, p. 25.

22 Daniel Defoe, *The Complete English Tradesman* [1726] (Gloucester: Alan Sutton, 1987), p. 132.

23 The desire to build a good reputation may drive people to make wrong decisions which are advantageous in the short term, but not in the long term. Equally the 'bad' player may act 'good' in the short term in order to get into the 'pool' of those with a good reputation (gatekeepers). Jeffrey C. Ely and Juuso Välimäki, 'Bad Reputation', *Quarterly Journal of Economics*, 118:3 (Aug. 2003), 785–814; Partha Dasgupta, 'Trust as a Commodity', in Gambetta, *Trust*, pp. 49–72, esp. 67–70.

24 Avner Offer, 'Between the Gift and the Market: The Economy of Regard', *EcHR*, new ser., 50:3 (Aug. 1997), 450–76. Offer agrees that regard is difficult to measure. It is clear that modern theorists believe reputation can be measured – as the difference between market capitalization and the liquidation value of assets. See Doorley and Garcia, *Reputation Management*, p. 7.

25 Henry Laurens to John Tarleton, 3 Sep. 1764, *HLP*, Vol. IV.

26 Henry Laurens to John & Thomas Tipping, 4 Dec. 1764, *HLP*, Vol. IV.

27 Serious faults might lead to expulsion. See below, pp. 103–4, 107–9, 116–21.

of Liverpool clearly felt that West Indian houses that bought slaves from ships for resale to other islands were not following good practice (by driving up prices), and that underselling to friends was equally unethical.[28] It is a sign of the cultural milieu of the mid-eighteenth century that engaging in the slave trade was not at odds with 'moral' behaviour, or indeed a good reputation, although this was to change towards the end of the period.[29] Clemens therefore saw no irony in his comment. Such generalised morality and ethical behaviour included making allowances in difficult times, such as credit crises, to those whose predicament was not of their own making. Manchester merchant Thomas Johnson wrote to Andrew Clow during the credit crisis of 1793 that in such difficult times, great allowances had to be made.[30] This sense of obligation was an important element of the business culture, and is the subject of the next chapter. It is clear that self-interest, regard and morality were all part of the reputational nexus. At the same time, the large distances around the Atlantic meant that it was not possible to know, or know of, everyone personally, by *direct* reputation. This meant that *indirect* reputation mechanisms were often used.[31] This included membership of groups, communities or even nations, which acted as 'seals of approval', or gatekeepers.[32]

Reputations were also deconstructed, and an important way in which this was achieved was through gossip and scandal. Whilst gossip can be benign, 'a slow scanning of the total information of the group', once the discussion moves into the public arena, it becomes scandal.[33] What people gossip about, of course, is a reflection of the group's particular interests and stress points. For our merchants, gossip and scandal obviously revolved around business probity, competence and particularly financial failure. Merchants also occasionally wrote about more private aspects of their peers' behaviour, and indeed their families, especially where such behaviour might impinge upon the ability to pay. However, this did not appear to be a major

---

28 James Clemens to William Speers, 3 Jun. 1767, Ships Papers, DTP.

29 See the chapter on crises, pp. 214–24.

30 Thomas Johnson to Andrew Clow, 30 Mar. 1793, Folder Thomas Johnson and Henry Norris, Andrew Clow & Co. Business Correspondence, CWU. For a good overview of the causes of credit crises in the eighteenth century see Julian Hoppit, 'Financial Crises in Eighteenth-Century England', *EcHR*, new ser., 39:1 (Feb. 1986), 39–58.

31 Iris Bohnet and Steffen Huck, 'Repetition and Reputation: Implications for Trust and Trustworthiness When Institutions Change', *American Economic Review*, 94:2, Papers and Proceedings of the One Hundred Sixteenth Annual Meeting of the American Economic Association (May 2004), 362–66, p. 363.

32 Shearmur and Klein, 'Good Conduct in the Great Society', p. 36.

33 Sally Engle Merry, 'Rethinking Gossip and Scandal', in Klein, *Reputation*, pp. 47–74.

preoccupation for merchants in the later eighteenth century.[34] Furthermore, whilst true friendships were often built up through trusting one another, likability was not an essential feature for trade. Stephen Girard and Andrew Clow were both irascible characters but still had good business reputations. Clearly, following good business practice and being successful was more important than affability. Gossiping through letters and chatting in coffee houses, taverns and the Council House obviously had the positive effect of reducing information and transaction costs, but the fact that the business community was a *relatively* homogenous group meant that it could enforce its own sanctions because it had a strong sense of group identity.[35] This meant that gossip and scandal was a way of controlling behaviour – a form of social control. Only the extremely poor, or the very rich, who were outside the gambit of gossip, could afford to ignore it.[36]

Sanctions and punishments for misbehaviour such as non-payment could be bilateral, but multi-lateral punishments were more useful because they then worked even in non-repeat trade.[37] That is, they had effect in Bristol, New York or Kingston, and not only in the port where a merchant was 'wronged'. Punishment mechanisms might have included not paying debts on the transgressor's behalf, not paying one's own debts due to the transgressor, not selling goods on their behalf already in possession, and the ultimate sanction – cancelling trade relationships (exclusion).[38] Transgressors might also have been taken to court in order to enforce payment. Bad reputations hung around for a long time in the 'network memory', therefore such punishments encouraged members of the network to abstain from malfeasance and opportunism, made the networks more efficient, and promoted their growth.[39] They seem to have worked as a significant deterrent, because punishments – whether withdrawing service, expulsion or legal measures –

---

34 Muldrew argues that the reputation of the whole household was very important earlier in the seventeenth and early eighteenth centuries, *The Economy of Obligation*, passim.

35 They therefore did not have to be truly moral. Mark S. Granovetter, 'Business Groups and Social Organization', in Neil J. Smelser and Richard Swedberg, *The Handbook of Economic Sociology*, 2nd edn (New York and Oxford: Princeton University Press, 2005), pp. 429–50, p. 433.

36 Merry, 'Rethinking Gossip and Scandal', p. 48.

37 Platteau, 'The Role of Public and Private Order Institutions', pp. 553–57.

38 Greif, 'Reputation and Coalitions', p. 869.

39 Hancock, 'The Trouble with Networks', p. 479; Werner Raub and Jeroen Weesie, 'Reputation and Efficiency in Social Interactions: An Example of Network Effects', *AJS*, 96:3 (Nov. 1990), 626–54, pp. 626–30. Carnevali agrees that cooperation leads to efficiency gains, but her case study shows that high profits can deter cooperation. Carnevali, 'Crooks, Thieves and Receivers'; Offer, 'Between the Gift and the Market', pp. 452, 463.

were rarely required in contrast to the amount of business conducted around the Atlantic. Therefore, if merchants wanted to be involved in continuous dealing, they had strong incentives to establish and preserve their character or reputation. If a merchant chose a non-cooperative option, he might soon find out that he had no-one with whom he could cooperate.[40]

Personal Reputations

Entry to the Market

Merchants gained entry to the market via the protection of, or promotion by, another's reputation – reputation by association. This could be through family or simply another connection where the protector felt comfortable promoting the protected. Such protection was usually personal and unqualified and is a good example of direct reputation mechanisms where a large amount of personal knowledge about a person is known.[41] The community knew the protector well, and he in turn knew the protected well. Douglass North calls this activity 'the dressing up of one man in the reputation of another'.[42] Such entry to the market could be made at dinner parties, at the tavern, counting house or social clubs, but much was done through letters of introduction. Family connections were used where available and appropriate. Isaac Wikoff stressed the good qualities of his brother William Wikoff Junior when introducing him to John Ewer in London; William had set up a house in New York and needed to build up correspondents there. Isaac stressed that he had been apprenticed under another brother (perhaps Peter), and that they had observed his conduct properly. William was a 'sober Carefull [sic] Industrious frugal young Man' capable of carrying on any business.[43]

Non-familial contacts were also useful, perhaps even more so. In 1783 John & Thomas Hodgson introduced their second mate Mr Turner to Richard Miles, Governor of Cape Coast Castle, as 'the son of a respectable Family' whom they held in great regard. They obviously envisaged helping Turner over the long term because they noted that they might promote him when he was capable (when he had built up competency trust).[44] John and Thomas

---

40 Tullock suggests that possibly only 'mental pathology' might make someone play a non-cooperative strategy. Tullock, 'Adam Smith and the Prisoners' Dilemma', pp. 23, 28.

41 Bohnet and Huck, 'Repetition and Reputation'.

42 Douglass C. North, 'Transaction Costs in History', *Journal of European Economic History*, 14:3 (1985), 557–76, p. 562.

43 Isaac Wikoff to John Ewer, 25 Oct. 1770, Folder Isaac Wikoff to John Ewer, CBP.

44 John & Thomas Hodgson to Richard Miles, 15 Nov. 1783, CRA, Vol. I.

Hodgson's extensive experience in the slave trade and their business at Factory Island meant that their recommendations carried weight.[45] In another letter to Miles regarding a shipment of slaves to the Coppels in Jamaica, they stated 'they cannot be in better hands, for they are good Young Men, and their Guarantee, Mr James France, of this Town, is an undoubted safe Man'.[46] France obviously conformed to the required standards of behaviour. Likewise, Henry Laurens helped out his former clerks when they started out on their own in 1764. Writing to his Liverpool correspondents Laurens stressed their integrity, honesty, knowledge and contacts in Charleston, adding that, 'everybody will trust them in the general way'.[47] Interestingly, he noted that the only issue they faced was not having a large capital. He managed to turn this into a positive however, noting that this would 'make them better Servants to those who shall be pleas'd to intrust [sic] them'.[48] Virginian merchant Robert Brent introduced Charles Carroll to Andrew Clow's house in Philadelphia and asked that it place the same confidence in Carroll as it would place in him, saying that he would be equally answerable from whatever business he engaged in.[49] In this way Brent was promising to protect Clow, as well as Carroll.

Merchants understood the value and potential of such protection or promotion. Joseph Hadfield set himself up in the insurance business in London during 1790 and explicitly recognised that the patronage he received from friends in Liverpool and Manchester had been really helpful. He noted that being 'attended by Mr Hunter in Person whilst I have offered my Policies, has procured me the confidence, & attention of some of the first Characters in the Coffee House'.[50] Mr Roepel of Paramibo (Suriname) expressed his joy at hearing that his son had arrived safely at Providence and was 'protected by Men of Credit and Reputation'.[51] He was clearly hoping that Brown & Benson would train him as a clerk. Such introductions inspired trust. David Cay wrote to Andrew Clow in 1789 that Don Antonio of Ferrol

45 Bruce L. Mouser, ed., *A Slaving Voyage to Africa and Jamaica: The Log of the Sandown, 1793–1794* (Bloomington and Indianapolis: Indiana University Press, 2002), pp. 10, 31, 127.

46 John & Thomas Hodgson, 16 Mar. 1783, CRA, Vol. II. The Hodgson's were alluding to the guarantee system in the slave trade, see above, pp. 54–55.

47 Henry Laurens to John Knight & John Blackburne, 21 Dec. 1764, *HLP*, Vol. IV.

48 Henry Laurens to John Knight & John Blackburne, 21 Dec. 1764, *HLP*, Vol. IV.

49 Robert Brent to Andrew Clow & Co., 5 Sep. 1785, Folder Andrew Clow 1780–1785, Box 13, Andrew Clow & Co., CWU.

50 Joseph Hadfield to David Cay, 7 Jul. 1790, Folder, Joseph, John & Thomas Hadfield 1785–1788, Box 12, Andrew Clow & Co., CWU.

51 C. Roepel to Brown & Benson, 5 Oct. 1790, Folder 2, West India Correspondence, BFBR.

(Spain) had been recommended by Messrs Morrough & Co., who stated 'that we may with the utmost safety execute <u>any</u> Commission from Dⁿ Antonio del Anido' [emphasis in original].[52]

It was not only through letters of introduction that reputation by association was important. First-hand experience of the behaviour of someone associated with a mercantile house led to the belief that others connected with them would behave similarly. For example, Mr Faures of Cape Francois (St. Domingue) was very impressed with the way that Captain Munro had conducted himself in acquiring a cargo of molasses 'at A time when Molasses are as scarce as Dollars which is saying a great deal'.[53] Munro's actions inspired Faures to conduct business with his employers, Brown & Benson of Providence. Not all captains were such good representatives however. Henry Laurens wrote to John Knight that his captain McKie was pushing for hard terms in his sales of slaves on the *Jenny*, which was not reflecting Knight's true character as a man of 'judgment and generosity'.[54]

Some merchants had no qualms about 'puffing' themselves up in order to construct their reputation.[55] William Pollard began a correspondence with William Reynolds of London after Reynolds had been recommended by a Mr Barrett of Jamaica. Pollard however, was quick to refer to his *own* credentials in turn, noting that he had conducted business for several years past with Thomas Hodgson, Peter Holme and the Earles, all well-respected merchants of Liverpool. He also stressed the wide range of commodities in which he dealt.[56] Nor were well-established merchants averse to 'puffing', even with long-term correspondents. Henry Laurens wrote from Charleston in 1764 to John Knight in Liverpool stressing his hard work regarding a problematic shipment of textiles on the *Austin*. He wrote that 'It wou'd have too much the Act of Vanity in me to talk of the diligence in this affair.'[57]

52 David Cay to Andrew Clow, 19 Mar. 1789 (in fact Anido later refused a bill in their favour), Andrew Clow to David Cay, 4 Oct. 1709, Folder David Cay, Andrew Clow & Co., CWU.

53 Currency and Bills of Exchange were always scarce in the West Indies. F. Faures to Brown & Benson, 16 Sep.[?] 1790, Folder 2, West Indies Correspondents, BFBR.

54 Henry Laurens to John Knight, 12 Jun. 1764, *HLP*, Vol. IV. See voyage 91029, Eltis et al., *The Transatlantic Slave Trade Database*.

55 On 'puffing' see Neil McKendrick, 'George Packwood and the Commercialization of Shaving: The Art of Eighteenth-Century Advertising or "The Way to Get Money and be Happy"', in Neil McKendrick, John Brewer and J. H. Plumb, *The Birth of a Consumer Society: The Commercialization of Eighteenth-Century England* (Bloomington: Indiana University Press, 1985), pp. 146–94.

56 William Pollard to William Reynolds, 25 May 1772, WPL.

57 Henry Laurens to John Knight & Thomas Mears, 20 Jan. 1764; *South Carolina Gazette*, 17 Dec. 1763, Vol. IV, *HLP*.

Worrying about seeming vain did not preclude him from adding in his next letter to Knight & Mears that 'I do not know a Merchant in this place who wou'd have made a Sale of the same nature & effect upon the same terms & conditions.'[58] Joshua Johnson considered that merchants in London had not acted with enough spirit against the closure of the port of Boston after the 'tea party', but commented that 'no doubt they will puff away with you what they have done'.[59]

Some reputation by association was indirect, a little like what was referred to in the previous chapter as institutional (hyphenated) trust.[60] In the same way that ascribed trust relied on perceived characteristics, certain groups and institutions ascribed (hyphenated) reputations. People within tight-knit groups did not want to lose their reputation because malfeasance might mean the loss of access to their whole community, such as family, religious or community ties. For example, the Society of Friends expelled their members for all sorts of behaviour.[61] The group acted as the assessor, or gatekeeper, meaning that individuals did not always have to trust their own judgement – or even that of another individual – about someone. Not only did merchants fear *expulsion* from certain groups, they *joined* certain groups because of the reputation it conferred upon them. Not only might 'membership gain one assistance from within the group, but those *outside* the group may recognise characteristic features of group members and favour them accordingly'; a 'seal of approval' could therefore be gained via that membership.[62] Going to church, joining charities or literary societies, being members of town councils or trade associations, no doubt included an element of social climbing, but status, knowledge and experience could also be conferred through membership.[63] Therefore we find leading merchants on town councils, trade associations, chambers of commerce, libraries, literary and philosophical societies and drinking clubs.[64] For example, in Liverpool during the 1750s and 1760s, many merchants used other association members for co-investment as well as to gain access to membership of the town council.[65]

---

58 Henry Laurens to John Knight & Thomas Mears, 24 Feb. 1764, *HLP*, Vol. IV.
59 Joshua Johnson toWallace, Davidson & Johnson, 3 Apr. 1774, JJL.
60 See above, pp. 84–85.
61 Walvin, *The Quakers*, chapter 4, 'Money Matters'. William Rathbone of Liverpool was expelled from the society in 1805 for having written a tract criticising the society in Ireland. Rathbone, *A Narrative of Events*; Rathbone, *A Memoir of the Proceedings of the Society Called Quakers*.
62 Shearmur and Klein, 'Good Conduct in the Great Society', pp. 36, 43.
63 Tullock. 'Adam Smith and the Prisoners' Dilemma', p. 25.
64 See the discussion on institutional trust above, pp. 84–93.
65 Haggerty and Haggerty, 'The Rise and Fall of a Metropolitan Business Network'.

However, membership by association was not always a positive experience. Guilds and craft associations were often characterised by negative social capital in the early-modern period and sections of Liverpool's mercantile community experienced declining social capital even whilst it was the leader in the slave trade.[66] At the personal level, too, association could have its downside, and failure to live up to expectations could lead to a withdrawal of protection. Brown & Benson came to regret giving the Roepels' son a chance. In October 1790 they reported that he had become 'so much attached to Company and amusement that we apprehend we cannot render him that service which you expect'.[67] By March 1791 they had formed the opinion that he had 'an Unconquerable aversion to that assiduous applycation [sic] Which is necessary in order to acquire any extensive or accurate Knowledge of Commercial Transactions'.[68] They were quick to add that he had been introduced to the wrong people in order to avoid offense to his parents, but it was clear that they were no longer prepared to dress him up in their reputation. Poor James Lawson tried repeatedly to distance himself from the activities of his partner, John Semple. He believed that not only his own downfall, but the death of their friend Mr Hamilton, was due to Semple. He wrote to his wife, 'I wish I could forget that such a Man ever existed, or that I ever had heard or knew of him.'[69] Bankrupt David Cay caused Andrew Clow many problems. Having disgraced himself in London, he proved to be a rather poor businessman overall. Clow remonstrated with him for his lack of letters, and worried that this was because he was involved in speculation which brought about 'cursed cargoes'.[70] Clow was clearly worried about his

---

See also Mark C. Casson, 'An Economic Approach to Regional Business Networks', in John F. Wilson and Andrew Popp, eds., *Industrial Clusters and Regional Business Networks in England 1750–1970* (Aldershot: Ashgate, 2003), pp. 19–43; Carola Lipp, 'Kinship Networks, Local Government, and Elections in a Town in Southwest Germany, 1800–1850', *Journal of Family History*, 30 (2005), 347–65; Delia Baldassarri and Mario Diani, 'The Integrative Power of Civic Networks', *AJS*, 113:3 (Nov. 2007), 735–80.

66 See for example, L. N. Rosenband, 'Social Capital in the Early Industrial Revolution', *Journal of Interdisciplinary History*, 29:3 (1999), 435–57; Sheilagh Ogilvie, 'Guilds, Efficiency, and Social Capital: Evidence from German Proto-Industry', *EcHR*, new ser., 57:2 (May 2004), 286–333.

67 Brown & Benson to C. Roepel, 11 Oct. 1790, Folder 2, West India Correspondents, BFBR.

68 Brown & Benson to C. Roepel, 23 Mar. 1791, Folder 2, West India Correspondents, BFBR.

69 James Lawson to Mrs Lawson, 14 Jan. 1773, James Lawson Letterbook 1770–76, and *passim*.

70 Andrew Clow to David Cay, 21 Oct. 1790, Clow Papers 1720, Hagley Museum and Library.

reputation by being associated with Cay's behaviour; with due cause, because in 1790 Peter Clement wrote that he wished 'that all DC's actions were as consistent with the Character of a prudent tradesman as his faith is'.[71]

Constructing and Maintaining a Reputation

In the long term, of course, merchants had to prove their own worth. New starters realised that whilst introductions might gain them entry into the business community, staying there was up to them. On the death of his partner in December 1759, Nathaniel Phillips had been trading from Jamaica for less than a year. He was therefore quick to assure his correspondents that not only would he satisfy the demands against the partnership, but would 'give content' to his correspondents in the future.[72] Those new to business on their own account often tried to 'acquire some heritage by association'.[73] Buchanan & Benn started their own commission house in Liverpool in 1808 and assured their correspondents that they had each served their apprenticeships in well-known mercantile houses. However, they continued, 'we trust we shall prove ourselves deserving of your confidence', and for good measure added that people could apply to their bankers in Liverpool and London for further details regarding their respectability.[74]

There were a number of ways in which merchants could construct their reputation. These included demeanour and behaviour in coffee houses and taverns, prompt and regular attendance at the 'Change, owning 'fine ships' that were admired by others, and delivering good quality products.[75] Most

---

71 Peter Clement to Andrew Clow, 6 Sep. 1790, Folder P. Clement, Andrew Clow & Co., CWU.

72 Nathaniel Phillips to James Hibbert & Son, 16 Feb. 1760; Nathaniel Phillips to George Maynard, 16 Feb. 1760, Mailhet & Phillips Letterbook 1759–?.

73 Milne notes this 'almost genealogical concern for the career paths of senior businessmen' in the nineteenth century. Graeme J. Milne, 'Reputation, Information and Ethics', in W. R. Lee, ed., *Networks of Influence and Power: Business, Culture and Identity in Liverpool's Merchant Community, c.1800–1914* (Aldershot: Ashgate, forthcoming).

74 The houses in question were J. & A. Lodge and Rathbone, Hughes & Duncan, and the banks, Leyland & Bullins and Masterman, Peters & Co. Buchanan & Benn to Brown & Ives, 20 Oct. 1808, Folder 16 Buchanan & Benn, BFBR. Products could also have particular reputations. Charles Stewart Parker noted in 1798 that 'cotton with that mark has here & in Liverpool acquired a good character'. Charles Stewart Parker to John Campbell Senr & Co., 6 Sep. 1798, Folder 920 PAR III 26/12. See also David Hancock, 'Self-Organized Complexity and the Emergence of an Atlantic Economy, 1651–1815', in Coclanis, ed., *The Atlantic Economy*, pp. 30–71, and Max S. Edelson, 'The Character of Commodities: The Reputations of South Carolina Rice and Indigo in the Atlantic World', in Coclanis, ed., *The Atlantic Economy*, pp. 344–60.

75 Regarding fine ships see Clow & Co. to Rathbone & Benson, 2 Nov. 1790, Folder

important, however, was performance in terms of business skills and sense, and above all – payment on time, or as Adam Smith put it, probity, prudence and punctuality.[76] Past behaviour was extremely important and was the empirical basis on which an actor's reputation was based.[77] There were therefore strong history or memory effects, which recorded both good and bad behaviour.[78] This section concentrates on how merchants built up their own individual 'seal of approval' via their 'performance'.[79]

'Good performance' meant conforming to a range of accepted norms and practices. Letter writing is a good example of this as business correspondence became more standardised over the eighteenth century. Letters have to be understood in their particular context, which was as an integral part of trading practice.[80] Defoe advised that mercantile letters should 'be plain, concise, to the purpose; no quaint expressions, no book-phrases, no flourishes, and yet they must be full and sufficient to express what he means, so as not to be doubtful, much less unintelligible'.[81] There was a standard format which most merchants conformed to, but not all correspondents followed good practice, especially when writing to long-term acquaintances. For example, we have already seen how in the previous chapter Samuel Bean of Jamaica chatted about his love affairs and getting drunk.[82] Nor was elite merchant Henry Laurens above mixing business news with gossip. In one of his many letters to John Knight, and after a particularly long perusal of several houses in Charleston, he wrote that, 'I have talked very freely to you, Sir, & long enough upon the present occasion You will perceive that your service only & no Interested views hath prompted my pen & if my thoughts are inoffensively impertinent the paper to which they are committed may still be made

Admin 1789–1790, CWU; John Angus to David Cay, 8 May 1790, Folder Capt Angus, Andrew Clow & Co., CWU.

76 Smith, 'Lecture on the Influence of Commerce on Manners', p. 18.

77 Raub and Weesie, 'Reputation and Efficiency', p. 629.

78 Bohnet and Huck, 'Repetition and Reputation', pp. 363–65.

79 Shearmur and Klein, 'Good Conduct in the Great Society', p. 36.

80 Ogborn, *Indian Ink*, pp. 22–23.

81 Defoe, *The Complete English Tradesman*, p. 18. Trevillato in *The Familiarity of Strangers*, stresses the increasing uniformity of style and of rhetorical norms in letters in the eighteenth century, and argues that we should not take such terms too literally. For example, the term 'friend' was increasingly used to cover a wide range of relationships. In contrast, Ditz stresses the performance and theatricality of merchants' letters. 'Shipwrecked'; 'Secret Selves, Creditable Personas'. For an overview of business handbooks in the eighteenth century see Rabuzzi, 'Eighteenth-Century Commercial Mentalities'. Letters also needed to be timely. See Haggerty, 'Trade and the Trans-Shipment of Knowledge'.

82 See above, p. 68.

useful in various ways'![83] Laurens realised that it was not good business practice to witter thus in business letters. There is no doubt that letters were an important way in which merchants expressed themselves – their successes and failures – but they were also important in the transmitting of information and confirming the performance of 'contractual trust'.[84]

More subtle messages about acceptable behaviour or performance were also relayed in letters. For example, Henry Laurens stressed the importance of a cargo, in this case slaves, going to the original intended agents. He wrote to Edward Martin in Liverpool that changing the house to which shipments were consigned:

> may be more injurious to your credit than the loss of double the Amount of Commission, arising by another kind of misadventure, for when tis given out that a House expects such a Cargo of Negroes & that same consignment is seen to go by another House it must occasion whispers & conjectures amongst Trading Men to lessen the reputation of the first.[85]

Changing consignees obviously cast doubt on the creditability of both houses concerned and created gossip. Rathbone & Benson were also concerned about the image presented by advertising. They advised Andrew Clow against advertising two different ships as being the first spring ship to sail from Liverpool to Philadelphia in 1790, not only because they both could not be first, but also because they knew other merchants would advertise in much the same way, and so none of the adverts would actually be believed.[86] Making false claims would raise doubts about all of your general business performance. Therefore, the *way* in which business was conducted, in terms of such self-enforcing agreements, was important.[87]

Writing in an acceptable format and keeping to subtle business practices were clear signals of reliability, but perhaps the most important way in which a merchant established his reputation was by keeping good accounts and making prompt payment. These were interdependent because not 'casting up shop' hinted that you were worried about your financial circumstances and did not want to know the truth, had something to hide such as fraud, or were simply morally lax. In contrast, exact bookkeeping was the mark of respectability and of a man who intended to thrive.[88] Merchants were often keen

---

83 Henry Laurens to John Knight, 12 Jun. 1764, *HLP*, Vol. IV.

84 On contractual trust, see above, pp. 77–81.

85 Henry Laurens to Edward Martin, 27 Jun. 1764, *HLP*, Vol. IV.

86 Rathbone & Benson to Andrew Clow, 15 Dec. 1790, Folder Admin 1789–90, Andrew Clow & Co., CWU.

87 Raub and Weesie, 'Reputation and Efficiency', pp. 632, 647.

88 Beverly Lemire, *The Business of Everyday Life: Gender, Practice and Social Politics in*

to stress that anyone could examine their books at any time as evidence of their honesty.[89] When it transpired that Andrew Clow had not made entries concerning the sales of some stock for William Wilson it was considered 'a circumstance truly surprising considering the extencive [sic] line of business in which that house was concerned'.[90] Such a reputable house was supposed to keep reputable accounts. Reports that John Semple had not written up his books for two years gave James Lawson yet another reason for concern. He wrote to Semple in February 1760 that it was 'hurting your character in not sending home a State of the books before this time'.[91] A link between not keeping one's books in order and business failure was more explicitly made by Clement Biddle regarding an insolvent merchant, John Relfe. Relfe's clerk had told him that Relfe had kept no records in his books of the goods in question – candles, 'but on loose papers &ᶜ and in his pockets'.[92] The implication was that the failure to keep good accounts was the reason why there was little prospect of his creditors receiving a dividend. This may also be why one of his creditors had put Relfe in debtors' prison.

Prompt payment was the best way to impress people and stop them from wanting to look at your books in the first place. Curtis Brett found that his new partner in Jamaica had been 'somewhat wild before' and his friends wanted proof of his prudence and care before they would advance him further credit.[93] Payment was always an issue for those new to the trade, as Ralph Eddowes realised when he started up business in Philadelphia in November 1794. He wrote to William Roscoe that he was worried about his credit, because being new to Philadelphia he could not afford to have a bad reputation.[94] He was still not sure of his position in 1802, but was grateful that the 'safe and seasonable arrival of my goods has so established my character for punctuality as it is probable will double my orders for the next season'.[95]

Of course, when things *were* going well, comments were made less often and were less remarkable. Compared to the extensive critcisms written when

---

England, c.1600–1900 (Manchester: Manchester University Press, 2005), chapter seven.

89 Defoe, *The Complete English Tradesman*, pp. 187, 197; Ditz, 'Secret Selves, Creditable Personas', pp. 222–27.

90 To the Worshipful Court of Frederick County ..., n.d. post 1794, Folder Andrew Clow & Co., Legal 1793–99, Andrew Clow & Co., Baker Library.

91 James Lawson to John Semple, 21 Feb. 1760, Letterbook 1758–62.

92 Clement Biddle & Co. to Nicholas & John Brown, 4 Feb. 1769, Folder 6, Correspondence with Francis & Relfe, BFBR.

93 Curtis Brett Autobiography, 1775, p. 21 (in private hands).

94 Ralph Eddowes to William Roscoe, 10 Nov. 1794, 920 ROS 1330, RP.

95 Ralph Eddowes to William Roscoe, 21 May 1802, 920 ROS 1337, RP.

merchants felt harmed, let down or betrayed, complements (when not part of letters of introduction) were less common. Therefore, we usually find very brief comments, such as from Charles Parker to John Bolton that, 'the sales are as usual exact and the whole transaction to my satisfaction'.[96] John Leigh praised Isaac Barker at St. Vincent, who he said had 'behaved very honourable in sales and remittances' on the *Narcissus'* last voyage.[97] In 1779 William Davenport noted that a bill had been paid two months before it was due.[98] This seemingly innocuous comment is remarkable not only because bills were not usually paid early, but because, like Leigh's contact, it was a West India house, normally known for late payment. Of course, the best compliment and confirmation of good performance was the continuance of the trading relationship.

Deconstructing Personal Reputations

Gossip was an important method by which information about people was spread, both by letter and in person. The coffee house and tavern were obviously important for local, oral transmission, but Toby Ditz has shown how private letters were actually often meant for public consumption. The authors of such letters knew that clerks and others would spread the information around, if not the addressees themselves.[99] Gossip using 'network memory' helped merchants find out about each other's long-term records on delivery and payment, as well as the latest insolvencies and bankruptcies, and other intelligence that could reduce information and transaction costs. Much of this 'information sharing' gossip was non-judgemental, although not always, and was occasionally malicious.[100] For example, Clow was well known to be a grumpy and disagreeable man. Joseph Hadfield noted in 1790 that 'vexatious Matters have put <u>Clow</u> so much out of humour' [stress in original], but this did not seem to affect people's willingness to do business with him because he was good at his job.[101] However, his success did cause jealousy, and gossip about him aggressively engrossing business in Philadelphia was heard as far away as London.[102] Philadelphia merchant Stephen Girard was also known as a callous, aloof, despotic personality, but because he was a trader with

---

96 Charles Stewart Parker to John Bolton, 9 May 1798, Folder 920 PAR III 25/4, PP.
97 John Leigh to Captain Brown, 22 Sep. 1806, John Leigh Letterbook 5 Jul. 1806–7 Mar. 1807.
98 William Davenport to Willock & Messon[?], 30 May 1779, WDL.
99 Ditz, 'Shipwrecked'.
100 Merry, 'Rethinking Gossip and Scandal', p. 51.
101 Joseph Hadfield to David Cay, 15 Dec. 1790, Folder Joseph, John & Thomas Hadfield 1785–88, Andrew Clow & Co., CWU.
102 Peter Clement to David Cay, 7 Jul. 1790, Folder Peter Clement, Andrew Clow & Co., CWU.

high standards, his personality did not really affect his business reputation.[103] Other relatively harmless gossip might concern a person's attitudes towards money. Finding a merchant uncivil during a trip to New York in 1771, Curtis Brett noted that, 'He is indeed, esteemed one of the most penurious Men in this Place, yet exceeded by his Wife in Poverty and Meanness of Spirit.'[104] Note that Brett justified his comment by referring to the merchant's well-known reputation in New York. Such gossip was less judgmental because these behaviours did not necessarily affect their 'performance' as merchants, and they were not sanctioned or expelled for this behaviour. It may even have been a way of humanizing or even belittling, otherwise successful merchants. Clearly, whilst an attractive personality could help people in business, Stephen Girard and Andrew Clow demonstrate that it was not as essential as good performance.

Gossip becomes scandal once 'everyone knows that everyone knows', and it is often precipitated by a public confrontation which forces the transgressor to own up and deal with his behaviour.[105] This may have occurred quite suddenly and may also have led to the ultimate sanction – exclusion. When merchants stepped outside the bounds of commercial norms and expectations, such gossip was mightily enjoyed. In 1774 Curtis Brett wrote to his friend John Mead in Jamaica recommending him to be conciliatory in a financial affair. He continued:

> For when two People, who have been so closely united in Interest, and are consequently supposed to know each other best, come to an open Rupture, and bespatter each other with Virulence, their common Enemies enjoy it in a high Degree, & make the most bitter Reflections both on themselves, their Connection and their Country.[106]

Brett was obviously also worried about his own reputation by association with Mead.

Scandals were occasionally made very public. George Baillie, part of a large Scots–West India network, accused John Bolton of being the cause of his ruin, by printing a book about him in 1809 entitled *Interesting Letters Addressed to John Bolton*.[107] Baillie castigated Bolton for being ungrateful to

103 Doerflinger, *A Vigorous Spirit*, pp. 1–2, 336, 350.
104 Curtis Brett to David Chambers, 13 Mar. 1771, CBL.
105 Merry, 'Rethinking Gossip and Scandal', p. 51.
106 Curtis Brett to John Mead, 20 Sep. 1774, CBL.
107 George Baillie, *Interesting Letters Addressed to John Bolton Esqr, Merchant, and Colonel of a Regiment of Volunteers* (London: Printed and Published by J. Gold, 1809). The Baillie network is discussed in some detail within Hamilton, *Scotland, the Caribbean and the Atlantic World*.

those that had helped him rise in business, and especially by not extending Baillie credit in difficult times. Baillie was a well-known 'friend' of Bolton, and when Bolton called on Baillie's securities over a debt, it of course alarmed the wider mercantile community, which assumed that something was amiss with Baillie's credit. Interestingly, Baillie noted Bolton's meanness to his common-law wife and children of colour in Jamaica. This may not have been enough on its own to ruin his reputation, but spoke about his character more generally, and turning against a person who had helped you in the past was unforgivable. As Adam Smith argued, 'The man who does not recompense his benefactor, when he has it in his power, and when his benefactor needs his assistance, is no doubt, guilty of the blackest ingratitude.'[108] In contrast to John Bolton, Robert Rainford left money and presents to his common-law wife and children of colour in Jamaica. However, his will was contested because his family in England did not think that they should have been provided for.[109] Attitudes in Britain towards personal relationships between whites and people of colour in the colonies clearly changed to suit their purposes. Profits from empire were collectively for the (white) family, not for an individual to do with as they wished.[110]

Wider economic allegiances might also produce comment. Following the Jay Treaty, many of the leading merchants who had been involved in the negotiations were lambasted in a publication called *The Philadelphia Jockey Club: Or Mercantile Influence Weighed*. Based on the assumption that they had been too generous with Britain, Robert Morris was called treacherous for having 'commercial connextions [sic] ... with Great Britain ... so indissoluble', and John Nixon was called a coward, because he had allegedly 'retreated to the shelter of an impenetrable haystack' whilst involved in a skirmish during the American Revolution. Likewise, finding William Crammond's good qualities was said to be similar to trying 'to pluck a nosegay from a foil over-run with weeds'.[111]

---

108 Adam Smith, *The Theory of Moral Sentiments* [1759], ed. Knud Haakonssen (Cambridge: Cambridge University Press, 2002), p. 91.

109 The Complaint of Joseph Rainford ..., 21 Feb. 1810, C13/132/35, TNA.

110 Finn, 'Anglo-Indian Lives', p. 57.

111 Timothy Tickler, *The Philadelphia Jockey Club; Or, Mercantile Influence Weighed. Consisting of Select Characters Taken from the Club of Addressors* (Printed for the Purchasers, 1795), pp. 7–9. The merchants were only identified by the capitals of their first and surnames, the original has some, but not all, of the full names inscribed by a contemporary reader. Many accused may have been recent immigrants, such as Philip Nicklin described as 'a weed of European extraction', p. 9. There was in fact a real Jockey Club in Philadelphia, though no doubt this publication referred to the 'racing' itself. See Charles Stewart to Aitchison & Parker, 15 Oct. 1767, 920 PAR I 27/16, PP.

However, much gossip and scandal was about controlling behaviour and self-monitoring, especially in a *relatively* homogenous group such as merchants.[112] Whilst the mercantile community could be wide ranging in terms of wealth and status, its members all had the same problems of supply and demand to deal with, and were so interdependent that their interests were very similar.[113] Sally Engle Merry describes four conditions for gossip controlling social control, which are evident in these merchants' business culture: it was a bounded social system where costs of defection were high (loss of profits through inability to trade); members were interdependent (extensive credit made this so); a community consensus was produced which was converted into actions (insolvency, bankruptcy, exclusion or expulsion); and extensive consensus about normative behaviour were evident (payment on time, timely delivery of correct goods, performance of obligations).[114] Accordingly, much gossip and scandal surrounded issues of business and socio-cultural norms particular or central to the mercantile community. For example, before James Mailhet died in 1759, he assigned a bond for £1200 over to a Miss Evans. However, as his estate was not very large this caused problems when trying to pay off his debts after his death. His partner Nathaniel Phillips noted that 'it must be a slur upon any Man's Character, that should give away any of his Estate, untill [sic] his debts should be satisfied'.[115] Mailhet was supposed to have considered what he owed to *all* his creditors, rather than favour one particular person by assigning a legally binding bond which would have been given precedence over his book debts.[116] However, whilst merchants were supposed to put their debts to the wider community first, imprudence regarding their family was also frowned upon, if not central.[117] James Bogle of London commented that a Mr Beard's effects were in a sorry state, and that, given the opportunities he had been given in Africa, he must have been an extravagant man, not to have left some for his relations

---

William Crammond was one of Clow's competitors. See for example David Cay to Andrew Clow, 3 Jul. 1790, Folder Admin 1789–1790, Andrew Clow & Co., CWU.

112 Merry, 'Rethinking Gossip and Scandal', pp. 52–53; Toby L. Ditz, 'Formative Ventures: Eighteenth-Century Commercial Letters and the Articulation of Experience', in Rebecca Earle, ed., *Epistolary Selves: Letters and Letter Writers, 1600–1945* (Aldershot: Ashgate, 2000), pp. 59–78, p. 68.

113 Haggerty, *The British-Atlantic Trading Community*. See also Granovetter, 'Business Groups and Social Organization'.

114 Merry, 'Rethinking Gossip and Scandal', p. 70.

115 Nathaniel Phillips to Hilton & Biscoe, 10 Jun. 1760, Mailhet & Phillips Letterbook, 1759–?.

116 On various financial instruments see Kerridge, *Trade and Banking*.

117 In Pennsylvania, however, the law seemed to work against provision for widows and families. Salmon, *Women and the Law of Property*, pp. 24–35, 92–104, 160–68.

who were in need of money.[118] Even apparently small transgressions would cause outrage. William Earle complained sarcastically that 'The Very great Mr Dallows has presumed to draw upon me for some £20 more than I owe him ... if the world be not soon convinced of the insincerity & unintegrity [sic] of that Man I am much mistook.'[119] Whilst merchants overdrew on each other quite often, and £20 was not a lot of money to William Earle, it was polite to at least notify the payer in advance of such payments. Indeed such over payments were common, but usually only within the context of a successful, ongoing relationship.

Gossip at the local level was also very important. Counting houses, town council meetings, trade associations, drinking clubs, literary and philosophic societies and of course coffee houses and taverns, may have been good places to network and in some cases confer reputation, but they also provided excellent breeding grounds for gossip.[120] No doubt whilst many a deal was done over rum, many reputations were *undone*.[121] Defoe noted that coffee houses 'seem to be places of new invention for a depravation of our manners and morals, places devoted to scandal and where the characters of all kinds of persons and professions are handled in the most merciless manner, where reproach triumphs'.[122] Joshua Johnson noted that he had just returned from the exchange where 'it's current that the Glasgow Banks is stopped'.[123] It may well have been talk in a Philadelphia coffee house that led to what Daniel Clark called a 'Birth to a Report that my goods come very high'.[124] Thomas Leyland was clearly worried about the opinions of his Liverpool peers concerning some puncheons of rum that he thought had been smuggled into Liverpool on one of his vessels without his knowledge. Leyland wrote to John Shannon in Ross (Ireland) in the 'strictest friendship & confidence', adding 'I assure you I am very unhappy, because such an affaire [sic] here, is considered as scandalous, as if I had picked my neighbours pocket'.[125] Merchants were

---

118 James Bogle to Richard Miles, 14 Jul. 1783, CRA, Vol. I.

119 William Earle to Witter Cummings, 21 Feb. 1760, Letterbook of William Earle, Jan. 1760–Sep. 1761, 2/2, EC.

120 Cowan argues that the mercantile community helped to legitimise the drinking of coffee. Barry Cowan, 'Publicity and Privacy in the History of the British Coffeehouse', *History Compass*, 5:4 (2007), 1180–1213, p. 1884, http://www3.interscience.wiley.com/journal/118491914/abstract?CRETRY=1&SRETRY=0, accessed Feb. 2010.

121 Peter Thompson, *Rum Punch and Revolution: Taverngoing and Public Life in Eighteenth-Century Philadelphia* (Philadelphia: University of Pennsylvania Press, 1999), p. 96.

122 Defoe, *The Complete English Tradesman*, pp. 133–34.

123 Joshua Johnson to Wallace, Davidson & Johnson, 22 Jun. 1772, JJL.

124 Daniel Clark to William Neale, 16 Oct. 1760, DCL.

125 Thomas Leyland to John Shannon, 3 Aug. 1786, TLL.

not averse to smuggling, but being *caught* taking advantage by avoiding excise duties was bad news.[126]

Gossip therefore helped to spread information about cheating as well as poor performance.[127] It also had a judgmental quality, and attitudes towards certain behaviour shaped responses, and might have meant the difference between insolvency, bankruptcy, imprisonment for debt, or expulsion.[128] For example, William Davenport considered that a Mr Garbet[?] was taking unfair advantage of the Statute of Limitations. In writing that 'if he presses this Method it must be Assuredly an infinite disgrace to himself' he was spreading gossip about him.[129] Similarly, when the captain of the *Minerva* died whilst in Jamaica in 1801, the Kingston agents for the owner of the vessel, Charles Angus, took advantage of this. They had the vessel condemned and then sold it to themselves for £700. Angus made sure that others knew that they had used their 'own Creatures' to engineer this outcome, and condemned it as 'Villainous Conduct'.[130] It is not clear whether Angus penalised his Jamaican agents by no longer dealing with them, but the experience would have been added to the network memory for future reference.

The impact of gossip, of course, could be fatal. Just one lapse in behaviour, or even a perceived lapse, could lead to a drastic revision of a merchant's reputation, and possibly exclusion.[131] Because of the centrality and importance of credit, the most usual reason for loss of reputation was for non-payment, or – talk of (potential) non-payment. Therefore, merchants went to great lengths to avoid this problem. John Perhouse wrote to his brother from Philadelphia in 1805 that if a bill was rejected, he 'might be utterly ruined', even if he had plenty of money in the bank.[132] John then requested that his brother James go to Manchester to talk to his agents there to ensure that none of

---

126 On the customs and excise see Ashworth, *Customs and Excise*. On smuggling see T. C. Barker, 'Smuggling in the Eighteenth Century: The Evidence of the Scottish Tobacco Trade', *Virginia Magazine of History and Biography*, 62:4 (Oct. 1954), 387–99; Hoh-Cheung Mui and Lorna H. Mui, 'Smuggling and the British Tea Trade before 1784', *American Historical Review*, 74:1 (Oct. 1968), 44–73.

127 Greif found that information flows were important in finding out about cheating, 'Reputation and Coalitions', p. 879.

128 Regarding changing attitudes towards insolvency and bankruptcy see Hoppit, *Risk and Failure*, chapter two.

129 William Davenport to Joseph Wimpey, 19 Mar. 1779, WDL.

130 Charles Angus to Mr Thomas, 28 Jan. 1801. A William Angus had been present in Jamaica in 1799, but it is not clear that this was his agent in 1801; Charles Angus to William Angus, 26 Sep. 1799, Charles Angus Letterbook 1799–1851.

131 This was still true in the nineteenth century. Galassi and Newton, 'My Word is My Bond', p. 18.

132 John Perhouse to James Perhouse, 25 May 1805, John Perhouse Journal 1800–1838.

his bills would be rejected. Similarly, Thomas Leyland remonstrated with a correspondent in Ireland regarding a protested bill, adding that 'I would not have let such a disgrace happen to me, If I could have raised a penny under the Heavens.'[133] This sort of disgrace could easily lead to expulsion from the group as a punishment.[134] Joseph Hadfield wrote to David Cay in 1793 that Donald & Burton's 'Acceptances are like waste paper – I have now to caution you against D&B's name and Agents every where' [emphasis in original].[135] Hadfield was worried because he was caught up in a chain of credit with Donald & Burton, and told Cay to draw on him before the failure became known publicly – that is, became a scandal. As the French Wars had just begun, everyone was jittery in any case. In the meantime, everyone was to exclude Donald & Burton by not trading with them.

Financial failure did not always come with an attachment of blame, but if people were seen to be overtrading, were deemed to have taken unnecessary risks, or had been involved in unethical behaviour, talk was far more judgemental. For example, a Mr Kennion, a London merchant, had failed, but had been allowed to continue as long as he confined himself to the 'Manchester' trade. However, by 1763 it was considered that he had 'launched deeper than ever, and falls now unpitied'.[136] As noted above, David Cay – by absconding from London and not facing his creditors – also received little sympathy.[137] However, as we have seen, Cay was able to recover from his bankruptcy by hanging onto Andrew Clow's shirttails, and John Leigh of Liverpool started up in business again after his bankruptcy in the early nineteenth century.[138] In fact, many merchants were able to recover from financial failure if perceptions about the causes of that failure were benign. The Liverpool house of Buchanan & Benn, heavily involved in the trade to North America, failed in 1811. However, Daniel Buchanan was trading again by February 1812. In a circular he stressed that one of their agents had caused a temporary injury to the credit of the house, which led to them being unable to insure a cargo. When that cargo was wrecked, it brought on their failure. All this sounds rather spurious, and normally not insuring a vessel would be

133 Thomas Leyland to Henry McDowell, 11 Aug. 1786, TLL.
134 Greif, 'Reputation and Coalitions', p. 868.
135 Joseph Hadfield to David Cay, 17 Feb. 1793, Folder Joseph, John & Thomas Hadfield 1785–88, Andrew Clow & Co., CWU.
136 Charles Stewart to Aitchison & Parker, 15 Nov. 1763, Folder 920 PAR I 27/3.
137 See above, p. 82.
138 When Peter Clement wrote to Cay in 1790 that he was perfectly satisfied with his resources and success, he was really referring to Clow as his partner. Peter Clement to Andrew Clow & Co., 20 Feb. 1790, Folder 1785–98, Andrew Clow & Co., CWU; John Leigh Letterbook, Jul. 1806–Mar. 1807.

considered reckless behaviour.[139] However, his friends had lent him enough capital to start up on his own, and had entrusted him with winding up the old firm, so his version of events must have been believed.[140] In contrast to Kennion's overtrading in 1763, the dislocation caused by the American War of Independence was perceived as the cause of Mr Shoolbred's failure in 1783. The Hodgsons wrote to Richard Miles that:

> No unfortunate man was ever so treated with more respect by his Creditors: His affairs are left in his own direction, under inspectorship, & it is generally believed that he will have a good fortune after paying all his debts.[141]

Good reputations were therefore important in responses to failure, and *not* being sanctioned or expelled.

In times of general financial difficulty, having a well-established reputable house was an advantage. Of course the reputations of houses were constructed from those of its individual partners, but houses were sometimes referred to separately. Large, well-known houses such as the Browns, Rathbone & Benson, and Henry Laurens, were given some leeway regarding payment in a crisis. As noted above, reputation is, and was, a form of capital which allows actors to believe others will pay in the future. In a crisis this gave elite merchants room to breathe, which other, lesser houses did not have. Curtis Brett realised that his partnership with Francis Allwood was still small and new in 1764 and wrote that 'we are too inconsiderable in Character to put off any Bills when become due'.[142] This is not to say that large, well-known houses never received negative comment, although this was possibly as a consequence of jealousy. It was noted above that Andrew Clow had been accused of trying to engross too much trade in Philadelphia, and Charles Angus complained that Applethwaite & Co. had not thought to advise him of the arrival of a vessel at Barbados. He wrote: 'I did not know till lately that they were an old overgrown rich People, such as are not fit correspondents for a Young House.'[143] Likewise, James Lawson felt that Haliday & Dunbar clearly demarcated between 'new' and 'old' houses, and that because they were an 'old' house, they had charged Lawson more for their (supposedly

---

139 Insurance policies were often taken out whilst a vessel was away from port, or had started the intended voyage. They may not therefore have been able to stop the vessel from sailing without insurance.

140 Printed Price Current and Circular, 22 Feb. 1812, Folder 16 Buchanan & Benn, B.53, BFBR.

141 John & Thomas Hodgson to Richard Miles, 11 Feb. 1783, CRA, Vol. II.

142 Curtis Brett to Francis Allwood, 23 Jan. 1764, CBL.

143 Charles Angus to Messrs Bagley & Wells, 21 Feb. 1799, Charles Angus Letterbook.

superior) services.[144] No doubt such 'benign' gossip did not cause any real damage to these large houses, but it is clear that for many, idle talk was 'hardly of idle significance'.[145]

Community Reputations

A s the reputation of business communities, places and countries were also constructed and deconstructed over time, it is worth briefly considering them here. They represent an even higher level of indirect reputation, often being even further removed from the individuals themselves than that of institutional reputations. The examples given here do not equate to a quantitative analysis, but they do demonstrate that various community reputations existed and fluctuated over time, which often affected how people dealt with them. As with individuals, the reputation of a community, and indeed state, was important in the ability to gain credit, and in responses to failure. At the state level, reputation, prestige, and 'regard' on the world stage was often one reason amongst others for conflicts; for example, the American War of Independence, the French Wars and the Anglo-American War. The 'community' reputation, like other reputations by association, could be a valuable asset to a merchant, but as we shall see, some community reputations were negative. Whilst some aspects of a community's reputation might be more or less static, reputations regarding credit often fluctuated according to the wider economic situation.

Liverpool's trading community as a whole had a good reputation throughout our period. Merchants there were known to be able to get generous credit terms, for having ready access to a variety of manufactures and for keeping costs low. Liverpool captains in the slave trade were so well respected for their knowledge that Bristol and London merchants used them for their slaving voyages.[146] London may have been the financial centre of Britain, but merchants in Liverpool were quick to defend the creditability of their own town in times of financial crisis, most famously in 1793 when the Corporation was allowed to issue its own notes to support credit in the town.[147] In 1810, there were many failures in London, but Buchanan & Benn noted that whilst this had affected confidence generally, they saw 'no cause to apprehend any

---

144 James Lawson to Haliday & Dunbar, 24 Nov. 1763, James Lawson Letterbook 1762–66.

145 Merry, 'Rethinking Gossip and Scandal', p. 70.

146 Behrendt, 'Human Capital'.

147 F. E. Hyde, B. B. Parkinson, and S. Marriner, 'The Port of Liverpool and the Crisis of 1793', *Economica*, new ser., 18:72 (1951), 363–78.

by which this town would be affected in any material degree'.[148] Maybe they helped protect Liverpool's reputation for a short while, but in fact the failures did eventually spread to the port, and as noted above, they failed themselves in 1811. Earlier on in the French Wars, William Roscoe must have been pleased to hear that there were no rumours regarding Liverpool's creditability in Philadelphia, though his friend Ralph Eddowes expressed concerns about Clarke's bank.[149] However, whilst Liverpool's reputation as a whole was mostly good throughout, a certain section of its community suffered from a loss in reputation – those involved in the slave trade. Whilst this section of the trading community had fulfilled its obligations to the state by investing in empire, the slave trade itself came to be vilified. Therefore, their involvement in it was condemned, even if they, as merchants *per se*, were not.[150] The massacre on the slave ship *Zong* did not help.[151] Grenville Sharp wrote to the Admiralty that the 'mercenary Business' had brought the wickedness of the 'impious Slave Dealers of Liverpool' to light [emphases in original].[152] A letter to William Roscoe in 1807 regarding possible compensation for the loss of the trade, castigated slave merchants in general who 'ought at least to have shown some moderation in the Pursuit of gain by such means'.[153] No doubt Liverpool merchants came in for special criticism being the leaders in the trade at this time.

Bristol did not appear to suffer from the same level of vilification as Liverpool for its involvement in the slave trade. Perhaps this was because its

---

148 Buchanan & Benn to Brown & Ives, 23 Aug. 1810, Folder 16 Buchanan & Benn, B.53, BFBR.

149 Ralph Eddowes to William Roscoe, 11 Jul. 1796, 920 ROS 1334, RP. In fact Clarke's bank may have been in some difficulties, as on the death of William Clarke in 1799 the bank only escaped bankruptcy by William Roscoe becoming a partner. In a later reincarnation of the business, Roscoe, Clarke & Roscoe went bankrupt in the post-war crash of 1816. John Hughes, *Liverpool Banks and Bankers 1760–1837* (Liverpool: Henry Young and Sons, 1906), pp. 56–65.

150 For a fuller discussion of this point, see the chapter on crises, pp. 214–24.

151 On the *Zong* see Anita Rupprecht, 'Excessive Memories: Slavery, Insurance and Resistance', *History Workshop Journal*, 64:1 (2007), 6–28; Jeremy Krikler, 'The Zong and the Lord Chief Justice', *History Workshop Journal*, 64:1 (2007), 29–47; Ian Baucom, *Specters of the Atlantic: Finance Capital, Slavery and the Philosophy of History* (Durham and London: Duke University Press, 2005). See also James Walvin, *The Zong: A Massacre, the Law, & the End of Slavery* (New Haven and London: Yale University Press, 2011), who has recently argued that the massacre was pivotal for the abolition movement.

152 Grenville Sharp to the Lords Commissioners of the Admiralty, 2 Jul. 1783, Documents Relating to the Slave Ship Zong, REC/19, National Maritime Museum. My thanks to Susanne Seymour for providing this reference.

153 T. Houlbrooke to William Roscoe, 12 Feb. 1807, 920 ROS 2154, RP.

merchants were gradually reducing their involvement in this trade, and by the second half of the eighteenth century seemed to be somewhat embarrassed by it.[154] Not that this deterred Bristol merchants from trading heavily in slave-produced sugar. Bristol's main problems with regard to reputation were that its merchants were perceived not to be able to keep their costs as low as in Liverpool, and their mercantile community was unable to work together in order to solve the problems with navigating the Avon as vessels got larger.[155] Lowbridge Bright, himself of Bristol, had to admit whilst on a visit to Liverpool that the credit terms offered to Liverpool were 'much better than I could get in Bristol' which allowed merchants there to offer generous credit times in turn.[156] The 'metropolis of the West' gradually lost out to Liverpool by around 1750, due to a lack of entrepreneurial spirit.[157] In 1773, a Bristol merchant recognised Liverpool's success, noting that 'The Liverpool people go on with such spirit. I wish we could get more into that track.'[158]

Traders in other places also came in for criticism, occasionally linked with particular commodities. London bills may always have been preferred, but Joseph Hadfield felt that tobacco traders in London were 'Cormorants' who laid great impositions on the trade; the commission business had led many to 'Mortgage the Tobacco long before its arrival' and the brokers were taking advantage of their distress.[159] Joshua Johnson felt that many London merchants were 'conjurors', that tobacco traders all told lies, and Charles Stewart Parker wrote of the 'premature pertness of a Cockney'.[160] East India merchants were also subject to derision around the Atlantic. John Perhouse wrote regarding a large house his brother recommended him to buy that, 'You must certainly take me for some east India nabob by recommending such as place as this to me.'[161] Indeed, East India Company officers had a bad reputation generally. They were accused of corruption, looting and

---

154 Madge Dresser, *Slavery Obscured: The Social History of the Slave Trade in an English Provincial Port* (London and New York: Continuum, 2001), chapters three and four.

155 David Richardson, 'Slavery and Bristol's "Golden Age"', *Slavery and Abolition*, 26:1 (2005), 35–54, p. 46; Morgan, *Bristol and the Atlantic Trade*, pp. 140–52.

156 Lowbridge Bright to Henry Bright, 20 Aug. 1773, *BMP*.

157 Katie McDade, 'A Particular Spirit of Enterprise': Bristol and Liverpool Slave Trade Merchants as Entrepreneurs in the Eighteenth Century (Unpublished PhD, University of Nottingham, 2011).

158 Lowbridge Bright to Bright, Milward & Duncombe, 5 Nov. 1773, *BMP*.

159 Joseph Hadfield to David Cay[?], 7 Jul. 1790, Folder Joseph, John & Thomas Hadfield 1785–88, CWU.

160 Joshua Johnson to Wallace & Davidson, 28 Dec. 1771; Joshua Johnson to John Davidson, 22 Jul. 1771, JJL; Charles Parker to George Rainy, 27 Apr. 1798, Folder 920 PAR III 25/2, PP.

161 John Perhouse to James Perhouse, 24 Oct. 1806, John Perhouse Journal 1800–38.

bribing, and its nabobs derided for buying into old landed families for political influence.[162] The Royal African Company also had a problematic reputation and its monopoly was often challenged. It was unable to protect or engross British trade on the African coast and its officers were accused of being corrupt and inefficient.[163] The Royal African Company had ceded its monopoly in 1698, but the Company remained contentious until the end of its charter in 1752.[164]

Scots merchants were also perceived to be endowed with certain qualities. One Scot used his own national stereotype to scold his brother for not writing: 'I am truly sorry you yet retain so much of your Scotch Silence as never once to write me since your Departure.'[165] Terse or not, the Scots had a reputation, with good reason, for engrossing the tobacco trade. Joshua Johnson continued his diatribe against certain sectors of the trading community, commenting that 'of course the Scotch will run away with all the trade' due to the many failures in London during the credit crisis in 1772.[166] Perhaps this reputation for being almost too good at business was one of the reasons why James Parker, having lived in Norfolk, Virginia, for twenty years, felt that his neighbours saw him as alien, as part of a despised minority.[167]

Nor did traders in American ports go without comment. Philadelphian William Pollard visited Charleston in 1774 and reported to one of his Manchester suppliers, B. & J. Bower, regarding one of their correspondents in the southern port. He wrote that whilst none of them were in immediate danger, 'I do not like their method of doing business here … there is but bad Encouragement to form connections in a Country where punctuality & Honour in making payments are discouraged.'[168] As mentioned above, Andrew Clow, who had plenty to say about everything, thought New Yorkers were a 'faithless pack' with whom he would rather not trade.[169]

---

162 Dirks, *The Scandal of Empire*, p. 9. The East India Company caused problems in terms of property rights; for example following the move from a commercial concern to a territorial power in the 1760s. For an individual East India merchant see Anthony Webster, *The Richest East India Merchant: The Life and Business of John Palmer of Calcutta 1767–1836* (Woodbridge: Boydell, 2007).

163 Davies, *The Royal African Company*.

164 See for example, Anon, *A Short View of the Dispute Between the Merchants of London, Bristol and Leverpool, and the Associates of a New Joint Stock Company, Concerning the Regulation of the African Trade* (London: Printed in the Year 1750).

165 Charles Angus to William Angus, 26 Sep. 1799, Charles Angus Letterbook.

166 Joshua Johnson to John Davidson, 30 Oct. 1772, JJL.

167 Keith Mason, 'A Loyalist's Journey: James Parker's Response to the Revolutionary Crisis', *The Virginia Magazine of History and Biography*, 102:2 (Apr. 1994), 139–66.

168 William Pollard to B. & J. Bower, 25 Jan. 1774, WPL.

169 See above, p. 69.

Perhaps the place in the British Atlantic with the worst reputation was the West Indies, and in particular, despite its importance for trade, Jamaica. Whilst the Jamaicans were well known for their hospitality, liveliness and friendliness, they were also renowned for keeping women of colour as 'housekeepers', for not going to church, opening up shop on holy days and being against Christianising their slaves.[170] Anne Storrow, having emigrated to Jamaica with her husband, thought the ladies well dressed, but that the handsome church in Kingston was 'little enough frequented' and little distinction made between Sunday and Monday.[171] John Stewart in his *Account of Jamaica* had plenty to say on these issues, amongst others. He allowed that many Jamaican merchants were 'respectable and useful characters', but added that Jamaicans as a whole were naturally litigious, read only trashy novels, were not fair in their business practices and were good at 'eluding the payments of their creditors'.[172] This latter point was a view that pervaded the Atlantic about the West Indians. Curtis Brett, involved in the Jamaica trade himself, noted in 1763 that 'Jamaica credit is worse than ever, and Bills from thence generally laugh'd at.'[173] Prompt payment was the primary issue, and whilst J. B. Moreton was reluctantly forced to admit that there were a 'few prudent sensible Creole men', it is clear that the Jamaicans' profligate lifestyle was seen as a factor in their poor 'performance of contract'.[174] The West Indian reputation was certainly bad enough to instigate the guarantee system, as was discussed above.[175] It is worth noting however, that Stewart also considered that 'A considerable share of the mercantile and retail business of this island is engrossed by the Jews; a people, who, in every part of the world where traffic exists, ensure to themselves, by their skill sagacity, and indefatigable diligence, success and profit.'[176]

---

170 See for example, John Venn to Bishop Sherlock, 15 Jun. 1751, Vol. XVIII (ii), Jamaica 1740–?; James White noted that the Jews kept their Sabbath however. James White to Bishop Gibson, 5 Mar. 1742/3, Vol. XVII(i), Jamaica 1661–1739, Fulham Papers, Lambeth Palace.

171 Ann Storrow to Mrs Brown, [?] May 1792, Folder 6, Anne Appleton Storrow Papers, MHS.

172 John J. Stewart, *An Account of Jamaica, and Its Inhabitants. By a Gentleman Long Resident in the West-Indies* (London: Printed for Longman, Hurst, Rees and Orme, 1808), pp. 148 and 2–12.

173 Curtis Brett to Francis Allwood, 10 Nov. 1763, CBL.

174 J. B. Moreton, *West India Customs and Manners: Containing Strictures on the Soil, Cultivation, Produce, Trade, Officers and Inhabitants* ... (London: Printed for J. Parsons, Paternaster Row; W. Richardson, Royal Exchange; H. Gardner, Strand; and J. Walter, Piccadilly, 1793), p. 106.

175 See above, pp. 54–55.

176 Stewart, *An Account of Jamaica*, p. 151.

Such reputations were not always a bar to trade; whilst people may have been jealous of the Liverpudlians' success in the slave trade or the Scots success in the tobacco trade, they were still trusted. In contrast, the suspect reputations of merchants in the Southern colonies/states and the British West Indies meant that they were often not trusted as a group. However, it is clear that certain individuals such as Henry Laurens managed to overcome this, and therefore, a good personal reputation might 'trump' a bad community one.

Reputation was also important at the national level because a good national reputation inspired institutional trust. As noted above, Malachy Postlethwayt was realistic about the need for the British government to borrow from the commercial classes, and so he thought it important that earlier debts should be paid off before new ones were contracted.[177] The policy of not doing so had 'changed honest Commerce into bubbling; our Traders into projectors'.[178] This was important because as Britain's wealth was mostly due to foreign commerce, its reputation both at home and internationally was extremely important. If the British state did not repay its debts, merchants, both at home and abroad, would not lend it money.[179] Furthermore, its merchants would be seen as mere stockbrokers or jobbers, a group with a very bad reputation.[180] Clearly the British state paid its debts in the long term, because by 1799 George Rose was able to praise the system of public debt and the way in which extra funding was being raised for the French war, stating that there was confidence in the whole system.[181] However, occasional changes in policy did affect Britain's reputation. We saw in the previous chapter that an overzealous re-interpretation of the Free Ports Act caused other nations to temporarily stop trading to the British West Indies, and that the Old Calabar debacle meant that Africans were less inclined to trust Europeans.[182] Postlethwayt also argued for regulating the trade with native Americans because British ill-usage towards them had given them a

---

177 See above, p. 86.

178 Postlethwayt, *Great Britain's True System*, 'Letter I: Of raising Public Supplies, by Encreasing the Public Debts Considered', pp. 1–24. See also Hoppit, 'Compulsion, Compensation and Property Rights'.

179 Postlethwayt, *Great Britain's True System*, 'Letter V: The Opinion that Some Foreigners Entertain of the National Debts, and the Public Credit of this Kingdom', pp. 86–111.

180 Bowen, '"The Pests of Human Society"'.

181 George Rose, *A Brief Examination into the Increase of the Revenue, Commerce, and Manufactures, of Great Britain, from 1792 to 1799*, 4th edn (London: Printed for J. Wright, No. 169 Piccadilly; J. Hatchard, No. 173 Piccadilly; and J. Sewell, Cornhill, 1799), The United States faced similar issues. See for example, Webster, *A Seventh Essay on Free Trade*.

182 See above, pp. 87–88, 92.

low opinion of British morals.[183] Such regulation would build up institutional trust. Mostly however, Britain, and its merchants, managed to retain a good reputation for trade.

The British, of course, had something to say about their biggest rivals in the eighteenth-century Atlantic. The French monarchy had long been criticised for not paying back loans; but in 1790 George Rose also accused the Republican government of wringing 'her supplies from taxes on her own inhabitants infinitely more oppressive than those under the monarchy' and withheld the interest on her debts.[184] Adam Smith argued that France had had a bad reputation since Louis XIV because its government did not worry about its 'character'. Furthermore, he added that because nations did not 'treat' with each other very often, there was a strong incentive to cheat (there was no shadow of the future).[185] In comparison to individual merchants, or communities of merchants, nations did not have to worry about repeat transactions and might 'gain more by one piece of fraud than [lose] by having a bad character'.[186] For example, the reaction to the French opening of more Free Ports during the French Wars was seen as outside the 'rule of war'.[187] In contrast however, the French had managed to gain the trust of the native Americans, which had not only facilitated trade, but had allowed them to spread the Catholic religion. In contrast to the low levels of institutional trust the native Americans placed in the British, the good reputation of the French had facilitated trade.

As was noted above, early on in the race for the Americas, Spain's empire of conquest was something to be emulated, for example by Cromwell's 'Western Design'.[188] However, mainland Spain's over-reliance on imports

---

183 Postlethwayt, *Britain's Commercial Interest Explained*, Vol. I, 'Dissertation XVI: A Succinct View of the Constitution of the British Plantations in America: and of the State and Condition Wherein They have Many Years Been; Wherein is Pointed out the Chief Causes of their Becoming the Present Seat of War; with Considerations How They May Recover their Strength and Stability, and Become a Match for our Enemies', pp. 421–60, p. 454. See above for regulation of trade with native Americans, p. 91.

184 Rose, *A Brief Examination*, pp. 40–41.

185 Smith was referring to such events as post-war treaties.

186 Smith, 'Lecture on the Influence of Commerce on Manners', pp. 17–18.

187 That is, nations should only carry on the same trade as they had in peace time. Stephen James, *War in Disguise; or, the Frauds of the Neutral Flags* (London: Printed by C. Whittingham, Dean Street, and sold by J. Hatchard, Piccadilly, 1805), p. 13. See also Gouverneur Morris, *An Answer to War In Disguise; Or, Remarks upon the New Doctrine of England, Concerning Neutral Trade* (New York: Printed for Hopkins and Seymour, 1806). Gouverneur Morris was an occasional partner of Robert Morris. Doerflinger, *A Vigorous Spirit*, p. 336, fn. 4.

188 See p. 15.

of silver meant it was either unwilling or unable to develop an empire of commerce, as was Britain, and the Spanish state was insolvent after 1790. Indeed, contemporaries thought that the Spaniards were backward, superstitious and slothful, with a languor that corroded the mother country. So powerful were these prejudices, ensconced in deep-seated anti-Catholic sentiment, that Elliott notes that they still pervade much of the historiography today.[189] Of course, the Spanish did try hard to profit from the Americas, as shown by the establishment of the *Casa de la Contración* in 1503 to control the trade to the West Indies. However, the granting of the *Asiento* to Britain in 1713 demonstrates that it was Britain that was making money out of trade even in the early-eighteenth century. Therefore, we find examples of expediency and cooperation, rather than competition, between these two empires. Roger Hope Elletson, whilst governor of Jamaica, wrote to the governor of Cuba in the 1760s over issues such as runaway slaves and the purchase of slaves.[190] Around the same time, Charles Stewart was trying to get an introduction to Spanish merchants in London. Some Spaniards he had met had promised to get him an introduction to the Spanish ambassador. When they did so and he found the ambassador was happy to introduce him to the 'first Spanish merchants in the city', he wrote that he was 'agreeably disappointed in our opinion of the honour of the Dons'.[191] Such cooperation was widespread. In 1786 merchants in Kingston argued that it had long been allowed for the Spaniards to enter anything for export, the nature of the trade with them requiring 'indulgence'.[192]

The reputation of the Americans changed over time and Stephen Conway argues that war was often a catalyst for changing perceptions of them, especially the perceptions of the British. Whilst the Americans were seen rather benignly as ungrateful children in mid-century, the Seven Years' War left the British with the perception that the Americans were a non-martial nation, no doubt one of the reasons for British arrogance during the American War of Independence. However, the Franco-American alliance of 1778 was crucial in turning the Americans into an enemy not to be trusted.[193] The

---

189 Elliott, *Empires of the Atlantic World*, p. 408, quoting Crévecouer, pp. 403–5.
190 Roger Elletson to Gobenador de Cuba, 10 Dec. 1766, Carta 12, Cuba 1051.N86, Correspondencia de los Capitanes Generales de Cuba, Archivo General de Indias, Seville.
191 Charles Stewart to [n/k], 29 Jan. 1764, 920 PAR I 27/6. See also Charles Stewart to Aitchison and Parker, 23 Nov. 1763, 920 PAR I 27/4 and Charles Stewart to Aitchison & Parker, 29 Jan. 1764, 920 PAR I 27/6, PP.
192 'To His honor Alured Clark …', extract of minutes, 24 May 1786, BoT, WI, BT6/75, f. 39.
193 Postlethwayt, *Britain's Commercial Interest Explained*, 'Dissertation XVII: Further

Americans' (successful) attempts to engross trade through sailing under neutral flags during the French and Napoleonic Wars won them no friends in Britain either, and eventually led to the Anglo-American War.[194] Their reputation regarding their creditability also fluctuated over time. There were low ebbs in the 1760s, as noted by Charles Stewart, and the repudiation of debts after the American War of Independence and the necessity of the Jay Treaty in 1795 simply made things worse.[195] In 1790, Andrew Clow wrote to Cay from London to 'be cautious in all your speculation until I can advise you of a change in the opinion of American credit'.[196] There were also many credit problems during the French Wars, and whilst they were not particular to the United States, Thomas Earle wrote regarding the many failures in America of 1802, 'Great Caution will be necessary in dealing with that Continent.'[197] Three years later, William Rathbone commented: 'more Caution is necessary in America than in England to guard against impositions from designing & dishonest persons'. [198] The problematic reputation of American bills was again raised in 1812.[199] Clearly such generalised perceptions of reputation affected the ability of merchants to trust each other where personal trust did not already exist.

Merchants and areas on the African coast also had varying reputations. As we saw in the discussion on institutional trust, Old Calabar and Bonny had good reputations for trade because Europeans trusted the debt enforcement institutions there. In West-Central Africa, the reputation of the Afro-Portuguese trading community also helped to solve issues of trading

---

Considerations on the Causes of the Present State of Our Affairs with America', pp. 461–80; Stephen Conway, 'From Fellow Nationalists to Foreigners: British Perceptions of the Americans, circa 1739–1893', *WMQ*, 3rd ser., 59:1 (2002), 65–100. See also *Common Sense: In Nine Conferences, between a British Merchant and a Candid Merchant of America, in their Private Capacities as Friends, Tracing the Several Causes of the Present Contests Between the Mother Country and her American Subjects, etc.* (London: 1775).

194 James, *War in Disguise*.

195 See above, pp. 94, 115. Merle Curti discusses various problems with the issue of the reputation of Americans in Europe in 'The Reputation of America Overseas (1776–1860)', *American Quarterly*, 1:1 (Spring 1959), 58–82.

196 Andrew Clow to David Cay, 15 Dec. 1790, Folder Joseph, John & Thomas Hadfield 1785–88, Andrew Clow & Co., CWU.

197 Thomas Earle to William Earle, 27 Jan. 1802, Letterbook Livorno, 2/3, EC.

198 William Rathbone to Thomas Rutter, 14 Mar. 1805, William Rathbone Letterbook.

199 Brian H. Tolley, 'The Liverpool Campaign Against the Orders in Council and the War of 1812', in J. R. Harris, ed., *Liverpool and Merseyside: Essays in the Economic and Social History of the Port and its Hinterland* (London: Frank Cass & Co. Ltd, 1969), pp. 98–146, p. 108.

with the 'other'.[200] In contrast, the reputations of particular European slave trade captains and merchant houses must have circulated on the African coast because many were involved in consecutive voyages. The reputations of certain European traders who were settled on the African coast also circulated around the Atlantic. For example, Richard Brew, a former agent of the Royal African Company had a bad reputation for not delivering slaves already paid for with bartered goods.[201] Reputation at the national level was therefore equally important, if not more so, when trading with the 'other' in facilitating trade and building up trusted relationships.

CONCLUSION

THE REPUTATIONAL NEXUS was not only made up of many different elements, it also functioned at the personal, community and national level. These levels of reputation roughly corresponded with individual trust, institutional trust (assurance) and confidence, thereby facilitating risk taking in turn. At the personal level, reputation was constructed in a variety of ways. Whilst concerns about personality, treatment and behaviour of family, and other moral issues were factors in a merchant's reputation, these were only of real concern to the extent that they affected his ability to pay. Performance of 'contract' in its various forms was the most important element. Associational membership could also 'confer' reputation on an individual in many instances, acting in a similar way to hyphenated (institutional) trust. However, when such group reputations were extended to a wider community, that reputation could often be far more complicated. Liverpool merchants were known to have positive human capital in the slave trade, but this was later to become a problematic reputation. Glasgow merchants were known to be good in the tobacco trade, but their success often led to them being vilified. East India Company 'nabobs' and officials of the Royal African Company also had bad reputations, but the worst community reputation was that of the West Indies, even causing new institutional forms to be invented. National reputations also mattered because they were linked to confidence. Despite some temporary setbacks, the British state managed to retain its positive reputation for creating an effective trading environment, although its relationship with its own merchants deteriorated towards the end of the period.

---

200 See above pp. 92–93.
201 Powell, Hardwar, Clemens & Stronge to David Tuohy, 9 Jul. 1768, Ships Papers, DTP. For Richard Brew see Margaret Priestley, *West African Trade and Coast Society: A Family Study* (London: Oxford University Press, 1969), chapters two to four.

If there was a hierarchy of reputations, the most important would be that at the personal level. This is because, as was discussed in the chapter on trust – and will be discussed further in the chapter on crises, personal trust and reputation often facilitated trade when levels of institutional trust, confidence and national reputation were low. Reputational mechanisms were socially embedded, as were the obligations that came with, as well as helped to construct, a good reputation. Many of these obligations were over and above the performance of 'contract' and it is to these that we now turn.

5

Obligation

I make no doubts, you are thoroughly sensible
of the late stagnation in Trade, and flatter my self
you will indulge me, with a further length of time.[1]

METCALF BOWLER OF PROVIDENCE wrote this rather begging letter
to elite merchants Brown & Benson in early 1784. By this time, the
post-war slump was already in progress and lesser merchants and shopkeepers
all along the eastern seaboard were experiencing financial difficulties. During
1784 Bowler paid what he could in a number of instalments of cash, but by
1785 he was reduced to paying Brown & Benson with various goods such as
molasses. In the end, he assigned all his real estate including his shop and
home to Brown & Benson as security for his debts, and his wife even had
to sign away her dower rights. The tone of his letters is obsequious, and
conformed to statements regarding the settling of all his debts to all his
creditors as discussed in the previous chapter. He played on their generosity,
kindness and reputation throughout. Only once did he complain that they
had 'crouded [sic] me rather too hard'.[2] Brown & Benson managed to gain
security for Bowler's debts (which no doubt made them unpopular with the
remainder of his creditors), but they did not pursue the collection of his
debts through the legal system. This story demonstrates the extraordinary
measures merchants took to be conciliatory, and to avoid the hassle and
expense of legal procedures which might in turn taint their own reputation.
Bowler's plight, however, reveals more than this. He played on the fact that
Brown & Benson were an elite, reputable mercantile house, and by being

---

1 Metcalf Bowler to Brown & Benson, 9 Mar. 1784, Folder 1, Metcalf Bowler 1783–93,
  BFBR.
2 Metcalf Bowler to Brown & Benson, 11 Jun. 1784, Folder 1, Metcalf Bowler 1783–93.

so, they owed obligations not only to him as a customer, but to the wider business community by not forcing lesser traders into bankruptcy. Bowler was asking for what Muldrew has described as 'forgiveness of debt'.[3] He pointed out that the security they had asked him for was 'trifling and of no consequence' to 'Person[s] of your multiplicity of Business', and that if they were kind he would be extremely grateful to such 'worthy men'.[4] Bowler's language demonstrates a clear sense of hierarchy and esteem, but he used this to stress *Brown & Benson's* responsibility as elite merchants to indulge him. To keep a good reputation one had to not only fulfil financial obligations, but moral ones too. However, obligations also stretched further than immediate correspondents, and even the wider trading community. Merchants also had a reciprocal relationship with the state.

This chapter could possibly have been entitled reciprocity, sociability, social capital or even gifting. However, these terms often have positive connotations and this chapter is concerned as much with the burdens the business community encountered, as the benefits it sought. This chapter therefore begins with an explanation of the decision to use obligation as a theoretical framework. It then describes how these obligations were fulfilled through a discussion of daily business procedural norms, payment, and what contemporaries called 'indulgence'.[5] Last, it looks at the obligatory relationship elite merchants had with the wider community in which they worked; including the state.

WHY OBLIGATION?

ENGAGING in social and commercial exchange creates diverse future obligations. These are often non-specific, and it is not known when the return of favours might be received. Significantly, they might not be received in the same form.[6] Bourdieu describes the recognition of such non-specific indebtedness as gratitude.[7] There is, however, an expectation

3 Muldrew, *The Economy of Obligation*, p. 82.

4 Metcalf Bowler to Brown & Benson, 1 Jun. 1784; 24 Sep. 1785, Folder 1, Metcalf Bowler 1783–93.

5 In the literature on the history of more modern businesses, the term routine rather than procedural norms is often used, but this term appears to apply to routines' *within* the firm rather than between firms. For a good example of this see Jones, 'Routines, Capabilities'.

6 Molm et al., 'Risk and Trust in Social Exchange', p. 1402; for reciprocal exchange see above, pp. 53–54, 74–79.

7 Bourdieu, 'The Forms of Capital', p. 106.

that such gratitude will be expressed in reciprocal action at some point in the future, whatever form that might take.[8] Merchants were acutely aware of the *expectations* on them and the *obligations* they were under. This distinction is made because whilst merchants were managing to fulfil expectations without any problems, they were not necessarily expressed as obligations. However, as soon as difficulties arose, those expectations clearly became felt as more burdensome obligations. As Donald Muir and Eugene Weinstein note, 'It is only when the relationship breaks down that the underlying obligations are brought to light.'[9] Obligation is therefore used here because of its connotation with burdens and negativities that other terms do not have.

Reciprocity involves a number of supportive actions, not necessarily of the same kind, and over an uncertain period of time. For example, Obadiah Brown & Co. had 'no objection' to the favour of advancing Francis & Relfe of Philadelphia $2000 in 1761.[10] However, in return they expected Francis & Relfe, in addition to paying back the loan of course, to send certain commodities to them, to allow them the income from the shipping of those goods on to London, as well as the commission on the sale of goods they sold on their behalf. Failure to reciprocate led to feelings of exploitation, resentment or unfairness, and Francis & Relfe in turn felt betrayed when Brown & Co. purchased dry goods from another house in Philadelphia.[11] The inability to reciprocate also exacerbates power differences, as we saw earlier in Metcalf Bowler's story. Reciprocity therefore often infers an exchange between two people, or perhaps a small, known 'triangular' group, but this does not explain the variety of obligatory relationships within the trading community.[12]

Bourdieu argues that the reproduction of social capital 'presupposes an unceasing effort of sociability', in which a series of exchanges endlessly reaffirm relationships; and there is no doubt that in business, sociability was, and still is, important in reducing transaction costs and supporting

---

8 Robert Putnam, *Bowling Alone: The Collapse and Revival of American Community* (New York and London: Simon and Schuster paperbacks, 2000), p. 20.

9 Quoted in Donal E. Muir and Eugene A. Weinstein, 'The Social Debt: An Investigation of Lower-Class and Middle-Class Norms of Social Obligation', *American Sociological Review*, 27:4 (Aug. 1962), 532–59, p. 533.

10 Francis & Relfe to Obadiah Brown & Co., 4 Mar. 1761; Folder 9, Francis & Relfe, Correspondence with Francis & Relfe, BFBR.

11 Francis & Relfe to Obadiah Brown & Co., 12 Mar. 1761, Folder 9, Francis & Relfe, Correspondence with Francis & Relfe.

12 Theo Van Tilberg, Eric Van Sonderen and Johan Ormel, 'The Measurement of Reciprocity in Ego-Centred Networks of Personal Relationships: A Comparison of Various Indices', *Social Psychology Quarterly*, 54:1 (Mar. 1991), 54–66.

self-governing institutions such as trade associations.[13] Indeed, Muldrew states that sociability had become equated with commerce as early as the late sixteenth century.[14] However, the term still has links to what Georg Simmel and Everett Hughes call 'play'; that 'Whilst all human associations are entered into because of some ulterior motives, there is in all of them a residue of pure sociability for its own sake.'[15] When Henry Laurens partially retired from business, he thanked Thomas Mears of Liverpool for past favours, and then added that he would be 'glad of your permission to continue our correspondence' – to continue talking for the sake of it.[16] In fact he did not appear to keep in contact with Thomas Mears, although he did keep in contact with John Knight, Mears' partner, no doubt because Knight's nephew, Knight Giball, went into partnership with Edmund Head, one of Lauren's protégés.[17] Merchants developed true friendships with their correspondents, and therefore wanted them, and their children, to be successful. Maintaining such friendships would keep those links open for the next generation. There is no doubt that merchants enjoyed their clubs, dinner parties and visits to the tavern as recreation, but we must not forget Simmel and Hughes' ulterior motives. Merchants wanted access to friendships as well as resources.

Those resources were often acquired through accessing social capital.[18] After all, money cannot buy 'all those social assets that enable one to attract respect, generate confidence, evoke affection, and draw on loyalty in a specific setting'.[19] Social capital has often been seen by historians and social scientists as self-evidently positive, though recently more sophisticated analyses have been posited.[20] However, it is clear that donors of resources

---

13 Bourdieu, 'The Forms of Capital', p. 104; Fukuyama, *Trust*, pp. 11, 325.

14 Craig Muldrew, 'The Culture of Reconciliation: Community and the Settlement of Economic Disputes in Early Modern England', *Historical Journal*, 39:4 (Dec. 1996), 915–42, p. 942.

15 Georg Simmel and Everett C. Hughes, 'The Sociology of Sociability', *AJS*, 55:3 (Nov. 1949), 254–61, pp. 254–55.

16 Henry Laurens to Thomas Mears, 22 Dec. 1764, *HLP*, Vol. IV.

17 *HLP*, Vols. V and VI make no reference to Thomas Mears; Henry Laurens to John Knight, 23 Oct. 1769, fn. 5, *HLP*, Vol. IV.

18 Social capital represents *access* to resources, not the resources themselves. Bourdieu, 'The Forms of Capital', p. 106 and *passim*. Social capital does not exist of itself, and certainly does not have agency as suggested in Ann M. Carlos, Karen Maguire and Larry Neal, '"A Knavish People ...": London Jewry and the Stock Market During the South Sea Bubble', *BH*, 50:6 (Nov. 2008), 728–48, p. 733.

19 Pamela Walker Laird, *Pull: Networking and Success since Benjamin Franklin* (Cambridge, MA and London: Harvard University Press, 2006), p. 2.

20 Historians have on the whole been far more sceptical of social capital than networks.

have motivations in providing information, credit or other assistance. These motivations might include conforming to social norms, expressing solidarity, or reacting to group sanctions, but the favour they give still creates an obligation of future reciprocity, of access to resources in turn.[21] Social capital can also be negative. When communities, or communities within communities, establish what Putnam calls bonding capital, this can lead to the exclusion of 'others' from the group. David Tuohy, a Liverpool slave trader who never managed to enter the elite group, grumbled in 1772 that he felt he was 'Strongly opposed by a party of Gent who would fair Monopolise that trade'.[22] Such exclusion and isolation can cause restricted access to opportunities, restrictions on individual freedoms, excessive claims on group members, and downward spiralling norms.[23] This is because, as Coleman suggests, social capital can create social norms whereby individuals forego self-interest in the interests of the collective. Therefore one of the forms social capital can take is the fulfilment of obligations to the community.[24] This can, however, have bad effects for the wider community as a whole if the sub-group becomes closed.

Due to the uncertainty surrounding the return of favours, gifting and counter-gifting are also extremely important in obligation networks. This is because gifts can be used to construct, maintain or reactivate dormant ties and 'provide the social basis for a moral economy'.[25] Gifts, whatever the form, 'assert the status of the giver and the value of the recipient in the giver's view'.[26] The person receiving the gift therefore becomes a social debtor. Gifts can come in several guises although some may literally be presents. For example, Henry Laurens liked to send his friend Thomas Mears a turtle every spring (a delicacy on English tables at this time), and Samuel Rainford

Rosenband, 'Social Capital in the Early Industrial Revolution'; Ogilvie, 'Guilds, Efficiency, and Social Capital'; Dario Gaggio, 'Do Social Historians need Social Capital?', *Social History*, 29:4 (Nov. 2004), 499–513, and the articles in the special edition of *BH*, 50:6 (Nov. 2008).

21 Alejandro Portes, 'Social Capital: Its Origins and Applications in Modern Sociology', *Annual Review of Sociology*, 24 (1998), 1–24, pp. 5–8.

22 David Tuohy to Mr Chilcott, 15 Dec. 1772, Letters Out, 380 TUO 2, DTP.

23 Putnam also uses the term bridging social capital, which is akin to Granovetter's weak ties. *Bowling Alone*, chapter 22; Portes, 'Social Capital', pp. 15–18.

24 Coleman, 'Social Capital in the Creation of Human Capital', pp. 101–5.

25 Asaf Darr, 'Gifting Practices and Interorganizational Relations: Constructing Obligation Networks in the Electronics Sector, *Sociological Forum*, 18:1 (Mar. 2003), 31–51, p. 33; Muir and Weinstein, 'The Social Debt', p. 535. In arguing that gifts can be used to construct, maintain or reactivate dormant ties, Darr agrees with Portes, 'Social Capital', p. 5.

26 Darr, 'Gifting Practices and Interorganizational Relations', p. 33.

of Jamaica liked to send ginger, pickled mangoes and sweetmeats to the wife of his friend and colleague Edward Chaffers.[27] Joshua Johnson sent magazines and papers to the wife of a correspondent in 1772.[28] However, gifts can also be in the form of information, free samples, drinks or dinner, letters of introduction, or even time taken to conduct an errand. Gifting therefore involves behaviour that does not have to be done, but still creates future obligations. For example, in 1772 William Pollard was the consignee for goods sent to Philadelphia by Thomas & Clayton Case of Liverpool. When Pollard could not sell all of their goods quickly enough, he bought the remainder on his own account, at his own risk, in order to finalise the accounts.[29] This was certainly not expected behaviour, and in fact, was quite unusual (an example of constructing goodwill trust). When Richard Bright of Bristol visited Liverpool in 1769 and stayed as a guest of the Heywood family, it was no doubt expected that at least some future commissions would be sent via Liverpool.[30] Whilst this behaviour may not seem efficient in a formal sense, because of the delay in gifting, it helped to build personal trust. Gifting was therefore often strategic, as opposed to purely emotive, because it helped to promote networks and create obligations in the long term.[31]

It is clear that reciprocity, sociability, accessing social capital and gifting contribute to obligations in various ways, hence why this chapter uses the term obligation. The term obligation also facilitates the investigation of expectations through a multiplicity of relationships, demonstrating that for our merchants, obligations involved far more than simply one-to-one reciprocity. For example, Henry Laurens wrote to John Knight in 1764 regarding the loading of a vessel, the *Knight*. Laurens stressed that he could not have loaded her with rice without the help of Mr Manigault, Mr Savage and others who had enabled him to 'get the better of every competitor'.[32]

---

27 Henry Laurens to Thomas Mears, 22 Dec. 1763, *HLP*, Vol. IV; Samuel Rainford to Edward Chaffers, 21 Jan. 1794, 920 CHA/1/10, PEC.

28 Joshua Johnson to Wallace & Davidson, 18 May 1772, JJL.

29 William Pollard to Thomas & Clayton Case, 19 Jun. 1772, William Pollard Letterbook.

30 The Brights and the Heywoods were Unitarians. In fact this connection was to be long lasting. Richard Bright became good friends with Benjamin Arthur Heywood and Nathaniel Heywood during their time as students at Warrington Academy, and Richard Bright later married Sarah Heywood, daughter of Benjamin Heywood. Samuel Heywood also later visited the Brights in 1771. Benjamin Heywood to Henry Bright, 4 Aug. 1771; Henry Bright to Richard Bright, 23 Dec. 1769, and 'Introduction', *BMP*, pp. 57–58. For the Heywoods' banking activities see George Chandler, *Four Centuries of Banking* (London: B. T. Basford Ltd, 1964), chapter four.

31 Offer, 'Between the Gift and the Market', p. 450; Muir and Weinstein, 'The Social Debt', p. 533; Darr, 'Gifting Practices', pp. 31–34.

32 Henry Laurens to John Knight, 8 Dec. 1764, *HLP*, Vol. IV.

Laurens had used his social capital, no doubt built up through reciprocity and sociability, to gain access to a scarce resource at a good price. At the same time, not only had Laurens created obligations for himself, he was letting Knight know that he too in turn was obliged not only to Laurens for his efforts, but to others in Laurens' network.

Obligations therefore came in various guises, and were called upon and repaid in various forms. As we saw above, when obligations were not fulfilled, there were serious repercussions. Furthermore, in time of difficulty, elite merchants were often asked for 'debt forgiveness', but they were also expected to protect and promote their local community and to work with the larger community of the state. The 'tangle of obligation was all enveloping'.[33]

FULFILLING EXPECTATIONS AND OBLIGATIONS

CERTAIN GROUPS OF PEOPLE had particularly high expectations of each other. These might include family members who were expected to help out their own first by way of 'implicit contract'.[34] When Charles Stewart Parker went to Grenada in 1789 he found that he was unable to get a place at Thornton, Baillie & Co. or Munro's 'from their having always such a Multiplicity of Nephews Cousens [sic] &c of their own to provide for'.[35] Nathaniel Phillips, having developed his trading networks through his father, found that he was obliged to advise his London correspondents Hilton & Biscoe of all his plans, ranging from entering into partnership to helping out his sister financially.[36] Yet employing family was far from always being a sound idea. Jeremiah Meyler in Jamaica drew on his uncle in Bristol without good cause, and Robert Bright, also in Jamaica, left large debts on his death in 1759 which his family had to deal with.[37] Samuel Rainford's very drunken elder brother John in Liverpool was a positive liability, he was said to have 'fits of inebriety'.[38] In 1805 William Rathbone advised his friend John Ashe

---

33 Muldrew, *The Economy of Obligation*, p. 189.

34 Ben-Porath, 'The F-Connection', p. 1. On the failure of this 'implicit contract' see Sheryllynne Haggerty, '"You promise Well and Perform as Badly": The Failure of the "implicit contract of family" in the Scottish Atlantic', *International Journal of Maritime History* 23:2 (Dec. 2011), pp. 1–15.

35 Charles Parker to Patrick Parker, 3 Dec. 1789, Folder 920 PAR 1 46/1, PP.

36 Nathaniel Phillips to Hilton & Biscoe, 16 Feb. 1760; 15 Jun. 1762, Mailhet & Phillips Letterbook, 1759–?.

37 Richard Meyler II to Jeremiah Meyler, 31 Oct. 1754; Gerard Nash to Henry Bright, 3 Feb. 1759; Richard Meyler II to Meyler & Hall, 22 Nov. 1763, *BMP*.

38 Edward Chaffers to the Honble Ct of Chancery, 4 Apr. 1810, 920 CHA/1/18, PEC.

in business at Trieste that as Ashe's brother's business 'was positively going backwards', Ashe might have to provide for him.[39] However, seeing as he had not been successful so far, Rathbone recommended that Ashe put his brother on a salary rather than take him on as a partner. Clearly the brother was deemed a risky proposition. Other groups that had expectations almost by default were religious or ethnic groups.[40] When Quaker Pim Nevins visited Philadelphia in 1802, Joshua Gilpin (another Quaker) invited him to stay at his house, and introduced Nevins to Thomas and Miers Fisher, Nicholas Walne, and Thomas P. Cope – all leading Quakers.[41] When Ralph Eddowes arrived in Philadelphia he had also expected the help of fellow Quakers the Fishers, but was disappointed. He found instead that Philip Nicklin was far more helpful.[42] Whilst such groups might have high expectations of one another, those expectations were of a similar nature to those of all correspondents; that is, to follow procedural norms, to pay on time, and to give some leeway where necessary. We saw in the previous chapter that certain procedural norms or performances were required, and because of the interconnected nature of reputation and obligation, we revisit some of those themes here.

Procedural Norms

Most expectations or obligations were fulfilled as part of everyday business. Although it is difficult to assess to what extent these norms were internalized

---

See also Sheryllynne Haggerty, 'I "could do for the Dickmans": When Networks Don't Work', in Gestrich and Schulte Beerbühl, *Cosmopolitan Networks in Commerce and Society*, pp. 317–42.

39 William Rathbone to John Ashe, 25 Jul. 1805, William Rathbone Letterbook.

40 Religious groups may have felt more morally obliged to assist as opposed to conforming to social norms alone. John C. Ortberg Jr., Richard L. Gorsuch and Grace J. Kim, 'Changing Attitude and Moral Obligation: Their Independent Effects on Behaviour', *Journal for the Scientific Study of Religion*, 40:3 (2001), 489–96, p. 489. Muldrew argues that in the seventeenth century notions of duty and contract were still combined with Christian notions of neighbourliness and belief. *The Economy of Obligation*, p. 146.

41 Pim Nevins, *Journal of a Visit to America, 1802–3, 9th Month, 11th, 13th, 14th 1802 and 12th Month, 4th, 1802*, 917.3.N41, APS.

42 Ralph Eddowes to William Roscoe, 3 Nov. 1794, 20 ROS 1329, RP. It is unlikely that Philip Nicklin was a Quaker because he was a director of the Bank of Pennsylvania which was dominated by Anglican merchants. *The American Kalendar; or, United States Register, for New Hampshire, Vermont, Massachusetts, Rhode Island, Connecticut, New York, New Jersey, Pennsylvania, Delaware, Maryland, Virginia, Kentucky, North Carolina, South Carolina, Georgia, and Tennessee, for the year 1798. To be continued annually, And will be carefully corrected to the Time of Publication* (London: Printed for J. Debrett, 1798), p. 139; Doerflinger, *A Vigorous Spirit of Enterprise*, p. 119.

or simply performed, the system must have worked because there was a high level of order to be found in the market.[43] Certainly the embeddedness of business within social relations meant that network partners were motivated to share private resources.[44] These could take the form of sharing capital in order to establish a merchant house or engage in a particular venture – as we saw in the chapter on risk – or it could involve time taken to find information, extra effort to procure shipping, or perhaps giving up the opportunity cost of dealing with another merchant. Such ties and common interests also meant that the trading community was involved in a high level of 'self-enforcing governance' through fulfilling expectations and obligations.[45] As mentioned above, whilst these expectations were being fulfilled, the sense of burden was relatively light. However, as soon as there was doubt over the ability to reciprocate, these expectations clearly came to be felt as obligations.

One basic expectation or procedural norm was for correspondents to keep each other informed of the state of the markets, the arrival and departure of vessels, bankruptcies, and other business news. Merchants were also expected to notify their agents of when vessels would be arriving so that they could deal with them properly. Henry Laurens asked John Tarleton in 1763 to ensure that his West India agents notified him in advance of vessels coming to Charleston from thence, as this would 'enable me to serve you with more ease to myself & what is of more consiquence [sic] more advantage to you'.[46] In 1792 William Wilson asked Andrew Clow to keep him informed of any rise and fall in the stocks in which they had invested. Wilson requested that if there was any particular change in the stocks and no post was leaving Philadelphia for Alexandria, that Clow use the express post to keep him updated.[47] Captain Bowers must have dreaded the reaction of his employers Brown & Ives when his vessel was taken by a French privateer in 1807. However, he knew he had to keep them informed, and he wrote to them in full from Cuba about the event and its aftermath, noting gloomily that he thought it would be at least three months before it was all sorted out.[48] Information on prices and the state of the market was important even when trade was suspended, as

43 Coleman, 'Social Capital in the Creation of Human Capital', p. 105; Granovetter, 'Economic Action and Social Structure', p. 502.
44 Brian Uzzi, 'Embeddedness in the Making of Financial Capital: How Social Relations and Networks Benefit Firms Seeking Financing', *American Sociological Review*, 64:4 (Aug. 1999), 481–505, p. 481.
45 Uzzi, 'Embeddedness in the Making of Financial Capital', p. 483.
46 Henry Laurens to John Tarleton, 27 Dec. 1763, *HLP*, Vol. IV.
47 William Wilson to Andrew Clow & Co., 27 Jan. 1792, Folder One, Andrew Clow & Co., Letters Received, Baker Library.
48 George Bowers to Brown & Ives, 13 May 1807, Folder 8, Brig Argus, B.492, BFBR.

demonstrated by the many price currents sent to the United States between 1807 and 1812, during which time various embargoes and non-Intercourse acts were in place.[49] Particular notice was to be given when one merchant drew on another by bill of exchange. James Chisholme had a plantation in Jamaica and he used Moses Benson of Liverpool as his agent to import his sugar into England. He used the credit from those transactions to draw on Benson, but he always carefully notified him in advance.[50] Henry Laurens apologised to Thomas Mears in 1763 for having drawn on him unexpectedly. He noted the express obligation he had created commenting that, 'I asked it rather as a matter of favour than right.'[51] Not advising a correspondent could cause huge embarrassment, as Andrew Clow found out when his incompetent partner Cay failed to notify George Fox of Falmouth of bills he had drawn on him. Fox informed Clow that, not having been advised in advance, he had noted them for non-acceptance.[52] When Samuel Rainford realised that money had been withdrawn from accounts at his businesses's sister house in Liverpool without notification he complained: 'do you call this giving us the usual and necessary advices according to the usage and Custom of Merchants and what is common in the Mercantile Houses'.[53]

Correspondents were also expected to work expeditiously for their principals. It was anticipated they would not only arrange for goods of the correct quality to be delivered, but to be shipped as quickly as possible in order to be ahead of the market; or at least not behind it. Peter Wikoff received goods in plenty of time from John Ewer in the Spring of 1772. He wrote, 'I am Obliged to you for the pains you took to get my goods on the first Vessell [sic] which has been a particular advantage to me.'[54] The return shipments east were equally important. Henry Laurens was upset that it had taken so long to load and get a vessel ready for sea in the spring of 1764. Even though it was not his fault, he wrote to Joseph Manesty in Liverpool that the *Barter* was ready for sea 'after a detaintion [sic] as gauling too as unexpected'.[55] Liverpool slave trader Robert Bostock was on the receiving end of a delay and

---

49 For more on this see the chapter on crises, pp. 224–33.

50 See for example, James Chisholme to Moses Benson, 11 Jul. 1793; 24 Nov. 1793; 28 Nov. 1793; Letterbook 5476, Chisholme Papers, NLS.

51 Henry Laurens to Thomas Mears, 22 Dec. 1763, *HLP*, Vol. IV.

52 George Fox to Andrew Clow, 9 Sep. 1790, Folder George Fox, Andrew Clow & Co., CWU.

53 Samuel Rainford, Jonathon Blundell and Robert Rainford to Blundell, Rainford & Co., 9 Jun. 1798, 920 CHA 1/25, PEC.

54 Peter Wikoff to John Ewer, 30 Apr. 1772, Folder Peter Wikoff to John Ewer, CBP.

55 Henry Laurens to Joseph Manesty, 17 Mar. 1764. See also Henry Laurens to Joseph Manesty, 24 Feb. 1764; Henry Laurens to John Haslin, 15 Mar. 1764, *HLP*, Vol. IV.

was annoyed with his agents in Antigua, Lightfoot, Mills & Co. They had apparently kept his captain waiting for accounts when his vessel was ready and could have sailed. 'I think I am not well us'd' he complained to them.[56] To add insult to injury Bostock thought the rum they had sent to Liverpool was not of good enough quality and they had made a poor average on the sale of slaves.[57] Whereas Henry Laurens and Joseph Manesty had an effective long-term relationship which allowed them to overlook the disappointment of the late ship, Bostock's alliance with Lightfoot, Mills & Co. was not so well established, and this may have caused issues regarding trust. Similarly, James Lawson was cross with his agents in Liverpool, Haliday & Dunbar, when they did not ensure that forty-four of his hogsheads of tobacco were shipped to Holland in 1760. Lawson felt sure that he must have been one of the first to sign up for freight with them and wrote to another house that 'If Mess[rs] Haliday & Dunbar have Shipt or allowed any other to Ship Rice or any other Goods on board that Vessel, I think they have used me Ill.'[58] Lawson dealt with this non-compliance by shifting his business to another Liverpool house, Rumbold & Walker.

The shadow of the future, however, meant that most correspondents did their utmost to fulfil their obligations and that subsequent good relations led to what Lawler and Yoon call 'staying behaviour'.[59] Using one faithful agent was obviously a risk-reduction strategy, but it was expected behaviour nonetheless. William Pollard advised Brian Bentley in Kingston during 1773 that 'our old settlers have got their old Correspondents which they do not like to leave'.[60] Boston merchants Nathaniel & Francis Thayer obviously felt that their correspondents Champion & Dickason of London should have used them to ship their 1784 spring goods, especially as they had just made a payment to them in August of 1783. They wrote: 'We are Greatly disappointed in not receiving the commission of your goods.'[61] Presumably another house had received them. Perhaps the Thayers had not sold the goods quickly enough or had not paid on time. However, they were clearly not in a position to be able to 'punish' Champion & Dickason. In May 1786 they were still

56 Robert Bostock to Lightfoot, Mills & Co., 15 Oct. 1788, RBL.

57 Slave traders often judged the success of a slaving voyage by the 'average' of all the slave sales from a vessel. This allowed them to make a quick comparison by sales in various markets and with their competitors.

58 James Lawson to Rumbold & Walker, 27 Feb. 1761; James Lawson to Haliday & Dunbar, 27 Feb. 1760, James Lawson Letterbook 1997.

59 See above, pp. 75–79.

60 William Pollard to Brian Bentley, 9 Mar. 1773, WPL.

61 Nathaniel & Francis Thayer to Champion & Dickason, 16 Jun. 1784, Nathaniel & Francis Thayer Letterbook 1783–1790, MHS.

hoping to do business with them, and wished them 'Success in Remittances from this Country'.[62] Staying behaviour also had some potentially negative consequences by cutting off other opportunities. For example, Daniel Gordon of Glasgow preferred, along with most other merchants, to send goods via small frequent shipments on various vessels which spread the risk of loss by sea as well as financial failure of correspondents. However, regarding the trade from Grenada, he wrote that 'we must have one large Cargo Yearly on Account of the Douglas or any other ship which our Friends may have in that Trade'.[63] Merchants were therefore obliged to use not only the 'houses' of their friends, but their vessels as well. Occasionally merchants wanted to avoid such obligations. In 1798 Charles Stewart Parker notified John Bolton that he might have to extend the credit he received from him. He explained that this was because he 'did not want to lay myself under obligations to any person in London, as consignments to this Port would in return be expected, & what I have determined against doing'.[64] Equally, Parker realised that building up a bank of favours was useful in other cases. Five years later he wrote to his Glasgow partner recommending giving an order to the Barradailes 'as we shall no doubt have to apply for them for money to pay duties'.[65]

Some obligations were rather awkward to negotiate. John Leigh carefully advised the captain of his shipment of slaves not to mention to his factor in Barbados, John Gordon, that he also had guarantees for certain houses in St. Vincent and Grenada. This was because Leigh was worried that if Gordon knew the vessel was going on to these islands he would expect the sales to go through his [Gordon's] particular friends. Of course Leigh wanted only to sell through the houses for which he had guarantees.[66] People were generally aware of such obligations. Therefore when Joseph Hadfield pressured Andrew Clow to use him for his insurance business, saying that 'You cannot be under any particular Obligation to Perrot', this was dubious practice.[67] Although Perrot's name does not occur many times in Clow's records, it was not for Hadfield to judge Clow's obligations to him. People also kept their friends advised of their obligations, as we saw above with Henry Laurens' use of his

62 Nathaniel & Francis Thayer to Champion & Dickason, 24 May 1786, Nathaniel & Francis Thayer Letterbook 1783–1790.

63 Daniel Gordon to George Robertson, 24 Nov. 1791, Folder 920 PAR I 50/3, PP.

64 Charles Stewart Parker to John Bolton, 27 May 1798, Folder 920 PAR III 25/ 10, PP.

65 Charles Stewart Parker to James McInroy, 20 Dec. 1803, Folder 920 PAR III 26/20, PP.

66 John Leigh to Captain Brown, 15 Jul. 1806, John Leigh Letterbook 1806–1807. On guarantees in the slave trade see Morgan, 'Remittance Procedures'.

67 Joseph Hadfield to Andrew Clow, 15 Jan. 1790, Folder Joseph, John & Thomas Hadfield, Box 12, Andrew Clow & Co., CWU.

friends on behalf of John Knight. Likewise Curtis Brett had obviously been given a letter of introduction to merchants in New York by a friend David Chambers. Following the use of this letter, Brett wrote that Chambers was under no obligation to his friends in New York on his account as he had received very little civility from them.[68] These examples demonstrate that obligations were built up and paid back in various ways, and certainly not always in 'like kind'. They were also of a rather circular nature. There were occasions when merchants avoided obligations of this sort, but most found having obligations to call on in the future extremely useful.[69]

Payment

Of course, the largest and most significant expectation or obligation was prompt payment. This was important on two levels. Clearly, merchants were obliged to pay their debts at the bilateral level, but the interconnected nature of credit also meant that this was usually a complicated matter and involved (multiple) third parties, especially with regard to bills of exchange. Similarly to Laurens and the non-financial obligations he called upon mentioned above, making payments sometimes incurred new obligations as well. William Wilson, who was mortified concerning his reputation at the beginning of the last chapter, made this explicit when he stated 'We have made a very good shift to pay All your Bills and our own without Any obligations to the Banks, but not without infinite Obligation to kind friends.'[70] He had avoided a debit balance with the bank, but had presumably had to pressurise friends either to lend him some money, or to agree to allow Wilson to defer his payment to them.[71] Family and partners were occasionally given more leeway in making payments. Charles Stewart Parker wrote concerning his partner in Grenada in 1798 that 'George [Robertson] has as my father says been unmerciful in his drafts, the payment of which keeps me amused in my Leisure hours.'[72] It may have been his partner drawing on him, but he still had to pay the bills when they became due. Thomas Leyland was less polite, but made the same point in June 1786. Some fruit he had imported from Seville was of such poor

---

68 Curtis Brett to David Chambers, 13 Mar. 1771, CBL.

69 For a later example of obligation avoidance see Forbes Munro and Tony Slaven, 'Networks and Markets in Clyde Shipping: The Donaldsons and the Hogarths 1970–1939', *BH*, 43:2 (Apr. 2001), 19–50.

70 Observations and Extracts of Affairs, 9 Jul. 1793, Folder Legal, Andrew Clow & Co., Baker Library.

71 Wright argues that banks only really gave loans via discounting bills. However, many account holders went overdrawn and so became borrowers by default. Wright, 'Bank Ownership and Lending Patterns'.

72 Charles Stewart Parker to James McInroy, 15 Aug. 1798, Folder 920 PAR III 26/8, PP.

quality that he wished his agents had rather thrown it over board because he was mortified to have to pay the duty and freight on such bad produce. He explained that to make matters worse, 'I will have to settle these matters with a set of people who will be very rigid in their demands.'[73] No doubt Leyland was cross because he always tried to be very careful regarding his obligations. Responding to a request for a loan just a couple of months later he wrote, 'experience has compelled me to decline all money engagements that exceed the funds in my possession'.[74]

If people wanted to keep a good reputation, they needed to fulfil their obligations to pay even in difficult times. Philadelphian Margaret Duncan imported goods from London via John Ewer from 1771 onwards. She was clearly aware of the importance of having her goods arrive early in the season. Not only did she ask Ewer to ship her chintzes on the first vessel, she even asked him to load them last so that she could get them off first.[75] She paid Ewer regularly using bills of exchange on the best names in Philadelphia. In 1774 it was obvious from her comments about 'our British Task Masters' that she supported the non-importation agreements in principal, but she still promised to try to make a remittance; and indeed she did so in June 1775.[76] As late as September of the same year, another customer of John Ewer, Owen Biddle, sent seven bills of exchange totalling £580.[77] Whether or not Margaret Duncan and Owen Biddle believed full-scale war was coming, they were still determined to pay their debts, which must have proved very difficult. Whether they realised it or not, such acts promoted personal trust and were extremely important in restarting business on independence, when institutional trust was low.[78]

Worrier James Lawson provides a splendid example of the lengths people went to in order to fulfil their obligations. Towards the end of the Seven Years' War, he found the impending peace yet another difficult situation with which he had to deal. He wrote to his partner John Semple to 'exert yourself to settle secure & collect our debts, in the best manner you can think of'.[79] However, in 1765 he still had to write to James Gildart in Liverpool that he

73 Thomas Leyland to Cahill & White, 3 Jun. 1786, TLL.
74 Thomas Leyland to John Cullimore, 12 Aug. 1786, TLL.
75 Margaret Duncan to John Ewer, 23 Nov. 1771, Folder Margaret Duncan to John Ewer, CBP.
76 The non-importation agreement had however, severely hurt her business. Margaret Duncan to John Ewer, 5 Dec. 1774; 3 Jun. 1775, Folder Margaret Duncan to John Ewer, CBP.
77 Owen Biddle to John Ewer, 5 Sep. 1775, Folder Owen Biddle to John Ewer, CBP.
78 On the different levels and types of trust see chapter two.
79 James Lawson to John Semple, 10 Sep. 1762, James Lawson Letterbook 1762–66.

had not received the promised remittances from Semple and did not know of a way to raise the money he owed him.[80] By 1774, having been to Virginia to try to sort out the mess his partner had caused, Lawson wrote that he hoped his creditors were satisfied that he had done all he could: 'when you consider that I have spent nine years of my life to procure that Sum without doing any other thing for myself'.[81] James Lawson's behaviour may have been exemplary, or even excessive, but his story highlights that merchants realised the importance of *being seen* to be doing everything they could to pay off their debts and fulfil their obligations. This was important in gaining some leniency from their fellow merchants, what contemporaries often called 'indulgence'.

Indulgence

The increasing complexity and volume of commerce meant that more and more people were pursuing their debts through the legal system.[82] One has only to look at the large numbers of cases in Chancery in London, the courts in Jamaica, or the debtors' lists for Philadelphia and Liverpool to see evidence of this. At the same time however, the web of credit relations meant that people went to extraordinary lengths to avoid taking disputes through the courts, and so we find that many potential conflicts were resolved by the 'embeddedness of business in social relations'.[83] Many traders and merchants were given extended periods of credit in times of personal or general crisis, and in both Liverpool and Philadelphia, it was often found expedient to give special dispensations to female traders, especially widows. There may have been an element of self-interest here – it was probably more expensive to support women in the poor house than through the extension of credit.[84] Eventually however, debts had to be paid. Insolvents were often handled by local assignees who dealt with the case semi-formally – that is, outside the law – but many tried to stop events going that far in the first place to avoid

---

80 James Lawson to James Gildart, [?] Aug. 1765, James Lawson Letterbook, 1762–66.

81 James Lawson to Thomas Phelps & Co., [?] Sep. 1774, James Lawson Letterbook 1770–76.

82 Muldrew noted that this started in the seventeenth century. See 'The Culture of Reconciliation'. For debtors' prisons and small claims courts see Finn, *The Character of Credit*, chapters three and five.

83 Granovetter, 'Economic Action and Social Structure', p. 497.

84 Women were highly involved in credit and investment at the local and regional level, though some were also involved in international trade. See Haggerty, *The British-Atlantic Trading Community*, chapter five. See also Patricia Cleary, *Elizabeth Murray: A Woman's Pursuit of Independence* (Amherst: University of Massachusetts Press, 2000). In Kingston, Jamaica, women were often given jobs such as Beadle or were paid to house pensioners for much the same reasons. See for example Kingston Vestry Minutes 1765–1770, 2/6/4–5, Jamaica National Archives, Spanishtown.

the financial cost and any potential scandal.[85] Therefore we find that William Davenport used the term indulgence when he found out about the death of a partner in a firm he dealt with, Vance, Caldwell & Vance. The death had caused delays in their payments and he wrote that although the slow payment fell heavy on his house, they would give them every indulgence in their power.[86] William Earle was arbitrating between a John Humphreys and Mr Maine in 1760. His attempts to mediate were not going well, however, and Maine had 'flew off' when Earle had offered Humphrey's terms for the payment of some goods. Earle told Humphreys, 'I wish you wou'd come over yourself. I am sure I shall not settle that Acco[tt] without a Quarrel.'[87] Curtis Brett also tried to mediate between John Mead and David Chambers. He told Mead to let the arbitrators sort it out, that it was better to lose a few hundred (pounds) and that being conciliatory was more likely to lead to happiness.[88] David Tuohy was hardly an elite merchant in Liverpool, but even he accepted that sometimes it was better to simply cut your losses. In 1771 he wrote 'its [sic] better to get anything from this Woman than suffer it to be lost'.[89] Debt forgiveness was clearly not always given with grace.

At the same time, some merchants hoped that threatening to go to court might encourage payment. A year later, David Tuohy wrote to a Mr Southart complaining that he had not sent accounts or payments for a shipment of corn. He added that as he had already deprived him of profits and interest for four and a half months, that he would take unpleasing steps if he did not hear from him soon.[90] In 1786 Thomas Leyland was in a similar situation. He wrote to John Shannon in Ross asking whether Lamphier & Allen had fallen out. Even if they had, he explained, this was no reason not to pay him. Leyland had lost £240 on a deal with them and felt 'compelled to take some disagreeable step to recover from them'.[91] He added that he was determined to expose them in the newspapers or sue them, thereby creating a scandal, telling Shannon that he could show Lamphier & Allen the letter if he thought it would help make them pay. Some disputes could not be settled, and indulgence had its limits. Buchanan & Simson noted that there was likely to be a disagreement with Haliday & Dunbar of Liverpool, the

---

85 For gossip and scandal, see above, pp. 113–21.

86 William Davenport to Vance, Caldwell & Vance, 24 Mar. 1780, WDL.

87 William Earle to John Humphreys, 2 Jul. 1760, Letterbook of William Earle, 2/2, EC.

88 Curtis Brett to John Mead, 20 Sep. 1774, CBL.

89 David Tuohy to Allick Livingstone, 25 Oct. 1771, Letters from David Tuohy, 380 TUO 2/1.

90 Edward Tuohy to Mr Southart, 27 Feb. 1772, Letters from Edward Tuohy, 380 TUO 2/1 DTP.

91 Thomas Leyland to John Shannon, 25 Jul. 1786, TLL.

idea of which they clearly did not relish.[92] James Lawson recognised that his creditors had been indulgent, but as early as February 1765 wrote that 'their patience are all worn out'.[93]

Indulgence was expected even when the status of the correspondents was relatively equal. If someone fulfilled their obligation (in whatever form) this implied an equality of status, whereas not to provide a fair return implied inferiority.[94] Such a sense of inferiority was clearly evident in Metcalf Bowler's begging letters to Brown & Benson, quoted earlier, where he highlighted the relative smallness of his debt to their large fortune and wrote in an extremely subservient tone. Perhaps he truly felt inferior, but it is also just as likely that he used this tone to play on ideas of obligation to the wider community. He was calling on wider socio-cultural understandings of the role of more successful merchants. Elite merchants were respected not only because of their wealth *per se*, but because it was recognised that by investing their capital they promoted both trade and manufacturers.[95] Furthermore, because everyone knew everyone was interconnected, pushing a small trader towards bankruptcy might start a very dangerous 'domino effect'. Whilst the house pressing for payment might survive, many of their other customers in turn, and others in the credit chain, might not. Therefore, elite merchants and others further up the economic ladder were under pressure to tolerate unpaid debts for some time. As we as we have already seen with risk, 'power relationships cannot be neglected'.[96]

Merchants were obviously aware of this sense of hierarchy, both in their own communities and across others. For example, David Tuohy wrote that he did not want to take any favours of a Mr Shaw, 'an opulent merchant', because he did not want to be obliged to him.[97] John Leigh wrote to his correspondent in Barbados, John Gordon, asking him to use his influence to get a Mr Barker to pay his bills.[98] Unfriendly but successful Andrew Clow provides some excellent examples of power relationships and indulgence. He received many letters clearly playing on the power that he had over

---

92 Buchanan & Simson to Capt Buchanan, 29 May 1761, Buchanan & Simson Letterbook.

93 James Lawson to JS [John Semple], 7 Feb. 1765, James Lawson Letterbook 1762–1774.

94 Eugene A. Weinstein, William L. DeVaughan and Mary Glenn Wiley, 'Obligation and the Flow of Deference', *Sociometry*, 32:1 (Mar. 1969), 1–12, p. 1.

95 See discussion above, pp. 1–2, 26.

96 Granovetter, 'Economic Action and Social Structure', p. 502.

97 David Tuohy to Chris Sullivan. c. Apr. 1772, Letters from David Tuohy, 380 TUO 2/1, DTP. There are too many merchants named Shaw in the Liverpool trade directory for 1774 to identify this person. John Gore, ed., *Liverpool Trade Directory* for 1774 (Liverpool: Printed for John Gore, 1774).

98 John Leigh to John Gordon, 5 Nov. 1805, John Leigh Letterbook Apr. 1805–Jul. 1806.

others.[99] William Harris wrote to him from Yorktown in March 1787 begging him not to sue, and promising that he would convince Clow that he would do what was just and right – that is, pay all his bills.[100] Samuel Ryland of Birmingham, England, also wrote to Clow in 1788 in the midst of the many failures of that year, begging him to stop proceedings against Messrs Gilchrist.[101] The Gilchrist's failure would clearly have affected Ryland in some way. Clow was also given a power of attorney by Josef Inardi of Rota, Spain, to collect debts from (and imprison if necessary) Charles Mulvey of Philadelphia. Mulvey wrote to Inardi in December 1789 when he realised that the full details of his situation and debts had been revealed to Clow. Like Bowler, his exasperation showed a little, but the tone was mostly subservient. He played on the fact that Inardi had helped him 'when a poor forlorn Creature' [emphases in original].[102] He tried to explain that a bad sale of Inardi's goods had been made against his [Mulvey's] will, arguing that if he 'should be obliged to turn Bankrupt, as they term it in English, you'll take away from me for ever the means to pay you'.[103] Mulvey had also got married and clearly wanted to allay any fears that he might use this to secure assets in his wife's name, to avoid payment.[104] He added that being married did not mean that he was suddenly a bad man. Mulvey also tried to make himself and his plight identifiable, which often mitigated and constrained those in authority.[105] Inardi was clearly not convinced. 'How can you think that I should have Confidence in You to send you any thing on Your own Acc^t, or for mine, when the first things you solicited to begin with ended so badly.'[106]

---

99 It is not certain that despite his surly nature, that Clow was particularly prone to litigiousness. He does not appear in my sampling of the Pennsylvania debtors' lists except by virtue of his executors. See Exors of Andrew Clow v. William Wilson, 21 Mar. 1797, and Clow & Co., v. Wignall & Reinangle, 18 Mar. 1799, RG33–55 (14–4600) W 1789–1805, Pennsylvania Historical Museum and Commission.

100 William Harris to Andrew Clow, 12 Mar. 1787, Folder Mar.–Apr. 1787, Andrew Clow & Co., SGC.

101 Samuel Ryland to Andrew Clow, 3 Jun. 1788, Folder May–Jun. 1788, Andrew Clow & Co., SGC.

102 Charles Mulvey to Josef Inardi, 10 Dec. 1789, Folder Andrew Clow 1786–89, Andrew Clow & Co., CWU.

103 This was not strictly true. Debtors put in jail for insolvency were even more unlikely to be able to pay their debts than those handled through bankruptcy proceedings. See Hoppit, *Risk and Failure*, chapter three.

104 Generally under British law, debtors could use separate estates to secure money from the claims of creditors. However, in fact, this was rarely upheld in Philadelphia. Salmon, *Women and the Law of Property*, pp. 92–104.

105 Granovetter, 'Economic Action and Social Structure', p. 494.

106 Josef Inardi to Charles Mulvey, 5 Feb. 1790, Folder Andrew Clow 1786–89, Andrew Clow & Co., CWU.

Inardi was angry that Mulvey had not declared the many debts he owed at the start of their relationship, and that he had concealed his marriage (adding to suspicions that he might try to secrete money away). To some extent his begging letter worked, however, perhaps because Inardi wanted to protect his own reputation as a member of the elite in both Rota and Philadelphia. He made an arrangement by which Mulvey, by public deed, would agree to pay Clow the money he owed Inardi in three equal instalments over thirty months. If he agreed to this, Inardi would not prosecute at that time. This, Inardi argued, demonstrated that he possessed 'more humanity than Vigour & that it is not my Intention to hurt any one'.[107] Clearly, Clow, Inardi and Mulvey were aware of the hierarchical nature of their relationships, of Mulvey's obligation to perform his 'contract' and pay, but also Inardi's responsibility not to bring the 'house of cards' of credit tumbling down.[108]

COMMUNITY OBLIGATIONS

WE SAW in the chapter on reputation that people sought a seal of approval through associational networks such as the town council, trade associations, literary and philosophical societies and drinking clubs. The sociability that such membership offered worked as a vital support not only for the individuals, but for the institutions themselves.[109] However, whilst holding these positions increased the reputation of the individual, and sometimes vice versa, they also involved certain responsibilities, or obligations. These could be to the wider trading community, or everyone in the merchant's port who benefitted from the commercial system. Importantly, there was also an obligatory relationship between the mercantile community and the state. As was discussed above, this relationship was important in the construction of assurance (institutional trust), as well as for the reputation of the state itself.[110] The social capital of the various mercantile communities arose and disappeared as by-products of other activities, but merchants created a bank of favours with the state, as well as within their own community, on which they expected to be able to call in times of need.[111] This relationship was often complicated because as Portes points out, whilst social capital can be used by communities as well as individuals,

107 Josef Inardi to Charles Mulvey, 5 Feb. 1790, Folder Andrew Clow 1786–89, Andrew Clow & Co., CWU.
108 The nature of contracts is dealt with above, see pp. 77–84.
109 Fukuyama, *Trust*, p. 325.
110 See above, pp. 86–88, 93–95, 126–27 .
111 Coleman, 'Social Capital in the Creation of Human Capital', p. 118.

the two are not necessarily compatible.[112] Indeed, whilst slave traders in Liverpool were accessing their individual positive social capital through their formal networks, they also created negative social capital for themselves as a group by becoming increasingly isolated and inward-looking.[113] This helps to explain why some power structures are established and maintained, even when past their usefulness.[114] The point is that in order to maintain these individual and community reputations, it was important that individuals within them did something over and above their own immediate interest, and worked for the greater good as well. Each member was therefore a custodian of the group in turn.[115] Adam Smith is worth quoting at length on this point.

> The Man who has performed no single action of importance, but whose whole conversation and deportment express the justest, the noblest, and most generous sentiments, can be entitled to no very high reward, even though his inutility should be owing to nothing but the want of an opportunity to serve. We can still refuse him without blame. We can still ask him, What have you done? What actual service can you produce, to entitle you to so great a recompense? We esteem you, and love you, but we owe you nothing.[116]

Smith clearly saw that some form of service to the wider community was necessary. The obligations that elite merchants might be expected to perform could take many forms. It is not possible to cover all the issues and debates in which elite merchants acted for their community, but a few examples will make the point. Merchants from London, Liverpool, Glasgow and Bristol represented their cities in relation to London, but so too did Jamaicans, and after Independence, United States communities did the same. For example, just before the American War of Independence, Samuel Haliday, John Dobson and John Walker attended parliament in order to defend Liverpool's interest with regard to the impending conflict.[117] The abolition movement gave rise to the Society of West India Planters and Merchants, a London-based pro-slavery group representing the 'West India Interest'. This group

112 Alejandro Portes, 'The Two Meanings of Social Capital', *Sociological Forum*, 15:1 (Mar. 2000), 1–12. p. 4.
113 See Haggerty and Haggerty, 'The Rise and Fall of a Metropolitan Business Network'.
114 Michael Woolcock, 'The Place of Social Capital in Understanding Social and Economic Outcomes', in John F. Helliwell, ed., *The Contribution of Human and Social Capital to Sustained Economic Growth and Well-Being: International Symposium Report* (Canada: OECD and Human Resources Development, 2001), pp. 65–88. Williams may not have used the term social capital, but this is the argument made by him regarding the West India Interest in *Capitalism and Slavery*.
115 Bourdieu, 'The Forms of Capital', p. 104.
116 Smith, *The Theory of Moral Sentiments*, p. 125.
117 'An Abstract of the Proceedings and Resolutions … 1777'.

lobbied parliament against abolition, but also regarding duties and drawbacks on items such as sugar and rum.[118] A variety of Liverpool merchants also gave evidence in the run up to Dolben's Act, including Edgar Corrie, Robert Norris, John Matthews and Archibald Dalziel.[119] Edgar Corrie was in fact in a difficult position because he was against the slave trade, but was an avid collector of trade statistics and so was very useful to the government.[120] We therefore find him corresponding with Baron Hawkesbury (later Lord Liverpool), the President of the Board of Trade, regarding the Corn Laws in the 1790s.[121] Liverpool merchants also petitioned the government on various issues, including restrictions on the exportation of sugar and drawbacks in 1799, and trade to captured West India islands during the French Wars.[122]

Similarly, Philadelphia's Chamber of Commerce also petitioned the government of the United States on various issues. These included the Charter of the Bank of the United States.[123] There were also many petitions during the French and Napoleonic Wars, including the concern with arming vessels during the Napoleonic Wars, and duties on the tonnage of foreign vessels which protected and promoted American shipping.[124] Another problem was the increasing belligerence of the British state. The British government was hostile to neutral shipping, and, the Philadelphians argued, was applying new

---

118 See Ryden, *West Indian Slavery*, passim.

119 Edgar Corrie to Baron Hawlesbury [n.d., c.1788]; Robert Norris, John Matthews, and Archibald Dalziel to Baron Hawkesbury, 5 Jul. 1788, LP, Add. 38416. On Liverpool's reaction to Dolben's Act see F. E. Sanderson, 'Liverpool Abolitionists', in Roger Anstey and P. E. H. Hair, eds., *Liverpool, the African Slave Trade, and Abolition* (Liverpool: Historic Society of Lancashire and Cheshire, Occasional Series, Vol. 2, 1976), 196–238. See also the evidence given in person to the BoT, AQ, I, *passim*.

120 Sydney G. Checkland, *The Gladstones: A Family Biography, 1764–1851* (Cambridge: Cambridge University Press, 1971), pp. 17–18.

121 See for example, Edgar Corrie to Baron Hawkesbury, 23 Jul. 1791, LP, Add. 38226 and *passim*. Charles Jenkinson was made Baron Hawkesbury in 1786 and the first Lord Liverpool in 1796. He was president of the Board of Trade 1786–1804. John Cannon, 'Jenkinson, Charles, first earl of Liverpool (1729–1808)', *Oxford Dictionary of National Biography Online*, accessed 30 Dec. 2010.

122 'The Memorial of the Merchants, Ship Owners and Sugar Refiners and Tradesmen of Liverpool, Whose Names are Hereunto Subscribed', 1799, 380 MD 129, LivRO; Baron Hawkesbury to John Tarleton, 19 Sep. 1794; 28 Nov. 1794, LP, Add. 38310. There are various petitions and memorials from the merchants of Liverpool at TNA under T1 on various subjects including regarding the Royal African Company.

123 Memorial of the Members of the Chamber of Commerce of Philadelphia relative to the Bank of the United States, 1810, LCP.

124 Representation of the Philadelphia Chamber of Commerce; Memorial of the Philadelphia Chamber of Commerce (Printed by order of the Senate of the United States, 25 Jan. 1803), LCP.

principles to justify its behaviour and had 'every sail stretched, to collect the unwary Americans'.[125] Philadelphia merchants also stressed their importance to the economy of the United States in December 1810. In petitioning against the revival of the Non-Intercourse Act they emphasised the amount of capital they had invested in the trade with British merchants. They also highlighted the 'habitual' nature of the trade which allowed them to import supplies on good terms, which was beneficial to the country at large.[126] Interestingly, this is very similar to the arguments made by the British slave traders against abolition.[127] Leading merchants such as Thomas Fitzsimmons, the Philadelphia Chamber's president, were expected to lead the community and take the initiative, as well as put their names to these documents.[128]

Each of the West India islands had agents to represent their interests in London. Stephen Fuller was the agent for Jamaica and also gave evidence to Baron Hawkesbury.[129] Although the rhetoric of the Society of West India Planters and Merchants changed often to suit their current purpose – so much so that Ryden calls the West India interest collectively 'Uncommitted Mercantilists' – they were also 'businessmen who were accustomed to using a rhetoric that emphasized government's obligation' to serve them.[130] We saw in the chapter on reputation that merchants from Jamaica petitioned the British government regarding the effects of stricter enforcement of the Free Ports Act. This was signed by fifty-three merchants or merchant houses, including the Hibberts, Stephens & Raester, and Rainford, Blundell & Rainford.[131] Various merchants from Jamaica also sent letters to their

---

125 They went on to criticise the Spanish and French as well. *Memorial of the Merchants and Traders of Philadelphia*, 15 Jan. 1806 (Washington, 1806).

126 Petition of Sundry Merchants of Philadelphia Praying Exemption from the Provisions in the Non-Intercourse Law, 11 Dec. 1810 (Washington City: Printed by R. C. Weightman, 1810).

127 For the communal response of the Liverpool merchants to abolition, see below, pp. 214–24.

128 Fitzimmons was an energetic leading provisions merchant and as such also represented Pennsylvania at the 1787 Constitutional Convention in Annapolis. Fitzimmons, like Robert Morris, speculated during the American Revolution and eventually went bankrupt. Doerflinger, *A Vigorous Spirit of Enterprise*, pp. 66, 141, 255, 261, 277, 288, 289. Another six of the state's representatives were also leading merchants, Robert Morris, Thomas Mifflin, George Clymer, James Wilson, Gouverneur Morris, Tench Coxe.

129 Stephen Fuller to Baron Hawkesbury, 14 Jul. 1788, LP, Add. 38416. For Fuller and the other West Indian Agents see Ryden, *West Indian Slavery*, esp. pp. 75–81.

130 Indeed, they sometimes attacked the mercantilist system when it suited them. Ryden, *West Indian Slavery*, chapter five, p. 104.

131 The Memorial and Petition of the Merchants of Kingston, c. May 1786, BoT, WI, BT 6/75, f. 44.

correspondents in London to be shown to parliament as evidence regarding hardships in the islands following the American War of Independence. The West Indies had been used to receiving flour and lumber from the northern colonies and now the British wanted them to import from Nova Scotia, the United States no longer being part of the British Empire.[132] These memorials included one from the Council and Assembly of Jamaica, and of course the island's agent, Stephen Fuller, made his representation too.[133]

The various ports in Britain are usually thought of as being in competition with one another at this time, but they did occasionally work together on various issues. In 1783 the merchants of Glasgow's Chamber of Commerce drew up petitions and sent them to Bristol and Liverpool 'in order to have their assistance in procuring redress', regarding the tobacco, sugar, herring and iron trades.[134] The merchants of Liverpool, Manchester and Glasgow had also clearly been working together against the East India Company monopoly before the French Wars pushed other matters to the fore. William Rathbone IV picked up the thread in 1808.[135] He was also called upon in that year to give evidence to the House of Commons regarding the 1807 Orders in Council, along with fellow Liverpool merchants Thomas Martin and Thomas Cropper. Many merchants, brokers and manufacturers from London, Manchester, Wakefield and Paisley also gave evidence at these inquiries.[136]

There was therefore a complex web of obligations between the various trading communities and the state. Moreover, elite merchants were under many obligations to protect and represent their trading communities. Whilst it is true they were protecting their own interests at the same time, these obligatory duties were often time-consuming, involved staying away from

---

132 See the various letters in BoT, America and West Indies: Commercial Intercourse, BT 6/83, Vols I and II, TNA.

133 The Humble Memorial and Petition of the Council and Assembly of Jamaica, 11 Dec. 1784, f. 19; The Representation of Stephen Fuller, Esq, Agent for Jamaica to His Majesty's Minister, f. 23, 8 Mar. 1785, BoT, America and West Indies: Commercial Intercourse, BT 6/83, Vol. I. For more on the relationship between the British West Indies and the United States following 1783 see Alice B. Keith, 'Relaxations in the British Restrictions on the American Trade with the British West Indies, 1783–1802', *Journal of Modern History*, 20:1 (1948), 1–18. For the West India lobbyists see Andrew. J. O'Shaughnessy, 'The Formation of a Commercial Lobby: The West India Interest, British Colonial Policy and the American Revolution', *The Historical Journal*, 40:1 (1997) 71–95.

134 Minutes, 18 Feb. 1783; 7 Mar. 1783, Chamber of Commerce and Manufacturers in the City of Glasgow, Vol. I, 1783–88.

135 William Rathbone to Lord Lauderdale, 10 Oct. 1808; 17 Oct. 1808, William Rathbone Letterbook.

136 Minutes of Evidence, HCPP, 1801 (119), pp. 260, 229, 259 and *passim*.

home and a good deal of concentration and effort in not only writing up these memorials and petitions, but in personally answering questions in parliament as well. Having invested their time and money into not only their own port, but the empire more widely, merchants expected the British state to reciprocate. When these relations became too strained, they often led to conflicts, such as the American War of Independence, the abolition of the British slave trade and the Anglo-American War (these three events are discussed in detail in the chapter on crises). There was clearly an important relationship between the mercantile communities which provided much of the finance for empire, and the state.[137] Through investing in empire, the various trading communities built up a stock of social as well as financial capital with the state, whether in Britain or the United States. Indeed, many merchants in Britain also had an investment in the eastward empire too. This was a positive investment strategy, promoted by the state, and merchants expected to be able to call on the state to support them in return for these 'gifts', and in a demonstration of mutual knowledge and respect.[138] We saw in the chapters on trust and reputation that the laws and institutions of the state were an important part of establishing assurance which facilitated trade in the absence of personal trust. The government was therefore expected to protect mercantile investments by protecting their property in its various forms.

In this regard the merchants of Liverpool found Baron Hawkesbury to be an extremely useful ally, and they offered him the freedom of the city in 1796 (the same year he was made Lord Liverpool). His response clearly elucidates the relationship between merchants and the state. He wrote that being sensible of the high complement paid to me:

> by a Corporation so respectable as that of Liverpool, for it affords a proof of their Approbation of my Endeavours to be of Service to the Commerce and Navigation of this Country ... and I shall feel a pride in bearing with the Arms of my Family, those of a Corporation composed of many wealthy, intelligent and respectable Merchants who by their extraordinary Industry and Enterprize, have contributed in so great a Degree to [a]ugment the Commerce and Navigation of Great Britain.[139]

This augmentation was achieved both by involvement in trade, and through investing in empire more directly by purchasing government bonds and consuls, and shares in chartered companies. Simply being involved in overseas

---

137 Bowen, *Elites, Enterprise*, p. 47.
138 Bourdieu, 'The Forms of Capital', p. 103.
139 Lord Liverpool to Thomas Naylor, 16 Jul. 1796, LP, Add. 38310.

trade as an elite merchant required a large amount of capital. A minimum of £1,000 was needed to set up a merchant house, more commonly around £5,000 was necessary, and sometimes up to £10,000 was required. Merchants also built up capital over time and some Glasgow firms involved in the lucrative tobacco trade acquired capital of up to £50,000.[140] Collectively the credit extended overseas by British merchants was impressive: in 1766 the debts owed to Britain from the American mainland totalled £4,450,000, and in 1791 it was estimated that over £4,984,655 5s. 8d. was still owed by Americans to some 200 British firms.[141] During the abolition debates it was claimed that the value of investment in the British West Indies was somewhere around £70–80 million.[142] Indeed, Liverpool alone was said to have around £200,000 invested in the slave trade in 1750, which increased to £2,641,200 by 1807.[143] One merchant, William Davenport of Liverpool, invested £60,000 in slave voyages between 1757 and 1784 on his own account.[144]

As mentioned previously, Malachy Postlethwayt realised the importance of mercantile investment in bonds and consuls in supporting the war effort.[145] Indeed, the British national debt grew from £16.7 million in 1697 to £242.9 million in 1784 and many merchants were heavily involved in funding this.[146] Samuel Rainford charged his friend Edward Chaffers with investing in bonds on his behalf, as did many others.[147] The Americans were involved in similar investments in their own government. William Wilson, in financial trouble as we have already seen, heavily invested in bonds.[148] A Philadelphia merchant house, Reed & Forde, invested in £1,436 worth of securities between January 1785 and December 1788, and made sales worth £2,577 over the same period.[149] Others invested in chartered companies. For example,

---

140 Bowen, *Elites, Enterprise*, pp. 57–58.

141 Bowen, *Elites, Enterprise*, pp. 93–94.

142 Evidence of George Hibbert, 20 Mar. 1790, HCSP, Vol. 72; Roger Anstey, *The Atlantic Slave Trade and British Abolition 1760–1810* (London: Macmillan, 1975), p. 309.

143 Kenneth Morgan, 'Liverpool's Dominance in the British Slave Trade, 1740–1807', in Richardson et al., *Liverpool and Transatlantic Slavery*, pp. 14–42, p. 15.

144 David Richardson, 'Profits in the Liverpool Slave Trade: the Accounts of William Davenport, 1757–1784', in Anstey and Hair, *Liverpool, the African Slave Trade*, pp. 60–90, p. 64.

145 See pp. 86–87.

146 Bowen, *Elites, Enterprise*, p. 83.

147 See for example Samuel Rainford to Edward Chaffers, 26 Aug. 1796, 920 CHA/1/2, PEC.

148 See the letters between William Wilson and Andrew Clow, Folder One, Andrew Clow & Co., Letters Received 1790–93, Baker Library.

149 Doerflinger, *A Vigorous Spirit of Enterprise*, p. 310. These were investments in federal securities, but accounts in the United States were still usually kept in sterling.

anyone, including foreigners, could purchase East India Stock. By the early nineteenth century, the company had a capital of £6 million, made up of investments as small as the 8s 10d. invested by spinster Ann Wright, to as much as £40,000 by Elijah Pereira Davidz.[150] It is clear that investments from merchants were important to the British imperial enterprise and to the early American Republic.

Having invested in empire or state in various ways, an activity promoted by the British government through colonial 'policy' such as chartered companies and the navigation acts, merchants expected that investment to be protected.[151] Whilst there have been debates as to whether 'mercantilism' ever existed as a policy, contemporaries certainly thought it did, or at least that some obligatory relationship based on these ideas pertained.[152] The purpose of wars was not only the aggrandizement and honour of the British Empire *per se*, but the increase of its commerce, and therefore the wealth of the empire and its mercantile citizens. Merchants regarded the Royal Navy as an instrument of this trade policy.[153] This dynamic was well expressed by McKnight & McIlwrath of Ayr when they wrote to their New York correspondent in 1800. 'We have taken Malta and will soon kick Bounapartes fava[r]ite expedition out of Egypt Where we will establish a depot for our eastern Commodities'; he added for good measure, 'Bounaparte is blowing the Coal and inviting everyone to bite us who can as he can only bark.'[154] However, it was not enough to simply take territory, it should also be advantageous to the British economy. In 1796 *The Times* had argued that peace should not be made if the conditions set by our enemies were disgraceful, rather peace should 'secure to us every channel of foreign commerce'.[155] Two years later an editorial in

150 Bowen, *The Business of Empire*, pp. 97, 85.
151 Policy is in inverted commas because there is a debate as to what extent not only mercantilism existed, but if so, whether it ever constituted a policy as such. See the essays in Coleman, *Revisions in Mercantilism*.
152 See the points made above, pp. 4, 17.
153 Patricia Crimmin, 'The Royal Navy and the Levant Trade c. 1795-c.1805', in Jeremy Black and Philip Woodfine, eds., *The British Royal Navy and the Use of Naval Power in the Eighteenth Century* (Leicester: Leicester University Press, 1988), pp. 221–36.
154 McKnight was referring to the Levant trade. McKnight & McIlwrath to Andrew Smith, 20 Oct. 1800, McKnight & McIlwrath Letterbook, NAS. France dominated the European trade to the Levant and was strong in the region. Napoleon had invaded Egypt in 1798 in order to protect France's interests there. Crimmin, 'The Royal Navy'.
155 *The Times*, 10 Dec. 1796, p. 2. For arguments about the policy behind wars in the period see Jeremy Black, *Trade, Empire and British Foreign Policy, 1689–1815* (New York: Routledge, 2007); Richard Pares, 'American versus Continental Warfare, 1739–1763', *The English Historical Review*, 31:203 (Jul. 1936); 429–65; Baugh, 'Great Britain's "Blue-Water" Policy'.

The Times during the French Wars said that it was all very well celebrating Nelson's victory at Aboukir Bay (Egypt), but whilst we must think about peace, 'it must be a solid, advantageous, and honourable peace'.[156]

Once taken, merchants trading from and to these newly-gained territories, along with established ones, wanted protection for their shipping because they felt vulnerable to attack from the enemy. The most usual way in which this was done was through the convoy system. Convoys had been used to protect British trade since the Restoration against the Barbary corsairs. They were used increasingly, and more effectively, throughout the eighteenth century.[157] They were finally formalized by the Convoy Act (1793) and Compulsory Convoy Act (1798).[158] Not that merchants were always satisfied with these arrangements. In 1815 various papers were presented to the House of Commons including memorials from the London Assurance Companies, the Merchants of Liverpool, Bristol, Port Glasgow and Greenock, and those with particular interest in the Irish trade. They were generally complaining about the losses to American privateers and cruisers due to the 'insufficient protection of the Trade at Sea'.[159] Note that by this point in time American shipping had grown to the extent that the Americans were perceived in Britain as the predominant threat from privateering. American privateers were seen off the coast of Lundy (an island just off the north coast of Devon in south-west England). Even worse, the American privateers had lately taken to burning vessels that they could not get back to a port; sacrilege to shipowners. Moreover, insurance premiums were also becoming excessive. A petition of the merchants of Glasgow in 1815 was signed by 554 persons who complained that they felt that they had been treated with 'coldness and neglect' by His Majesty's Government.[160] Not that the Americans were the only ones engaged in privateering of course. During the Seven Years' War over 1,679 vessels were involved in privateering authorised by the British

---

156 *The Times*, 10 Oct. 1798, p. 2. Not that such conquests and investments always went well, as Ryden has shown. Whilst many West India islands were taken during the wars, this caused problems with prices; 'aggregate demand and supply for sugar was constantly changing', as did prices of land and slaves. Ryden, *West Indian Slavery*, chapter nine, p. 236.

157 See for example the references to convoys in Mouser, *A Slaving Voyage*, pp. 111–12, 116–17, 119.

158 J. R. Jones, 'Limitations of British Sea Power in the French Wars, 1689–1815', in Black and Woodfine, *The British Royal Navy*, pp. 33–49.

159 Papers Presented to the Honourable House of Commons, 1 Feb. 1815, Papers Relating to the War with America: 1815, HCPP, 1814–15 (45) (60).

160 [Copy of] Petition of the Merchants, Manufacturers, Ship Owners, and Underwriters of the City of Glasgow, [n.d.], Papers Relating to the War with America: 1815, HCPP, 1814–15 (45) (60).

government. London sent out 648 of these, Bristol 253, Liverpool 246 and Glasgow and Dublin 21 each. In addition, 3 were sent from Jamaica, 3 from New York, 1 from Philadelphia and another from Quebec. During the American Revolution London was responsible for 719, Bristol 20, Liverpool 390 and Glasgow 123. A further 8 belonged to occupied New York, 7 from Jamaica and 204 from all around Ireland. The numbers were even higher during the French and Napoleonic Wars.[161]

These complaints demonstrate that when the state did not fulfil its obligations to them, the mercantile community felt betrayed. Obviously there was a great deal of posturing going on here, but such complaints and feelings increased at the turn of the nineteenth century. The merchants in these port cities had had a powerful voice in government, through their reputations as successful places of trade, as well as through lobbying or parliamentary representation, but the situation was changing. Chartered companies were becoming less powerful on the whole – the East India Company excepted, and even its role had changed considerably.[162] Mercantilist policy, real or imagined, was on the decline and this was changing the nature of the obligatory relationship between the mercantile community and the state. Early signs of this were seen during the debates on abolition, when it was clear that merchants thought that colonial law was being violated.[163] The 'West India Interest' at least had found that its social capital had been spent and it was no longer to be indulged by the state.[164]

CONCLUSION

O BLIGATIONS were an important part of the business culture in this period. Clearly understood procedural norms led to an environment of realistic expectations as to how people would perform. Moreover, Metcalf Bowler's story highlights the fact that obligations involved far more than one-to-one reciprocity, and that power and reputation also came into play. Gifts were often given in terms of time, services performed, or credit

---

161 More vessels were always commissioned than actually fitted out. Starkey, *British Privateering Enterprise*, pp. 165, 200, 322–23. For more on Liverpool see Williams, *History of the Liverpool Privateers*; Bristol often concentrated on privateering to the detriment of its normal commerce. Morgan, *Bristol and the Atlantic Trade*, pp. 19–22.
162 See above pp. 15, 18, 20.
163 Ryden notes that their argument that changing the rules of colonisation was unconstitutional is often forgotten. *West Indian Slavery*, p. 196. See below, pp. 215–18.
164 Fukuyama argues that habits and customs are clung onto for a long time, but once social capital is spent, it takes a long time to rebuild. *Trust*, p. 321.

advanced, but the fact that actual presents were also given demonstrates that affective relationships were established and maintained, even at a distance. The performance (and occasionally over-performance) of procedural norms protected present and future reputations, but also created an environment of expectations which everyone understood. However, these expectations clearly became obligations when they were not performed and in these cases indulgence was often called upon. Indulgence was, however, a rational form of cost-effective behaviour.[165] For our merchants, avoiding the legal system kept transaction costs low, but such behaviour was shaped by socio-cultural norms concerning the role of elite merchants. The sociability afforded, and social capital accessed by, formal and informal institutions, whilst conferring status on merchants, also entailed performing obligatory services for others reliant on commerce, including negotiating with the state on their behalf. This obligatory relationship with the state, although more contested at the end of the period, was important for the creation of assurance and confidence. Reputational mechanisms and obligations therefore helped to create an environment in which the trading community was involved in a high level of 'self-enforcing governance' through fulfilling expectations and obligations.[166] We shall now see how these elements worked when tested by the merchants' own networks and crises.

---

165 Uzzi, 'Embeddedness in the Making of Financial Capital', p. 484.
166 Uzzi, 'Embeddedness in the Making of Financial Capital', p. 483.

6

Networks

The trade of this Country and City I apprehend
will go into New Hands so I hope to have a
fair Chance as the oldest settler.[1]

ALEXANDER JOHNSTON wrote this comment about New York to a correspondent in Scotland in 1783. Johnston had decided to set up in business there having travelled around the Atlantic sorting out his financial affairs. He obviously saw that new opportunities would be available to men like him following the American War of Independence. In order to organise his new trading venture as best as possible, he had set up a new partnership in St. Kitts where he had been in business for some time with his brother and a Mr Moore, and another house, under the name of John Stewart & Co., in St. Eustatia. Johnston had also visited London, Baltimore and Philadelphia in the previous two years, but he clearly sensed, quite prophetically, that New York's role as a port city was going to be increasingly important.[2] Johnston reasoned that because many established merchants were leaving the city, it would be easier to construct new networks.[3] Interestingly, he also noted that the habits, manners and customs of people in New York were quite European,

---

1 Alexander Johnston to Thomas Gordon, 3 Dec. 1783, AJL.
2 New York took over from Philadelphia as the leading eastern seaboard port by the first decade of the nineteenth century. Doerflinger, *A Vigorous Spirit of Enterprise*, p. 342.
3 Many British factors and loyalists left the city, others would have been forced out by the dislocation of war, and new opportunities for building networks were also created by the new states no longer being under the jurisdiction of the Navigation Acts. See Margaret E. Newell, *From Dependency to Independence: Economic Revolution in Colonial New England* (Ithaca and London: Cornell University Press, 1998), chapter fourteen.

and that this was agreeable to him. Presumably this common cultural ground made it easier to trust people.

Johnston's comments raise many of the issues covered in previous chapters. He was prepared to risk establishing a new business despite the changing institutional framework. He had constructed personal trust with enough people in order to set up in business and clearly general levels of trust were returning. Johnston needed to build up his own reputation, no doubt using existing ties with people he had met during his travels, but the fact that many established merchants were leaving New York meant that many old obligational relationships were being severed in the city, giving him the chance to build up his own. The whole situation highlights the constantly changing nature of networks. They are dynamic and instrumental.

This chapter is the first of two, based around case studies, which bring the themes of risk, trust, reputation and obligation together. The term network(s) is the most often borrowed by historians from socio-economics, but much of the analysis remains broadly positive.[4] In contrast, this chapter stresses two points: the problems of networks and how they can hinder progress or are otherwise detrimental, and how they change over time.[5] This chapter therefore first outlines various existing definitions and the function of networks, including positing a definition of business networks for use here. It then considers some of the problems associated with networks. Three case studies are then presented which highlight these issues, before concluding. Using case studies facilitates an understanding of how the actions of individuals interface with, react to, and help to develop, the wider economy.

Networks: Definition and Function

Despite the recent interest in using networks for historical analysis, the concept is nothing new.[6] Eighteenth-century merchants were well aware of the use, benefits and problems of networks, they simply called the other actors 'friends' or 'correspondents'.[7] However, social scientists have been much more active than historians in defining networks, in terms of both membership and function. Laurel Smith-Doerr and Walter Powell

---

4 See below, pp. 165–69.

5 Smith-Doerr and Powell have called for this approach. Laurel Smith-Doerr and Walter W. Powell, 'Networks and Economic Life', in Smelser and Swedberg, *The Handbook of Economic Sociology*, pp. 379–402, pp. 395, 389, 393.

6 Paul Duguid, 'Networks and Knowledge: The Beginning and End of the Port Commodity Chain, 1703–1860', *BH*, 79 (Autumn 2004), 492–526, p. 493.

7 Hancock, 'The Trouble with Networks', pp. 472–73.

define them as 'a set of actors, with specific types of connections to one another'.[8] Mark Casson in a chapter on regional business networks simply defines them as *a set of high-trust linkages connecting a set of people* [stress in original].[9] Joel Podolny and Karen Page consider them to be *any collection of actors (N≥2) that pursue repeated, enduring exchange relations with one another and, at the same time, lack a legitimate organizational authority to arbitrate and resolve disputes that may arise during the exchange* [stress in original].[10] Some have posited definitions of networks for certain groups such as James Rauch who defines co-ethnic networks as 'communities of individuals or businesses that share a demographic attribute such as ethnicity or religion'.[11] Stanley Wasserman and Katherine Faust contend that a social network 'consists of a finite set or sets of actors and the relation or relations defined upon them'.[12] All of these definitions use the terms connections or relationships. Indeed, Wasserman and Faust argue that this relational information – the relationship between the actors – is the critical and defining feature of a network. We cannot therefore simply say because a group of people know each other that they belong to a network. There has to be something that binds them together, that makes them instrumental.

Networks therefore have a purpose or function. In terms of business networks, Podolny and Page argue for three. First they should promote the rapid transfer of information, which may also be synthesized and yield new knowledge or understanding. Second, membership of a network may infer status and legitimacy (we saw clear evidence of this in the chapters on reputation and obligation). Third, there should be economic benefits such as lower information and transaction costs and the ability to adapt to environmental changes – of which there were plenty in our period.[13] Rauch adds that networks should promote international trade by alleviating problems of contract enforcement and asymmetrical information, and by providing information about new trading opportunities.[14] Renzulli et al. also stress the active nature of business networks, arguing that they should provide

8 Smith-Doerr and Powell, 'Networks and Economic Life', p. 381.

9 Casson, 'An Economic Approach to Regional Business Networks', p. 28.

10 Joel M. Podolny and Karen L. Page, 'Network Forms of Organization', *Annual Review of Sociology*, 24 (1998), 57–76, p. 59.

11 James E. Rauch, 'Business and Social Networks in International Trade', *Journal of Economic Literature*, 39 (Dec. 2001), 1177–1203, p. 1178.

12 Stanley Wasserman and Katherine Faust, *Social Network Analysis: Methods and Applications* (Cambridge: Cambridge University Press, 1994), p. 20.

13 Podolny and Page, 'Network Forms of Organization', pp. 62–66. On information and transaction costs see Casson, 'Institutional Economics and Business History'.

14 Rauch, 'Business and Social Networks', p. 1200.

instrumental support, as opposed to 'background' networks which should provide more general support.[15] Usually of course, business and personal networks overlapped and intertwined, then as now. Smith-Doerr and Powell therefore argue that economic networks represent informal relationships where social and economic ties are interwoven in such a way that purposeful activity becomes entangled with friendship, reputation and trust. Networks should therefore influence and not simply facilitate economic activity. Moreover, it is clear that individual networks should not only benefit the actors within it, but produce wider economic benefits as well. However, it is worth noting that whilst these networks represent formal exchanges, resource provision or pooling that lead to interdependence and a form of relational governance, for example, through reputation mechanisms, they can also be tapped to the detriment of others through negative social capital.[16]

Networks are of course, constructed, used and abused in historically-specific contexts. Therefore, none of the above definitions quite suit the context of eighteenth-century Atlantic commerce. Smith-Doerr and Powell's, and Wasserman and Faust's are too vague, and Rauch's is too limiting considering the vast amount of cross-cultural trade that occurred in our period. Casson's simplistic stress on trust will not do either because as we saw in the chapter on trust, levels and types of trust fluctuated over time and interacted with one another. At the same time, there were often (though not always) institutions in place that provided our merchants with assurance should their personal trust relations fail; which also makes Podolny and Page's definition inadequate. Therefore, for the purposes of this book business networks are defined as *a group or groups of people that form associations with the explicit or implicit expectation of mutual long-term economic benefit*. This definition does not exclude cross-cultural trade but does allow for familial, religious or ethnic ties and predominantly socio-cultural relationships where they existed. The potentially long-term nature of networks and the changing institutional environment are allowed for. It also encompasses the fact that there were many different, but often interlinked, networks around the Atlantic. Finally, it defines their instrumental nature. Merchants wanted to build trade and thereby make money.

---

15 Linda A. Renzulli, Howard Aldrich and James Moody, 'Family Matters: Gender, Networks, and Entrepreneurial Outcomes', *Social Forces*, 79:2 (Dec. 2000), 523–46, p. 537; Laird, *Pull*, pp. 28–29.

16 Smith-Doerr and Powell, 'Networks and Economic Life', pp. 379–80. See the discussion on social capital above, pp. 135–36.

PROBLEMATIZING NETWORKS

Now THAT WE HAVE a definition and function of business networks, it is possible to assess their potential for success over time and consider the problems associated with them. One issue is what Yoram Ben-Porath calls the 'implicit contract of family'.[17] The 'kinship nexus' persists as a positive feature of networks in historical research because it is assumed to reduce moral hazard.[18] It has also been posited that the reason why small businesses did not adapt to limited liability quickly was because the family firm, with its implicit trust, was an adaptable business model.[19] However, as Graeme Milne has shown for the mid-nineteenth century, joint stock companies were seen as a last resort for struggling traders or as 'risky schemes for great wealth'.[20] They were therefore adopted only cautiously – whether or not family firms were involved – because they had negative connotations for reputation. It may also have simply been that small partnerships, whether family-based or not, could adapt to change more quickly.[21] Certainly our merchants were often involved in a variety of partnerships at any one time. Furthermore, Renzulli et al. have argued that kinship ties can be restrictive by providing only low levels of new information, based as they are on strong ties, and Tilly demonstrates that ethnic networks can be similarly problematic.[22] Such networks do provide support, but also mean that members do not consider other, potentially better, options.[23] In fact, contemporaries were more pragmatic than historians sometimes give them credit for. For example, the networks of elite Marylanders went far beyond personal and marriage ties, and as early as the seventeenth century, economic exigency trumped ethnic, national and religious ties for Massachusetts merchants.[24] Whilst it is true that family, ethnic or religious networks may have provided strong

---

17 Ben-Porath, 'The F-Connection', p. 1.
18 Mathias, 'Risk, Credit and Kinship'.
19 Rose, 'The Family Firm in British Business'.
20 Graeme J. Milne, *Trade and Traders in Mid-Victorian Liverpool* (Liverpool: Liverpool University Press, 2000), p. 162.
21 Smith-Doerr and Powell, 'Networks and Economic Life', p. 389.
22 Renzulli et al., 'Family Matters', p. 525. Charles Tilly, 'Transplanted Networks', in Virginia Yans-McLaughlin, ed., *Immigration Reconsidered: History, Sociology, and Politics* (New York and Oxford: Oxford University Press, 1995), pp. 79–95, p. 84.
23 Maria Jacqueline Hagan, 'Social Networks, Gender and Immigrant Incorporation: Resources and Constraints', *American Sociological Review*, 63:1 (Feb. 1998), 55–67, p. 55.
24 Trevor Burnard, 'A Tangled Cousinry? Associational Networks of the Maryland Elite, 1691–1776', *Journal of Southern History*, 61:1 (Feb. 1995), 17–44; Marsha L. Hamilton, *Social and Economic Networks in Early Massachusetts: Atlantic Connections* (Pennsylvania: Pennsylvania University Press, 2009), especially introduction and chapter four.

reputational mechanisms and specific cultural market information, they also faced ostracism.[25] This certainly occurred in the cases of Jews and Quakers in our period, despite the fact that the latter were perceived to have a highly moralistic business culture.[26] This has caused Rauch to conclude that the exclusiveness of ethnic networks has been exaggerated, and that the stress on them is due to observability rather than primacy of importance.[27] If family, ethnic and religious ties are insufficient to explain networks, it is clear that merchants needed to build up and develop their weak ties over time. In Pamela Laird's terms, they needed to establish peer and authority networks in addition to their background ones.[28] Irishman David Tuohy maintained many family and ethnic trading correspondents throughout his career. However, after having spent many years as a slave ship captain he settled in Liverpool. By 1784 he had constructed new and wider ties and co-invested with others in the slave trade, as well as continuing to help out his family and other Irish contacts.[29] In developing such ties, and in order to develop their business, people such as Tuohy created new identities and networks along the way.[30]

The fact that actors are always developing new (and losing existing) ties shows that networks are dynamic. It also means that actors within networks have different values to the central actor (from the analyst's point of view), what Granovetter has called weak and strong ties. Clearly, not all ties are equally valuable or comparable, and ties may well be used for different purposes, through a number of different interlinking networks. For example,

---

25 See for example, Walvin, *The Quakers*, Tolles, *Meeting House and Counting House*; Prior and Kirby, 'The Society of Friends'; Rauch, 'Business and Social Networks', pp. 1184–86. See also Hamilton on the Scots, *Scotland, the Caribbean and the Atlantic*; Greif on the Maghrabi, *Institutions and the Path to the Modern Economy*; Søren Mentz, 'The Commercial Culture of the Armenian Merchant: Diaspora and Social Behaviour', *Itinerario*, 28:1 (2004), 16–28.

26 The Quakers in Philadelphia experienced the wrath of other merchants for their anti-war stance for example. Doerflinger, *A Vigorous Spirit of Enterprise*, pp. 218–23; Tolles, *Meeting House and Counting House*, pp. 17–19, 24–27. See also Trivellato, *The Familiarity of Strangers*.

27 Rauch, 'Business and Social Networks', pp. 1183, 1178.

28 Laird, *Pull*, pp. 28–29.

29 See for example, Ships Papers, Ingram, 380 TUO 4/10. He co-invested with John Clemison, John Kaye, George Johnston, James Carruthers, Ingram & Butler and George McMinn, DTP passim. He invested in a total of ten slave trade voyages between 1781 and 1788, centred around Francis Ingram, Christopher Butler, John Clemison, James Ingram, but also with Thomas Parke and Benjamin Heywood amongst others. See Eltis et al., *The Trans-Atlantic Slave Trade Database*, voyages 80578, 80579, 80581, 81028, 81148, 81247, 81248, 81249, 81906, 81907.

30 Hagan, 'Social Networks', p. 60–64; Tilly, 'Transplanted Networks', p. 85.

at the local level a merchant might have used the exchange to get the latest trade information from a relatively weak tie, used his friends at a charitable institution to build up his civic reputation, and built up a denser network of ties in the taverns and inns with those who had money to invest. Indeed, dense ties are often used to facilitate lending and sponsorship, especially in high-risk scenarios, but this is not to say that they are unproblematic.[31] Tim Crumplin has shown that dense networks can become opaque, meaning that cliques of members can get out of control, and therefore have dubious benefits.[32] At the other end of the scale, building up weak ties was especially important if the weak tie acted as a bridge to other networks.[33] For example, in Liverpool, it was useful to know the Heywoods and Leyland & Bullins, because both houses had good contacts in London, with Denison's and Masterman's banks respectively. This made them good bridges or brokers, with the potential to best synthesize information and thereby have good ideas.[34] As rich merchants and bankers with links to institutions such as the Town Council and the African Company of Merchants Trading from Liverpool, they were also in a powerful position in a variety of local networks.[35] At the same time, as Hancock and Andrew Popp have demonstrated, both strong and weak ties can be expensive and time-consuming to construct and maintain.[36] Furthermore, family members might expect siblings or children to spend lots of time with them, and as we have seen, certain members of the Bright-Meyler network in the West Indies caused problems for their compatriots in Bristol. Even useful friendships centred around social clubs or the Exchange might also be time-consuming to maintain, and power relationships may still come into play. Therefore we cannot simply equate strong ties with positive ties, or assume that strong ties are less problematic and more reliable than weak ones.

It is clear that relationships within a network are not equal. This means

---

31 Smith-Doerr and Powell, 'Networks and Economic Life', pp. 383–84.

32 Tim E. Crumplin, 'Opaque Networks: Business and Community in the Isle of Man, 1840–1900', *BH*, 49:6 (Nov. 2007), 780–801.

33 As Granovetter highlights, not all weak ties are useful ties, 'The Strength of Weak Ties', p. 1364.

34 Ronald D. Burt, 'Structural Holes and Good Ideas', *AJS*, 10:2 (2004), 349–99.

35 Thomas Leyland was elected onto the council as a Bailiff in 1796 and served as Mayor in 1798 and 1814. The Heywood family were on the Committee of the African Company from the early 1750s into the 1790s. Minutes of the Town Council; Minutes of the Committee of the African Company of Merchants Trading from Liverpool.

36 Hancock, 'The Trouble with Networks'; Andrew Popp talks of the 'punishing schedule' involved, 'Building the Market: John Shaw of Wolverhampton and Commercial Travelling in Early Nineteenth-Century England', *BH*, 49:3 (May 2007), 321–47.

that power relationships also play a role.[37] In the previous chapter we saw the begging letters sent to the Browns in Providence and Andrew Clow in Philadelphia. These merchants were seen to have the power in those relationships. Whilst Lawler and Yoon suggest that equal power should produce positive effects such as reduced hostility and more concessions, it is obvious that conversely, unequal power can cause friction.[38] This is not to say that only the elite have power. The Browns and Clow were quite wealthy individuals, but power is relative; it is the degree of dependency that is important.[39] As Bonacich argues, 'Power comes from being connected to those who are powerless'; someone with less options than you.[40] Being relatively powerless affects people's behaviour. Actors are likely to concede more when excluded, or when there is a threat of exclusion from a network. Once included, actors will often reduce their offers to other actors.[41] For example, when Henry Lauren's protégés Hest & Head were starting up in business in Charleston, they would probably have accepted any commission business sent their way.[42] Later on, when established, they would have been able to pick and choose who to do business with based on past experience and present opportunities. Being powerful within a network therefore gives an actor more independence and freedom of choice, but does not necessarily means that they are a powerful actor within the larger networks around the Atlantic.[43] The actor's position within the network is important, but they do not necessarily need to be at the centre in order to have power. Moreover, an actor can be relatively powerless in one network, but relatively powerful in another.

Earlier chapters have demonstrated that networks were mostly positive. Repeated exchange helped turn weak ties into strong ties, and real friendships were formed, even when two merchants had either never met, or saw each other only very infrequently. For many, the emotional buzz caused by successful iterative exchange relations led to real affective commitment which

---

37 It is possible to measure these power relationships. See Haggerty and Haggerty, 'Visual Analytics'; Wasserman and Faust, *Social Network Analysis*.

38 Lawler and Yoon, 'Commitment in Exchange Relations'.

39 Smith-Doerr and Powell, 'Networks and Economic Life', p. 383.

40 Phillip Bonacich, 'Power and Centrality: A Family of Measures' *American Journal of Sociology*, 92:2 (Mar. 1987), 1170–82, pp. 1171, 1776.

41 Shane R. Thye, Michael J. Lovaglia and Barry Markovsky, 'Responses to Social Exchange and Social Exclusion in Networks', *Social Forces*, 75:3 (Mar. 1997), 1031–47, pp. 1031–33.

42 See above, pp. 40, 77.

43 Linton C. Freeman, 'Centrality in Social Networks: Conceptual Clarification', *Social Networks*, 1 (1978–79), 215–39.

led to gift giving, 'staying' and contributing together.[44] For example, we saw above that Samuel Rainford, Joshua Johnson and Henry Laurens liked to send gifts to their friends around the Atlantic.[45] In 1801 George Plumstead of Philadelphia sent a doll to a little girl known to a correspondent, and Liverpudlian Thomas Mears sent Henry Laurens' wife roots and seeds for her garden.[46] We have also seen that there was a preference for staying with established, reliable correspondents. Peter Wikoff did 'not chuse [sic] to differ with old correspondents' and John Leigh stayed with Isaac Barker of St. Vincent because the latter made prompt remittance.[47] There are also countless instances of contributing (co-investing) which highlight the affective and trusting nature of these relationships even at a distance. Joseph Wharton of Philadelphia and Joseph Manesty of Liverpool co-owned the *Barter* in 1764.[48] Again in the 1760s, Chaloner Arcedeckne in Bath (but who owned an estate in Jamaica) joined forces with Chisholme Laing (a ship's captain) and George Chandler in London, amongst others, in a vessel to be stationed at Morant Bay, Jamaica.[49] However, it is important to recognise that such relationships were entangled and complicated and that they changed over time. The purpose here is not to argue that networks are not useful. Rather it is to play Devil's Advocate to the positive slant in the historiography on networks. Furthermore, exceptions can help to prove the rule. The case studies presented here are not necessarily representative. They are the stories of those who highlight the issues with which this chapter is concerned. The case studies therefore focus on the themes of kinship and ethnicity, the time required to build up networks, the problematic nature of weak and strong ties, and power relationships within networks. They also facilitate the consideration to what extent these networks were instrumental in fulfilling their purpose for both the individual and the wider trading community.

---

44 Lawler and Yoon, 'Commitment in Exchange Relations', p. 90. See also Smith-Doerr and Powell, 'Networks and Economic Life', pp. 384–86.

45 See above, pp. 136–37.

46 Samuel Barber to George Plumstead, 14 Jul. 1801, Misc Letters 361, Winterthur Museum Library; Thomas Mears to Henry Laurens, 22 Dec. 1763, *HLP*, Vol. IV.

47 Peter Wikoff to John Ewer, 29 Dec. 1772, Folder Peter Wikoff to John Ewer, CBP; John Leigh to Isaac Barker, 16 Sep. 1806, John Leigh Letterbook 5 Mar. 1806–7 Mar. 1807.

48 *HLP*, Vol. IV, p. 83, fn. 4.

49 George Chandler & Co. to Chaloner Arcedeckne, 3 Sep. 1765; Simon Taylor to Chaloner Arcedeckne, 24 Jan. 1767, Correspondence of WI Agents, Arcedeckne Papers, Cambridge University Library. Such trans-Atlantic investment in shipping declined with American Independence because American ships were thereafter classified as foreign. This was codified by Lord Liverpool's Act of 1786. F. Neal, 'Liverpool Shipping in the Early Nineteenth Century', in Harris, ed., *Liverpool and Merseyside*, pp. 147–81, p. 148.

FAMILY MATTERS: JAMES LAWSON[50]

JAMES LAWSON may have had a natural disposition towards worrying, but it is clear that he had plenty to worry about. The fact that his partner and brother-in-law failed to be prudent highlights the fact that the implicit contract of family can be broken. Lawson came from Strathaven in Lanarkshire, Scotland, but was based in Glasgow. Having married John Semple's sister, he was first in business in the firm of Jamieson, Semple & Lawson. When Jamieson left the firm in 1754 for reasons unknown, Lawson and Semple started a new partnership.[51] Lawson ran the Glasgow house, whilst Semple ran the store at Port Tobacco, Charles Co., Maryland.[52] Their main business was in tobacco, which they imported via Glasgow, Liverpool and occasionally London, but they were also involved in importing sugar, rum and cotton from the West Indies, and in exporting items such as linen, hats and yarn in return. This may have been during Glasgow's 'Golden Age' of Tobacco, but it was not a propitious time to set up in business. War was looming, with its attendant boom and bust, there was a general fall in tobacco prices due to over-production, and later, impressment of sailors for the Navy.[53] Despite this, by 1760, Semple had opened further stores in Alexandria (Virginia) and Leonardtown (Maryland). Semple also suggested becoming involved in the slave trade in 1759, for which they could not get backers, but Lawson was at a loss to stop Semple dabbling in the domestic slave trade, over-purchasing tobacco, or investing in iron furnaces and land speculation.[54] Semple consistently over-extended his credit and stubbornly quarrelled with his neighbours, despite the fact that they provided the only

---

50 A longer version of this case study is available at Haggerty, "'You Promise Well and Perform as Badly'".

51 The accounts of the original concern were not settled until 1772. See Statement of Accounts 1750–1774, f. 19.

52 For the store system whereby Scottish merchants set up a store in the Chesapeake, run by their own factor, through which they directly purchased tobacco, and in turn provided vital credit and consumer goods to the colonists and planters in those areas see Jacob M. Price, 'The Rise of Glasgow in the Chesapeake Tobacco Trade, 1707–1775', WMQ, 3rd ser., 11:2 (Apr. 1954), 179–99.

53 Devine, 'The Golden Age of Tobacco'; James Lawson to John Semple, 10 Aug. 1759, Letterbook 1758–1762, SJLP.

54 Lawson wrote to James Clemens asking how many 'Negroes' Semple had purchased, as he had not been advised. James Lawson to James Clemens & Co., 20 Feb. 1761, Letterbook 1758–1762; James Lawson to John Hamilton, 27 Jun. 1767, Letterbook 1766–67. For a fuller account of Semple's dealings in America see David Curtis Skaggs, 'John Semple and the Development of the Potomac Valley, 1750–1773', Virginia Magazine of History of Biography, 92:3 (Jul. 1984), 282–308.

access to water and pig iron for his iron forge.[55] David Skaggs writes of one of Semple's business partners, John Ballandine, that he 'was a man of extraordinary vision and small business acumen'.[56] The same could be said of Semple, who never seemed to be in touch with the reality of his finances or abilities. It is a testament of the obligation to family that Lawson persisted in extending credit to Semple until at least 1764. Indeed, Semple's rather over-enthusiastic assessment of his prospects in iron meant that he was able to raise a total of £5,000 in total advances from Lawson, John Hamilton and another Glasgow house, George Pagan and Mathew Crawford, in order to start up his iron business. John Hamilton no doubt felt obligated by virtue of being married to another of Semple's sisters.[57]

James Lawson & Co. was not the biggest Glasgow firm importing tobacco, but the house was significant. In 1760 James Lawson imported 792 hogsheads of tobacco at Port Glasgow and Greenock. The largest importer, John Glassford & Co., imported a total of 4,945 hogsheads, but there were seven firms (out of those importing 500 hogsheads or more) that imported less than Lawson.[58] By November 1759, and only five years after setting up in business together, Lawson was complaining to Semple that he was sending far too much tobacco back to England, especially considering that it was a falling market.[59] The prospect of a good crop meant that noone was buying tobacco in Glasgow or Liverpool. Semple's behaviour was even causing his neighbours in Maryland to comment in their letters home that he was 'a Surprise to all around you this last season in buying such quantities of Tobacco at such prices'; Lawson seethed that he was 'foolish and unprudent [sic]'.[60] Whether it was due to Semple's exasperating behaviour at this particular time, or Lawson's worrying nature, Lawson set off to Liverpool on 3 December 1759 to personally receive 285 hogheads of tobacco sent there by Semple. Considering that his correspondents were leading Liverpool merchant houses Rumbold & Walker and Haliday & Dunbar, this meddling was hardly necessary and displayed a level of mistrust.[61] Lawson's complaints about the tobacco

---

55 Skaggs, 'John Semple', passim.

56 Skaggs, 'John Semple'. Skaggs seems rather in awe of men such as Semple as entrepreneurs, but Semple's behaviour was certainly not celebrated by his contemporaries.

57 Skaggs, 'John Semple', p. 291.

58 They were the only firm to import only from Maryland, which highlights the restricted nature of Lawson's networks. Price, 'Buchanan & Simson', p. 14.

59 James Lawson to John Semple, 30 Nov. 1759, Letterbook 1758–1762.

60 James Lawson to John Semple, 14 Jan. 1760, Letterbook 1758–1762.

61 William Haliday was wealthy enough to be elected on to Liverpool's Council in 1760 and Thomas Rumbold in 1771, Minutes of the Town Council.

trade in general, and Semple's poor behaviour in particular, continued into 1760. Eventually, in an attempt to control Semple's behaviour, two of John Hamilton's sons, Alexander and Francis, were sent to Maryland, and another friend, Alexander Lithgow, was sent to operate one of the stores.[62] They had little effect.

Much of the tobacco imported into Britain by Lawson and Semple would have arrived through Glasgow. Over 30 per cent of all British tobacco imports arrived via Scotland by 1758, but some were sent via Liverpool as well.[63] Lawson therefore used national networks in order to distribute his tobacco, as well as Osnaburghs and rice. This was not unusual. Glasgow merchants Buchanan & Simson also imported and transhipped tobacco through Liverpool, as well as sugar and pig iron.[64] Much of the tobacco imported via Liverpool and Glasgow was meant for transhipment to the Dutch and French markets, the latter via the bulk-buying monopoly Farmers General of the French Customs.[65] Lawson had a Scots correspondent in Rotterdam, William Davidson, to whom he liked to ship, but by the end of 1759 this was becoming problematic, and Lawson wrote to Haliday & Dunbar in Liverpool and James Russell in London in December 1759 about the possibilities of selling to the French.[66] Lawson had a lot of expensive tobacco to dispose of thanks to Semple and he must have exasperated his Liverpool correspondents. He often wrote to them reminding them to always send good bills on London as they were considered the best (of which they would have been well aware) and asking repeatedly about prices.[67] Indeed, Lawson eventually managed to

62 Skaggs, 'John Semple', p. 297.
63 Devine, 'The Golden Age of Tobacco', p. 143. James Lawson to Haliday & Dunbar, 19 Nov. 1759, Letterbook 1758–62; James Lawson to Rumbold & Walker, 16 May 1763, Letterbook 1762–66. Occasionally he sold his tobacco via London, Edinburgh, Bremen and Copenhagen. James Lawson to James Crawford, 2 Aug. 1762; James Lawson to William Alexander & Sons, 9 Jul. 1762, Letterbook 1758–62; James Lawson to Frederick Schroder, 22 Aug. 1760, Letterbook 1758–62; James Lawson to George Langston, 3 May 1763, Letterbook 1762–66
64 In addition to Haliday & Dunbar, Buchanan & Simson used James Gildart, Arthur & Benjamin Heywood, Crosbies & Trafford, and Ellis & Robert Cunliffe. Buchanan & Simson Letterbook 507, passim, NAS. See also Buchanan & Simson in Account with James Lawson, Ledgers 1758–59, f. 31, SJLP.
65 For more on the French monopoly see Devine, 'The Golden Age of Tobacco', pp. 148–50.
66 James Lawson to Haliday & Dunbar, 27 Dec. 1759; James Lawson to James Russell, 3 Dec. 1759, and passim, Letterbook 1758–1762. Davidson had a reputation for being able to charter neutral vessels. The French monopoly sales were important for liquidity because they bought in cash and short bills, but expected a low price in return.
67 See for example, James Lawson to Haliday & Dunbar, 27 Dec. 1759, Letterbook 1758–1762.

fall out with Haliday & Dunbar over forty-four hogsheads of tobacco that they had not shipped in the vessel he had expected them to (possibly about 5 per cent of his imports), and he felt that they had overcharged him as well.[68] Following this dispute he increasingly did business with Rumbold & Walker of Liverpool instead.[69]

These Scots networks were very interlinked. Buchanan & Simson and Lawson not only used the same correspondents, they also sometimes imported on the same vessels such as the *Venus*.[70] They were aware of each other's movements and seemed to provide 'mutual restraint and ... mutual aid' rather than being in out-and-out competition.[71] Buchanan & Simson wrote to James Gildart on 5 December 1759 that their friend James Lawson was with them in Liverpool, asked for information about how he was doing, and requested that they help him.[72] Semple clearly caused Lawson many problems, but for a while at least, Lawson managed to retain a good reputation in order to cooperate with his local, national and international networks, as shown in Figure 6:1. At this point it is clear that Lawson had correspondents in the north west of England, as well as in London and Bristol. Besides his contacts for the tobacco trade in Maryland and Holland he also had a number of correspondents in the West Indies. He had strong ties with his family, other Scots firms, and also with Haliday & Dunbar in Liverpool.

James Lawson continued to beg Semple to make payments back to England and eventually stated that he wanted to withdraw from the problematic tobacco trade. By 1762 Lawson had turned the problem of war on its head and was worried about the prospects of the trade in peacetime.[73] His difficulties with Semple were to get far worse however, once Semple started investing in iron furnaces and land speculation. In April 1762 Semple entered into a series of agreements with John Ballendine, despite the fact that the latter was increasingly gaining a reputation for dishonesty,

---

68 James Lawson to Haliday & Dunbar, 27 Nov. 1763, Letterbook 1762–66. This may not have been all down to Lawson's excessive worrying however, as Buchanan & Simson also expected to have a dispute with them in 1761. Buchanan & Simson to Capt Buchanan, 29 May 1761, Buchanan & Simson Letterbook 507.

69 James Lawson Letterbook 1198.

70 Buchanan & Simson to Haliday & Dunbar, 31 Oct. 1759, Buchanan & Simson Letterbook 507; James Lawson to Haliday & Dunbar, 19 Nov. 1759, Letterbook 1197.

71 T. M. Devine, 'Glasgow Merchants and the Collapse of the Tobacco Trade 1775–1783', *Scottish Historical Review*, 52 (1973), 50–74, p. 67.

72 Buchanan & Simson to James Gildart, 5 Dec. 1759, Buchanan & Simson Letterbook 507.

73 See for example James Lawson to John Semple, 10 Sep. 1762, Letterbook 1762–66.

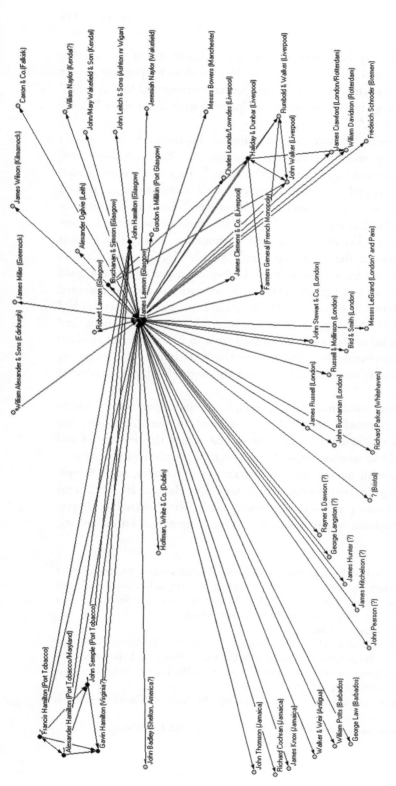

Key: • Strong ties   ◦ Weak ties.

FIGURE 6:1 JAMES LAWSON'S NETWORKS C.1760–63

Note: Granovetter defines a strong tie as a 'combination of the amount of time, the emotional intensity, the intimacy (mutual confiding), and the reciprocal services which characterize the tie', 'The Strength of Weak Ties', p. 136I.

I am defining a strong tie as an emotionally-intensive tie as opposed to one based on frequency or financial value.

Source: James Lawson Letterbooks: 1758–62; 1762–66; 1762–74; Ledger 1758–59; Buchanan & Simson Letterbook 507.

N.B. All the network diagrams in this chapter created using Pajek, available at http://vlado.fmf.uni-lj.si/pub/networks/Pajek/ (accessed 19 Sep. 2011).

and Lawson's exhortation that 'It would be madness to plunge into a new Branch [of trade] at such precarious times.'[74] Semple however, was clearly a risk taker and continued to live in a state of denial. In May 1763 Lawson wrote to him that 'We have been wading over our Head and Ear's [sic] these several years past … You imagine that when you send Home Tobacco or Iron they are as good as Cash, but in that you are far mistaken.'[75] He added that it took six to nine months to turn them into cash. Lawson was not alone in this predicament. The end of the war was accompanied by a credit crisis and many well-established Glasgow families saw their fortunes disappear.[76] In 1763, realising that John Hamilton's sons were totally unable to rein in Semple (in fact Alexander Hamilton went into business with him for some time), Gavin Hamilton, John Hamilton's brother, was sent to Maryland to try to control him.[77] Lawson wrote to Gavin Hamilton in the January of 1763 that 'Mr Semple I am afraid pushes by far too fast and without thought of how money is to be raised here.'[78] He wrote later the same year in much the same vein to Alexander Hamilton adding if Semple disgraced himself it was his own fault as he continually ignored all of his advice.[79] Even this failed and Lawson was forced to send his son Robert to Maryland in 1764.[80] In August 1765 Lawson assessed that he had advanced Semple £8–9,000 for his iron works in Maryland.[81] By 1769 Semple owed Lawson at least £14,066 and 150,633 bags of tobacco.[82] It is clear that although Lawson did not want to invest in the iron furnaces, his credit extension meant that he was inextricably linked and forced to take risks with the project, even though he never wanted or received shares in any of the concerns.[83] Indeed, in February 1765 Lawson had begged Semple to keep the books of the concerns separate. Semple was receiving lots of information from Lawson, but acted against this

74 Skaggs, 'John Semple', p. 289; James Lawson to John Semple, 10 Sep. 1762, Letterbook 1762–66.
75 James Lawson to John Semple, 9 May 1763, Letterbook 1762–66.
76 T. M. Devine, *The Tobacco Lords: A Study of the Tobacco Merchants of Glasgow and their Trading Activities* (Edinburgh: John Donald Publishers, 1975), p. 7.
77 James Lawson to Jno Thomson, 2 Jan. 1764, Letterbook 1762–74; Skaggs. 'John Semple', p. 297.
78 James Lawson to Gavin Hamilton, 13 Jan. 1763, Letterbook 1762–74.
79 James Lawson to Alexander Hamilton, 3 Sep. 1763, Letterbook 1762–74.
80 James Lawson to John Russell, 16 Jun. 1768, Letterbook 1767–69.
81 James Lawson to James Gildart, [?] Aug. 1765, Letterbook 1762–66.
82 Skaggs, 'John Semple', p. 292. This is a significant but not unusual amount. The capital of Glasgow tobacco firms ranged from £5,000–20,000. Devine, *The Tobacco Lords*, p. 75.
83 James Lawson to Rumbold & Walker, 24 Nov. 1763; James Lawson to Thomas Phelps & Co., [?] Sep. 1774, Letterbook 1203.

advice. Despite family ties, this was a case of moral hazard, not asymmetrical information. Semple used the implicit contract of family against Lawson.

Despite Lawson's concerns over Semple's iron activities, he clearly felt obligated to try to sell the iron he sent. In March 1763 Lawson wrote to Rumbold & Walker in Liverpool asking about the prospects for Virginia bar iron of 'fine soft quality suitable for ship work'.[84] He sent £254 2s. 2d. worth of bar iron to them from Glasgow in June 1763, adding that there was more if this trial worked out.[85] Only just over a month had passed, and not being able to help himself, he wrote to them for information about the sales of the iron.[86] Despite his constant worrying, over the next two years he continued to send iron to them and James Gildart of Liverpool, as well as continuing to stress the need for 'good London bills'.[87] However, by 1765 Lawson was complaining about Semple to his Liverpool correspondents. Maybe he was simply frustrated, but he may also have been trying to defend and disassociate himself from Semple in their eyes. He wrote to James Gildart that he was 'truly much pinched with Mr Semples bills for *his* iron work concern' [my emphasis], bemoaning Semple's lack of remittances, and admitting his ignorance in the iron business.[88] Whilst stressing his desire to keep his obligations with Semple, he was clearly trying to separate their reputations. More telling of the problems Semple was causing is that by 1765 Lawson's networks had started to decline, as shown in Figure 6:2. The number of his contacts in the West Indies had shrunk, and there was less correspondence with those with whom he was still in contact. Indeed, it appears that most of this correspondence was regarding the collection of debts and less concerned with acquiring products for sale in America.[89] This accounts for many of the contacts in Figure 6:2, and those in mainland America existed predominantly because he had been physically there from 1765 (see below). Therefore, as the crisis with Semple came to a head it seemed to take up more and more of his time. This occurred despite the fact that he had extended family ties in America whom he should have been able to trust. He had also fallen out with Haliday & Dunbar, and Rumbold & Walker were now his strong ties in Liverpool. It is clear that Lawson's family ties were a disaster for him,

---

84 James Lawson to Rumbold & Walker, 21 Mar. 1763, Letterbook 1762–66, Semple. In fact, Lawson complained about the quality of the iron. Skaggs, 'John Semple', p. 297.

85 James Lawson to Rumbold, Walker & Co., 27 Jun. 1763, Letterbook 1762–66.

86 James Lawson to Rumbold & Walker, 29 Jul. 1763, Letterbook 1762–66.

87 Letterbook 1198, passim; James Lawson to Rumbold & Walker, 4 Jun. 1764, Letterbook 1762–66.

88 James Lawson to James Gildart, 27 Feb. 1765; [?] Aug. 1765, Letterbook 1762–66.

89 See for example James Lawson to James Knox, 14 Jan. 1763; James Lawson to Richard Cochran, 2 Jan. 1764; James Lawson to James Reid, 23 Apr. 1764, Letterbook 1762–74.

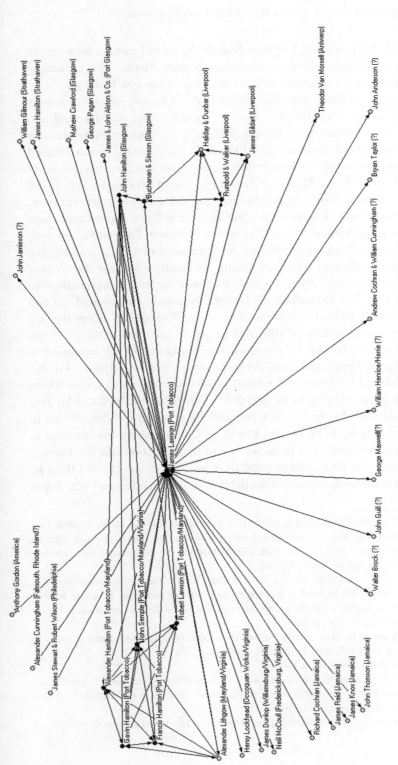

FIGURE 6.2 JAMES LAWSON'S NETWORKS C.1765–67

Key: ● Strong ties   ◇ Weak ties

Source: James Lawson Letterbooks; 1762–66; 1762–1774; 1766–67; 1767–1769; 1769–1770; Ledger 1758–59.

particularly his brother-in-law John Semple. None of Lawson's pleas or the extended family networks were able to stop Semple. Rather than expanding over time, Lawson's networks were on the verge of collapse by 1767.

As Semple's situation worsened, so did that of Lawson, who was relatively powerless within this network. Lawson wanted to go to Maryland and sort out the problems with Semple personally as 'Our creditors are now raising prosecutions against me.'[90] Indeed, as his extended family realised they would not be able to recoup their money from Semple, they turned to Lawson instead. Even Alexander Hamilton pressed him for money, as did John Hamilton's widow.[91] At first his creditors did not want to let him leave, fearing that he would never return, but eventually Lawson convinced them to let him go in September 1765.[92] However, even with Lawson face-to-face, Semple continued to be obstinate. The furnaces and forges were standing idle, but he 'hid' at the iron concerns, forcing his creditors to meet there rather than in Port Tobacco.[93] By 1771 Semple had been confined by his creditors to prison at Dumfries (Maryland?).[94] Despite this, and being around £21,000 in debt, Semple refused to sell any of his estate.[95] Unable to accept that his reputation was in tatters, he still tried to get his creditors to advance even more money in order to get the iron works going again. Semple continued to try to keep his family and other networks involved in his schemes. Finally, Lawson learned his lesson and refused to advance more money, over which Semple had the audacity to be annoyed.[96] When Semple died c. May 1774 Lawson assessed that he had lost £10,000. He returned to Glasgow and in September 1774 wrote to Thomas Phelps & Co. describing the situation in a letter very reminiscent of those we saw in the obligation chapter. Lawson made it clear that he wanted to fulfil all of his obligations. He told them he had come home with as many of the debts as he could collect and with hopes

---

90 James Lawson to John Semple, 7 Feb. 1765, Letterbook 1762–74. Under Scottish Law the partnership was a separate legal entity, which meant that they could draw up regulations to control the members. Clearly this was not in operation here. Devine, 'The Golden Age of Tobacco', p. 154.

91 She was his second wife. Skaggs, 'John Semple', p. 302. The family did not appear to secure these debts by bond or mortgage which was the usual way to secure debts in this period. See for example, Smith, *Slavery, Family and Gentry Capitalism*, p. 146.

92 Skaggs, 'John Semple', p. 298.

93 James Lawson to Mrs Lawson, 14 Jan. 1773, Letterbook 1770–76, James Lawson to John Semple, 7 Feb. 1765, Letterbook 1762–74.

94 There is also a Dumfries in Virginia.

95 Skaggs, 'John Semple', p. 300. This was complicated by the fact that Semple did not have good title to the land he owned in the various colonies. James Lawson to Alston & Moreton, 15 Jan. 1771, Letterbook 1770–76.

96 James Lawson to John Alston & James Morton, 31 Jan. 1773, Letterbook 1770–76.

that he could pay twenty shillings in the pound (i.e. all of his debts), stressing that he had spent nine years of his life trying to procure the money.[97]

In 1770 Lawson received a letter from his wife Nancy expressing concerns that she would never see him again.[98] He wrote that he hoped to be back that year, but in fact it was another four years until he was able to return to Scotland. He wrote in January 1773 that he and Robert were both well, but it is clear he was anxious to return home.[99] Lawson may have been a natural worrier, but his family obligations meant that he extended himself much further than he otherwise might have done, embroiled him in a risky business and a set of credit relations that he had desperately tried to avoid, and put his reputation into question. Staying with these family networks certainly did not protect him from moral hazard because Semple chose to ignore the information and advice he received. Importantly, Lawson's networks were not flexible enough to enable him to cope with the changing situation, locked as he was into obligatory family ties.[100] After at least twenty-five years in business, and approaching old age, Lawson was brought almost to bankruptcy by the very network he should have been most able to rely upon. As he put it himself, 'it is hard to be brought to poverty in our old age by a Brother in whom we placed all our confidence'.[101]

FALLING OUT: SAMUEL RAINFORD[102]

SAMUEL RAINFORD was the eldest son of a farming family. Perhaps knowing that his inheritance would be small (he eventually received £116 18s. 7d.), rather than take over the farm, he took the risk of setting up as a merchant in Jamaica.[103] Using his Liverpool networks to gain credit, and his experience as a ship's captain, he was settled in Kingston by 1774.[104] He was initially in a loose partnership with his long-term friend Edward Chaffers,

---

97 James Lawson to Thomas Phelps & Co., [?] Sep. 1774, Letterbook 1770–76.

98 James Lawson to Mrs Lawson, 5 Jun. 1770, Letterbook 1769–70, SJLP.

99 James Lawson to John Alston & James Morton, 31 Jan. 1773, Letterbook 1770–76.

100 Casson, 'An Economic Approach to Regional Business Networks', p. 23.

101 James Lawson to John Semple, 7 Feb. 1765, Letterbook 1762–74.

102 For fuller versions of this case study see Haggerty and Haggerty, 'Visual Analytics'; and Haggerty, 'I "could do for the Dickmans"'.

103 Account Book of Thomas and Elizabeth Rainford, 920 CHA/1/2, PEC.

104 Rainford was captain of the ship Liver, owned by Joseph and Jonathon Brookes in 1763, and apparently visited Jamaica in 1764. Henry Laurens to John Knight, 17 Aug. 1763, HLP, Vol. III; Henry Laurens to Thos Mears, 8 Dec. 1764, HLP, Vol. IV; Samuel Rainford to Edward Chaffers, 7 Jan. 1775, 920 CHA/1/10, PEC.

but by 1775 Rainford was expanding his trade and exporting sugar and pimento to Liverpool, and importing a wide variety of goods such as candles and butter into Kingston.[105] Much of this trade was via Jonathon Blundell Senior of Liverpool, and by 1778 Rainford was involved in the slave trade as well, mainly backed by Blundell.[106] By 1779 Samuel Rainford had also set up in partnership with his brother Robert and Jonathon Blundell Junior. This close relationship with the Blundells was instrumental in helping the Rainfords initially, but was later to prove extremely problematic.

Jonathon Blundell Senior was useful to Samuel Rainford because he had good connections in Jamaica, having imported sugar and rum from there since at least 1763.[107] He was also well connected in Liverpool at this time, listed in the trade directories as a merchant and sugar-baker, and having run a stocking manufactory from as early as 1766. Blundell Senior was also a member of various institutions such as the Committee of African Merchants between 1750 and 1798.[108] Although he had not owned vessels in the slave trade for many years, he still had vital connections to investors in the trade.[109] No doubt Rainford thought that such an eminent merchant would be predictable and reduce his risk.[110] When Samuel Rainford set up in business with his brother Robert and Jonathon Blundell Junior on 9 August 1779, Samuel's lack of capital meant that Blundell Senior held all

---

105 Samuel Rainford to Edward Chaffers, 7 Jan. 1775, 920 CHA/1/10, PEC. It has not been possible to determine the exact relationship between Rainford and Chaffers, or indeed how Rainford knew the Blundells. They did not appear in the same clubs or institutions at the same time. There was a Peter Rainford on the Liverpool Council who died in 1750, but no connection has been made. Edward Chaffers did not invest in slave trade vessels, but was a member of the Liverpool Chamber of Commerce established in 1774 alongside Jonathon Blundell, and Chaffers and Blundell invested in canal development together. Eltis et al., *Trans-Atlantic Slave Trade Database*; Robert J. Bennett, *The Voice of Liverpool Business: The First Chamber of Commerce and Atlantic Economy, 1774–c.1796* (Liverpool: Liverpool Chamber of Commerce, 2010), pp. 150, 154.

106 Jonathon Blundell to Samuel Rainford, 16 Oct. 1783, 920 CHA/1/1, PEC.

107 Case and Southworth Sales Ledger 1763–69; Case and Southworth Jamaica Sales 1754–61, Case & Southworth Papers, LivRO.

108 J. Gore, ed., *Liverpool Trade Directory* for 1766 (Liverpool: Printed by W. Nevitt and Co. for J. Gore, Bookseller near the Exchange, 1766); Minutes of the African Committee. Jonathon Blundell only served briefly on the Liverpool Council (1764–66), but his grandson Henry Blundell Hollinshead was elected to the Council in 1802, Liverpool Town Books.

109 He did invest in a one off slave voyage in 1780, but the *Hero* was taken by the French. Voyage number 81813. Elits et al., *Trans-Atlantic Slave Trade Database*.

110 Lawler and Yoon, 'Commitment in Exchange Relations', p. 104.

the power in this relationship.[111] Indeed, his son's involvement may have been the price for the increasing credit extended to the Kingston house. By September 1783 the Kingston house owed Blundell senior £15,820 16s. 1½d.;[112] not an inconsiderable sum when it took around £5–10,000 to set up a new house from scratch.[113] This injection of money certainly helped. The Kingston house imported 258 slaves on the *Rumbold* in 1779, and a further 475 on the same vessel in 1780.[114] Rainford, Blundell & Rainford also imported textiles, groceries and hardware on the *Dalling* from London, groceries from Cork on the *Mary* from Liverpool in 1780, and acted as agents for the *Modeste* sailing to Liverpool from Kingston in the same year. In return they exported sugar, cotton, coffee and silver dollars.[115] During the 1780s Rainford, Blundell & Rainford did business with several of the Liverpool elite, including William Earle, Thomas Staniforth, Francis Ingram, Thomas Parke, Charles Pole and Thomas Leyland. This allowed the Kingston house to increase its activity in the slave trade and it was involved in a total of thirty-seven slave trade voyages between the arrival of the *Rumbold* in 1779 and the start of the French Wars in 1793.[116] In 1779 they imported 10.17 per cent of all slaves imported into Jamaica, and as late as 1791 they still imported over 8 per cent of the total, although it would appear they stopped trading in slaves in August 1793.[117] They also created weak ties with New York, Bristol and London. The Rainfords' commodity portfolio and their networks were therefore increasing. Figure 6:3 shows their various links in Jamaica, with the

---

111 [Copy of] Memorandum of an agreement … 13 Jul. 1789, 920 CHA/1/36, PEC.

112 Rainford, Blundell & Rainford in Account Current with Jonathon Blundell, 9 Aug. 1779 to 29 Jun. 1782, 920 CHA/1/21, PEC. It has not been possible to assess whether any capital as opposed to credit was advanced at the beginning of the dealings between Blundell Senior and Rainford, Blundell & Rainford.

113 Campbell, *The London Tradesman*, p. 336.

114 Eltis et al., *The Trans-Atlantic Slave Trade Database*, voyages 92449 and 92450; see also Rainford, Blundell & Rainford Pocket Ledger MG-54-No 74, National Library and Archives Canada.

115 *The Royal Gazette*, 8 Jul. 1780, 30 Sep. 1780, 5 Aug. 1780, Rainford, Blundell & Rainford Account with Jonathon Blundell, 6 Nov. 1785. The shipments in 1780 had obviously been arranged before the new partnership, as they were advertised as Blundell & Rainford only.

116 The following analysis is based on Rainford, Blundell & Rainford Pocket Ledger MG-54-No 74, National Archives Canada and Eltis et al., *The Trans-Atlantic Slave Trade Database*. The voyage numbers on the Database are 92449, 92450, 83975, 83259, 81670, 81141, 81988, 83624, 82853 (London-based voyage), 81606, 83977, 81989, 80848, 82770, 81671, 81921 (London-based voyage), 83918, 81672, 83814, 82156, 80255, 81673, 81182, 82626, 80256, 81561, 83272, 82627, 80516, 80257, 83757, 83273, 81008, 80517, 80862, 83984, except where noted.

117 Haggerty and Haggerty, 'Visual Analytics', p. 6.

Hibberts in Manchester, and the Brights in Bristol – leading houses in their respective cities. They also had contact with various dry goods merchants in Liverpool. Especially important to note is the access to the dense Liverpool slave trade networks through Blundell Senior. Note also that Rainford's family ties (the Harrisons in the bottom right) are weak ties in terms of business (and indeed personally) and his dealings with them were mostly via Edward Chaffers.[118]

The alliance with the Blundells was successful at first. Rainford, Blundell & Rainford reduced their balance owing to Blundell Senior to £764 9s. 3½d. by 1785.[119] However, it seems that the power imbalance soon became clear in the way that Blundell Senior's house treated the Kingston concern, and that Blundell Senior had a strong sense of the obligations due him by the Rainford brothers. For example, he charged more for guaranteeing bills than other firms in Kingston were charged by their Liverpool correspondents, charged commission on accepting bills as soon as they were accepted (rather than when paid) and charged extra for protested bills. Samuel Rainford considered none of these practices normal.[120] Even clerical arrangements caused problems as Blundell Senior's clerk insisted on adding bills together before crediting the Kingston house so that they did not know which bills had been paid and which had not. They wrote in 1784, 'Bid your clerk make an Account out specifying each particular Bill, that is, the drawers name, who upon, and the amount of each Bill.'[121] This was indeed lazy, or even misleading, practice.

In 1789 a sister house of the Kingston concern was set up in Liverpool.[122] The partnership document detailed that one of the three men was to be resident in Liverpool at any one time and to conduct the business of the house there; 'that is to accept and pay all bills that may be drawn on the House here for the payment of negroes they may dispose of ... and Negociate [sic]

---

118 For more on Rainford's family see Haggerty, 'I "could do for the Dickmans"'.

119 Rainford, Blundell & Rainford in Account Current with Jonathon Blundell, 6 Nov. 1783 to 6 Nov. 1785, 920 CHA 1/1, PEC.

120 See the complaints and replies at Rainford, Blundell & Rainford to Jonathon Blundell, 13 Feb. 1784; Jonathon Blundell to Rainford, Blundell & Rainford, 20 Feb. 1784; Rainford, Blundell & Rainford to Jonathon Blundell, 19 Jun. 1790, 920 CHA 1/1.

121 Rainford, Blundell & Rainford to Jonathon Blundell, 13 Feb. 1784, 920 CHA 1/1.

122 This was a relatively unusual step but not unknown. Another Kingston firm, Hibbert & Jackson, also had subsidiary houses, in London, Hibbert, Purrier & Horton, and in Manchester. Trevor Burnard, '"The Grant Mart of the Island": The Economic Function of Kingston, Jamaica in the Mid-Eighteenth Century', in Kathleen E. A. Monteith and Glen Richards, eds., *Jamaica in Slavery and Freedom: History, Heritage and Culture* (Mona, Jamaica: University of West India Press, 2002), pp. 225–41, p. 232.

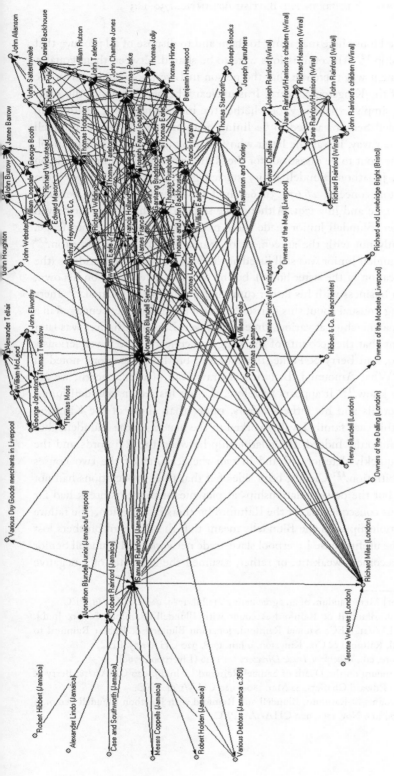

Key: ● Strong ties ◇ Weak ties

FIGURE 6:3 SAMUEL RAINFORD'S NETWORKS C.1774–1778

Source: Papers of Edward Chaffers; Rainford, Blundell & Rainford Pocket Ledger MG–54–No 74; Eltis et al., *The Trans-Atlantic Slave Trade Database.*

all Bills the House here may remit to them and to dispose of all produce that they may ship'.[123] All commissions were to be shared between them equally. The agreement was therefore that the person in Liverpool should act in the interests of the Kingston concern. It is unclear whether setting up the sister house was simply expediency, or whether the increasingly poor relationship with Blundell Senior had led to declining relations with Jonathon Blundell Junior. Either way, it was the latter who first took up the post in Liverpool, which turned out to be disastrous for the Rainford brothers. Immediately on his return, Jonathon Blundell Junior started giving his father money from the Kingston concern: £6,676 3s. 6d. in four separate payments between November 1789 and July 1791. Although he stated that this was money owed to his father, Blundell Junior made these payments without the knowledge, and certainly not with the agreement of, Samuel Rainford in Kingston.[124] By 1796 Blundell Junior was still listed at the St. George's Street address (the original location of the sister house), but he was also listed there on his own, and was in business with his father running a coal office at 1 Canal.[125] There was nothing unusual about this in itself, as most merchants were engaged in a variety of partnerships at various times. However, Edward Chaffers was later to comment that the accounts of the Kingston concern were never seriously attended to, and Berry & Parke, the Rainford brothers' executors, noted in 1804 that 'What Amount J, B, Junr has drawn out of the Concern, we are at a loss to know.'[126] It appears therefore, that on his return Blundell Junior looked after his and his father's affairs, rather than those of the Kingston house. In this case family loyalty worked to the benefit of the Blundells, but not the Rainfords. Indeed, the relationship between the Rainfords and the Blundells quickly deteriorated and in 1791 the accounts of the two houses were in arbitration.[127] Clearly, both sides felt that their expectations had not been met, but the power relationships at play meant that this break had far more serious consequences for the Rainford brothers in Kingston. The failure of the relationship with the Blundells meant that the Rainford brothers lost access to the useful dense Liverpool slave-trade networks and Blundell Senior had now become a weak tie, or rather, assumed the character of a negative

---

123 [Copy of] Memorandum of an agreement … 13 Jul. 1789, 920 CHA/1/36, PEC.

124 Rainford, Blundell & Rainford Account with Blundell, Rainford & Co. [n.d.], 920 CHA/1/21, PEC; Samuel Rainford, Jonathon Blundell & Robert Rainford to Blundell, Rainford & Co., Kingston, 9 Jun. 1798, 920 CHA/1/25, PEC.

125 John Gore, ed., *Liverpool Trade Directory* for 1796 (Liverpool, 1796).

126 Memorandum on the Death of Samuel Rainford … [n.d.], 920 CHA/1/18; Berry & Parke to Edward Chaffers, 22 Mar. 1804, 920 CHA/1/14, PEC.

127 The Accounts of Rainford, Blundell and Rainford with Jonathon Blundell Senior, 6 Nov. 1779 to 6 Nov. 1791, 920 CHA/1/21, PEC.

strong tie. Samuel Rainford was no longer used by any of the Liverpool worthies from 1788 onwards, except Thomas Hodgson, the Gregsons, George Case (and then only once each) and John Backhouse. This was despite the fact that men such as Thomas Leyland and Francis Ingram continued to invest heavily in the slave trade. It is probable that the Blundells in Liverpool were gossiping about Rainford to such an extent that his reputation was in decline there and many people felt that they could no longer do business with him, highlighting the importance of information flow through local and informal networks. It could also be that the powerful Blundell Senior compelled them to withdraw their business from the Rainfords. Certainly they were unceremoniously dropped by the majority of Liverpool's slave traders, as is shown in Figure 6:4.[128]

Although the Rainfords clearly lost access to the dense Liverpool slave trade networks, ties were not severed by all their Liverpool contacts. Furthermore, they managed to increase their networks elsewhere, turning weak ties into strong ties. Clearly Rainford appears more central to his network in Figure 6:4. In terms of the slave trade, it is interesting to note that they did continue to do business with the small (and non-elite) investment group of Thomas Seaman, William Percival and William Boats.[129] In fact, this group allowed the Rainfords to increase the number of slaves they imported into Jamaica in the early 1790s.[130] This continued tie may have been due to face-to-face contact via Thomas Seaman, who had captained one of their vessels, the *Gregson*, to Jamaica in 1783, and also because William Boats had owned at least seven of the slave trade vessels sent to Rainford, Blundell & Rainford individually.[131] Perhaps being a relative outsider on the Council meant that Boats did not feel the need to buckle under Blundell Senior's influence. Other Liverpool people also continued to do business with the Rainford Brothers. These included Arthur Heywood & Co. and Moses Benson.[132] The well-known Liverpool merchant

---

128 Note that Robert Rainford had two 'reputed sons' in Jamaica via his common-law wife Bella Hall. Bella Hall was a brown woman, his housekeeper. The Complaint of Joseph Rainford ... 21 Feb. 1810, C13/132/35. For more on housekeepers in Jamaica see Trevor G. Burnard, *Mastery, Tyranny, and Desire: Thomas Thistlewood and his Slaves in the Anglo-Jamaican World* (Chapel Hill and London, 2004); Hilary McD. Beckles, *Centering Woman: Gender Discourses in Caribbean Slave Society* (Kingston, Jamaica: Ian Randle, 1999), chapter three.

129 William Boats was on the Council, but he was clearly not accepted as one of the elite as he never served as mayor. Minutes of the Town Council.

130 See Haggerty and Haggerty, 'Visual Analytics', p. 6.

131 Rainford, Blundell and Rainford Pocket Ledger.

132 Samuel Rainford to Edward Chaffers, 31 Jul. 1792, 920 CHA 1/10; Samuel Rainford to Edward Chaffers, 10 Jun. 1797, 920 CHA 1/13.

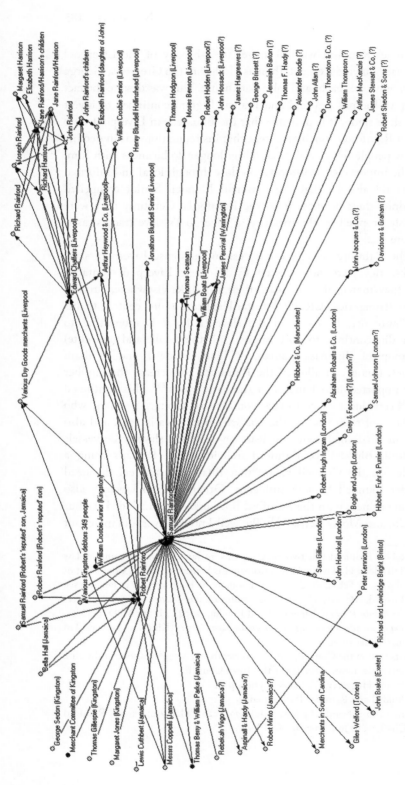

FIGURE 6:4 SAMUEL RAINFORD'S LATER NETWORKS

Key: ● Strong ties ○ Weak ties

Source: Papers of Edward Chaffers; Rainford, Blundell & Rainford Pocket Ledger MG-54-No 74; Eltis et al., *The Trans-Atlantic Slave Trade Database*; The Complaint of Joseph Rainford ..., 21 Feb. 1810, C13/132/35, TNA.

William Crosbie also sent his son to train as a clerk at the Kingston house.[133] Furthermore Samuel Rainford turned his weak ties the Brights in Bristol into stronger ties and started up a direct trade with South Carolina.[134] He also established ties with many houses in London by clearing his bills though them.[135] Over time Samuel Rainford also built up his reputation in Jamaica; the house sold the slaves they imported to a wide range of people in Jamaica. Their pocket ledger lists sales to 349 different people, many of which were respectable merchants and well-known Jewish shopkeepers.[136] As early as 1780 he acted as executor for Robert Holden in Jamaica and was working as an attorney for others as well.[137] He was also on the Committee of Merchants which in 1781 sought to alleviate the problems with scarcity of money on the island, and was a signatory on a memorial sent to the Board of Trade in 1786, alongside elite merchants Alexander Lindo and Robert Hibbert.[138] In turn, merchants Thomas Berry and William Parke became Samuel's executors on his death in 1798.[139] This suggests that whilst Rainford had little power within the Liverpool slave trade network, he did have power in other Liverpool networks, elsewhere in the Atlantic, and especially in Jamaica. Edward Chaffers was also a stalwart friend to Samuel Rainford. He took care of Samuel's large family in Liverpool, acted as a bank for the Rainfords, dealt with their investments in government bonds, bought lottery tickets for them, arranged for the purchase of property and even sent out spectacles for Samuel.[140] In return Samuel often sent Chaffers and his wife gifts such as sweetmeats.[141] Their affective commitment was demonstrated by real presents, and in gifts of time spent helping each other in various ways.

---

133 Edward Chaffers to Samuel Rainford, 13 Feb. 1794, 920 CHA/1/11, PEC.

134 Samuel Rainford to Edward Chaffers, 23 Feb. 1793, 920 CHA 1/10; Samuel Rainford to Edward Chaffers, 920 CHA 1/18; *The Royal Gazette, Supplement*, 8 Nov. 1783.

135 See CHA/1/10–13, PEC, passim.

136 Rainford, Blundell & Rainford Pocket Ledger. On the Jews in Jamaica see Mordechai Arbell, *The Portuguese Jews in Jamaica* (Kingston, Jamaica: Canoe Press, 2000).

137 *The Royal Gazette, Supplement*, 2 Dec. 1780; David Duncomb to Lowbridge Bright, 17 Jun. 1790, *BMP*.

138 *The Royal Gazette, Supplement*, 27 Jan. 1781. This memorial was part of the reaction to direct trade no longer being possible with the newly-formed United States under the Navigation Acts. To his Honor Alured Clarke ... Copy of a letter from a Committee of the body of Merchants [n.d]; To his Honor Alured Clarke ... Memorial and Petition of the Merchants of Kingston, 1786; BoT: West Indies, BT 6/75, ff. 40, 45.

139 Accounts Related to the Estate of Samuel Rainford, 920 CHA/1/18, PEC.

140 See correspondence from Samuel Rainford to Edward Chaffers, 920 CHA/10–13, PEC.

141 Samuel Rainford to Edward Chaffers, 21 Jan. 1794, 920 CHA/1/10.

Samuel Rainford's story demonstrates the problems that can occur due to over-reliance on one strong tie. The fact that the Rainfords fell out with the Blundells led to a negative instrumentality on the long-term development of Samuel Rainford's networks. Clearly the failure to meet expectations led to strong feelings and the implicit family of contract worked to the disadvantage of those outside it. When Samuel Rainford died in 1798 he left an estate worth £22,000 Jamaican currency (about £15,700 sterling), a pen (small farm) on the outskirts of Kingston, another parcel of land, and two stores at the corner of Harbour and Princes Street.[142] This was not that much money considering the initial extension of credit from Jonathon Blundell Senior and that Rainford traded for over twenty-four years on the island. However, his story also highlights that through developing weak ties into strong ties over the long term and by being reliable and building his reputation, Samuel Rainford created other opportunities by developing alternative networks. Even the fall out with the Blundells did not damage his reputation with everyone in Liverpool, nor in Jamaica or elsewhere around the Atlantic. Rainford's story demonstrates that many networks were active at the same time, and that this is important for the survival of business networks in a time of crisis, personal or otherwise. Blundell Senior's power within Liverpool's slave trade networks did have serious repercussions for Rainford's involvement with that trade and at the height of Liverpool's involvement in it, but Samuel Rainford had forged himself other options.

NETWORKING ON THE EDGE: ANDREW CLOW

EDGEWORKER ANDREW CLOW was ambitious, a workaholic, not very likeable, but obviously an astute businessman.[143] He always seemed keen to take the initiative and liked to take the risk of new opportunities, and to keep them secret from others on occasion. For example, in 1788 he berated his partner David Cay for having discussed future plans with other people.[144] Yet his success in trade seems to have meant that people were happy to continue trading with him despite his rather grumpy

---

142 Jamaica Currency was the local currency valued at 140 per cent of pounds sterling. i.e. £140 Jamaica Currency was equal to £100 sterling. Robert Rainford to Edward Chaffers, 4 Aug. 1798, 920 CHA/1/25, PEC.

143 For edgeworking see above, pp. 41–42. Andrew Clow also appeared in my *British-Atlantic Trading Community*, pp. 234–39, but he has fascinated me for years and there is new data presented here.

144 Andrew Clow to David Cay, 14 Apr. 1788, Folder Mar.–Apr. 1788, Andrew Clow & Co., SGC.

disposition.[145] Clow originally came from Manchester and was still in business there in early 1784. At some point before 1783 he conducted business (either formally or informally) with London-based merchant David Cay.[146] Cay committed an act of bankruptcy around 1785 when he absconded from London deeply in debt.[147] Whether his financial problems were due to the economic fluctuations caused by the American War of Independence is not evident. However, Clow certainly saw the United States as an opportunity. By July 1784 he had established a presence in Philadelphia, having his mail directed to Mrs Bertrams, Front Street.[148] By December of that year he was settled at his own house at Front Street at the corner of Chesnut.[149] He exported wheat, flour and lumber and imported textiles and hardware from England, which he also redistributed coastwise.[150] He eventually went (back) into business with David Cay, despite the fact that it is clear from his letters that he had little competency trust in him, or indeed in many other people. As his friend Joseph Hadfield noted in a letter to Clow in 1790, 'I have as great an aversion as you to Partnerships.'[151] It was obvious to others that 'Clow of course superintends all the affairs of the House' in Philadelphia, and

---

145 Casson suggests that a reputation for integrity will lead to a person becoming a trusted leader. 'An Economic Approach to Regional Business Networks', p. 32.

146 A letter of February 1784 shows Andrew Clow & Co. still in Manchester. William Rathbone & Son, 21 Feb. 1784, Folder 1785–98, Andrew Clow & Co., CWU. James Bradshaw called Cay Clow's partner in 1784, James Bradshaw to Andrew Clow, 13 Nov. 1784, Folder Oct.–Dec. 1784, Andrew Clow & Co., SGC. According to Doerflinger, Clow went broke when he first went to Philadelphia, though I did not come across evidence for this. A Vigorous Spirit of Enterprise, p. 245. Matson suggests they were in formal partnership together before 1785, 'Accounting for War and Revolution', pp. 182–84.

147 Cay was still trading in London in February 1784. David Cay to Andrew Clow, 25 Feb. 1784, Folder Jan.–Sep. 1784, Andrew Clow & Co., SGC; Andrew Howkin to David Cay, 29 May 1786, Folder Jan.–Jun. 1786, Andrew Clow & Co., SGC. For more on David Cay's bankruptcy see Folder 1784–1790, Andrew Clow & Co., SGC. On acts of bankruptcy see Hoppit, Risk and Failure, chapter three.

148 James Renwick to Andrew Clow, 28 Jul. 1784, Folder Jan.–Sep. 1784, Correspondence 1784–90, Andrew Clow & Co., SGC.

149 George Mitchell to Andrew Clow, 3 Dec. 1784, Folder Oct.–Dec. 1784, Correspondence 1784–90, Andrew Clow & Co., SGC; Francis White, ed., The Philadelphia Trade Directory for 1785 (Philadelphia: Printed by Young, Stewart and McCullock, 1785). In 1791 Cay was listed at a separate address, 71 Front Street, with Clow at number 20 Front Street. Clement Biddle, ed., The Philadelphia Directory for 1791 (Philadelphia: Printed for James and Johnson, 1791).

150 For Clow's trade in general see Andrew Clow & Co. papers in SGC and CWU.

151 Joseph Hadfield to Andrew Clow, 15 Jan. 1790, Folder Joseph, John & Thomas Hadfield, Andrew Clow & Co., CWU.

it is unclear what connection obliged Clow to stay with David Cay.[152] Clow wrote on occasion that he had visited with Cay's family but it has not been possible to ascertain whether their families had intermarried.[153] Indeed, both Clow and Cay made little reference to their family or kin. The only family Clow seemed to have had was a sister and a daughter Mary, but family did not play any real part in Clow's business networks.[154]

Despite Cay's financial demise, Clow clearly retained a good reputation because he was able to set up in Philadelphia without any apparent difficulty and was also solicited for business and given power of attorney to act for others within his first few years there.[155] Perhaps it was due to a lack of family networks, but Clow clearly felt driven to proactively network far more intensively than other merchants. Having been brought up, as he claimed, in the manufacturing line, he first used his connections in Manchester, Liverpool and London for supply.[156] However, he developed his networks not by simply writing to people from Philadelphia, getting letters of introduction, or relying on his reputation, but by personal visits.[157] Once they had set up their own house most merchants became relatively static, having developed their skills and networks whilst a captain or supercargo; but Clow personally visited as many of his correspondents as possible even after he had set up the house in Philadelphia. For example in 1786 he visited Manchester, Birmingham, Glasgow, Paisley, Edinburgh, various places around Yorkshire,

---

152 Joseph Hadfield to David Cay, 15 Dec. 1790, Folder Joseph, John & Thomas Hadfield, Andrew Clow Papers, CWU.

153 See for example, Andrew Clow to David Cay, 2 May 1786, Folder Jan.–Jun. 1786, Andrew Clow & Co., SGC.

154 David Cay to Andrew Clow, 7 Jun. 1784, Folder Correspondence, CWU. Mary had been quite sickly from at least 1786. In December 1786 she was staying with Mr Renwick, who advised that she was 'improving fast'. David Cay to Andrew Clow, 30 Dec. 1786, Folder Nov.–Dec. 1786, Andrew Clow & Co., SGC. Clow was 'sadly distressed' by his daughter's death. Their old friend Joseph Hadfield had to break the news to him. Joseph Hadfield to David Cay, 7 Jul. 1790, Folder Joseph, John & Thomas Hadfield, Andrew Clow & Co., CWU. I have not been able to ascertain whether Clow or Cay married and therefore whether Mary was legitimate or not. The fact that Clow and Cay shared a house in Philadelphia for some time would suggest not. Marriage was one element of 'commercial masculinity'. Smail, 'Coming of Age', pp. 244–46.

155 James Bunyie & Co. to Andrew Clow, 25 Sep. 1784; Folder Jan.–Sep.; Deed by James Bradshaw dated 14 Nov. 1785, Folder Oct.–Dec. 1784, Andrew Clow & Co., SGC.

156 Lithgow & Harrison to Andrew Clow & Co., 11 Feb. 1785, Folder 1785–98, Andrew Clow & Co., CWU.

157 This was an increasing trend. Kenneth Morgan, 'Business Networks in the British Export Trade to North America, 1750–1800', in McCusker and Morgan, *The Early-Modern Atlantic Economy*, pp. 36–62.

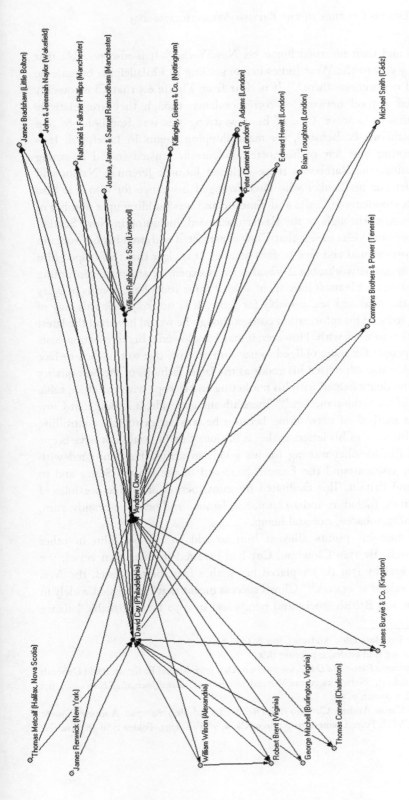

FIGURE 6.5   ANDREW CLOW'S NETWORKS C.1787

Key: ● Strong ties   ⬡ Weak ties

Sources: Andrew Clow & Co, SGC; Andrew Clow & Co, Business Correspondence, CWU; Andrew Clow & Co, Baker Library; Clow Papers, Hagley Library.

London and then returned home via New York.[158] It is also possible that he paid a visit to the West Indies before settling in Philadelphia because he also had connections there.[159] It is clear from Figure 6:5 that Clow quickly developed a good network of correspondents, though they are relatively few at this early stage. One of his few strong ties was Rathbone & Son (later Rathbone & Benson), his main shipping agents in Liverpool. It is worth noting how few of his correspondents he trusted (noted as strong ties). Besides the Rathbones these included John & Jeremiah Naylor and Peter Clement his banker who later arranged insurance for him. He also had correspondents in Cádiz and Tenerife and was building up a number of correspondents throughout the Eastern seaboard, including in Nova Scotia.

His personal visits meant that Clow constructed and used his networks in a very instrumental and face-to-face manner. It is clear that this helped him to build up his networks, but it was also a very expensive and time-consuming way of doing so. He must have spent at least three and a half months of every year on the road and sea, possibly far more. It is unlikely that this way of working reduced his information costs, although he would have had the latest information to work with. However, it may have lowered his transaction costs because people felt more obliged to pay him on time due to this face-to-face contact. He also advertised his goods as the latest fashions of the best quality and this no doubt helped with his marketing and to cope with the changeable demand of the fashion market.[160] These advantages aside, it is clear that Clow used this method of networking because he was an extremely controlling person. The tone of his letters makes it obvious that he could not have borne to sit in Philadelphia waiting for his goods to arrive. He continued with his yearly visits around the Eastern Seaboard of the United States and to and around Britain. This facilitated the construction of a wide portfolio of commodities, including Indian corn, tea, lemons and oranges, brandy, rum, sugar, coffee, tobacco, rice and hemp.

Over time his profits allowed him to add to his portfolio in other ways as well. By 1789 Clow and Cay had invested in their own vessel, the *Adriana*, and by 1791 they replaced her with a new, better vessel, the *New Adriana*, valued at £5,000.[161] Clow's success meant that he invested widely in American and British stocks and bonds and in 1790 had a sizeable balance

---

158 Folder Jan.–Jun. 1786, Andrew Clow & Co., SGC.
159 I could not find evidence to prove this.
160 *Pennsylvania Packet and Daily Advertiser*, 19 Oct. 1787; Rachel E. Kranton and Deborah F. Minehart, 'Networks versus Vertical Integration', *Rand Journal of Economics*, 31:3 (2000), 570–601, p. 572.
161 David Cay to Andrew Clow, 19 Jun. 1789, Folder Admin 1789–1790, Andrew Clow & Co., CWU; Peter Clement to Andrew Clow, 26 Feb. 1793, Folder 1785–98, Andrew

of $1,138.74 at the Bank of North America, with $61,123.57 going through the partnership's account in the following year. Fellow merchant Joshua Gilpin had $49,111 through his account in the same year, whilst leading Quaker merchants Samuel and Miers Fisher had a comparatively low $30,823.10.[162] Nor was this the total of their cash flow as they also cleared bills through Peter Clement in London. At this time war was a constant threat with the continuing naval race and competition between Britain and France.[163] Clow, ever alert to new opportunities, went on a new face-to-face networking drive in the Mediterranean in 1789. He visited Bilbao, Coruña, Lisbon, Gibraltar and Algiers. This meant that along with the various correspondents he had developed over the years, by 1793 he had an impressive number and distribution of contacts, as shown in Figure 6:6. It is clear that he had significantly increased his contacts in the north west of England for the textile trade and along the Eastern seaboard. There were also far more contacts in the West Indies, including Haiti and St. Croix. Furthermore, Clow had vastly extended his contacts around Europe and the Mediterranean, with contacts in France, Spain, Portugal, Germany and Algiers. He was clearly able to take advantage of turmoil in both the Caribbean and Europe at this time. In 1790 the elite Liverpool house of Corrie, Gladstone & Bradshaw wrote that it was sensible of his 'weight in Philadelphia which will make us desirous of cultivating a Correspondence'.[164] Clearly he had built up a good reputation. At the same time, he still had relatively few strong ties; Rathbone & Benson, Joseph Hadfield & Sons, James, John & Ben Potter, Watson, Myers & Co. and Peter Clement appeared to be the only trusted correspondents. However, his aggressive style made him enemies in some circles. In the same year his friend Peter Clement heard gossip to the effect that people were being advised 'not do business with Mr Clow … it was a passion with the People there [in Philadelphia] in general that he must very soon get to the end of his chain' [i.e. he was extending his credit too far].[165] Success was not without its jealousies.

Clow & Co., CWU. I have not been able to ascertain what shares they held in the vessel. Given Clow's personality, it is likely they held all of the 64ths.

162 This was a sizeable balance because merchants always tried to re-invest their money as soon as possible rather than leave it lying idle. Andrew Clow & Co., Letters Received, Baker Library; Personal Ledgers, Bank of North America.

163 Michael Duffy, 'World-Wide War and British Expansion, 1793–1815, in Marshall, *The Eighteenth Century*, pp. 184–207.

164 Corrie, Gladstone & Bradshaw to Andrew Clow & Co., 10 Jul. 1790, Folder Jan.–Jul. 1790, Andrew Clow & Co., SGC.

165 Peter Clement to David Cay, 7 Jul. 1790, Folder P. Clement, Andrew Clow & Co., CWU.

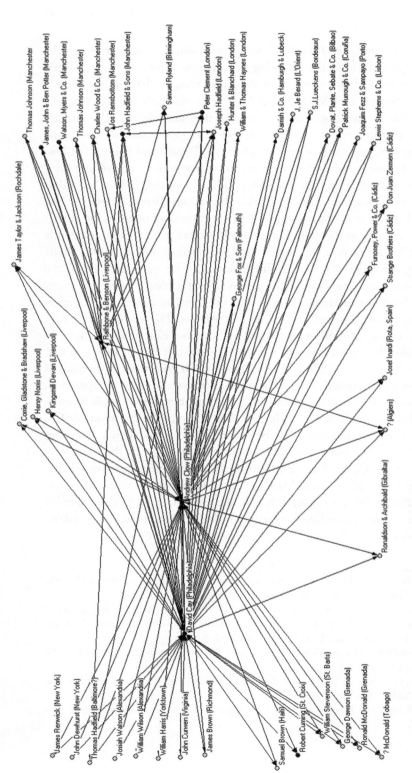

FIGURE 6:6   ANDREW CLOW'S NETWORKS C.1793

Key: ● Strong ties   ◎ Weak ties

Sources: Andrew Clow & Co., SGC; Andrew Clow & Co., Business Correspondence, CWU; Andrew Clow & Co., Baker Library; Clow Papers, Hagley Library.

Clow's proactive strategy worked for him as he successfully extended his role in international trade over time, despite the turmoil of this period. He did not use family networks, rather he used personal visits to develop and cement weak ties. At the same time, he was clearly not a likeable man, nor easy to get along with, and so his reputation must have been based on his business acumen and record for prompt payment. Certainly people trusted him more than he trusted others in return. His lack of trust in people and the need to control meant that he was extremely mobile. This, along with his irascible character meant that whilst he had a large number and geographical spread of correspondents, by necessity he almost shunned local associational networks which may have given him status and prestige in other, more cultural or social ways. The more static Cay probably did most of the local networking for the firm. Neither did Clow seem to develop much affective commitment through his business dealings. He did 'stay' and seem friendly with those he trusted such as the Rathbones, Joseph Hadfield, Peter Clement and a few suppliers, but there only seemed to be one example of gift-giving, and that was from others to him.[166] His erstwhile partner Cay quite clearly exasperated Clow, whilst Joseph Hadfield in London was obviously wary of him despite the fact that Clow sometimes travelled with him in England on his yearly visits.[167] Furthermore, apart from being in business with Cay, it would appear that he only co-invested with others twice. Once for one voyage with Robert Cuming in an adventure from St. Eustatius, and the second time he co-owned the *Kitty* in 1789 along with Joseph Hadfield and George Dawson on an adventure to Antigua and Grenada.[168] His lack of personal ties and his inability to trust others makes one wonder how many felt truly obliged, rather than simply in awe of him. How many people truly mourned for him when he and Cay both died from the yellow fever epidemic

---

166 The female members of Thomas Johnson's Manchester family wanted to send Clow some stilton cheeses. Thomas Johnson to Andrew Clow, 24 Jan. 1790, Folder Thomas Johnson and Henry Norris, Andrew Clow & Co., CWU.

167 Joseph Hadfield to David Cay, 15 Dec. 1790, Folder Joseph, John & Thomas Hadfield 1785–88, Andrew Clow & Co., CWU.

168 Account sales ... on Joint Account of Messrs A. Clow & Co. and R. Cuming, 26 Jul. 1793, Folder Parrish & Co., Andrew Clow & Co., Business Correspondence, CWU. Cuming was based at St. Croix. See Folder R. Cuming, Andrew Clow Papers, CWU; Sales of Sundry Merchandise ..., [n. d.], Folder Kitty, 1789–94, Business Correspondence, Box 13, Andrew Clow & Co. CWU. It appears that Clow did ask George Fox & Sons of Falmouth to take an interest in a cargo of flour, but they declined. George Fox & Sons to Andrew Clow & Co., 3 Sep. 1790, Folder George Fox, Andrew Clow & Co., CWU. St Eustatius was taken from the Dutch in 1781, although there had been a Scottish presence there from as early as the 1750s. Hamilton, *Scotland, the Caribbean and the Atlantic World*, pp. 43, 71.

in Philadelphia in 1793?[169] If he had reached the end of his credit before he died, would anyone in his network have stepped in to help him? At the same time, how much more could he have achieved if he had not died so suddenly? Clow is an enigma. Unlikeable but with a reputation for business acumen, untrusting but obviously trustworthy, and a successful edgeworker always on the outskirts of society. His networks did not so much help him; rather he developed and used them in a far more pro-active, even aggressive way, than did others. Certainly networks need a change agent such as Clow, who developed international networks and thereby promoted trade.[170] He was successful, despite not relying on family, ethnicity or religious networks. Whether this success made him happy or content however, seems unlikely.

Conclusion

THESE CASE STUDIES challenge the rather benign view often taken of networks. It is fair to say that they are not representative – most networks worked well. However, studying networks which do not fulfill their potential highlights many points. Lawson's story demonstrates that being locked into kin or ethnic ties could have serious repercussions. Certainly the implicit contract of family was broken by Semple, whilst Lawson was powerless to stop himself being embroiled in risks for which he had no appetite and was unable to create new options. In contrast, although Rainford was on the wrong end of strong family ties, he was able to survive because he had built up many independent weak ties and established his reputation over time. Whilst he was relatively powerless in relation to Jonathon Blundell Senior, he was powerful in a number of other networks. This variety was clearly vital to the regional and international economy.[171] Clow was a risk taker and a change agent. He may not have built many affective ties, but he did spend a vast amount of time cultivating his networks not only around the Atlantic but in the Mediterranean as well. Such activity was especially important in developing international trade in times of institutional change or crisis.

This chapter also shows that these networks comprised groups of people that formed associations with the explicit or implicit expectation of mutual benefit. Their success in doing so varied greatly. Some were better than

---

169 Invoice, Ruddack & Co., Funeral Charges, Andrew Clow Business Correspondence, 1790–96, CWU.
170 John F. Wilson and John Singleton, 'The Manchester Industrial District, 1750–1939: Clustering, Networking and Performance', in Wilson and Popp, *Industrial Clusters*, pp. 44–67, pp. 44–45.
171 Casson, 'An Economic Approach to Regional Business Networks', p. 34.

others at transferring and synthesising information, some gained status and legitimacy, whilst others lost theirs. Information and transactions costs were not always lowered and the ability to adapt to environmental changes varied widely. Some merchants promoted international trade through their networks whilst others did not. What is clear is that familial, religious and ethnic networks are not always a boon, dense networks can be problematic, various networks are not only active at one time but necessary, networks are dynamic and changing all the time, and that power relations are very important. The fact that most networks worked well is a testament to the majority of merchants being able to handle these challenges in these difficult times. With that in mind, we can now see how they coped in periods of crisis.

7

Crises

We are War Merchants and
We cannot judge the Effects of Peace[1]

McKNIGHT & McILWRATH'S COMMENT highlights the fact that there were many wars during this period; and that many merchants were used to, and comfortable with, coping in a war economy. Indeed, the Treaty of Amiens in 1801, to which this quote refers, created only a temporary lull in the French Wars. McKnight & McIlwrath were trading from Ayr, Scotland, but John Perhouse of Philadelphia noted a similar attitude a few weeks later, commenting that the merchants there were in despair having planned for a long war.[2] Clearly, some merchants were more prepared, willing, or able to conduct business in a difficult business environment. Moreover, some such as McKnight & McIlwrath and Andrew Clow, positively thrived on these situations or involved themselves in speculation. In contrast, others such as James Lawson were clearly uneasy trading during periods of conflict.

Whilst war was a major phenomenon throughout the eighteenth century, there were other types of crises as well. These included imagined crises, natural crises, economic crises and financial crises.[3] Often financial crises were caused by 'real' crises.[4] These had both positive and negative features and outcomes, all of with which merchants had to cope. Personal trust

---

1 McKnight & McIlwrath to John McDonald, 5 Oct. 1801, McKnight & McIlwrath Letterbook 1800–1802.

2 John Perhouse to James Perhouse, 2 Dec. 1801, John Perhouse Journal.

3 Of course there were many individual bankruptcies or insolvencies which meant a personal financial crisis, but here I am concerned with those crises which affected the whole business community.

4 Mark Casson, 'Crises and Globalisation: The Consequence of Mistaken Judgments'

was an extremely important element of the business culture at such times. Communications were even slower and less reliable than usual, levels of institutional and general trust were low, and uncertainty high.[5] An existing good reputation was important during these periods, and many tried to keep to their obligations in order to enhance that reputation and thereby enable them to trade in the future. In these difficult times networks were retrenched, but at the same time, merchants created various institutions which helped them to combat the challenges facing them.

This chapter first explores what constitutes a crisis, before discussing 'imagined' crises, natural crises, war, and financial crises. Three case studies are then investigated: the American War of Independence, the abolition of the British-Atlantic slave trade, and the build-up to the Anglo-American War. These case studies facilitate a discussion of how the business culture helped both individuals and business communities cope with, and react to, such events. They also highlight the changing relationship between the trading communities in Britain, the mainland colonies/states and the British West India colonies, and importantly, especially within Britain, between the mercantile community and the state. Therefore this chapter stresses the resilience of the business culture, but also how it altered and helped merchants cope over time. It also highlights how risk, trust, reputation, obligation and networks played out in this environment.

WHAT IS A CRISIS?

DECIDING whether a certain event is a crisis depends on your definition.[6] However, Freddie Heylen and Lorenzo Pozzi argue that a general definition of a crisis does not exist, and that evidence of crises are 'scarce and ambiguous'.[7] Louis Cullen notes that whilst it may be easy to define the French Revolution as a political crisis for example, economic crises are not always so easy to categorise.[8] It is clear however, that eighteenth-century merchants 'knew a crisis when they saw one'.[9] Whilst Hoppit is referring to

---

(Unpublished paper given at Association of Business Historians conference 2010). My thanks to Mark Casson for sight of the full text.

5 See the chapter on trust above, *passim*.

6 Hoppit, 'Financial Crises', p. 40.

7 Freddie Heylen and Lorenzo Pozzi, 'Crises and Human Capital Accumulation', *Canadian Journal of Economics*, 40:4 (Nov. 2007), 1261–85, pp. 1263, 1262.

8 L. M. Cullen, 'History, Economic Crises and Revolution: Understanding Eighteenth-Century France', *EcHR*, new ser., 45:4 (Nov. 1993), 635–57, p. 635.

9 Hoppit, 'Financial Crises', p. 40.

financial crises, rather than natural crises such as hurricanes, or man-made crises such as war or policy changes, these events were normally concomitant with, caused by, or vice versa caused, general economic or financial crises. Eventually they end up relating to the economy by affecting total factor productivity, often leading to a decline in physical capital, or a period of inflation.[10] For example, boom and bust characterised post-war periods in the eighteenth-century Atlantic. Sometimes various types of crises happened at the same time which created an even more complex situation. For example, Charles Stewart Parker in London noted in 1798 that prices 'may have rose in consequence of convoys ... & several ships being from the shortness of Crops disappointed in getting loaded'.[11] Given that merchants reacted to, and coped with, crises in order to maximise their profit (or reduce their risk) Doorley and Garcia's definition of a crisis in business is helpful. 'A crisis is not necessarily a catastrophic event, but rather an event that, left to usual business processes and velocities, causes significant reputational, operational, or financial harm.'[12] This encompasses a wide variety of crises, but demonstrates that in order to survive, or benefit from a crisis economically, merchants had to alter their business practices or patterns, at least in the short term.

Some crises are imagined into existence – they are in our heads.[13] For example, rumours about an individual might lead to people calling in their debts and making that person insolvent unnecessarily. Similar events can cause a run on a bank. Such rumours abound in situations of uncertainty leading to a kind of self-fulfilling prophecy.[14] Often however, crises provoke a response. The Bubble Act of 1720 could be seen as a response to a moral panic over speculation which effectively put 'an end to such a frenzy'.[15] Kenneth Thompson argues that our contemporary world 'is the age of moral panic', but some of today's perceived crises such as that in trust, also arose in the eighteenth century.[16] For example, it is possible to frame the Boston Tea Party as a moral panic, or 'a general frenzy'.[17] Because confidence in the

---

10 Heylen and Pozzi, 'Crises and Human Capital Accumulation', pp. 1263, 1269.

11 Charles Parker to John Bolton, 16 Aug. 1798, 920 Par III 25/22.

12 Doorley and Garcia, *Reputation Management*, p. 328. Casson in contrast sees a crisis as an unexpected event that requires urgent action, 'Crises and Globalisation'.

13 Ulrich Beck, 'Living in the World Risk Society', *Economy and Society*, 35:3 (Aug. 2006), 329–45, p. 333.

14 Doorley and Garcia, *Reputation Management*, p. 338.

15 Hoppit, 'The Myths of the South Sea Bubble', p. 145.

16 Kenneth Thompson, *Moral Panics* (London and New York: Routledge, 1998), p. 1; Fukuyama, *Trust*; O'Neill, *A Question of Trust*.

17 *An Impartial History of the War in America* ... (London: Printed for R. Faulder,

system or regime (general trust) is important, stability is maintained whilst it exists, but a loss in that confidence may well lead to a crisis.[18] This is because 'events are more likely to be perceived as fundamental threats ... if the society, or some part of it, is in crisis or experiencing disturbing changes giving rise to stress'.[19]

Perceptions of threats are therefore important, and personal or collective past experiences feed into this. If certain events have happened under particular conditions, and those conditions arise again, it is reasonable to expect a repetition. For example, a history of tensions and animosities will increase the likelihood of eruptions of a new conflict, and indeed, expectations of it.[20] Similarly, if a merchant witnessed increasing speculation during a war, experience would tell him that boom and bust would follow. Such perceptions vary widely according to personality, age and other factors, as was discussed in the chapter on risk. For example, Matson argues that Stephen Girard perceived that running commercial risks, even during wartime, was less risky than investing in manufactures, finance or real estate.[21] Others saw such activities as diversification and risk spreading.[22] At the same time, to be risk averse, to prepare one's self for the worst, as did James Lawson, is entirely rational, because ignorance of a possible crisis or a decision can exacerbate the situation.[23] For example, the Americans did not know that the British had revoked the Orders in Council in 1812, and therefore declared war.[24]

Natural crises were also common throughout the eighteenth century. Calamities such as earthquakes, epidemics, fire, crop failure, and hurricanes were rarely entirely unexpected, but still 'wrought havoc in all the British colonies'.[25] Not only did hurricanes ruin crops, they damaged port facilities

Bookseller, New Bond-Street and J. Milliken, Bookseller, Carlisle, 1780), in Markman Ellis, ed., *Tea and the Tea Table in Eighteenth-Century England* (London: Pickering and Chatto, 2010), 4 vols, Vol. IV: Ben Dew, ed., *Tea and Politics: The Boston Tea Party (1773) and the Commutation Act (1784)*, p. 148. My thanks to Ben Dew for giving me early sight of this volume.

18 Hoppit, 'Financial Crises', pp. 51, 53.

19 Thompson, *Moral Panics*, p. 8.

20 Jens Rydgren, 'The Power of the Past: A Contribution to a Cognitive Sociology of Ethnic Conflict', *Sociological Theory*, 25:3 (Sep. 2007), 225–44, pp. 235, 239.

21 Matson, 'Accounting for War and Revolution', p. 187.

22 See above, pp. 62–64.

23 Beck, 'Living in the World Risk Society', p. 330.

24 See below, p. 226.

25 Clarke and Short, 'Social Organization and Risk', p. 378; Matthew Mulcahy, '"Melancholy and Fatal Calamities": Disaster and Society in Eighteenth-Century South Carolina', in Greene et al., eds., *Money, Trade and Power*, pp. 278–98, p. 238. Certain areas such as Asia and the tropics are particularly vulnerable to these events,

and housing, and sometimes claimed the lives of slaves as well.[26] Food shortages also increased the likelihood of slave uprisings, a continuous potential threat in the plantation economies.[27] These all affected prices in markets for merchants to deal with, or conversely, speculate on.[28] For example, Ryden notes that the 'sugar crisis' at the end of the eighteenth century followed a 'speculative mania' in sugar production.[29] Whilst such failures are in some ways endogenous to the business cycle, they are also exacerbated by human behaviour.[30] Misfortune, miscalculated risk or wasted capital may all play a part.[31] Natural crises therefore have a negative relationship with short-term economic activity, but there can also be a 'positive association between the number of disasters and economic growth'.[32] For example, Mulcahy has demonstrated that the fire in Charleston of November 1740 and the hurricane of September 1752 provided an opportunity to improve the city.[33] Similarly, when Port Royal, Jamaica, crumbled into the sea in 1692, it stimulated the updating of capital stock, and promoted the move to Kingston.[34]

Rather strangely, war is not cited very often in the socio-economic literature

---

and whilst humans do not have ultimate control over these events, they placed themselves in the position of having to deal with hurricanes by migrating to the southern and West Indian colonies. Mark Skidmore and Hideki Toya, 'Do Natural Disasters Promote Long-Run Growth?', *Economic Inquiry*, 40:4 (2002), 664–87, p. 666; Mulcahy, '"Melancholy and Fatal Calamities"', p. 279.

26 Mulcahy, 'Weathering the Storms', pp. 641–43.

27 On slave revolts see Michael Mullin, *Africa in America: Slave Acculturation and Resistance in the American South and the British Caribbean, 1736–1831* (Urbana: University of Illinois Press, 1992); Gelein Matthews, *Caribbean Slave Revolts and the British Abolitionist Movement* (Baton Rouge: Louisiana State Press, 2006).

28 Of course a bumper harvest could also affect markets, as in 1790 when price of both meat and grain fell following a good harvest. George Fox to Andrew Clow, 3 Jun. 1790, Folder George Fox, Andrew Clow & Co., CWU. On speculation during the run-up to the Anglo-American war see below, pp. 228–29.

29 Ryden, *West Indian Slavery*, p. 273.

30 Fabio Canova, 'Were Financial Crises Predictable?', *Journal of Money, Credit and Banking*, 26:1 (Feb. 1994), 102–24, p. 104.

31 Canova, 'Were Financial Crises Predictable?', p. 104. See also Trivellato, *The Familiarity of Strangers*, chapter ten.

32 However, such benefits do not come from geological disasters. Skidmore and Toya, 'Do Natural Disasters Promote Long-Run Growth?', pp. 665, 672.

33 The way in which they went about this with regard to the use of slaves was also conditioned by larger social processes and relations such as slavery. Mulcahy, '"Melancholy and Fatal Calamities"'.

34 Colin Clarke, *Kingston, Jamaica: Urban Development and Social Change, 1692–2002* (Jamaica: Ian Randle Publishers, 2005), chapter two; Nuala Zahediah, 'The Merchants of Port Royal, Jamaica, and the Spanish Contraband Trade, 1655–1692', *WMQ*, 43:4 (Oct. 1986), 570–93.

on crises, and yet it is clear that for contemporaries, war was ever present.[35] As wars came to be fought on land and sea, and became more expensive, they affected a larger section of the population. In our period alone and within the Atlantic context there were thirty-four years of war: 1756–1763, 1775–1783, 1793–1802 and 1803–1815; and this does not even include periods of international tension such as non-importation acts and embargoes.[36] As was discussed in the chapter on obligation there was an 'intimate interdependence of war and trade', and merchants as a community, in Britain at least, were often happy for wars to be fought if the outcome brought commercial advantages, such as gaining the Ceded Islands in the Treaty of Paris in 1763.[37] Of course, wars were horrific in themselves, but they also disrupted patterns of trade, as well as creating other problems. For example, British merchants and residents in Grenada and Tobago appealed to the British government for help between 1779 and 1782, having lost property and needing provisions as a result of the French capture of the islands.[38] Even periods of tension such as non-importation, embargoes or blockades 'required a different level of commitment and sacrifice', and often pressure was put on merchants to comply.[39] At the same time however, elite merchants often found periods of non-importation a useful time in which to offload excess stock. This usually had the effect of weeding out the weaker merchants – or 'cleansing the market', leaving the survivors stronger.[40]

Of course some merchants approached periods of war with eager anticipation. For example, privateering was an alternative way of making money.

---

35 An exception is Rydgren, 'The Power of the Past'.

36 Huw W. Bowen, *War and British Society, 1688–1815* (Cambridge: Cambridge University Press, 1998), pp. 1–10.

37 Seeley, *The Expansion of England*, p. 110; see above, pp. 154–59; Richard Sheridan, 'The British Credit Crisis of 1772', *Journal of Economic History*, 20:2 (Jun. 1960), 161–86, p. 165; Pearce, *British Trade with Spanish America*, p. 41. On strategy and policy of eighteenth-century wars see Pares, 'American versus Continental Warfare'; Baugh, 'Great Britain's "Blue-Water" Policy'.

38 See the letters at CO 101/24, Grenada: Original Correspondence, ff. 2–5, 19–37, 131–32, TNA. The British took Tobago and Grenada during the Seven Years' War but Tobago was given back to the French under the Treaty of Paris in 1783, Bruce P. Lenman, 'Colonial Wars and Imperial Instability, 1688–1793', in Marshall, *Oxford History of the British Empire*, Vol. II, pp. 151–68, pp. 164, 166.

39 Newell, *From Dependency to Independence*, p. 282. See for example the suggested standard letter for cancelling orders from Britain dated 7 Nov. 1765, MSS Relating to Non-Importation Resolutions 1766–1775, Vol. I, 1765–66, 973.2 M31, APS.

40 Sheridan, 'The British Credit Crisis', p. 170; Ricardo J. Caballero and Mohamad L. Hammour do add that such cleansing is not necessarily desirable, 'The Cleansing Effect of Recessions', *American Economic Review*, 85:5 (Dec. 1994), 1350–68, p. 1365; Smith-Doerr and Powell, 'Networks and Economic Life', p. 383.

It was shown in the chapter on risk that merchants in Bristol and Liverpool enthusiastically engaged in the practice, and New England merchants such as the Huntingdon family also 'invested heavily in privateering as an alternative to normal exchange'.[41] Merchants in the West Indies did the same. Bermuda fitted out twenty-four vessels 'Against the War with France' between the commencement of the war and 21 November 1791.[42] The interruptions to trade caused by war meant that many brokers withheld stock until the optimum time to sell, creating false dearths in markets and pushing up prices. Such speculation was particularly rife during the tension between the United States and Britain over the period 1807 to 1812.[43] Entrepreneurs such as Andrew Clow could take advantage of such possibilities, even if they were seen as upstarts and were unpopular.[44] As Clow sought new markets in the Mediterranean with the onset of the French wars, so others in Philadelphia redirected their trade via Boston and New York during the American War of Independence. After the war some merchants such as Stephen Girard tried to develop trade with China and India.[45] Robert Morris, for example, sent the first American vessel to Canton in 1784.[46] Indeed, Doerflinger argues that the shock of war accelerated economic development in the Delaware valley.[47] Others profited directly from providing the army with food, clothes or arms.[48] It is also possible that merchants such as Philadelphian Jabez Fisher, who travelled to England to learn from merchants there during the American War of Independence, increased their human capital, thereby benefitting in the long term.[49] Therefore wars, and indeed other crises, can be seen as events which promote Schumpeter's 'creative destruction' by forcing merchants to adapt their mercantile habits.

---

41 Newell, *From Dependency to Independence*, p. 300.

42 'A List of Ships and Vessels Commissioned …', to 21 Nov. 1791, CO 37/44, Bermuda: Original Correspondence, ff. 187–88, TNA.

43 See below, pp. 228–29.

44 Joseph A. Schumpeter, *The Theory of Economic Development: An Inquiry into Profits, Capital, Credit Interest, and the Business Cycle*, Harvard Economic Studies, Vol. XLVI [1911] (Cambridge, MA: Harvard University Press, 1934), pp. 88–90.

45 Matson, 'Accounting for War and Revolution'.

46 Doerflinger, *A Vigorous Spirit of Enterprise*, p. 284.

47 Doerflinger, *A Vigorous Spirit of Enterprise*, p. 197.

48 See below, p. 211. See the University of Greenwich/National Maritime Museum project *Sustaining the Empire: War, the Navy and the Contractor State* at http://www.nmm.ac.uk/researchers/research-areas-and-projects/sustaining-the-empire/, accessed 24 Sep. 2010.

49 Kenneth Morgan, ed., *An American Quaker in the British Isles: The Travel Journals of Jabez Maud Fisher, 1775–1779* (Oxford: Oxford University Press, 1992); Heylen and Pozzi, 'Crises and Human Capital Accumulation'.

All of these 'real' crises usually affected the general economy and financial markets in some way, which meant that financial crises were a commonplace occurrence. They were often triggered by an event such as war or the bankruptcy of an important merchant or banking house.[50] Even rumours of these events might have fostered enough uncertainty to create the sudden change in expectations necessary to trigger an 'imagined' financial crisis. Within our period, there were financial crises in Britain in 1761, 1763, 1772, 1778, 1788, 1793 and 1797, most of which spread around the Atlantic. There were also domestic crises in the Americas for example, in 1778–79, 1785, 1792 and 1797.[51] It is clear that many of these dates correlate with bubbles such as post-war booms.[52] Gossip about such events was easily spread around the Atlantic. Joshua Johnson wrote to his partners in Maryland during June 1772 that the breaking of the Scots bank of Fordyce & Co. had stagnated business and that 'there is doubts about the Scotch [Ayr] Bank'.[53] The eventual failure of the house started a trans-Atlantic wide crisis on the back of a boom which followed the ending of the earlier non-importation agreements in the thirteen colonies.[54]

As with other crises, financial crises usually have the effect of 'cleansing' the trading community of those who are not so financially viable or knowledgeable, such as Temin and Voth's 'greater fools' during the South Sea 'bubble'.[55] Such radical problems can make radical measures 'acceptable'. The Bubble Act of 1720 has already been mentioned, but the various Acts under George III dealing with insolvency, and the developing law of bankruptcy,

---

50 Hoppit, 'Financial Crises', p. 39; Franklin Allen and Douglas Gale, 'Bubbles and Crises', *Economic Journal*, 110:460 (Jan. 2000), 236–55, pp. 238, 236.

51 Sam Bass Warner, *The Private City* (Philadelphia: University of Pennsylvania Press, 1968), chapter two; Doerflinger, *A Vigorous Spirit of Enterprise*, p. 262; David J. Cowen, 'The First Bank of the United States and the Securities Market Crash of 1792', *Journal of Economic History*, 60:4 (Dec. 2000), 1041–60; Richard Sylla, Robert E. Wright and David J. Cowen, 'Alexander Hamilton, Central Banker: Crisis Management during the U.S. Financial Panic of 1792', *BHR*, 83 (Spring 2009), 61–86; Richard S. Chew, 'Certain Victims of an International Contagion: The Panic of 1797 and the Hard Times of the Late 1790s in Baltimore', *Journal of the Early Republic*, 25 (Winter 2005), 565–613.

52 Allen and Gale, 'Bubbles and Crises', p. 236.

53 Joshua Johnson to Wallace & Davidson, 22 Jun. 1772, JJL. See also Henry Hamilton, 'The Failure of the Ayr Bank', *EcHR*, new ser., 8:3 (1956), 405–17.

54 The plantation economies were the worst affected. Sheridan, 'The British Credit Crisis'.

55 The most famous bubble is of course the South Sea Bubble. See Carswell, *The South Sea Bubble*; Hoppit, 'The Myths of the South Sea Bubble'; Peter Temin and Hans-Joachim Voth, 'Riding the South Sea Bubble', *American Economic Review*, 94:5 (Dec. 2004), 1654–68. On bubbles more generally see Garber, *Famous First Bubbles*.

are obvious examples of policy development reacting to increasing financial failures.[56]

Crises of various sorts were therefore endemic to the Atlantic economy in this period. Many merchants lost out because of them, some survived, and others thrived. Many crises affected the wider economy and financial markets drastically. However, in the long term, these events often caused positive outcomes for some, if not all. This included new laws enacted by the state, but also new institutions developed by the mercantile community in order to represent themselves to the state.

THE AMERICAN WAR OF INDEPENDENCE

WHATEVER THE CAUSES of the American War of Independence, the increasing tension between the colonists on the mainland and the British state caused merchants wide ranging problems.[57] Following the various non-importations of 1765–66, 1768–70 and 1774–76 and the Boston Tea Party, attitudes tended to harden. By 1780 the colonists were being called 'obstinate bigots' with 'factious and turbulent' spirits.[58] However, the trading community tended to be rather more pragmatic, partially no doubt, because conflict often hurt the finances of merchants, even if they supported non-importations ideologically. For example, in 1774 Philadelphian Margaret Duncan, who so assiduously paid her debts, noted that the non-importations had 'been a great disadvantage' to her.[59] Yet she, like many others, was

---

56 Allan Drazen and Vittorio Grilli, 'The Benefit of Crises for Economic Reforms', *American Economic Review*, 83:3 (Jun. 1993), 598–607, p. 598. See also Ron Harris, 'The Bubble Act: Its Passage and its Effects on Business Organization', *Journal of Economic History*, 54:3 (Sep. 1994), 610–27; Hoppit, *Risk and Failure*, chapter three. See also Finn, *The Character of Credit*, chapters three and four; Peter J. Coleman, *Debtors and Creditors in America: Insolvency, Imprisonment for Debt, and Bankruptcy, 1607–1900* (Madison: State Historical Society of Wisconsin, 1974). See Thomas Max Safley, 'Business Failure and Civil Scandal in Early Modern Europe', *BHR*, 83:1 (Spring 2009), 35–60 for the tightening up of restrictions in eighteenth-century Germany in response to failures.

57 For a brief introduction to the range of views on the causes of the war see: Bailyn, *The Ideological Origins of the American Revolution*; Nash, *The Urban Crucible*; Egnal, *A Mighty Empire*; Gordon S. Wood, *The American Revolution: A History* (London: Weidenfeld & Nicholson, 2003); Timothy H. Breen, *The Marketplace of Revolution: How Consumer Politics Shaped American Independence* (New York: Oxford University Press, 2004).

58 Dew, *Tea and Politics; An Impartial History of the War in America* ..., pp. 140–41.

59 Margaret Duncan to John Ewer, 5 Dec. 1774, Folder Margaret Duncan to John Ewer, CBP.

determined to stand by them. Peter Wikoff of the same city noted that 'many persons here are very Anxious to stick to our Resolutions'.[60] He added that he was importing only necessities and that 'We still stand firm.'[61] Others found themselves in difficulties, such as James & Drinker and Isaac & Thomas Wharton, who were interviewed by the Philadelphia Committee in their capacity as agents for the East India Company, and were no doubt pressurised to comply with non-importation. Whilst the Whartons clearly gave suitable answers, they were still pressured to resign as agents for the East India Company, and tensions continued to run high with regard to James & Drinker.[62] There was similar pressure in New York where importers from Great Britain were accused of frustrating 'the laudable efforts' of patriotic people.[63]

Despite the fact that various British polemical tracts argued against the colonists, much of which was rather patronising, a conciliatory view was still proposed by some, including the political œconomist George Chalmers.[64] Furthermore, some merchants in Britain, having partners in the colonies, broadly supported the Americans.[65] For example, in 1763 Charles Stewart wrote to his colleagues in his sister house in Norfolk, Virginia, declaring himself a warm advocate of their country.[66] A year later he commented regarding the American Bill (presumably the Stamp Act passed the following year) that Grenville had 'cut your throats with a feather'.[67] There is no doubt however, that by 1772, the reputation of American merchants as a group was suspect. Joshua Johnson in London wrote to his partners in Maryland that merchants in London were 'so suspicious of America that I had the utmost

---

60 Peter Wikoff to John Ewer, 12 May 1770, Folder Peter Wikoff to John Ewer, CBP.

61 Wikoff to John Ewer, 19 May 1770, Folder Peter Wikoff to John Ewer, CBP.

62 'A Committee was Appointed ...', 17 Oct. 1773; Letter dated 17 Oct. 1773, Manuscripts Relating to Non-Importation Resolutions, 1766–1775, 973.2 M31; James & Drinker signed a Broadsheet for Repeal of the Stamp Act in 1766. 'From the Merchants and Traders of Philadelphia, 1766', Manuscripts Relating to Non Importation Resolutions.

63 'Whereas a Number of Persons ...', Broadside Advertisement, New York, 12 Jun. 1770.

64 Postlethwayt, *Britain's Commercial Interest Explained*, 'Dissertation XVI: A Succinct View', pp. 421–26; *A Letter from a Merchant in London to His Nephew in North America* ... (Printed for J. Walter, Charing Cross, London, 1766); George Chalmers, *An Estimate of the Comparative Strength of Britain* ... (London: Printed for C. Dilly in the Poultry and J. Bowen in New Bond Street, 1782). Chalmers was a lawyer who had lived in Baltimore and Maryland before the war. A good overview of the tensions in the American port towns is Nash, *The Urban Crucible*.

65 It has been argued however, that support came mainly from artisans, retailers and wholesalers rather than merchants. John Sainsbury, 'The Pro-Americans of London, 1769–1782', *WMQ*, 3rd ser., 35:3 (Jul. 1978), 423–54, p. 447.

66 Charles Stewart to Aitchison & Parker, 11 Sep. 1763, 920 PAR 1 27/2.

67 Charles Stewart to Aitchison & Parker, 23 Mar. 1764, 920 PAR 1 27/8.

difficulty to procure a friend'.[68] Trade continued to decline over the next two years along with a 'stoppage of credit' and far fewer goods were sent to both Philadelphia and Maryland.[69] In this way, merchants retrenched their networks and their financial assets as the situation worsened. This is not to say that despite the large amounts owing to Britain by the Americans – somewhere between £2 and £6 million sterling at the outbreak of the war – respectable merchants did not try to pay their debts.[70] As mentioned above, Margaret Duncan and Owen Biddle made great efforts to pay their debts and in this way protected their reputation and ensured personal trust continued despite the tension.[71]

By 1775, however, the choice whether to trade with the mainland colonies was out of the merchants' hands. Bristolian Lowbridge Bright lamented the fact that 'The Present Situation in America shutting up so many markets'; too many were sending slave vessels to Jamaica as an alternative option.[72] David Tuohy in Liverpool also told his Irish correspondents that all the African ships were laid up in September 1775 due to the American disturbances. This was because arms and gunpowder, which formed a significant part of the African cargo, were prohibited from export at that time.[73] In 1774 Bostonian Thomas Peck wrote to his London correspondents that the port was entirely blocked by Men of War. 'Such a Cruel Cursed act Could not have been Contrived but in Hell' he wrote, adding that this would cause great alienation.[74] In the same letter however, he added that he should not have any problems paying his debts. Merchants clearly made a distinction between the actions of the state, and the actions of their correspondents. Moreover, American merchants realised the influence that British merchants might have with the state, and implored them to use it. In 1775, in a letter in which he stressed he was trying to collect all his debts, Owen Biddle wrote

---

68 Joshua Johnson to Wallace & Davidson, 27 Aug. 1771, JJL.
69 Joshua Johnson to Wallace, Davidson & Johnson, 2 Sep. 1772, JJL.
70 Sheridan, 'The British Credit Crisis', p. 166.
71 See above, p. 145.
72 Lowbridge Bright to Benjamin Heywood, 23 Jan. 1775, *BMP*. It was important to keep heavily capitalised equipment such as ships busy.
73 David Tuohy to Stephen Fagan, 18 Sep. 1775; David Tuohy to Ryan & Begone, 5 Oct. 1775, Letters from David Tuohy, 380 TUO 2/4, DTP. Suitable cargoes to various areas of the West African coast are discussed in David Richardson, 'West African Consumption Patterns and Their Influence on the Eighteenth-Century English Slave Trade', in Henry A. Gemery and Jan S. Hogendorn, eds., *The Uncommon Market: Essays in the Economic History of the Atlantic Slave Trade* (New York and London: Academic Press, 1979), pp. 303–30.
74 Thomas Peck to Sharp & Davis, 7 Jun. 1774, Thomas M. Peck Letterbook 1763–1776, MHS.

to John Ewer that he hoped the merchants and manufacturers of Great Britain would 'interest themselves universally to put a stop to a Civil War which can hardly produce any advantages to the Ministry'.[75] The deed of the Liverpool Chamber of Commerce established in 1774 does not expressly state its objectives, but its activities clearly show that it was concerned with lobbying parliament and acting as a voice on behalf of Liverpool commerce.[76] The Liverpool merchants also used this institution in order to garner support from other trading towns, especially with regard to the 'precarious nature of British property in America at this time'.[77] In addition they sent delegates to London to lobby on their behalf – on this and other issues.[78] Glasgow merchants used their own Chamber of Commerce, established on 10 January 1783, in much the same way. Indeed, their first act was to draw up a memorial regarding the tobacco and sugar trades to send to Bristol and Liverpool.[79] In doing so, they were holding to their fourth resolution, which expressly noted that its aim was 'To afford aid to Members whether as individuals or otherwise who may apply for assistance in negotiating any matters of business, whether local, or of a nature which requires the weight & influence of the Directors, in making application to the Board of Trustees, to the King's Ministers, or to Parliament.'[80] New York merchants had also set up their own Chamber of Commerce in 1768, again during a period of tension.[81]

Trade between Britain and the thirteen colonies did not completely stop during the war, but it was obviously drastically reduced.[82] However, there were other ways of using shipping, such as privateering. During the years 1777–1783, London had 719 vessels involved in privateering, Liverpool 390, Bristol 390, and Glasgow 123. Ireland as a whole had 204 vessels involved.[83] Merchants all around the Atlantic engaged in this activity. For example, Connecticut's river ports and coastal towns sent out 380 ships with Letters of Marque during the war, and Marblehead, Newburyport and Salem together

---

75 Owen Biddle to John Ewer, 2 May 1775, Folder Owen Biddle to John Ewer, CBP.
76 Bennett, *The Voice of Liverpool Business*, pp. 7–8.
77 'An Abstract of the Proceedings and Resolutions ... 1777', p. 4.
78 Mr Dobson, Mr Haliday and Mr Walker comprised the delegation. 'An Abstract of the Proceedings and Resolutions ... 1777', p. 26.
79 18 Feb. 1783, Minutes of the Chamber of Commerce and Manufactures in the City of Glasgow, Vol. I, 1783–1788.
80 List of Resolutions, Minutes of the Chamber of Commerce and Manufactures in the City of Glasgow, Vol. I, 1783–1788.
81 Priest, 'Law and Commerce', p. 412.
82 Mitchell and Deane, *Abstract of British Historical Statistics*, pp. 310–11.
83 Starkey, *British Privateering Enterprise*, p. 200.

captured fifty-five British merchant and arms supply vessels in the first year of the war.[84] Of course privateering caused problems and the merchants again pressurised the state to protect their normal trade by convoy. A petition from the merchants of Liverpool in 1777 requested the government to 'persue [sic] such Measures as the Importance of the case may appear to require'.[85] This petition was not from the American merchants however, but from West Indian traders, no doubt prompted by the taking of John Tarleton's vessel, the *Mary*, in the Caribbean in March of that year.[86] Many in the West Indies also profited from privateering at this time. By November 1781, 4,784 hogsheads of sugar had been taken and sold from prize vessels in Jamaica alone, and merchants such as John and William Coppell and Robert Hibbert were profiting nicely from exporting these goods to England.[87]

Others, such as Stephen Girard of Philadelphia, engaged in smuggling in an attempt to keep their ships busy. This included filling hogsheads of rice from Charleston 'secretly with flour' and sending them to French Caribbean islands in contravention of French decrees.[88] Such activities required large amounts of personal trust. When the French later opened up their ports to free trade in 1784, Girard was 'jubilant' and continued to try to redirect some of his trade in this manner into the 1790s.[89] Owen Biddle (again with a letter remitting bills of exchange) wrote to John Ewer in London defiantly in September 1775, that 'all the British Navy cannot exclude us from a Trade with the Foreign Islands and I hope the Ministry will be convinced of the futillity [sic] of their attempts'.[90] Others relocated themselves instead; many loyalist merchants moved to Jamaica. In 1784 the Assembly noted that there were over seventy such merchants in Kingston who, by profiting from a law which allowed them to stay tax free in Jamaica, were quite wealthy and practising 'commerce to a considerable extent'.[91] As we have already seen, Alexander Johnston also spent most of the period of the American War of

---

84 Newell, *From Dependency to Independence*, p. 300.
85 The Memorial of the Merchants of Liverpool, 10 Jun. 1777, Secretaries of State: State Papers Foreign: France, f. 332, TNA.
86 Extract of a Letter to Gill Slater, 10 Mar. 1777, f. 334; see also Copy of a letter to John Dobson, 23 May 1777, Secretaries of State: State Papers Foreign: France, f. 335.
87 Journals of the Assembly of Jamaica, Vol. 7, 16 Nov. 1781, f. 410.
88 Quoted in Matson, 'Accounting for War and Revolution', p. 187.
89 Quoted in Matson, 'Accounting for War and Revolution', pp. 189, 196. See also Silvia Marzagalli, 'The Failure of a Trans-Atlantic Alliance? Franco-American Trade, 1783–1815', *History of European Ideas*, 34 (2008), 456–64.
90 Owen Biddle to John Ewer, 5 Sep. 1775, Folder Owen Biddle, CBP.
91 Journals of the Assembly of Jamaica, Vol. 8, 30 Nov. 1784, f. 32. It was not possible to ascertain to which law they were referring.

Independence traversing the Atlantic, and Jabez Fisher used the opportunity to increase his knowledge of trade in England.[92]

Others on both sides of the Atlantic attempted to benefit from the war more directly by supplying the Army in an even more explicit relationship between merchants and the state. Philadelphian Thomas Mifflin was the first quarter-master general of the Continental Army. As early as the end of 1777 when the British occupied Philadelphia he had earned himself a profit of £6,106.[93] Daniel Parker of Watertown near Boston supplied the Continental Army from 1777 onwards.[94] In 1783 he noted a credit balance from provisions supplied to the army of $386,348.68, and earned about the same amount again from his other trading activities.[95] There is no doubt however, that many suffered from bankruptcies caused by the war, 'cleansing' the trading community of its less successful members. Lowbridge Bright of Bristol noted in 1775 that 'I am afraid the Bankruptcies in Liverpool & the very great distress consequent thereon will be the means of forcing a deal of what is now on hand into the market & reduce the price [of sugar] still further.'[96] Nathaniel Phillips was on the other side of the sugar market in the same year. He wrote from Kingston, 'I cannot help deploring the distressed & perplexed situation of our public affairs, & if something does not turn upon our favour in the course of this year, I very much fear, the Sugar Colonies, as well as the state, will be involved in very great difficulties.'[97]

When hostilities ended, those that were still able were anxious to start trade again. George Chalmers cynically noted that 'they [the Americans] will sacrifice their Resentment to their Interest'.[98] Even in New York, occupied during much of the war, Alexander Johnston commented in 1784 that the 'prejudices of the minds of people begin to wear off by degrees'.[99] Indeed many, including Johnston and Andrew Clow, as we saw in the chapter on networks, saw the post-war period as one of opportunity.[100] William Sitgreaves of Philadelphia was also anxious to start up in business, and took his son into partnership. However, he kept his networks of people and range

---

92 See above, pp. 161–62 and p. 204.

93 Doerflinger, *A Vigorous Spirit of Enterprise*, p. 210.

94 See Daniel Parker Papers, passim, MHS.

95 Daniel Parker in Account with Daniel Parker & Co., 1783–84, Folder 5, Daniel Parker Papers.

96 Lowbridge Bright to David Duncombe, 24 Apr. 1778, *BMP*.

97 Nathaniel Phillips to Hibbert, Purrier & Horton, 22 Jul. 1778, Nathaniel Phillips Letterbook 1775–?, National Library of Wales.

98 Evidence of George Chalmer, 6 Apr. 1784, f. 141, BoT, BT6/83, Vol. I.

99 Alexander Johnston to Samuel Gardiner, 10 Feb. 1784, AJL.

100 See above, pp. 161–62 and pp. 188–96.

of commodities small until he felt the situation was more settled. No doubt the fact that Philadelphia had been overstocked with muslin as early as June 1783 led him to be cautious (his experience told him to expect a bust to follow).[101] In Boston too, Nathaniel & Francis Thayer picked up their trade via their London correspondents, Champion & Dickason. They must have been conducting some trade with them during the war, because on 20 August 1783 the Thayers sent them a bill of Exchange for £110 and two months later another for £532.[102]

Personal trust was obviously a key factor in facilitating the recommencement of trade, because institutional trust was of course a concern at such a politically sensitive time. It was noted above that correspondents expected each other to put pressure on their respective governments in order to resolve such issues.[103] In particular, British merchants were keen to know to what extent the new legislatures in the United States were going to enforce debts owed to the British from before the war. For example, Sparling & Bolden of Liverpool wrote to their sister house in Virginia that:

> We hope to hear your Assembly have repealed the Law relative to the Nonpayment of Debts due and owing from the Inhabitants of your State to British subjects, otherwise all Credit and Confidences whatever betwixt Britain & Virginia will cease, as no person here will in future give any Credit or trust their property to a Country who[se] inhabitants cannot be compelled by the Laws to pay their just Debts.[104]

The rush back to trade caused a boom, which of course, was followed with a bust just as Sitgreaves had anticipated. By February 1784 Kingston was 'overtock^d with all sorts of Good$^{s'}$.[105] The next year Nathaniel & Francis Thayer wrote to send only half of the goods they had ordered and in 1785 and 1786 there were many bankruptcies in Philadelphia.[106] By 1788 there

---

101 William Sitgreaves to Haliday & Dunbar, 13 Oct. 1783 f. 32; William Sitgreaves to Thomas Brammall, 28 Nov. 1783, f. 43; Sitgreaves to William Little, 4 Jun. 1783, f. 19, William and John Sitgreaves Letterbook 1783–94. The Treaty of Paris was not signed until 3 September 1783, but trade had re-commenced some time before. A preliminary treaty had been signed 30 November 1782.
102 Nathaniel & Francis Thayer to Champion & Dickason, 20 Aug. 1783; 28 Oct. 1783, Nathaniel & Francis Thayer Letterbook 1783–1790.
103 See above, pp. 208–9.
104 Sparling & Bolden to Sparling, Lawrence & Co., 29 Jan. 1788, Sparling & Bolden Letterbook.
105 Jacob Samson to Levy Cohen, 22 Feb. 1784, Lowe v Cohen, C105/19.
106 Nathaniel & Francis Thayer to Champion & Dickason, 5 May 1785, Nathaniel & Francis Thayer Letterbook; Doerflinger, *A Vigorous Spirit of Enterprise*, p. 262.

were widespread bankruptcies in Britain too, with failures in Manchester in particular.[107]

The war did cause one particular long-term problem. The Orders in Council of 2 July, 5 September and 22 December 1783 prohibited importation of American produce into British islands except in British vessels.[108] One contemporary commented sarcastically that 'it is not expected that the Sons of Freedom will condescend to Trade with Us on these Terms'.[109] An absentee planter added that 'The Americans will be willing to supply our islands whatever their government decides'.[110] Others were equally realistic about the strength of personal trust networks: 'the supplies for the Islands can be got only from the United States ... the true Question is by what mode the Supplies from the United States shall be procured, whether clandestinely, or upon a fair footing'.[111] Alexander Johnston in New York agreed: 'of course the Connections between those colonies [British West Indies] and this Continent though under different Government will continue to be very great'.[112] This was because the West Indies had previously relied on fish and flour from the northern colonies. The idea of the orders was that these supplies should come from Nova Scotia, but the merchants in the West Indies wanted to continue trading with the correspondents they already knew and trusted, arguing that Nova Scotia could not supply sufficient quantities, nor quickly enough.[113] West India pamphleteers were very active in this period, printing their petitions for general circulation and writing letters to British newspapers, but they were generally unsuccessful.[114] The only concessions they managed to gain was that certain products such as oil, or naval stores of interest to the empire, could be imported and governors were exempt from infringing the navigation laws by importing directly from the United States when there were severe food shortages, such as following a hurricane.[115] The Caribbean weather and the governors of the various islands managed to ensure that this latter exception applied as often as possible, but excessive lobbying by the British West-India Interest failed to overturn

---

107 Peter Clement to David Cay, 4 Jun. 1788; Joseph Ramsbotham to Andrew Clow, 25 Aug. 1788, Folder May–Jun. 1788, Andrew Clow & Co., SGC.
108 See Keith, 'Relaxations in the British Restrictions'.
109 Extract from three letters, 12 Oct. 1783, BoT, BT6/83, f. 121, Vol. II.
110 Evidence of Mr Knox, f. 51, BoT, BT6/83, Vol. I. On Knox see Ryden, *West Indian Slavery*, pp. 77–78.
111 At the Council Chamber, 17 May 1788, f. 172, BoT, BT6/83, Vol. I.
112 Alexander Johnston to Thomas Gordon, 3 Dec. 1783, AJL.
113 See Records of the BoT: America and West Indies, BT6/83, Vols. I and II.
114 O'Shaughnessy, *An Empire Divided*, p. 241.
115 A great amount of illicit shipping also took place. Keith, 'Relaxations', pp. 2–3.

the basics of this policy. In taking this stance, the West India lobby were of course challenging mercantilist principles, but as Ryden has noted, they easily altered their views throughout this period to best suit their purposes.[116] Merchants were always pragmatic men.

The American War of Independence forced merchants to retrench their networks and redirect their trade. Most however, attempted to fulfil their obligations in order to preserve their reputations. This allowed trade to recommence easily at the end of the war. Personal trust was extremely important in facilitating this. At variance with the state, merchants set up institutions such as chambers of commerce in order to exert pressure on the government. At the end of the American Revolution relations between the British state and the remaining British mercantile community were not impaired to any great extent, but abolition of the British slave trade was to put new strains on that relationship.

ABOLITION OF THE BRITISH-ATLANTIC SLAVE TRADE

L IVERPOOL'S REPUTATION has inevitably been linked with its role in the slave trade and there have long been debates over the wealth derived from the trade.[117] Many reasons have been posited for Liverpool's success including excellent transport links, good access to manufactures for barter, market power on the African coast and human capital.[118] Contemporaries also argued that it was due to the 'enterprizing Spirit of the Merchants'.[119] However, whilst the abolition movement has been covered in detail in the historiography, relatively little has been said about the defence of the trade, especially as it pertained to the leading port in the trade at that time – Liverpool.[120] For slave traders (and indeed, manufacturers and planters),

---

116 O'Shaughnessy, *An Empire Divided*, p. 241; Ryden, *West Indian Slavery*, chapter five.

117 F. E. Hyde, B. B. Parkinson and S. Marriner, 'The Nature and Profitability of the Liverpool Slave Trade', *EcHR*, new ser., 5:3 (1953), 368–77; Richardson, 'Profits in the Liverpool Slave Trade'.

118 Lamb, 'Volume and Tonnage', p. 91; Morgan, 'Liverpool's Dominance in the British Slave Trade'; Behrendt, 'Human Capital in the British Slave Trade'.

119 Anon [Robert Norris], *A Short Account of The African Slave Trade* (Liverpool: Printed at Ann Smith's Navigation Shop, Pool Lane, 1788), p. 10.

120 Classic abolition literature would include: Thomas Clarkson, *The History of the Progress, and Accomplishment of the Abolition of the African Slave Trade by the British Parliament* (London: Longman and Co., 1808); Reginald Coupland, *William Wilberforce: A Narrative* (Oxford: Clarendon Press, 1923); Lowell J. Ragatz, *The Fall of the Planter Class in the British Caribbean, 1763–1833: A Study in Social and Economic History* (New York and London: Century Co., 1928); Williams, *Capitalism and Slavery*; Anstey,

abolition was a political and economic crisis rather than a moral one. Investigating Liverpool's response to this challenge, especially during the height of the first abolition movement and petition campaign of 1788, facilitates a discussion of reputation, both of the Liverpool slave trade community and of the trade itself, and the relationship between this sector of the trading community and the state. As we saw earlier, reputation was based on socially-constructed ideals.[121] The Liverpool slave traders had built a collective reputation, and therefore made a collective response.[122] Whilst reputational ideals did not really change in terms of what constituted a good merchant, they certainly altered in relation to what was an acceptable 'cargo'. This heightened tensions both within the trading community, and between the slave traders and the state.

Liverpool's defence was based around the classic trio of economics, politics and morals.[123] Slow to react to Dolben's Bill at first, they eventually raised their defence by sending delegates to London to give evidence to the Board of Trade and the House of Commons in 1788, namely John Tarleton, Robert Norris (an American merchant trading out of Liverpool) and James Penny.[124] There was also an intense correspondence with Charles Jenkinson

---

The Atlantic Slave Trade; Seymour Drescher, *Econocide: British Slavery in the Age of Abolition* (Pittsburgh: University of Pittsburgh Press, and London: Feffer and Simons, 1977); J. R. Oldfield, *Popular Politics and British Anti-Slavery: The Mobilisation of Public Opinion Against the Slave Trade 1787–1807* (Manchester: Manchester University Press, 1995); Matthews, *Caribbean Slave Revolts*; Ryden, *West Indian Slavery*, chapter eight. See also F. E. Sanderson, 'The Liverpool Delegates and Sir William Dolben's Bill', in *Transactions of the Historic Society of Lancashire and Cheshire*, 124 (1972), 57–84.

121 See above, pp. 99–104.

122 Tullock, 'Adam Smith and the Prisoners' Dilemma'; Raub and Weesie, 'Reputation and Efficiency'.

123 Whilst Seymour Drescher also posits the notion of security in terms of slave rebellion in the British West Indies, Liverpool merchants did not tend to call upon this line of defence. Seymour Drescher, 'People and Parliament', *Journal of Interdisciplinary History*, 20:4 (1990), 561–80.

124 Lt. John Matthews RN, and Archibald Dalzel were also delegates but were less active. See Anstey, *The Atlantic Slave Trade*, pp. 290–91; Sanderson, 'The Liverpool Delegates'. Evidence of Robert Norris, 2 Jun. 1788, HCSP, Vol. 68, f. 4. Many of the arguments relayed here come from this early period, but the merchants' stance remained much the same right up to 1807. Dolben's Act was passed in 1788, the Slave Trade Carrying Act in 1799 (both of which reduced the number of slaves to tonnage ratio on slave vessels), and The Abolition of the Slave Trade Act (not slavery) was passed in 1807. In 1788, there were also eight Liverpool subscribers to the London Society for the Abolition of the Slave Trade: Jonathon Binns, Daniel Daulby, William Rathbone III, William Rathbone Junior, William Roscoe, William Wallace, John Yates, and one anonymous, whom Howman understands to be James Currie who was reluctant to openly criticise his fellow Liverpudlians. Sanderson, 'Liverpool

(Baron Hawkesbury from 1791 and Lord Liverpool from 1796), who was Secretary of the Board of Trade 1786–1804.[125] Whilst a wide range of people were involved in the defence of the slave trade and slavery, the Liverpool merchants were not so keen to defend the interests of the London absentees and planters. Rather, they concentrated on defending the slave trade itself, and of themselves as merchants.[126]

The importance of the trade to the economy of both Liverpool and Britain as a whole was obviously the Liverpool merchants' primary and strongest defence. This argument may also be one of the reasons why high profits from the trade have been exaggerated. Clearly Liverpool remained an important port after 1807, but the disastrous effects of abolishing the trade were stressed at the time.[127] For example, in 1788 James Penny told the Board of Trade that 'should this Trade be Abolished it would not only greatly affect the Commercial Interest, but ... more particularly the Town of Liverpool, whose fall in that Case would be as rapid as its rise has been

---

Abolitionists', p. 198; Howman, 'Abolitionism in Liverpool'. See also J. Trepp, 'The Liverpool Movement for Abolition', *Journal of Negro History*, 13 (1928), 265–85.

125 John Cannon, 'Jenkinson, Charles', Oxford Dictionary of National Biography online, accessed 30 Dec. 2010.

126 Ryden, *West Indian Slavery*, p. 194.

127 Merchants in Liverpool, especially those who had been involved in the slave trade used their human capital to trade in palm oil on the African coast (including James Penny) which they dominated and expanded their trade in sugar, rum, cotton and tobacco. Anthony Tibbles, 'Oil not Slaves: Liverpool and West Africa after 1807', in Anthony Tibbles, ed., *Transatlantic Slavery: Against Human Dignity* [1995] (Liverpool: Liverpool University Press, 1994), pp. 73–77. Liverpool merchants also responded to new opportunities in Central and South America. For example George Hibbert (Manchester) possibly had a sister house in Buenos Aires in 1817 (ADM 1/23); Alexander Johnston possibly had a sister house in Bahia c.1809 (Wylie Papers), and James Penny may have had family connections in Mexico City in the 1830s (Owens and Sons Papers). My great thanks to Manuel Llorca-Jaña for this information. The extent of their involvement in the Latin American trade is still debated. David Eltis, 'The British Contribution to the Nineteenth-Century Transatlantic Slave Trade', *EcHR*, 2nd ser., 32:2 (May 1979), 211–27; D. C. M. Platt, *Latin America and British Trade 1806–1914* (London: Adam & Charles Black, 1972), part I; Manuel Llorca-Jaña, 'The Organisation of British Textile Exports to the River Plate and Chile: Merchant Houses in Operation, c. 1810–59', *BH*, 53:6 (2011), pp. 821–65, pp. 821–23. Many also continued to have investments in the Caribbean beyond 1807. See for example Legacies of British Slave Ownership Project. Claims: British Guiana 477 (William Earle); Jamaica St. James 276 (Thomas Hodgson); St Lucia 624 (Tarleton & Backhouse); St. Vincent 598A and 598B (Case family and John Bolton); Trinidad 1808 (Alexander Johnston). My thanks to Nick Draper and Rachel Lang of the Legacies of British Slave Ownership project for this information. See also the Parker family network above, pp. 31–32.

astonishing'.[128] John Tarleton also agreed that the town had been 'peculiarly fortunate'.[129] However, in response to accusations of very large profits he remarked that at least ten per cent was required to induce merchants into the trade due to the large credit advanced, and the risks involved in the trade.[130] Liverpool's slave traders had indeed invested large amounts of money in slaving voyages. William Davenport alone invested £60,000 between 1757 and 1784.[131] Liverpool as a whole had around £200,000 invested in the trade in 1750, which increased to £2,641,200 in 1807.[132] Thomas Hodgson was one of those with a 'factory' on the west coast of Africa.[133] Nor was it just in the slave trade *per se* in which these merchants and others had invested. Slave traders and manufacturers had also advanced credit for the purchase of plantations, building sugar works, and equipment and clothes for the slaves, amongst other items. The total debts due to British merchants and mortgagees were estimated to be about one third of the value of the British West Indies. As the total value of property investment in the British West Indies was estimated at somewhere around £70–80 million, this was a significant amount.[134] George Hibbert, a Manchester merchant with close connections to Jamaica, was one of many worried about the non-payment of debts should the trade be stopped. He argued that without new importations of slaves the labouring population of the West Indies would decline and production decrease dramatically.[135]

---

128 Evidence of James Penny, 10 Mar. 1788, BoT, AQ, Vol. I, f. 357. The importance of the Liverpool slave trade to the national economy had been stressed since as early as 1765. 'Memorial of the Merchants of Leverpoole trading to Africa desirs to have liberty to import from any parts of Europe East India Goods Rifles & Brandy for the African Trade', 16 Mar. 1765, T1/447/349–51, TNA.

129 Evidence of John Tarleton, 4 Mar. 1788, BoT, AQ, Vol. I, ff. 229–32.

130 John Tarleton to Charles Jenkinson, 9 Jun. 1788, LP, Vol. CCXXVII, Papers relating to the Slave Trade 1787–1823, f. 103. James Wallace argued that every kind of person was involved in the trade in Liverpool: *A General and Descriptive History of the Ancient and Present State of Liverpool* (Liverpool: Printed and Sold by R. Phillips, Castle Street, 1795), p. 229. However, due to the large capital requirements, those others than elite traders can only have advanced a few items for barter on the African coast.

131 Richardson, 'Profits of the Liverpool Slave Trade', p. 64.

132 Morgan, 'Liverpool's Dominance in the British Slave Trade', p. 15.

133 Miles Barber had owned a factory at Factory Island, which was taken over by John & Thomas Hodgson of Liverpool. Richard Horrocks was their agent there. Mouser, *A Slaving Voyage*, pp. 10, 41. Hancock's London associates owned Bance Island, another factory, near the mouth of the Sierra Leone River until 1784 when it passed to Richard Oswald's nephews John and Alexander Anderson. However, they ceased operations in 1811. Hancock, *Citizens of the World*, chapter six, esp. pp. 215–16.

134 Evidence of George Hibbert, 20 Mar. 1790, HCSP, Vol. 72, f. 386; Anstey, *The Atlantic Slave Trade*, p. 309.

135 Evidence of Robert Hibbert, 30 Mar. 1790, HCSP, Vol. 72, f. 362.

The West India planters already had a reputation for being slow and/or bad payers.[136] What would happen to this investment should their profits decline? A letter from Jamaica summed up this relationship: 'The Colonies would not exist without the African Trade. The Manchester & Sheffield Manufactories would instantly go to ruin & their people be set a starving.'[137]

Whilst the question of overcrowding, conditions, and high mortality on the 'middle passage' was a moral issue for many people, it was also an economic one for the slave traders. Here the slave merchants had an advantage over the abolitionists due to their human capital in the trade. Abolitionists were not so knowledgeable. Even the information of those who had been in the trade was out of date – Reverend John Newton had not been to Africa since 1754.[138] The main thrust of Dolben's Bill was to reduce the number of slaves per ton to a maximum of five slaves to every three tons (1.67 slaves per ton) in an attempt to reduce overcrowding. However, Tarleton argued that slave traders did not overload their vessels because it was inefficient. 'A Merchant would be mad to risk his Fortune on such a dangerous Speculation. If his ship will only carry 200 conveniently he will not crowd in 100 more to try the experiment of bringing 50 of that additional 100 to Markett & expose thereby the Health of the 200 to Disease or Death.'[139] It was therefore in the slave traders' interests to not overcrowd their vessels. Moreover, Tarleton argued that the proposed ratio would mean that only large ships would be efficient enough to carry on the trade at a profit. Whilst this would benefit those with larger vessels in the short term, having a ratio of less than two slaves per ton would effectively abolish the trade in the long term.[140] In order to stress this point he added that his own firm of Tarleton & Backhouse would be one of those that would benefit in the short term, 'but my attachment to my fellow Townsmen, a just sense of my duty as their delegate, and my regard for the welfare of my Country equally compel me to resist the proposed restrictions'.[141] Tarleton

---

136 For a good summary on lengthening payment times see Morgan, 'Remittance Procedures'.

137 Extract from a Letter from a Gentleman in Jamaica, 12 Apr. 1788, LP, Vol. CCXXVII, Papers Relating to the Slave Trade 1787–1823, f. 127.

138 Newton was due to go on his fourth voyage in 1754 but suffered from a temporary paralysis two days before. He took this as an answer to his prayers and decided not to go. Jonathon Aitkin, *John Newton: From Disgrace to Amazing Grace* (London and New York: Continuum, 2007), pp. 80–81.

139 Replies to Arguments advanced in Favour of the Bill for regulating the Transportation of Negroes, 1 Feb. 1788, LP, Vol. CCXXVII, f. 189.

140 Evidence of John Tarleton, 16 Jun. 1788, HCSP, Vol. 68, f. 50.

141 Tarleton to Charles Jenkinson, 25 May 1788, LP, Vol. CCXXVII, ff. 90–91. Tarleton did not mention that of course only the ports that could handle the larger vessels, such as Liverpool, would be able to handle the trade.

therefore used his own reputation and his obligations to Liverpool as a port and its trading community to give further credence to his evidence. There were further arguments against larger vessels. It was well known that a smaller vessel was loaded more quickly which facilitated a shorter stay on the African coast. This was important in reducing vulnerability to disease and therefore preserving the lives of blacks and whites alike.[142] Slave rebellions were also less likely if vessels moved from their loading area quickly.[143] Larger vessels would work against these advantages, meaning a less efficient timing of the voyage as a whole, leading to late arrival in the West Indies, which would in turn, ruin the next year's voyages. All this would reduce profits to an extent so as to ruin the trade entirely, argued Tarleton.[144]

The slave traders' second strand of defence was centred around political economy. John Tarleton argued that a consequence of the new tonnage to slave ratio would be 'a Removal to the Port of Havre, in France'.[145] Competition with other European nations in the slave trade was a serious concern given that none of them had ever secured a foothold on the African coast.[146] This meant that Europeans had not been able to determine the terms of trade there and had been compelled to adopt African credit institutions such as pawnship.[147] Furthermore, the Africans were sophisticated consumers and played the European traders off against one another.[148] Therefore, were the British to withdraw from the trade, it would simply move to the ports of 'France, Spain, Holland, Denmark and America and indeed be carried on with English credit but in foreign ships.'[149] The result would be that

---

142 See Richard L. Cohen and Richard A. Jensen, 'The Determinants of Slave Mortality Rates on the Middle Passage', *Explorations in Economic History*, 19 (1982), pp. 269–82; Herbert S. Klein and Stanley L. Engerman, 'Long-term Trends in African Mortality in the Trans-Atlantic Slave Trade', in David Eltis and David Richardson, *Routes to Slavery: Direction, Ethnicity and Mortality in the Atlantic Slave Trade* (London and Portland, OR: Frank Cass, 1997), pp. 36–48.

143 Tarleton to Charles Jenkinson, 9 Jun. 1788, LP, Vol. CCXXVII, ff. 103–4.

144 Tarleton to Charles Jenkinson, 9 Jun. 1788, LP, Vol. CCXXVII, ff. 103–4; Evidence of James Penny, 16 Jun. 1788, HCSP, Vol. 68, f. 40. For more on the importance of the timing of the trade see Stephen D. Behrendt, 'Markets, Transaction Cycles, and Profits: Merchant Decision Making in the British Slave Trade', *WMQ*, 3rd ser., 58:1 (2001), pp. 171–204.

145 Evidence of John Tarleton, 16 Jun. 1788, HCSP, Vol. 68, f. 50.

146 Davies, *The Royal African Company*, pp. 1–16.

147 Lovejoy and Richardson, 'Trust, Pawnship and Atlantic History'.

148 Thornton, *Africa and Africans*, p. 45; Richardson, 'West African Consumption Patterns', esp. pp. 318–19.

149 *The Times*, 4 Apr. 1789. The planters would still be in debt to English merchants. The trade did move to other nations despite the efforts of the anti-slave trade naval squadron, but the British were still heavily involved in providing goods and insurance

the British would end up subsidising the trade of their competitors, and particularly the French, who were supported by government bounties and had already pushed the British out of Angola.[150] Indeed, the French and Spanish were eagerly preparing to take advantage of British abolition. William Walton of Liverpool reported that Spanish agents had already been sent to London, Manchester and Liverpool to see how the trade was conducted.[151] The French were also collecting information specifically about the goods used for barter and had expressed their 'Surprize at the Quality and Price of these Goods, the expedition with which they can be furnished, and the Credit at which they were sold.'[152] It would be madness to give up a world-leading position in the slave trade, especially when there was a vibrant trade in slaves and manufactures to the Spanish colonies for which ships were being fitted out in Liverpool, London and Bristol.[153] This was important because the French and Spanish paid for their slaves and other merchandise with silver bullion.[154] In terms of the zero-sum game of mercantilism, taking such wealth from a competitor was very important.[155]

A crucial part of this 'impolitic' argument was the implicit contract between the slave traders and the state. Indeed, as Ryden points out, the part of the argument that ending the slave trade was unconstitutional is often forgotten.[156] The slave traders stressed that the large amounts of money they

---

for the slave trade, and before 1811, foreign vessels were occasionally fitted out in Britain. David Eltis, 'The British Trans-Atlantic Slave Trade after 1807', *Maritime History*, 4:1 (Spring 1974), 1–11.

150 Evidence of John Tarleton, 4 Mar. 1789, BoT, AQ, Vol. I, f. 236; Letter from a Bristol merchant to a gentleman in London, 25 Jan. 1788, LP, Vol. CCXXVII, f. 22.

151 William Walton to Charles Jenkinson, 24 Feb. 1788, LP, Vol. CCXXVII, f. 29.

152 Examination of Samuel Taylor Esquire, Merchant and Manufacturer of the Town of Manchester, 8 Mar. 1788, BoT, AQ, Vol. I, ff. 309–11.

153 This trade had started under the Treaty of Utrecht the *Asiento* of 1713 which had allowed the British to supply the Spanish colonies with 4,800 slaves per annum and send one trade ship to the Spanish colonies each year by which they could sell English manufactures. Despite the effective end of the *Asiento* in 1739 a clandestine trade with the Spanish continued. Pearce, *British Trade with Spanish America*, chapter one. Between 1 Jan. 1787 and 1 May 1788 Bristol was reported to have fitted out four ships for the French and Spanish colonies, London, six and Liverpool, four. Henry Wilckens to Charles Jenkinson, 15 Mar. 1788, LP, Vol. CCXXVII, f. 89.

154 Samuel Rainford to Jonathon Blundell, 13 Feb. 1784, 920 CHA/1/1, Robert Rainford to Edward Chaffers, 6 May 1800, 920 CHA/1/26, PEC.

155 For the benefits or otherwise of mercantilism see Stanley L. Engerman, 'Mercantilism and Overseas Trade, 1700–1800', in Roderick Floud and D. N. McCloskey, eds., *The Economic History of Britain Since 1700*, Vol. I, *1700–1860*, 2nd edn (Cambridge: Cambridge University Press, 1994), pp. 182–204, esp. pp. 199–203.

156 Ryden, *West Indian Slavery*, p. 196.

had invested in the slave trade and slavery had been in support of government policy. To abolish the slave trade was therefore a U-turn in British policy and a betrayal of the good intentions of the merchants and other creditors and mortgagees.[157] This was one of the arguments for compensation claims; that abolishing the slave trade would 'violate the system of Colonial law'.[158] Previous parliaments had passed laws sanctioning the trade and therefore the relationships between the slave traders, slave owners, and the state.[159] Changing policy now was therefore not only harmful to the economy, it was reneging on well-established obligatory relationships between the slave traders and the state.

Despite being on uncertain moral ground, even in an eighteenth-century context, Liverpool's merchants still managed to raise a defence in this area. There were charges against them in three main areas: that the terms of conditions of trade in Africa were unfair on the Africans; that the trade served to increase slavery in Africa; and that conditions on the 'middle passage' were poor, especially with regard to overcrowding and mortality rates.[160] With regards to the terms of trade the slave traders gave evidence of credit arrangements such as pawnship (an African institution adopted by Europeans), and also argued that they expressly forbade abuses such as kidnapping, unfair bartering and other interferences with local conditions. If 'cruel acts have been committed it has been against the instructions and without their knowledge' they stated.[161] Both John Tarleton and Henry Wilckens gave evidence that they supported regulation of the trade in order to reduce such abuses. Wilckens added that the 'Willful killing of slaves ... [and] The Kidnapping of free Negroes should likewise be made Capital [offences] because it is sure to cause the destruction of some white men in Return', known as panyarring.[162]

Arguing against the accusation that the trade was increasing slavery in Africa was a more difficult task. Liverpool slave traders may have had good

---

157 *The Times*, 4 Apr. 1789.

158 *The Times*, 27 Jan. 1807.

159 *A Treatise Upon The Trade From Great-Britain To Africa; Humbly Recommended To The Attention Of Government*, By An African Merchant (London: Printed for E. Baldwin, Paternoster Row, 1772), p. 11.

160 A last argument put forward in defence of the trade was basically a racialist one based on the alleged behaviour of the slaves in the West Indies. The Liverpool merchants however, did not use this line of defence and so it is not discussed here. For examples of this line of defence see: Evidence of Robert Hibbert, 20 Mar. 1790, HCSP, Vol. 72. ff. 360–63; Evidence of Charles Spooner, 1 Mar. 1788, BoT, AQ, Vol. I, ff. 182–83.

161 John Tarleton to Baron Hawkesbury, 11 Apr. 1792, LP, Vol. CCXXVII, f. 258.

162 Henry Wilkins to Charles Jenkinson, 15 Mar. 1788, LP, Vol. CCXVII, ff. 53–54.

knowledge about trade on the African coast, but not many whites ventured far enough inland to have a sound knowledge of the hinterland. Even those that lived permanently on the West African coast did not venture more than a few miles inland because the Africans were in control of the slave trade within Africa.[163] Therefore their main defence was that slavery had always existed in Africa. John Barnes, a former Governor of Senegal, stated that 'As far as I know of any history, I do not know a time when there were not Slaves there.'[164] He also added to the common argument that slaves had been enslaved by virtue of being thieves, murderers, adulterers, witches or by becoming debtors through gambling.[165] Therefore the enslaved had not been good citizens in any case. Robert Norris also argued that leaders such as the King of Dahomey were tyrants, and might kill thousands of slaves around the period of the poll tax if they had not been sold.[166] The implication was that the slaves were happy to be rescued and were headed for a better life.[167] This was rather disingenuous given their fate on the plantations in the West Indies.[168]

Thomas Clarkson's infamous drawing of the Liverpool slave ship *Brookes* meant that overcrowding and mortality during the 'middle passage' became the most well-known moral issue regarding the slave trade.[169] Once again the slave traders used their human capital as defence. Tonnage was important, but so also was ship design. Robert Norris argued that 'the African ships are peculiarly constructed for carrying a large Number'.[170] Moreover, Liverpool ships were well known by their special air vents or 'side scuttles and gratings' which fed air into the hold.[171] This careful construction of vessels in Liverpool, James Penny and John Tarleton argued, meant that slave mortality was usually less than five per cent from the Gold Coast and Whydah to Jamaica.[172] Robert Norris noted that vessels with larger tonnage

---

163 Klein, *The Atlantic Slave Trade*, p. 77.
164 Evidence of John Barnes, 26 May 1789, HCSP, Vol. 68, f. 73.
165 Evidence of John Barnes, 26 May 1789, HCSP, Vol. 68, f. 74.
166 Evidence of Robert Norris, 27 Feb. 1788, BoT, AQ, Vol. I, ff. 109–16.
167 *A Treatise Upon The Trade From Great-Britain To Africa*, p. 11.
168 Jack P. Greene, 'Society and Economy in the British Caribbean during the Seventeenth and Eighteenth Centuries', *American Historical Review*, 79:5 (1974), 1499–1517.
169 Historians are still debating the health effects of overcrowding and conditions on board the vessel, versus the length of time and where the slaves had to spend time on the coast. See Cohen and Jensen, 'The Determinants of Slave Mortality Rates'; Klein and Engerman, 'Long-term Trends in African Mortality'.
170 Evidence of Robert Norris, 2 Jun. 1788, HCSP, Vol. 68, f. 4.
171 Evidence of Captain Hall, 22 Feb. 1788, BoT, AQ, Vol. I, f. 73. Interestingly, Captain Hall proceeded to speak against the slave trade.
172 Evidence of James Penny, 13 Jun. 1788; Evidence of John Tarleton, 16 Jun. 1788, HCSP, Vol. 68, ff. 37, 46. Mortality rates were overall about 5.7 per cent at the end of the

did not benefit from a lower mortality rate.[173] He added that there was competition between the slave ship captains as to who kept the cleanest ship and had the lowest mortality rates, noting that 'every Man in Profession has a Point of Honour – it is their Emulation, and they value themselves upon it'.[174] Indeed, detailed instructions were often given for the care of the slaves.[175] It was therefore in the interests of both merchant and captain to keep the slaves in the best conditions.

The merchants' arguments regarding the importance of the slave trade to the British economy were believed, but still did not hold sway in the changing socio-economic environment in Britain at this time. More institutions were set up in response to this crisis: the Liverpool merchants set up a West India Association in 1799 and Glasgow did the same in 1807, but despite this the Abolition of the Slave Trade Act was passed in 1807.[176] However, the slave traders' defence highlights the importance of reputation and their changing relationship with the state. They defended their reputations as merchants very effectively. It was clear that the British (Liverpool as the leading port) were world-leaders in the trade. The reputation of Liverpool was secure enough for the government to allow it to issue its own bills during the credit crisis of 1793.[177] Moreover, by stressing their obligatory relationship with the state, the Liverpool merchants demonstrated that this was a government-sanctioned trade in which they had invested a lot of money. Under the mercantilist mode, this trade had served both merchants and the state well, yet the slave traders did not get compensation in 1807 as did those involved in slavery in 1833.[178] This may have been because they were trading a 'commodity' rather than owning land, but more importantly, notions of what the British Empire should be were changing. Not only were Adam Smith's ideas on free trade becoming more popular, but notions of British liberty, Christianity and humanitarianism were important concepts in which the African was

---

eighteenth century, although these were highly skewed, and the median was around 3 per cent. Herbert S. Klein and Stanley L. Engerman, 'Slave Mortality Rates on British Ships 1791–1797', in Anstey and Hair, *Liverpool, the African Slave Trade and Abolition*, pp. 113–25, p. 117.

173 Evidence of Robert Norris, 2 Jun. 1788, HCSP, Vol. 68, ff. 7–8.
174 Evidence of Robert Norris, 2 Jun. 1788, HCSP, Vol. 68, f. 9.
175 Additional Orders for Captain Speers, 3 Jun. 1767, Ships Papers, DTP.
176 Some of the Liverpool minutes deal with the overproduction of sugar. Minutes of the West India Association, 380 WES/1, LivRO; Chamber of Commerce and Manufacturers in the City of Glasgow, Vol. I, 1783–1788. See also 'The Memorial of the Merchants, Ship owners, Sugar Refiners', LivRO.
177 Hyde et al., 'The Port of Liverpool and the Crisis of 1793'.
178 Hoppit, 'Compulsion, Compensation and Property Rights'.

becoming more human, and less of a commodity.[179] Cultural constructions of what constituted a reputable merchant might not have changed, but cultural constructions of what constituted a reputable commodity had. The fact that the state concurred with this new framework no doubt left this particular sector of the trading community feeling embittered. It also caused the Liverpool merchants (and others) to set up further institutions through which they formalised their networks to facilitate a greater degree of political organisation, through which they could defend their interests vis-à-vis the state.[180]

THE ANGLO-AMERICAN CONFLICT

THE ANGLO-AMERICAN WAR was both played out against the backdrop of the French wars, and caused in part by actions taken in pursuance of the war by the French and British.[181] The Americans wanted to stay out of the conflict, and to profit from their neutral status. In 1793 Sparling & Bolden of Liverpool wrote to their partners in Virginia, 'We hope the American States will not engage in the quarrel, indeed we don't see they can gain any thing by it, but may lose much, and if they observe a strict neutrality they will have the whole carrying Trade to and from their respective States during the War, which will be a prodigious advantage to them.'[182] The Americans did indeed engross a large amount of the carrying trade, but not without complaint.[183] In 1805 Stephen James complained in *War in Disguise* that neutral nations should only be allowed to carry on the trade that they pursued in peacetime. Not only had France opened up all her colonial ports to all neutral nations, the Americans had rushed into this trade 'with avidity' and it was evident 'that the flag of the United States, was, for the most part,

---

179 Oldfield, *Popular Politics and British Anti-Slavery*, chapter four.
180 This was to continue into the 1840s for example joining with the Glasgow Chamber of Commerce to attack the East India Monopoly. Anthony Webster, 'The Strategies and Limits of Gentlemanly Capitalism: The London East India Agency Houses, Provincial Commercial Interests, and the Evolution of British Economic Policy in South and South East Asia, 1800–1850', *EcHR*, new ser., 59:4 (Nov. 2006), 743–64.
181 On the effects of the French Wars in Liverpool see Sydney G. Checkland, 'American Versus West Indian Traders in Liverpool, 1793–1815', *Journal of Economic History*, 18:2 (Jun. 1958), 141–60.
182 Sparling & Bolden to John Lawrence & Co., 14 Feb. 1793, Sparling & Bolden Letterbook.
183 William Rathbone estimated that 9/10ths of Anglo-American shipping was built in the United States. Evidence of William Rathbone, Minutes of Evidence, Vol. 119 (1808), pp. 77–78, ff. 261–62, HCPP.

used to protect the property of the French Planter, not of the American Merchant'.[184] Indeed, the Liverpool merchants eventually reacted to this loss of shipping by setting up yet another institution, the Shipowners' Association in 1810. Its first president was a leading American trader, Samuel Holland.[185] The English were painfully aware that the Americans were also increasing their share of the China trade and were considered 'powerful competitors' in that area by 1807.[186] Shortages of corn due to bad harvests, accusations of speculation, impressment and Napoleon's continental blockade all served to heighten the tension.[187] This situation was made worse by British Orders in Council which, although in place for some time, were greatly stiffened in November 1807. Originally brought in as retaliation for Napoleon's blockade, these Orders allowed British Navy ships to stop and search neutral vessels for goods being freighted for the enemy and for British deserters.[188] Many people in Britain supported these Orders because of the perception that the Americans were taking advantage of their neutral flag: 'we *ought* to enforce our right of search for the persons of deserters' [stress in original], proclaimed *The Times*.[189] However, British merchants trading with the United States believed these measures would only harm British trade further and the difference of opinion led to criticism of Liverpool merchants by commentators in London.[190] Indeed, a resolution against the British government's attitude written by the Liverpool American Chamber of Commerce in 1807 was sent to Glasgow, Bristol, Hull, Leeds, Sheffield, Birmingham, Manchester, and London.[191]

Matters were brought to a head when the British frigate *Leopard* fired

---

184 This stance was based on Britain's 'rule of 1756' which barred neutrals from trading with enemy ports normally closed to them in peace time. James, *War In Disguise*, pp. 19, 20, 213, 13.

185 Brian H. Tolley, 'The American Trade of Liverpool in the Early Nineteenth Century and the War of 1812' (unpublished MA thesis, University of Liverpool: 1967), p. 91.

186 *The Times*, 1 Sep. 1807; see also *The Times*, 5 Sep. 1801; 8 Feb. 1813. The Philadelphians had started trade with India and China in the 1780s, as did merchants in New York. Doerflinger, *A Vigorous Spirit of Enterprise*, pp. 283–84, 336.

187 *The Times*, 14 Aug. 1800; Bowen, *War and British Society*, esp. chapter three.

188 The Orders decreed that all trading vessels, under whatever flag were to purchase a licence in a British Port. This greatly increased their costs of course. The British had also already enraged the Americans by impressing many of their sailors. John Merriman, *A History of Modern Europe: From the Renaissance to the Age of Napoleon*, 2nd edn (New York and London: W. W. Norton and Company, 2004), p. 539.

189 *The Times*, 14 Oct. 1807.

190 *The Times*, 14 Oct. 1807.

191 Minutes of the Liverpool American Chamber of Commerce, 11 Aug. 1807, 23 Jul. 1807. In Oct. 1807 they also joined with the West India Association against the new Dock Act, 1 Oct. 1807.

on, and then boarded, the USS *Chesapeake* on 22 June 1807 in order to retrieve deserters.[192] The Americans retaliated with an Embargo on the importation of British goods brought into effect 22 December 1807, which effectively cut out exports to Britain as well. This was replaced in March 1808 with the Non-Intercourse Act. In April 1808 the Erskine Treaty reopened trade between the two countries with effect from the 10 June, but this was never ratified by Britain and on 9 August 1809 the Non-Intercourse Act was reinstated. This was in turn repealed on 1 May 1810 but when the British failed to reciprocate by rescinding the orders it was replaced by the Non-Importation Act on 2 February 1811. On 4 April 1812 the Embargo was re-imposed and on 19 June 1812, war declared with Britain. The British revoked the orders on 16 June 1812, but by then it was too late to stop the United States declaring war on Britain.[193]

The increasing tension between the two states was not reflected however in the Anglo-American trading communities. This is not to say that there were not concerns. Liverpool house Morall & Borland sent out a Price Current to their American correspondents in November 1807 (before the December Embargo) which noted that 'there appears very little apprehension remaining. Credit however, has suffered much, and a distrust still operating has the effect of limiting transactions in our markets'.[194] Business was suffering due to low levels of institutional and general trust, but this had more to do with worries over goods being confiscated rather than with potential non-payment. The correspondence between Brown & Ives of Providence, Rhode Island, and Rathbone, Hughes & Duncan of Liverpool provides a prism for studying how the various trading communities coped in this period, and highlights that personal trust, as was the case during the American War of Independence, was very important in facilitating trade. Both firms were elite, well-established houses with good reputations, and had been conducting business together since at least 1803.[195] They traded in a wide

---

192 Silverstone argues that Jefferson could easily have got the United States into the War at this time because this was such an affront to American pride. Scott A. Silverstone, *Divided Union: The Politics of War in the Early American Republic* (Ithaca and London: Cornell University Press, 2004), pp. 74–75. See also Papers Presented to the House of Commons Relating to the Encounter Between His Majesty's Ships Leopard and the American Frigate Chesapeake, 1807–08 (1809), 45, HCPP.

193 Daniels, 'American Cotton Trade'.

194 Morall & Borland Price Current, 14 Nov. 1807, Folder Morall & Borland 22 Apr. 1807–16 May 1812, B240.F9, BFBR. Morall & Borland had a contract to supply the British Army with timber, pragmatic as ever. Tolley, 'The Liverpool Campaign', p. 109.

195 For introductions to these families see above, pp. 28–31.

variety of goods re-exported via Providence to Liverpool, including cotton, sugar and mahogany, shipping British hardware in return.[196]

The Chesapeake Affair however, meant that they had to reassess their business environment. In November 1807, again just before the American Embargo was declared, Brown & Ives wrote to Rathbone, Hughes & Duncan that 'the late news from your side exciting considerable apprehensions that Hostilities may be resorted to – we shall suspend her sailing until the actual situation of things between the two Countries is known'.[197] With the Embargo in place, they never sent the vessel, but Rathbone, Hughes & Duncan understood their predicament. They wrote in January 1808 that 'We feel much indebted for your friendly dispositions towards us, and regret exceedingly the circumstances, which we presume have afterwards induced you to postpone the voyage proposed.'[198] Lowering levels of institutional trust also meant that people again retrenched their networks to those most trusted, and were not so likely to trust *new* correspondents. For example, Rathbone, Hughes & Duncan were happy to help out Amos Jenckes, introduced to them by Brown & Ives, but despite that recommendation, they were relieved not to have had to advance him credit: 'the unpleasant state of affairs, between your country and this caused us to be unusually cautious' they explained.[199]

The continuing state of affairs meant that there was little contact between the two firms between January 1808 and February 1809, when correspondence resumed in a friendly manner (the Liverpool firm now trading under the name of Hughes & Duncan, William Rathbone having died on 11 February 1809).[200] This meant that when the Erskine Treaty allowed trade during the summer of 1809, commerce between the two firms, and indeed other various houses involved in the Anglo-American business resumed. Between 11 June and 22 July 1809, 226 vessels arrived in Liverpool alone from the United States.[201] This included the *Mary*, with over 400 casks of flaxseed directed

196 See for example Brown & Ives to Rathbone, Hughes & Duncan, 4 Apr. 1803; 14 May 1803; 4 Apr. 1804, Folder Rathbone, Hughes & Duncan 11 Mar. 1803–22 Apr. 1807, B289.F3.

197 Brown & Ives to Rathbone, Hughes & Duncan, 14 Nov. 1807, Folder Rathbone, Hughes & Duncan 12 Aug. 1807–31 Jul. 1809, B289.F4, BFBR.

198 Rathbone, Hughes & Duncan to Brown & Ives, 30 Jan. 1808, Folder Rathbone, Hughes & Duncan 12 Aug. 1807–31 Jul. 1809, B289.F4.

199 Rathbone, Hughes & Duncan to Brown & Ives, 20 Oct. 1807, Folder Rathbone, Hughes & Duncan 12 Aug. 1807–31 Jul. 1809, B289.F4.

200 Rathbone, Hughes & Duncan to Brown & Ives, 13 Feb. 1809; Notice of Dissolution of Partnership, 28 Mar. 1809; Notice of New Partnership, 28 Mar. 1809, Folder Rathbone, Hughes & Duncan 12 Aug. 1807–31 Jul. 1809, B289.F4.

201 Hughes & Duncan to Brown & Ives, 22 Jul. 1809, Folder Rathbone, Hughes & Duncan 12 Aug. 1807–31 Jul. 1809, B289.F4.

from Brown & Ives to Hughes & Duncan, for which the latter thanked them 'for this new mark of friendship'.[202] Friendly relations continued despite the fact that both sides were aware that trade was very likely to be suspended again and believed that war was unavoidable.[203]

Some merchants of course aimed to profit from the uncertainty of trade between the two countries, although Hughes & Duncan clearly disapproved of such speculation, as did other reputable firms. During August 1809, as concerns rose over the non-ratification of the Erskine Treaty, there were 'considerable speculations ... undertaken by those who entertain it' in Liverpool.[204] Conway & Davidson, also of Liverpool, were equally critical. They gossiped that 'This Mercantile Fever has not subsided ... when the truth is told, it will be found, they [the speculators] were hard at Work All the following day (Sunday)' [emphasis in original].[205] When on 9 August 1809 the Non-Intercourse Act was indeed re-instated by President Madison, Brown & Ives and Hughes & Duncan continued to correspond with one another and to send regular Price Currents.[206] This was time-consuming but had the practical effect of keeping each other informed. It also promoted personal trust by fulfilling obligations even when trade was much reduced. Indeed, other Liverpool firms such as Conway & Davidson, Buchanan & Benn, Martin, Hope & Thornely and Morrall & Borland did the same throughout the period.[207] In this way networks and affective commitment were maintained throughout the crisis.

There were other ways to maintain business apart from direct trade of course. Hughes & Duncan continued to trade with Brown & Ives during 1810

---

202 Hughes & Duncan to Brown & Ives, 19 Aug. 1809, Folder Hughes & Duncan 5 Aug. 1809–31 Oct. 1809, B289.F5, BFBR.

203 Hughes & Duncan to Brown & Ives, 16 Aug. 1809; 19 Aug. 1809, Folder Rathbone, Hughes & Duncan 12 Aug. 1807–31 Jul. 1809, B289.F5; Hughes & Duncan to Brown & Ives, 3 Aug. 1811, Folder Hughes & Duncan 11 May 1811–2 Nov. 1811, B290.F1, BFBR.

204 Hughes & Duncan to Brown & Ives, 19 Aug. 1809, Folder Hughes & Duncan 5 Aug. 1809–31 Oct. 1809, B289.F5.

205 Conway & Davidson to Brown & Ives, 16 Sep. 1809, Folder Conway & Davidson 1809–1810, B64.F20.

206 See the letters in Folder William & Richard Rathbone 27 Mar. 1809–2 Jan. 1810, B284. F1 and Folder Hughes & Duncan 31 Oct. 1809–23 Dec. 1809, B289.F6, BFBR for example.

207 Folder Conway & Davidson 2 Aug. 1809–30 Jan. 1810, B64.F20; Folder Conway & Davidson 14 Feb. 1810–23 Jun. 1810, B64.F21; Folder Conway & Davidson 6 Jul. 1810–1 Dec. 1810, B64.F22; Folder Buchanan & Benn 20 Oct. 1808–25 Jun. 1812, B53. F16; Folder Martin, Hope & Thornely, 3 Feb. 1807–14 Apr. 1808, B233.F5 and Folder Martin, Hope & Thornely 30 Apr. 1808–20 Nov. 1811, B233.F6; Folder Morall & Borland 22 Apr. 1807–16 May 1812, B240.F9. Brown & Ives did not appear to respond to Conway & Davidson's request to start a correspondence.

via Cádiz, Spain, by which route Brown & Ives sent 600 casks of flaxseed and twenty-two bales of cotton on the *Charlotte*.[208] The use of such routes in an attempt to circumvent the embargoes was quite common. Hughes & Duncan calculated that eighty-six vessels had arrived in Liverpool between 6 and 23 June, of which fifty-six had arrived direct and presumably legally under the Erskine Treaty, whilst thirty others had arrived from 'Amelia Island [Canada], Madeira, Fayal [Portuguese Azores], Lisbon & by Nonintercourse breakers direct.'[209] Another common strategy was for vessels to have pretended to have 'been blown off the coast' in a barely-veiled attempt to disguise embargo breaking.[210] Indeed, in 1811, Brown & Ives' vessel the *Hazard* 'sprung a leak' and entered Liverpool, where conveniently, Hughes & Duncan sold the cargo on their behalf.[211] Merchants had a tradition of ignoring state regulations, but usually this occurred on the periphery rather than at the metropole.[212] This was a new level of flouting regulations.

On 25 June 1812, Hughes & Duncan wrote to Brown & Ives to inform them that those 'obnoxious acts', the Orders in Council, had been revoked on 16 June and that 'we do most heartily congratulate you on the auspicious opening it presents of an early termination of the differences between this country and the United States, and of the restoration of our usual commercial intercourse'.[213] Clearly the two firms wanted to resume business as normal.

---

208 Brown & Ives to Hughes & Duncan, 11 May 1810, 18 May 1810; Hughes & Duncan to Brown & Ives, 23 Jun. 1810, Folder Hughes & Duncan 24 Dec. 1809–27 Dec. 1810, B289.F7, BFBR. On trading conditions in Cádiz, see Lamikiz, *Trade and Trust*, chapter three.

209 These vessels carried cotton, wheat, flour, tobacco, flaxseed, beeswax and bark for example. Hughes & Duncan to Brown & Ives, 23 Jun. 1810, Folder Hughes & Duncan 24 Dec. 1809–27 Dec. 1810, B289.F7. Hughes & Duncan noted that it was legal to reship at Lisbon for 4 per cent duty ad valorem. Hughes & Duncan to Brown & Ives, 1 Dec. 1809, Folder Hughes & Duncan, 31 Oct. 1809–23 Dec. 1809, B289.F6, BFBR.

210 Quoted in Checkland, 'American Versus West Indian Traders', p. 155. Martin, Hope & Thornely mentioned in passing that a number of embargo breakers had lowered the price of the article. Martin, Hope & Thornely to Brown & Ives, 28 Jul. 1809, Folder Martin, Hope & Thornely 1807–1811, B233.F6, BFBR.

211 Hughes & Duncan to Brown & Ives, 7 Jun. 1811, Folder Hughes & Duncan 11 May 1811–2 Nov. 1811, B290.F1. Brown & Ives had previously had a vessel wrecked off the Liverpool coast, the *Robert Hale* in 1810. Hedges, *The Browns of Providence*, Vol. II, *The Nineteenth Century*, pp. 129–30.

212 See for example, Schnurmann, 'Atlantic Trade and American Identities'; Hatfield, 'Dutch and New Netherland Merchants'; Banks, 'Official Duplicity'.

213 British Foreign Minister Lord Castlereagh announced that the Orders in Council authorizing the seizures were suspended on 16 Jun. 1812, Silverstone, *Divided Union*, p. 71; Hughes & Duncan to Brown & Ives, 25 Jun. 1812, Folder Hughes & Duncan 12 Nov. 1811–29 Aug. 1812, B290.F2, BFBR.

However, the British were too late as war had been declared on Britain by the United States on 19 June 1812 (a clear case where lack of information made a crisis worse). Despite the failure in institutional and general trust, Hughes & Duncan continued to write to Brown & Ives during 1812, keeping them informed about the war on the continent and the prices of various commodities, and in December 1812 sent them payment for the goods they had sold off the *Hazard*.[214] It is a testament to the enduring relations between these two firms, and indeed the trans-Atlantic trading community, that they resumed their normal trade in January 1815 and were still trading together until at least 1824.[215]

The state of course took the position as argued by James Stephen in *War in Disguise*, and in fact ministers supplied materials for its composition and vetted the finished manuscript.[216] However, as demonstrated by the large number of embargo breakers and the continual correspondence between merchants in Liverpool and America, the American trade was too important to be simply brushed aside. The government's stance therefore brought it into conflict with certain sectors of the mercantile and manufacturing communities. The West India merchants supported the mercantilist game the government was playing, and indeed the November 1807 Orders which tightened those already in place were at the instigation of the West India Interest.[217] However, for those merchants trading to the United States, the Orders and Embargoes were devastating. William Rathbone IV led the mostly Quaker and Unitarian Liverpool-American traders in petitioning parliament against the Orders and in giving evidence to the House of Commons in 1808. Others giving evidence from Liverpool included Thomas Martin and James Cropper, but merchants from London, Manchester, Wakefield and Hull also gave evidence against the Orders. Rathbone assessed that for 1807, 'If the trade to Liverpool was divided into sixteenths, I believe it [the American Trade] would be about five sixteenth parts of the whole.'[218] He added that since the town had also been denied the Atlantic slave trade (which he judged at only two-sixteenths), and been effectively denied their trade to the Baltic, the northern and eastern ports of Europe, and Portugal, that only four-sixteenths, or one quarter of

214 Hughes & Duncan to Brown & Ives, 3 Dec. 1812, Folder Hughes & Duncan 5 Oct. 1812–10 Jun. 1814, B290.F3, BFBR.
215 Folder Hughes & Duncan 11 Jun. 1814–26 May 1815, B290.F4; Folder Hughes Duncan & Co. 18 Jun. 1816–3 Jan. 1824, B290.F8, BFBR.
216 Tom Holberg, 'The Acts, Orders in Council, &c. Of Great Britain [on Trade], 1793–1812', http://www.napoleon-series.org/research/government/british/decrees/c_britdecrees1.html, accessed 3 Jun. 2010.
217 Checkland, 'American Versus West Indian Traders', p. 151.
218 Evidence of William Rathbone, Minutes of Evidence (1808), 119, p. 76, HCPP.

their trade remained to them.[219] Rathbone had personally experienced the consequences of this decline in trade. His house had distributed £32,000 in profits in 1807, but only £13,000 in 1808.[220] The financial situation remained problematic. Buchanan & Benn noted the many failures in London, Liverpool and 'provincial manufacturing towns' in 1810, only to fail themselves in 1812.[221] Limited assistance was given by the state and its institutions. In 1810 Hughes & Duncan wrote to Brown & Ives that:

> The Commercial distresses of this Country have seldom been more alarming. In London it is understood that the Bank of England will afford some Accommodation to the Merchants, but as this will of course be confined to those only Who can make out a substantial claim to Confidence [those with good reputations], We expect that the relief which will be derived from it will be of a very limited nature.[222]

The following year they noted that the government itself had stepped in and that 'the issue of 6 millions in Exchequer Bills for the use of the Merchants & Manufacturers are likely we think to check in some degree the depression of the markets'.[223] Reputation was clearly functioning as a form of capital in this situation.[224]

Notwithstanding this support, these difficulties no doubt shaped the tone of those giving evidence to Parliamentary inquiries about the war, which gives an indication of the strained relationships between this sector of the trading community in Britain and the state. Petitions were normally polite and couched in servile tones, but in giving evidence to Parliament the British merchants trading to America were quite clear that they considered the blame for the present predicament lay with the British government.[225] Their interrogators attempted to establish that trade would recommence if

219 Rathbone added that most of the townsmen were happy for reasons of humanity to have lost the slave trade. Evidence of William Rathbone, Minutes of Evidence (1808), 119, p. 103.

220 This was still a substantial amount of money. Checkland, 'American Versus West Indian Traders', p. 154. See also Ryden, West Indian Slavery, p. 277.

221 Buchanan & Benn to Brown & Ives, 23 Aug. 1810; Buchanan & Benn Price Current, 22 Feb. 1812, Folder Buchanan & Benn 20 Oct. 1808–25 Jun. 1812, B53.F16.

222 Hughes & Duncan to Brown & Ives, 30 Jun. 1810, Folder Hughes & Duncan 17 Jul. 1810–26 Dec. 1810, B289.F8, BFBR.

223 Hughes & Duncan to Brown & Ives, 23 Mar. 1811, Folder Hughes & Duncan 27 Dec. 1810–23 Mar. 1811, B289.F9, BFBR.

224 See above, p. 99.

225 See for example, Memorial of the Merchants of Liverpool, 10 Jun. 1777, SP 78/302, f. 332; Petition of Messrs Rathbone Hughes & Duncan, 18 Jul. 1797, Non-colonial series of bundles 1797 (Jul. 1797), PC 1/39/125, TNA.

the American Embargo was lifted, but Rathbone replied rather sarcastically that he was 'of opinion, that the British Naval Force, employed to carry into execution the present Orders in Council, must effectually [sic] prevent all intercourse between America and the Continent' and totally destroy the trade.[226] Given that embargo breakers and circumventors were commonplace by the next year, he rather disingenuously added that there would be no contraband trade. Rathbone also said that he did not have enough knowledge to comment on the extent of trade of the United States to the colonies of France, Holland and Spain.

Thomas Martin was questioned particularly about the timing of the changes in trade following the various 1807 Orders and the December Embargo. Martin reported that news about the Embargo had not reached Liverpool until the 26 January 1808. However, he had visited Birmingham between the 9 and 13 January where every merchant whom he asked replied that they 'would not ship any goods; it was universal … it was perfectly clear to me, that the Orders in Council were the great and principal cause of their not exporting'.[227] He added for good measure that there was also an apprehension of war which could only have derived from the Orders in Council. Almost treacherously, he continued that he did not consider the Americans' Non-Importation Act even an act of hostility but 'solely a system of precaution'.[228]

It was not just the ports that were suffering. Without exports to America and indeed much of Europe, manufacturing was also in steep decline. William Wood of the long-standing Manchester firm Thomas Phillips & Co. also gave evidence. He noted that he had not been paid for his autumn 1806 shipment, which was mainly due to the fact that many of the bills sent in payment had been protested for non-payment, for which he blamed the interruption in trade between the two countries (rather than his correspondents, who after all, had attempted to pay). Moreover he had not made any shipment to the United States in 1808. This meant that he had had to limit the amount of work he could give to his workmen by half, a measure he had brought in during November 1807 – before the American Embargo. He also confirmed that he would not ship goods to the United States should the Embargo be lifted, only if the Orders in Council were removed.[229]

By 1812 the economic situation had worsened considerably and there was general unease throughout Britain. Even the West India traders who had

226 Evidence of William Rathbone, Minutes of Evidence (1808), 119, pp. 77, 79.
227 Evidence of Thomas Martin, Minutes of Evidence (1808), 119, pp. 80–82.
228 Evidence of Thomas Martin, Minutes of Evidence (1808), 119, p. 82.
229 Evidence of William Wood, Minutes of Evidence (1808), 119, pp. 1–4.

supported the Orders were becoming concerned about trading in a time of war.[230] The American merchants therefore felt the time was right for a further attack on the Orders. Another committee to hear evidence was held in 1812 where the merchants and others presented their case once again. This time the government listened and the Orders were revoked, but too late to prevent war with the United States. However, despite the tension between the governments of Britain and the United States, merchants trading between these two places remained on friendly terms. They coped with the declining levels of institutional and general trust by retrenching their networks to those of strong personal trust and changing and developing their shipping patterns (legally and illegally). Continuing to keep each other informed and making prompt payments ensured that obligations were met and personal trust was maintained. This allowed merchants to return to full and complete trading relations as soon as possible after the war. Gladstone might have said arrogantly in early 1812, 'When we have chastised the Americans, when we have humbled them, then we shall grant them peace', but the merchants themselves were far more pragmatic.[231] The run up to the Anglo-American war seems to have created a new level of disharmony between the mercantile community and the state.

CONCLUSION

THERE WERE MANY TYPES of crisis, but eventually, all crises had an economic impact with which merchants around the Atlantic had to deal. Importantly, these had both negative and positive aspects. Obviously the 'cleansing' of business communities was a dubious benefit, and definitely not one for those individuals that suffered because of it. However, the merchant community as a whole was forced to adapt and adjust in order to cope with changing conditions. As a crisis loomed, merchants relied more and more on long-term personal contacts as levels of institutional and general trust declined. Networks were retrenched at these times to those most trusted, reliable and reputable members of the trading community. Clearly, reputational mechanisms and fulfilling obligations were crucial to maintaining personal trust networks at such times.

These crises had wider ramifications however. The American War of Independence had not strained the relationship between merchants in Britain

---

230 Checkland, 'American Versus West Indian Traders', p. 158; Tolley, 'The Liverpool Campaign'.

231 Quoted in Checkland, 'American Versus West Indian Traders', p. 159.

and the West Indies and the British state because obligations had been kept on both sides (notwithstanding the Orders in Council of 1783). However, the abolition debates clearly show that government policy was shifting away from a 'mercantilist' framework, and that the West India Interest was losing influence. Indeed, abolitionist attacks may have 'cemented planter paranoia' about such issues.[232] At the same time, Anglo-American traders were equally uneasy about the ramifications of this shift, as was demonstrated by their reaction to the Orders in Council of 1807. This tension further highlighted the shifting balance of power between the West India Interest and the 'new' interests (including those looking to engross the East India trade) and the state.[233] This is not to say that the relationship with the state had completely broken down; the state still provided convoy protection, and financial support on occasion. However, the changing nature of this relationship and the increasingly complex business environment saw the formalisation of networks through the creation of many institutions. These were established in North America as well as Britain; for example, the Boston Society for Encouraging Trade and Commerce sometime before 1763, New York's Chamber of Commerce in 1768 and Philadelphia's in 1801.[234] However, the growth was even more marked in Britain: including the Liverpool Chamber of Commerce (1774), the Glasgow Chamber of Commerce (1783), the Liverpool West India Association (1799), the Liverpool American Chamber of Commerce (1801), the Glasgow West India Association (1807) and the Liverpool Shipowners' Association (1810). At the same time, the importance of the Anglo-American trade meant that merchants were keen to ensure positive relations with their American correspondents. Their business culture therefore enabled the British merchants to manage the 'renewal of a Commercial Intercourse so intimately connected with the welfare alike of your Country & ours'.[235]

---

232 Ryden, *West Indian Slavery*, p. 132.
233 Checkland, 'American Verses West Indian Traders', p. 159. In Liverpool the American and West India traders managed to work together for a short while at least, despite the tensions, and led the national campaign against renewal of the East India Company charter in 1813. In fact the early East India Association had many West India traders in it. Yukihisa Kumagai, 'The Lobbying Activities of Provincial Mercantile and Manufacturing Interests against the Renewal of the East India Company's Charter, 1812–1813 and 1829–1833' (unpublished Ph. D. thesis: University of Glasgow, 2008), pp. 158–60.
234 Newell, *From Dependency to Independence*, p. 270; The Philadelphia Chamber of Commerce was set up in 1801 '*for the purpose of aiding the Trade of the city of Philadelphia, by carrying into effect, such Rules and Regulations as may … be established with respect to our Commerce*' [emphasis in original], Articles of Association, Philadelphia Chamber of Commerce Minutes, 1801.
235 Martin, Hope & Thornely to Brown & Ives, 14 Apr. 1808, Folder Martin, Hope &

Conclusion:
A British Business Culture

As Commerce is what renders every Country rich and consequently
powerful; so the Merchant in this View, may be said to be the
most useful Member of the Society in which he lives.[1]

W HATEVER THE ORIGINAL MOTIVATIONS behind British expansion
and colonialism in the Atlantic, there is no doubt that the character
of this empire was 'commercial'.[2] Furthermore, during the eighteenth century
the 'cult of commerce became an increasingly important part of being British',
enhancing the role and reputation of merchants as a group.[3] If we think in
terms of informal maritime empire, one based on the economy rather than
sovereignty or dominion, there is no doubt that the British Empire was the
most successful at this point in time.[4] Even after Independence the United
States continued to be Britain's largest single trading partner. This success
was largely due to a business culture which facilitated trade despite long-term
structural changes and short-term crises. As Malachy Postlethwayt opined
in the quote above, commerce had made Britain rich and powerful, and its
merchants had facilitated this. Using socio-economic theory has provided
a nuanced understanding of how these merchants conceived of, and dealt
with, their complex and interdependent commercial relationships. Moreover,
applying that theory to the business records and actions of those men has
shown how those attitudes shaped the reality of their everyday decisions

---

Thornely 3 Feb. 1807–14 Apr. 1808, B233.F5.

1 Postlethwayt, *Great Britain's True System*, Letter I, 'Of Raising the Supplies, by
Encreasing the Public Debts, Considered', pp. 20–24, p. 22.

2 Armitage, *The Ideological Origins*, p. 8.

3 Colley, *Britons*, p. 67.

4 Armitage, *The Ideological Origins*, p. 102.

and experiences. This is important because it highlights their sophisticated understanding and management of their businesses. There is no doubt that these merchants wanted to make as much money as possible, but they were not pure 'economic men'. This is not to say that they were not rational, but neither were they atomized individuals; they had to work in the world around them.[5] As Granovetter would argue, this approach lets us thread through over- and under- socialized interpretations of economic relations.[6]

Risk, trust, reputation, obligation and networks were the 'institutional elements' of this successful business culture. Of course all these elements were interdependent. It was not possible to take risks without some level of trust; some aspects of trust were reliant on a good reputation; which was in turn dependent on fulfilling obligations. All these elements were both dependent on, and played out in, the networks of which these men were all a part. Importantly, these merchants were nuanced in their conception, and management of, these issues. Moral, natural and technical hazards were approached and managed differently. Personal was the most important level of trust, but merchants were acutely aware when assurance structures were in doubt thereby causing problems, and often contracted their networks when confidence was low. Personal reputations were carefully constructed and protected, and contemporaries were only too aware of how easily these could be lost. Gatekeepers such as town councils, chambers of commerce and trade associations were therefore one way in which to both bolster and confer reputations. Conforming to business etiquette and prompt payment were well known to be obligations that helped protect that reputation, but gift-giving in a variety of forms was also important and one way in which emotional bonds were cemented. Moreover, both creditors and debtors were aware of the obligations very successful merchants were under to the wider community. This all worked within a context in which a variety of networks were in action at any one given time, and merchants were conscious of the importance of their friends and associates. Mostly therefore, merchants were extremely active in increasing and developing their contacts over time as they pursued their business. Moreover, most of them were able to adapt their networks to cope with changing market conditions. All together these elements formed a business culture which was a successful private-order institution that facilitated trade in a difficult environment. This is clear from the way in which individual merchants, and indeed, communities of merchants, responded to crises. Merchants were nearly always able to return to trade at short notice, to work together to defend their trading interests,

---

5 Coleman, 'Social Capital in the Creation of Human Capital', p. 118.
6 Granovetter, 'Economic Action and Social Structure', p. 481.

to subvert laws and regulations at various opportunities, and to trust one another over vast geo-political spaces, whatever the inclinations of their government. There were rules to follow, and obligations to fulfill, but on the whole, there was a tough but forgiving mentality, which worked in the long term.[7]

The British state played an important role in this business culture. It mostly kept its obligations and therefore its reputation intact with the mercantile community at home and abroad. It paid back its loans, unlike the French monarchy, had a system of taxation which promoted re-exports on the whole, and was not overly interventionist, like the Spanish. The British state provided convoys, compensated for losses during war, and negotiated treaties that promoted commerce in addition to other 'imperial' ambitions. This all served to provide assurance and to promote confidence in the state and the general system of trade. This meant that despite all the short-term crises in this period, there was a sense of stability in the long term. However, the relationship between the British state and merchants in the former colonies, in Britain, and in the British West Indies, did change over this period, particularly towards the end. The American War of Independence, which of course broke bonds with merchants in the former colonies, perversely caused very few problems in assurance structures between merchants in Britain and the British West Indies, and the state. This was because although the British lost the war, the state upheld its implicit bargain with the merchants throughout that conflict, and indeed in the period following. In contrast, abolition of the British slave trade marked the impending end of the old colonial or mercantilist system. Whilst the slave traders may have felt the economic brunt of this change, it is clear that other British merchants trading in the Atlantic world soon realised the long-term implications and ramifications of this shift in policy. The old mercantile-state obligations could no longer be relied upon. This was clear from the response of the 'American' traders during the Anglo-American conflict. In siding with the Americans, merchants such as William Rathbone IV were ensuring that personal and indeed communal trust remained in place between merchants across the Atlantic, in a context where the institutional and social framework at home was changing. Abolition of the British Atlantic slave trade not only broke these former obligations between the merchant community and the state, the fact that enslaved persons were no longer considered a culturally-acceptable cargo highlighted a new identity for the British empire (at least in terms of its public façade). It was to become a civilising, Christianizing (Protestant) mission, one that was increasingly looking east towards Asia and

---

7 Casson, 'An Economic Approach to Regional Business Networks', p. 39.

Africa, rather than west, despite the fact that the United States continued to be its largest trading partner throughout the nineteenth century and that mercantilism experienced only a slow death.[8]

The betrayal felt by the West India, African and American merchants as a community mirrors the betrayal felt by individual merchants when obligations were not met. To some extent merchants were playing out a part – their role within a 'rationalised' business practice. The standardised format of petitions, the norms and procedures associated with letter writing, gossip in taverns and letters, all suggest that merchants were explicitly aware of the role they played towards each other, and of the expectations and obligations they were under. There was a sense of performance. Yet even if to some extent these men were acting out a 'mercantile' role, rather than being truly 'moral', it does not really matter. It was the public perception that was important.[9] To quote Axelrod, 'A moral person couldn't do much better.'[10] However, the records and actions of these men leave no doubt that they did internalise their business culture to a large extent and that their actions and beliefs were shaped by the cultural, social, political and legal milieu of the period. As Granovetter notes, 'Actors do not behave or decide as atoms outside a social context, nor do they adhere slavishly to a script written for them.'[11] Even if these merchants were aware of a sense of performance, they still truly enjoyed taking risks together, trusted one another, relished being associated with other reputable merchants, and really felt betrayed when obligations were not met. This made the business culture both emotional, as well as successful.

The fact that merchants were truly punished when they transgressed, and that failure was accompanied by complete financial failure, meant that this business culture worked despite the low-institutional environment of the early-modern Atlantic world. However, this is certainly not a call for a low-institutional environment in today's seemingly amoral business world. There was something different about the business world before limited liability, and when reputation was based on a more complicated reputational nexus than simply financial success. At the same time, certain elements of this business culture were not specific to the British in time or space. For example, Elliott has noted as many similarities as differences between the Spanish and English mercantile communities. Greif has shown that reputa-

---

8 Colley, *Britons*; Bayly, *Imperial Meridian*; Bayly, *The Birth of the Modern World*, pp. 136–36; Peter J. Cain and Anthony G. Hopkins, *British Imperialism: Innovation and Expansion 1688–1914* (London and New York: Longman, 1993), pp. 99–104.

9 Muldrew, *The Economy of Obligation*, p. 156; Granovetter, 'Business Groups and Social Organization', p. 433.

10 Axelrod, *The Evolution of Co-operation*, pp. 136–37.

11 Granovetter, 'Economic Action and Social Structure', p. 487.

tional mechanisms were an important part of the medieval business culture of the Maghrabi. Trivellato has demonstrated that networks of trust and business routines were essential for Jews involved in the Livorno trade in the seventeenth and early eighteenth centuries, and Gaggio has demonstrated the role of social capital in the twentieth-century Italian jewelry industry. So what was special about the early-modern British Atlantic? Why did Spanish œconomists urge their state and merchants to follow the British model of commercial empire?[12]

To some extent being a latecomer was an advantage. The British may have missed out on Aztec gold and Potosí silver, but what initially appeared to be poor pickings – plantation economies based on staple products – turned out to be the biggest money-making empire, with the ability to succeed over the long term. Their relative late arrival also meant that the British could learn from the Portuguese and Spanish experience, which whilst shaping their desire for empire, also shaped responses to interactions with native peoples and the environment in Africa and the Americas. More importantly, the other Atlantic empires, having early dominance, took a different approach in terms of political œconomy. All were in relative decline by the mid-eighteenth century, leaving the British dominant in the Atlantic in 1763.[13] Even if the British merchants *had* worked merely for money, working merely for gold and silver, as did the Spanish and Portuguese, was a far less successful strategy. As early as 1696 contemporaries realised that '*Trade* is a richer and more durable *Mine* than any in *Mexico* or *Peru*' [emphases in original].[14] Therefore, some of the British success can be attributed to timing and the decisions and policies made by other states, as part of a developmental cycle.[15]

However, the British were able to take advantage of this situation and its opportunities in a significant way. Whether this was the result of a coherent strategy or 'mercantilist' policy is debatable, but what is certain is that the British state and its merchants had a particular understanding which promoted long-term economic growth and allowed the mercantile community to deal with, react to, and even benefit from, the difficult economic environment in which they traded.[16] However, whilst the British state encouraged and supported Atlantic mercantile expansion, even if only to keep up with its competitors, it was the enterprise and tenacity of the merchants that were the real drivers behind British success. These merchants

---

12 Lamikiz, *Trade and Trust*, p. 14.

13 These arguments were set out more fully above, pp. 10–17.

14 C. K. quoted in Armitage, *The Ideological Origins*, p. 159.

15 Bayly, *The Birth of the Modern World*, p. 12.

16 Heckscher, 'Mercantilism'; Coleman, *Revisions in Mercantilism*; Coleman, 'Mercantilism Revisited'.

were not necessarily truly moral, kind, or generous men; their adherence to a 'do to others as you would have done to yourself' philosophy was conditioned both by their social mores and an eye to the shadow of the long-term future.[17] At the same time, the fact that their business culture was socially embedded also meant that much of this culture was truly internalized, making their business culture emotive as well as successful. This meant that they were able to regulate themselves to a large extent within the context of a relatively low-institutional environment. Such norms produce stability in themselves.[18] The business culture of merchants around the British Atlantic therefore provided a robust private-order institution in which merchants never worked 'merely for money'.

---

17 Axelrod, *The Evolution of Co-operation*, pp. 136–37.
18 Platteau, 'The Role of Public and Private Order Institutions', p. 541.

Bibliography

PRIMARY SOURCES

Britain

London

British Library
Liverpool Papers
Add.38310, Letterbooks of Charles Jenkinson.
Add.38226, Official Correspondence.
Add.38416, Papers Relating to the Slave Trade, 1787–1823.

Lambeth Palace
Fulham Papers
Vol. XVII(i), Jamaica 1661–1739.
Vol. XVIII(ii), Jamaica 1740–?.

National Maritime Museum
REC/19, Documents Relating to the Slave Ship Zong.

Public Record Office at The National Archives
Board of Trade Papers
BT6/9, Copies of certain of the evidence submitted to the Committee of Council
    for Trade and Plantations in the course of their enquiry into the State of the
    African Slave Trade, I and II.
BT6/75, West Indies.
BT6/83, America and West Indies: Commercial Intercourse.

Chancery Papers
C13/132/35, The Complaint of Joseph Rainford ..., 21 Feb. 1810.
C15/19, Lowe v Cohen.

C108/212, John Leigh Letterbook, 1803–5.
C108/213, Letterbook of John Leigh & Co. 1808–9.

Colonial Office Papers
CO37/44, Bermuda: Original Correspondence.
CO101/24, Grenada: Original Correspondence.

Exchequer Papers
E134/6Geo3/East4, Christie & Christie v Robinson.

High Court of Admiralty Papers
HCA26/5, Letters of Marque or Reprisals Against France from the 27 May 1756–16 Sep 1756.

Privy Council Papers
PC1/39/125, Petition of Messrs Rathbone Hughes & Duncan, 18 Jul. 1797, Non-colonial series of bundles 1797 (Jul. 1797).

State Papers Foreign
SP78/302, Memorial of the Merchants of Liverpool, 10 Jun. 1777.

Treasury
T1/447/349–51, Memorial of the Merchants of Leverpoole trading to Africa desirs to have liberty to import from any parts of Europe East India Goods Rifles & Brandy for the African Trade, 16 Mar. 1765.
T70/1549, Company of Royal Adventurers of England Trading to Africa and Successors, Parts I and II.

Regional

Barclays Bank Archives
0199–0060(2), Arthur Heywood Papers, Articles of Partnership, 26 Aug. 1776.

Cambridge University Library
VANNECK-ARC/1 Arcedeckne Papers, Correspondence of WI Agents.

Derbyshire Record Office
D157 M/3371 & M/3372, Insurance and Disbursement Book for the Molly.
D157 M/T 3375, John Stanton Private Account Book.

Liverpool Record Office
352/MD1, Committee Book of the African Company of Merchants trading from Liverpool, 1750–1820.
352 MIN/COU I 2/8, East India Trade Committee Minute Book 1812–1833.
367 SEF, Mock Corporation of Sephton.

380 AME(1), Minutes of the Liverpool American Chamber of Commerce, 1808–1908.
380 MD 33, Case and Southworth Journal 1754–1757.
380 MD 34, Case and Southworth Journal 1757–1761.
380 MD 35, Case and Southworth Jamaica Sales.
380 MD 36, Case and Southworth Sales Ledger 1763–1767.
380 MD 47, Herculaneum Potteries Minute Book 1806–1822.
380 MD 48, Herculaneum Pottery Ledgers 1806–1817.
380 MD 52, Log of the Madampookata and Count de Nord and Agamemnon.
380 MD 59, Thomas Leyland Letterbook 1786–1788.
380 MD 127, John Tomlinson's Account Current with John Knight.
380 MD 129, The Memorial of the Merchants, Ship owners, Sugar Refiners and Tradesmen of Liverpool Whose Names are Hereunto Subscribed, 1799.
380 TUO, David Tuohy Papers.
380 WES/1, West India Association, Miscellaneous Minute Books.
387 MD 54, Robert Bostock Letterbook 1779–1790.
920 CHA, Papers of Edward Chaffers.
920 PAR, Parker Papers.
920 ROS, Roscoe Papers.
MD 219–1, Sparling & Bolden Letterbook 1788–1799.
MIN COU I, Minutes of the Town Council.

Merseyside Maritime Museum Archives
D/CR, Cropper Family Collection.
D/DAV, William Davenport Papers
D/EARLE, Earle Collection.

Sydney Jones Library, University of Liverpool
RP II 1.169, William Rathbone IV Letterbook.

In private hands
Curtis Brett Autobiography, 1775.
Curtis Brett Letterbook 1762–1776.

Wales

National Library of Wales
11484, Nathaniel Phillips Letterbook 1775-?
11485, Mailhet & Phillips Letterbook 1759-?.

Scotland

Mitchell Library, Glasgow
TD 1670/1, Chamber of Commerce and Manufacturers in the City of Glasgow, Vol. I, 1783–88.
(Rare Books) Glasgow West India Association Minutes 1807–1969.

National Archives of Scotland, Edinburgh
CS96/502, 503, 507, Buchanan & Simson Papers.
CS96/619. McKnight & McIlwrath Letterbook.
CS96/1176–1203, Semple, Jamieson, Lawson Papers.

National Library of Scotland, Edinburgh
5476, Chisholme Papers, Letterbook.

United States

American Philosophical Society
917.3.N41, Pim Nevins, Journal of a Visit to America, 1802–3, 9th Month, 11th, 13th, 14th 1802 and 12th Month, 4th, 1802.
973.2 M31, Manuscripts Relating to Non-Importation Resolutions, 1766–1775.
B/P43.1, John Perhouse Journal 1800–1838.

Baker Library, Harvard University
Andrew Clow & Co., Letters Received.

Hagley Museum and Library, Wilmington
1720, Andrew Clow Papers.

Historical Society of Pennsylvania
1542/36B-C/Vol 6, Bank of North America Personal Ledgers.
1957, Willing, Morris & Co. Correspondence, Robert Morris Collection, Levis Collection.
Am 911, Daniel Clark Letter and Invoice Book 1759–1763.
Am 91121, Mifflin and Massey Ledger 1760–1763.
Am 125, William Pollard Letterbook 1772–74.
Andrew Clow & Co., Claude W. Unger Collection.
Andrew Clow & Co., Simon Gratz Collection.
Cadwalader Bond Papers.
Coll 50, #12, William and John Sitgreaves Letterbook 1783–1794, Thomas A. Biddle Business Books.

John Carter Brown Library, Brown University
Brown Family Business Records.

Library Company of Philadelphia
Am 1777 Liv Log 2252.0.11, An Abstract of the Proceedings and Resolutions of the Several Committees of the Chamber of Commerce for the Port of Liverpool, From the First Establishment on the 24th June 1774 to the 24th June 1777.
Am 1801 Phi Cha 50396.0.12, Articles of Association and Rules of the Philadelphia Chamber of Commerce, 1801.

Memorial of the Members of the Chamber of Commerce of Philadelphia relative to the Bank of the United States, 1810.

Phi Cha LCP (old Hsp) Wf* 301.VI, Representation of the Philadelphia Chamber of Commerce, 1804.

Rare Am 1802, Uni St a Press (b.w.) (2) 4077.0.27, Memorial of the Philadelphia Chamber of Commerce, 1803.

Massachusetts Historical Society
MS.N–657, Daniel Parker Papers.

MS.N–681, Thomas M. Peck Letterbook, 1763–1776.

MS.N–979 and N–980, Anne Appleton Storrow Papers.

MS.N–1656, Nathaniel and Francis Thayer Letterbook 1783–1790.

Pennsylvania Historical Museum and Commission, Harrisburg
RG33–55 (14–4600) W 1789–1805, Exors of Andrew Clow v William Wilson, 21 Mar. 1797, and Clow and Co., v Wignall & Reinangle, 18 Mar. 1799.

Widener Library
Jamaica Deeds, Articles of Agreement … Between John Bicknill … and George Nicholson, 20 May 1750.

Winterthur Museum, Garden and Library
Misc Letters 361, Samuel Barber to George Plumstead, 14 Jul. 1801.

Jamaica

Jamaica National Archives
2/6/4–5, Kingston Vestry Minutes 1765–1770.

National Library of Jamaica
MST 22A, Alexander Johnston Letterbook 1780–1783.

University of West Indies Archives, Mona
Reel 509 (Microfilm), Charles Angus Letterbook 1799–1851.

Spain

Archivo General de Indias, Seville
Carta 12, Cuba 1051.N86, Roger Hope Elletson to Gobenador de Cuba, 10 Dec. 1766, Correspondencia de los Capitanes Generales de Cuba.

Canada

National Library and Archives Canada
MG–54-No 74, Rainford, Blundell & Rainford Pocket Ledger.

Edited Editions

Ellis, Markman, ed., *Tea and the Tea Table in Eighteenth-Century England* (London: Pickering and Chatto, 2010), 4 vols, Vol. IV: Ben Dew, ed., *Tea and Politics: The Boston Tea Party (1773) and the Commutation Act (1784)*.

Fyfe, Christopher, ed., *Anna Maria Falconbridge, Narrative of Two Voyages to the River Sierra Leone with Alexander Falconbridge, An Account of the Slave Trade in Africa* (Liverpool: Liverpool University Press, 2000).

Lambert, Shiela, ed., House of Commons Sessional Papers of the Eighteenth Century (Wilmington, Delaware: Scholarly Resources, 1975), Vols. 68, 72.

Morgan, Kenneth, ed., *An American Quaker in the British Isles: The Travel Journals of Jabez Maud Fisher, 1775–1779* (Oxford: Oxford University Press, 1992).

Morgan, Kenneth, ed., *The Bright-Meyler Papers: A Bristol West India Connection, 1732–1837* (Oxford: Oxford University Press for the British Academy, 2007).

Mouser, ed., Bruce L., *A Slaving Voyage to Africa and Jamaica: The Log of the Sandown, 1793–1794* (Bloomington and Indianapolis: Indiana University Press, 2002).

Price, Jacob M., ed., *Joshua Johnson's Letterbook, 1771–1774: Letters from a Merchant in London to his Partners in Maryland* (London Record Society, 15, 1979).

Rogers, George C. Jr., ed., *The Papers of Henry Laurens*, Vols. IV, V, VI, VII (Columbia, SC: Published for the South Carolina Historical Society by the University of South Carolina Press, 1974).

Trade Directories

Biddle, Clement, ed., *The Philadelphia Directory for 1791* (Philadelphia: Printed for James and Johnson, 1791).

Gore, John, ed., *Liverpool Trade Directory* for 1766 (Liverpool: Printed by W. Nevitt and Co. for J. Gore, Bookseller near the Exchange, 1766).

Gore, John, ed., *Liverpool Trade Directory* for 1774 (Liverpool: Printed for John Gore, 1774).

Gore, John, ed., *Liverpool Trade Directory* for 1796 (Liverpool, 1796).

White, G. Francis, ed., *The Philadelphia Trade Directory for 1785* (Philadelphia: Printed by Young, Stewart and McCullock, 1785).

Newspapers

Billinge's Liverpool Advertiser and Marine Intelligencer (Liverpool, 21 Nov. 1796; 24 Nov. 1806).

Pennsylvania Packet and Daily Advertiser (19 Oct. 1787)

South Carolina Gazette (Charleston: 17 Dec. 1763).

The Royal Gazette (Kingston, Jamaica: 8 Jul. 1780; 5 Aug. 1780; 30 Sep. 1780; 2 Dec. 1780; 27 Jan. 1781; 8 Nov. 1783).

The Times (London: 4 Apr. 1789; 10 Dec. 1796; 10 Oct. 1798; 14 Aug. 1800; 5 Sep. 1801; 27 Jan. 1807; 1 Sep. 1807; 14 Oct. 1807; 8 Feb. 1813).

Printed Primary

Acts of Assembly, Passed in the Island of Jamaica, From the Year 1681 to the Year 1769 Inclusive: In Two Volumes (Kingston, Jamaica: Printed by Alexander Aikman, 1787).

A Letter from a Merchant in London to His Nephew in North America ... (Printed for J. Walter, Charing Cross, London, 1766).

The American Kalendar; or, United States Register, for New Hampshire, Vermont, Massachusetts, Rhode Island, Connecticut, New York, New Jersey, Pennsylvania, Delaware, Maryland, Virginia, Kentucky, North Carolina, South Carolina, Georgia, and Tennessee, for the year 1798. To be continued annually, And will be carefully corrected to the Time of Publication (London: Printed for J. Debrett, 1798).

Anon, *A Short View of the Dispute Between the Merchants of London, Bristol and Leverpool, and the Associates of a New Joint Stock Company, Concerning the Regulation of the African Trade* (London: Printed in the Year 1750).

Anon [Robert Norris], *A Short Account of The African Slave Trade* (Liverpool: Printed at Ann Smith's Navigation Shop, Pool Lane, 1788).

Anon, *West African Account*, n.d. British Library.

Baillie, George, *Interesting Letters Addressed to John Bolton Esqr, Merchant, and Colonel of a Regiment of Volunteers* (London: Printed and Published by J. Gold, 1809).

Boydell, James, *The Merchant Freighter's and Captains of Ships Assistant – Being Tables Calculated with the Greatest Accuracy* (Three King Court, Lombard Street, London, 1764).

Campbell, Robert, *The London Tradesman*, 3rd edn (London: Printed by T. Gardner, 1757).

Chalmers, George, *An Estimate of the Comparative Strength of Britain ...* (London: Printed for C. Dilly in the Poultry and J. Bowen in New Bond Street, 1782).

Chambers, Ephraim, *Cyclopædia: Or, Universal Dictionary of the Arts and Sciences. With A Supplement and Modern Improvements Incorporated in one Alphabet* (London: Printed for J. F. and C. Rivington, A. Hamilton, T. Payne and Son, W. Owen, B. White and Son (and 24 others in London), 1786–88).

Common Sense: In Nine Conferences, between a British Merchant and a Candid Merchant of America, in their Private Capacities as Friends, Tracing the Several Causes of the Present Contests Between the Mother Country and her American Subjects, etc. (London: 1775).

Barry Cowan, 'Publicity and Privacy in the History of the British Coffeehouse', *History Compass*, 5:4 (2007), 1180–1213, http://www3.interscience.wiley.com/journal/118491914/abstract?CRETRY=1&SRETRY=0, accessed Feb. 2010.

Cunningham, Timothy, *The Merchant's Lawyer: Or, the Law of Trade in General ... To Which is Added a Complete Book of Rates*, Vol. II, 2nd edn (London, 1768).

Defoe, Daniel, *The Complete English Tradesman* [1726] (Gloucester: Alan Sutton, 1987).

Fisher, G., *The American Instructor; or, Young Man's Best Companion* (Philadelphia: Benjamin Franklin and D. Hall, 1748).

Franklin, Benjamin *The Way to be Wise and Wealthy: Recommended to All; Applied, more particularly, and accommodated to the several Conditions and Circumstances of the Gentleman. The Scholar, the Soldier, the Tradesman, the Sailor, the Artificer, the Husbandman*, by a Merchant, 4th edn (London: Printed for L. Davis and C. Reymers, 1760).

Gordon, William, *The Universal Accountant and Complete Merchant. In Two Volumes.* (Edinburgh: Printed for the Author, and A. Donaldson, and sold by Donaldson at Edinburgh & Strand, London, 1763).

James, Stephen, *War in Disguise; or, the Frauds of the Neutral Flags* (London: Printed by C. Whittingham, Dean Street, and sold by J. Hatchard, Piccadilly, 1805).

Journals of the Assembly of Jamaica (Jamaica: Parliament Assembly to 1811–29), Vols. 7, 8.

The Liverpool Memorandum Book or, Gentleman's, Merchant's & Tradesmen's Daily Pocket Journal, For the Year 1753 (Liverpool: Printed by R. Williamson and sold by C. Hitch and L. Hawes, London, 1752).

Memorial of the Merchants and Traders of Philadelphia, 15 Jan. 1806 (Washington, 1806).

Montefiore, Joshua, *The Trader's and Manufacturer's Compendium; Containing the Laws, Customs, and Regulations, Relative to Trade; Intended for the use of Wholesale and Retail Dealers*, 2 vols, Vol. I (London: Printed for the author, 1804).

Moreton, J. B., *West India Customs and Manners: Containing Strictures on the Soil, Cultivation, Produce, Trade, Officers and Inhabitants* ... (London: Printed for J. Parsons, Paternaster Row; W. Richardson, Royal Exchange; H. Gardner, Strand; and J. Walter, Piccadilly, 1793).

Morris, Gouverneur, *An Answer to War In Disguise; Or, Remarks upon the New Doctrine of England, Concerning Neutral Trade* (New York: Printed for Hopkins and Seymour, 1806).

Petition of Sundry Merchants of Philadelphia Praying Exemption from the Provisions in the Non-Intercourse Law, 11 Dec. 1810 (Washington City: Printed by R. C. Weightman, 1810).

Postlethwayt, Malachy, *Britain's Commercial Interest Explained and Improved* [1757] (New York: August M. Kelly, 1968).

Postlethwayt, Malachy, *Great Britain's True System* [1757] (New York: August M. Kelly, 1968).

Rathbone, William, *A Narrative of Events That Have Lately Taken Place in Ireland Among the Society Called Quakers, With Corresponding Documents and Occasional Observations* (Liverpool: Printed by M'Creery, 1804).

Rose, George, *A Brief Examination into the Increase of the Revenue, Commerce, and Manufactures, of Great Britain, from 1792 to 1799*, 4th edn (London: Printed for J. Wright, No. 169 Piccadilly; J. Hatchard, No. 173 Piccadilly; and J. Sewell, Cornhill, 1799).

Sheridan, Thomas, *A General Dictionary of the English Language* [1780] (Menston: Scolar Press Limited, 1967).

Smith, Adam, *The Theory of Moral Sentiments* [1759], ed. Knud Haakonssen (Cambridge: Cambridge University Press, 2002).

Smith, Adam, *An Inquiry in the Nature of the Wealth of Nations* [1776] (Oxford: Oxford University Press, 1998).

Smith, Adam, 'Lecture on the Influence of Commerce on Manners' [1766] reproduced in Daniel B. Klein, ed., *Reputation: Studies in the Voluntary Elicitation of Good Conduct* (Ann Arbor: University of Michigan Press, 1997), pp. 17–20.

Stewart, John J., *An Account of Jamaica, and Its Inhabitants. By a Gentleman Long Resident in the West-Indies* (London: Printed for Longman, Hurst, Rees and Orme, 1808).

Tickler, Timothy, *The Philadelphia Jockey Club; Or, Mercantile Influence Weighed. Consisting of Select Characters Taken from the Club of Addressors* (Printed for the Purchasers, 1795).

The Tradesman: Or, Commercial Magazine (London: Sherwood, Neely & Jones, 1808).

The Tradesman; The Merchant's Guide (Liverpool: Printed by William Nevitt, 1774).

A Treatise Upon The Trade From Great-Britain To Africa; Humbly Recommended To The Attention Of Government, By An African Merchant (London: Printed For E. Baldwin, Paternoster Row, 1772).

Webster, Pelatiah, *A Seventh Essay on Free Trade and Finance* (Philadelphia: Printed by Eleazer Oswald at the Coffee House, 1785).

Whereas a Number of Persons ..., Broadside Advertisement, New York, 12 Jun. 1770.

Other

Eltis et al., eds., *The Trans-Atlantic Slave Trade Database*, http://www.slavevoyages.org/tast/database/search.faces.

House of Commons Parliamentary Papers Online, http://parlipapers.chadwyck.co.uk/marketing/index.jsp.

Pre 1900 Literature

Clarkson, Thomas, *The History of the Progress, and Accomplishment of the Abolition of the African Slave Trade by the British Parliament* (London: Longman and Co., 1808).

Seeley, John Robert, *The Expansion of England: Two Courses of Lectures* (London: MacMillan & Co., 1883).

Wallace, James, *A General and Descriptive History of the Ancient and Present State of Liverpool* (Liverpool: Printed and Sold by R. Phillips, Castle Street, 1795).

Williams, Gomer, *History of the Liverpool Privateers and Letters of Marque with An Account of the Liverpool Slave Trade 1744–1812* [1897] (Liverpool: Liverpool University Press, 2004).

SECONDARY SOURCES

Adger, W. Neil, 'Social Capital, Collective Action and Adaptation to Climate Change', *Economic Geography*, 79:4 (2003), 387–404.

Aitkin, Jonathon, *John Newton: From Disgrace to Amazing Grace* (London and New York: Continuum, 2007).

Allen, Franklin, and Douglas Gale, 'Bubbles and Crises', *Economic Journal*, 110:460 (Jan. 2000), 236–55.

Anderson, Jennifer L., 'Nature's Currency: The Atlantic Mahogany Trade and Commodification of Nature in the Eighteenth Century', *Early American Studies*, 2:1 (Spring 2004), pp. 47–80.

Anstey, Roger, *The Atlantic Slave Trade and British Abolition 1760–1810* (London: Macmillan, 1975).

Arbell, Mordechai, *The Portuguese Jews in Jamaica* (Kingston, Jamaica: Canoe Press, 2000).

Armitage, David, *The Ideological Origins of the British Empire* (Cambridge: Cambridge University Press, 2000).

Armytage, Frances, *The Free Port System in the British West Indies: A Study in Commercial Policy, 1766–1822* (London, New York, Toronto: Longmans, Green and Co., 1953).

Ashworth, William J., *Customs and Excise: Trade, Production and Consumption in England, 1640–1845* (Oxford: Oxford University Press, 2003).

Axelrod, Robert, *The Evolution of Co-operation* [1984] (London: Penguin Books, 1990).

Bailyn, Bernard, *The Ideological Origins of the American Revolution* (Cambridge, MA: The Belknap Press of Harvard University Press, 1967).

Bailyn, Bernard, *Atlantic History: Concepts and Contours* (Cambridge, MA and London: Harvard University Press, 2005).

Baldassarri, Delia, and Mario Diani, 'The Integrative Power of Civic Networks', *American Journal of Sociology*, 113:3 (Nov. 2007), 735–80.

Banks, Kenneth J., 'Official Duplicity: The Illicit Slave Trade of Martinique, 1713–1763', in Peter A. Coclanis, ed., *The Atlantic Economy during the Seventeenth and Eighteenth Centuries: Organization, Operation, Practice, and Personnel* (Columbia, SC: University of South Carolina Press, 2005), pp. 229–51.

Barber, Edwin Atlee, *Anglo American Pottery: Old English China with American Views*, 2nd edn (Philadelphia: Patterson and White, 1901).

Barker, Eirlys M., 'Indian Traders, Charles Town and London's Vital Link to the Interior of North America, 1717–1755', in Jack P. Greene, Rosemary Brana-Shute, and Randy J. Sparks, eds., *Money, Trade, and Power: The Evolution of Colonial South Carolina's Plantation Society* (Columbia, S. C.: University of South Carolina Press, 2001), pp. 141–65.

Barker, Hannah, 'Soul, Purse and Family: Middling and Lower-Class Masculinity in Eighteenth-Century Manchester', *Social History*, 33:1 (Feb. 2008), 12–35.

Barker, T. C., 'Smuggling in the Eighteenth Century: The Evidence of the Scottish Tobacco Trade', *Virginia Magazine of History and Biography*, 62:4 (Oct. 1954), 387–99.

Baucom, Ian, *Specters of the Atlantic: Finance Capital, Slavery and the Philosophy of History* (Durham and London: Duke University Press, 2005).

Baugh, Daniel A., 'Great Britain's "Blue-Water" Policy, 1689–1815', *International History Review*, 10:1 (Feb. 1988), 33–58.

Bayly, Christopher A., *Imperial Meridian: The British Empire and the World, 1780–1830* (Harlow: Longman, 1989).

Bayly, Christopher A., *The Birth of the Modern World, 1780–1914: Global Connections and Comparisons* (Malden, MA: Blackwell Publishing Limited, 2004).

Beck, Ulrich, 'Living in the World Risk Society', *Economy and Society*, 35:3 (Aug. 2006), 329–45.

Beckles, Hilary McD., 'A "riotous and unruly Lot": Irish Indentured Servants and Freemen in the English West Indies, 1644–1713', *William and Mary Quarterly*, 3rd ser., 47 (1990), 503–22.

Beckles, Hilary McD., *Centering Woman: Gender Discourses in Caribbean Slave Society* (Kingston, Jamaica: Ian Randle, 1999).

Behrendt, Stephen D., 'Markets, Transaction Cycles, and Profits: Merchant Decision Making in the British Slave Trade', *William and Mary Quarterly*, 3rd ser., 58:1 (2001), pp. 171–204.

Behrendt, Stephen D., 'Human Capital in the British Slave Trade', in David Richardson, Suzanne Schwarz and Anthony Tibbles, eds., *Liverpool and Transatlantic Slavery* (Liverpool: Liverpool University Press, 2007), pp. 66–98.

Bennett, Robert J., *The Voice of Liverpool Business: The First Chamber of Commerce and Atlantic Economy, 1774–c.1796* (Liverpool: Liverpool Chamber of Commerce, 2010).

Ben-Porath, Yoram, 'The F-Connection: Families, Friends and Firms and the Organization of Exchange', *Population and Development Review*, 6:1 (Mar. 1980), 1–30.

Bernstein, Peter L., *Against the Gods: The Remarkable Story of Risk* (New York: Wiley & Sons, 1996).

Black, Jeremy, *Trade, Empire and British Foreign Policy, 1689–1815* (New York: Routledge, 2007).

Bohnet, Iris, and Steffen Huck, 'Repetition and Reputation: Implications for Trust and Trustworthiness When Institutions Change', *American Economic Review*, 94:2, Papers and Proceedings of the One Hundred Sixteenth Annual Meeting of the American Economic Association (May 2004), 362–66.

Bonacich, Phillip, 'Power and Centrality: A Family of Measures' *American Journal of Sociology*, 92:2 (Mar. 1987), 1170–82.

Boulle, Pierre H., and D. Gillian Thompson, 'France Overseas', in William Doyle, ed., *Old Regime France 1648–1788* (Oxford: Oxford University Press, 2001), pp. 105–38.

Bourdieu, Pierre, 'The Forms of Capital', in Mark Granovetter and Richard Swedberg, eds., *The Sociology of Economic Life*, 2nd edn (Cambridge: Westview Press, 2001), pp. 96–111.

Bowen, Huw V., *War and British Society, 1688–1815* (Cambridge: Cambridge University Press, 1988).

Bowen, Huw V., '"The Pests of Human Society": Stockbrokers, Jobbers and Speculators in Mid-Eighteenth Century Britain', *History*, 78:252 (Feb. 1993), 38–53.

Bowen, Huw V., *Elites, Enterprise and the Making of the British Overseas Empire 1688–1775* (Basingstoke, London and New York: MacMillan Press, 1996).

Bowen, Huw V., *The Business of Empire: The East India Company and Imperial Britain, 1756–1833* (Cambridge: Cambridge University Press, 2006).

Boxer, Charles R., *The Portuguese Seaborne Empire 1415–1825* (London: Hutchinson, 1969).

Braddick, Michael J., *The Nerves of State: Taxation and the Financing of the English State, 1558–1714* (Manchester: Manchester University Press, 1996).

Braddick, Michael J., 'The English Government: War, Trade, and Settlement, 1625–1688', in Nicholas Canny, ed., *The Oxford History of the British Empire: Vol. I, The Origins of Empire* (Oxford and New York: Oxford University Press, 1998), pp. 286–308.

Brazendale, David, ed., *Georgian Liverpool: A Guide to the City in 1797* (Lancaster: Palatine Books, 2007).

Breen, Timothy H., *The Marketplace of Revolution: How Consumer Politics Shaped American Independence* (New York: Oxford University Press, 2004)

Burnard, Trevor, 'A Tangled Cousinry? Associational Networks of the Maryland Elite, 1691–1776', *Journal of Southern History*, 61:1 (Feb. 1995), 17–44.

Burnard, Trevor G., '"The Grant Mart of the Island": The Economic Function of Kingston, Jamaica in the Mid-Eighteenth Century', in Kathleen E. A. Monteith and Glen Richards, eds., *Jamaica in Slavery and Freedom: History, Heritage and Culture* (Mona, Jamaica: University of West India Press, 2002), pp. 225–41.

Burnard, Trevor G., *Mastery, Tyranny, and Desire: Thomas Thistlewood and his Slaves in the Anglo-Jamaican World* (Chapel Hill and London, 2004).

Burt, Ronald D., 'Structural Holes and Good Ideas', *American Journal of Sociology*, 10:2 (2004), 349–99.

Butel, Paul, *The Atlantic*, tr. Iain Hamilton Grant (London and New York: Routledge, 1999).

Caballero, Ricardo J., and Mohamad L. Hammour, 'The Cleansing Effect of Recessions', *American Economic Review*, 85:5 (Dec. 1994), 1350–68.

Cain, Peter J., and Anthony G. Hopkins, *British Imperialism: Innovation and Expansion 1688–1914* (London and New York: Longman, 1993)

Canova, Fabio, 'Were Financial Crises Predictable?', *Journal of Money, Credit and Banking*, 26:1 (Feb. 1994), 102–24.

Carlos, Ann M., and Jamie Brown Kruse, 'The Decline of the Royal African Company: Fringe Firms and the Role of the Charter', *Economic History Review*, new ser., 49:2 (May 1996), 291–313.

Carlos, Ann M., and Frank D. Lewis, 'Marketing in the Land of Hudson Bay: Indian Consumers and the Hudson's Bay Company, 1670–1770', *Enterprise & Society*, 3:2 (Jun. 2002), 285–317.

Carlos, Ann M., Karen Maguire and Larry Neal, '"A Knavish People ...": London Jewry and the Stock Market During the South Sea Bubble', *Business History*, 50:6 (Nov. 2008), 728–48.

Carlos, Ann M., and Larry Neal, 'The Micro-Foundations of the Early London Capital Market: Bank of England Shareholders During and After the South Sea Bubble', *Economic History Review*, new ser., 59:3 (Aug. 2006), 498–538.

Carnevali, Francesca, '"Crooks, Thieves, and Receivers": Transaction Costs in Nineteenth-Century Industrial Birmingham', *Economic History Review*, new ser., 57:3 (Aug. 2004), 533–50.

Carson, James Taylor, 'When Is An Ocean Not An Ocean? Geographies of the Atlantic World', *Southern Quarterly*, 43 (2006), 16–46.

Carson, James Taylor, *Making An Atlantic World: Circles, Paths, and Stories from the Colonial South* (Knoxville, TN: The University of Tennessee Press, 2007).

Carswell, John, *The South Sea Bubble* (London: Alan Sutton, 1960).

Casson, Mark C., *The Entrepreneur: An Economic Theory* (Oxford: Martin Robinson, 1982).

Casson, Mark C., *Entrepreneurship and Business Culture: Studies in the Economics of Trust* (Aldershot: Elgar, 1995).

Casson, Mark C., 'Institutional Economics and Business History: A Way Forward?', *Business History*, Special Issue on Institutions and the Evolution of Modern Business, 39:4 (1997), 151–71.

Casson, Mark C., 'An Economic Approach to Regional Business Networks', in John F. Wilson and Andrew Popp, eds., *Industrial Clusters and Regional Business Networks in England 1750–1970* (Aldershot: Ashgate, 2003), pp. 19–43.

Casson, Mark C., 'Crises and Globalisation: The Consequences of Mistaken Judgements' (Unpublished paper first given at Association of Business Historians conference 2010).

Castree, Noel, *Nature* (London and New York: Routledge, 2005).

Chandler, George, *Four Centuries of Banking* (London: B. T. Basford Ltd, 1964).

Checkland, Sydney G., 'American Versus West Indian Traders in Liverpool, 1793–1815', *Journal of Economic History*, 18:2 (Jun. 1958), 141–60.

Checkland, Sydney G., *The Gladstones: A Family Biography, 1764–1851* (Cambridge: Cambridge University Press, 1971).

Chew, Richard S., 'Certain Victims of an International Contagion: The Panic of 1797 and the Hard Times of the Late 1790s in Baltimore', *Journal of the Early Republic*, 25 (Winter 2005), 565–613.

Clarke, Colin, *Kingston, Jamaica: Urban Development and Social Change, 1692–2002* (Jamaica: Ian Randle Publishers, 2005).

Clarke, Lee, 'Context Dependency and Risk Decision Making', in James F. Short Jr. and Lee Clark, eds., *Organisation, Uncertainties and Risk* (Boulder, San Francisco and London: Westview Press, 1992), pp. 27–38.

Clarke, Lee, and James F. Short, 'Social Organisation and Risk: Some Current Controversies', *Annual Review of Sociology*, 19 (1993), 375–99.

Cleary, Patricia, *Elizabeth Murray: A Woman's Pursuit of Independence* (Amherst: University of Massachusetts Press, 2000).

Cockerell, Hugh Anthony Lewis, *The British Insurance Business 1547–1970: An Introduction and Guide to Historical Records in the UK* (London: Heinemann Educational Books Ltd, 1976).

Coclanis, Peter A., 'Atlantic World or Atlantic/World?', *William and Mary Quarterly*, 3rd ser., 63:4 (Oct. 2006), 725–42.

Cohen, Paul, 'Was there an Amerindian Atlantic? Reflections on the Limits of a Historiographical Concept', *History of European Ideas*, 34 (2008), 388–410.

Cohen, Richard L., and Richard A. Jensen, 'The Determinants of Slave Mortality Rates on the Middle Passage', *Explorations in Economic History*, 19 (1982), pp. 269–82.

Coleman, D. C., ed., *Revisions in Mercantilism* (London: Methuen, 1969).

Coleman, D. C., 'Mercantilism Revisited', *Historical Journal*, 23:4 (1980), 773–91.

Coleman, James, 'Social Capital in the Creation of Human Capital', *American Journal of Sociology*, 94, Supplement: Organization and Institutions: Sociological and Economic Approaches to the Analysis of Social Structure (1988), 95–120.

Coleman, Peter J., *Debtors and Creditors in America: Insolvency, Imprisonment for Debt, and Bankruptcy, 1607–1900* (Madison: State Historical Society of Wisconsin, 1974).

Colley, Linda, *Britons: Forging the Nation 1707–1837* (New Haven and London: Yale University Press, 1992).

Conway, Stephen, 'From Fellow Nationalists to Foreigners: British Perceptions of the Americans, circa 1739–1893', *William and Mary Quarterly*, 3rd ser., 59:1 (2002), 65–100.

Coupland, Reginald, *William Wilberforce: A Narrative* (Oxford: Clarendon Press, 1923).

Cowen, David J., 'The First Bank of the United States and the Securities Market Crash of 1792', *Journal of Economic History*, 60:4 (Dec. 2000), 1041–60.

Craig, R., and R. Jarvis, *Liverpool Registry of Merchant Ships* (Manchester: Printed for the Chetham Society, 1967).

Crimmin, Patricia, 'The Royal Navy and the Levant Trade c. 1795–c.1805', in Jeremy Black and Philip Woodfine, eds., *The British Royal Navy and the Use of Naval Power in the Eighteenth Century* (Leicester: Leicester University Press, 1988), pp. 221–36.

Crothers, Glenn A., 'Commercial Risk and Capital Formation in Early America: Virginia Merchants and the Rise of American Marine Insurance, 1750–1815', *Business History Review* (Winter 2004), 607–33.

Crumplin, Tim E., 'Opaque Networks: Business and Community in the Isle of Man, 1840–1900', *Business History*, 49:6 (Nov. 2007), 780–801.

Cullen, L. M., 'History, Economic Crises and Revolution: Understanding Eighteenth-Century France', *Economic History Review*, new ser., 45:4 (Nov. 1993), 635–57.

Curti, Merle, 'The Reputation of America Overseas (1776–1860)', *American Quarterly*, 1:1 (Spring 1959), 58–82.

Curtin, Philip D., *Cross-Cultural Trade in World History* (Cambridge: Cambridge University Press, 1984).

Daniels, G. W., 'American Cotton Trade with Liverpool under the Embargo and Non-Intercourse Acts', *American Historical Review*, 21:2 (Jan. 1916), 276–87.

Darr, Asaf, 'Gifting Practices and Interorganizational Relations: Constructing Obligation Networks in the Electronics Sector', *Sociological Forum*, 18:1 (Mar. 2003), 31–51.

Dasgupta, Partha, 'Trust as a Commodity', in Diego Gambetta, ed., *Trust: Making and Breaking Cooperative Relations* (New York and Oxford: Basil Blackwell Ltd, 1988), pp. 49–72.

Davidoff, Leonore, and Catharine Hall, *Family Fortunes: Men and Women of the English Middle Class 1780–1850* (London: Hutchinson, 1987).

Davies, K. G., *The Royal African Company* (London: Longmans, Green and Co., 1957).

Davies, Steve, 'Vertical Integration', in Roger Clarke and Tony McGuinness, eds., *The Economics of the Firm* (New York and London: Basil Blackwell Ltd, 1987), pp. 83–106.

Devine, T. M., 'Glasgow Merchants and the Collapse of the Tobacco Trade 1775–1783', *Scottish Historical Review*, 52 (1973), 50–74.

Devine, T. M., *The Tobacco Lords: A Study of the Tobacco Merchants of Glasgow and their Trading Activities* (Edinburgh: John Donald Publishers, 1975).

Devine, T. M., 'The Golden Age of Tobacco', in T. M. Devine and Gordon Jackson, eds., *Glasgow, Vol. I: Beginnings to 1830* (Manchester and New York: Manchester University Press, 1995).

Dickinson, G., 'Enterprise Risk Management: Its Origins and Conceptual Foundation', *The Geneva Papers on Risk and Insurance*, 26:3 (2001), 360–66.

Dirks, Nicholas B., *The Scandal of Empire: India and the Creation of Imperial Britain* (Cambridge, MA: Harvard University Press, 2006).

Ditz, Toby L., 'Shipwrecked; or, Masculinity Imperiled: Mercantile Representations of Failure and the Gendered Self in Eighteenth-Century Philadelphia', *Journal of American History*, 81:1 (Jun. 1994), 51–80.

Ditz, Toby L., 'Formative Ventures: Eighteenth-Century Commercial Letters and the Articulation of Experience', in Rebecca Earle, ed., *Epistolary Selves: Letters and Letter Writers, 1600–1945* (Aldershot: Ashgate, 2000), pp. 59–78.

Ditz, Toby L., 'Secret Selves, Credible Personas: The Problematics of Trust and Public Display in the Writing of Eighteenth-Century Philadelphia Mer-chants', in Robert Blair St. George, ed., *Possible Pasts: Becoming Colonial in Early America* (Ithaca and London: Cornell University Press, 2000), pp. 219–42.

Doerflinger, Thomas M., *A Vigorous Spirit of Enterprise: Merchants and Economic Development in Revolutionary Philadelphia* (Williamsburg, VA: University of North Carolina Press, 1986).

Doorley, John, and Helio Garcia, *Reputation Management: The Key to Successful Public Relations and Corporate Communication* (New York and London: Routledge, 2007).

Doyle, William, ed., *Old Regime France, 1648–1788* (Oxford: Oxford University Press, 2001).

Draper, Nick, 'The City of London and Slavery: Evidence from the First Dock Companies, 1795–1800', *Economic History Review*, 61:2 (2008), 432–66.

Drazen, Allan, and Vittorio Grilli, 'The Benefit of Crises for Economic Reforms', *American Economic Review*, 83:3 (Jun. 1993), 598–607.

Drescher, Seymour, *Econocide: British Slavery in the Age of Abolition* (Pittsburgh: University of Pittsburgh Press, and London: Feffer and Simons, 1977).

Drescher, Seymour, 'People and Parliament', *Journal of Interdisciplinary History*, 20:4 (1990), 561–80.

Dresser, Madge, *Slavery Obscured: The Social History of the Slave Trade in an English Provincial Port* (London and New York: Continuum, 2001).

Duffy, Michael, 'World-Wide War and British Expansion, 1793–1815', in P. J. Marshall, ed., *The Oxford History of the British Empire: Vol. II, The Eighteenth Century* (Oxford: Oxford University Press, 1998), pp. 184–207.

Duguid, Paul, 'Networks and Knowledge: The Beginning and End of the Port Commodity Chain, 1703–1860', *Business History*, 79 (Autumn 2004), 492–526.

Edelson, Max S., 'The Character of Commodities: The Reputations of South Carolina Rice and Indigo in the Atlantic World', in Peter Coclanis, ed., *The Atlantic Economy during the Seventeenth and Eighteenth Centuries: Organization, Operation, Practice, and Personnel* (Columbia, SC: University of South Carolina Press, 2005), pp. 344–60.

Eeckhoudt, Louis, and Harris Schlesinger, 'Putting Risk it Its Proper Place', *American Economic Review*, 96:1 (Mar. 2006), 280–89.

Egnal, Marc, *A Mighty Empire: The Origins of the American Revolution* (Ithaca and London: Cornell University Press, 1988).

Egnal, Marc, and Joseph Ernst, 'An Economic Interpretation of the American Revolution', *William and Mary Quarterly*, 3rd ser., 29:1 (1972), 3–32.

Elliott, J. H., *Empires of the Atlantic World: Britain and Spain in America, 1492–1830* (New Haven, Connecticut and London: Yale University Press, 2006).

Eltis, David, 'The British Trans-Atlantic Slave Trade after 1807', *Maritime History*, 4:1 (Spring 1974), 1–11.

Eltis, David, 'The British Contribution to the Nineteenth-Century Transatlantic Slave Trade', *Economic History Review*, 2nd ser., 32:2 (May 1979), 211–27.

Eltis, David, 'Atlantic History in Global Perspective', *Itinerario*, 23:2 (1999), 141–61.

Eltis, David, 'The Volume and Structure of the Transatlantic Slave Trade: A Reassessment', *William and Mary Quarterly*, 3rd ser., 58:1, New Perspectives on the Transatlantic Slave Trade (Jan. 2001), 17–46, p. 43

Ely, Jeffrey C., and Juuso Välimäki, 'Bad Reputation', *Quarterly Journal of Economics*, 118:3 (Aug. 2003), 785–81.

Emlen, Robert P., 'Nicholas Brown', in John A. Garraty and Mark C. Carnes, eds., *American National Biography* (New York and Oxford: Oxford University Press, 1999).

Engerman, Stanley, 'Mercantilism and Overseas Trade, 1700–1800', in Roderick Floud and D. N. McCloskey, eds., *The Economic History of Britain Since 1700*, Vol. I, *1700–1860*, 2nd edn (Cambridge: Cambridge University Press, 1994), pp. 182–204.

Enthoven, Victor, 'Early Dutch Expansion in the Atlantic Region, 1585–1621', in Johannes Postma and Victor Enthoven, eds., *Riches from Atlantic Commerce: Dutch Transatlantic Trade and Shipping 1585–1817* (Leiden and Boston: Brill Press, 2003), pp. 17–47.

Felix, Joël, 'The Economy', in William Doyle, ed., *Old Regime France, 1648–1788* (Oxford: Oxford University Press, 2001), pp. 7–41.

Finn, Margot, *The Character of Credit: Personal Debt in English Culture, 1740–1914* (Cambridge: Cambridge University Press, 2003).

Finn, Margot, 'Anglo-Indian Lives in the Later Eighteenth and Nineteenth Centuries', *Journal for Eighteenth-Century Studies*, 33:1 (Mar. 2010), 49–65.

Flower, Raymond, and Michael Wynn Jones, *Lloyd's of London: An Illustrated History* (Newton Abbott: David & Charles, 1974).

Fogelman, Aaron Spencer, 'The Transformation of the Atlantic World, 1776–1867', *Atlantic Studies*, 6:1 (Apr. 2009), 5–28.

Foreman, Amanda, *Georgiana, Duchess of Devonshire* (London: Harper Collins, 1998).

Forrestier, Albane, 'Risk, Kinship and Personal Relationships in Late Eighteenth-Century West Indian Trade: The Commercial Networks of Tobin & Pinney', *Business History*, 52:6 (2010), 912–31.

Freeman, Linton C., 'Centrality in Social Networks: Conceptual Clarification', *Social Networks*, 1 (1978–79), 215–39.

Fukuyama, Francis, *Trust: The Social Virtues and the Creation of Prosperity* [1995] (New York: Free Press Paperbacks, 1996).

Fulford, Tim, *Romantic Indians: Native Americans: British Literature, and TransAtlantic Culture, 1756–1830* (Oxford: Oxford University Press, 2006).

Gaggio, Dario, 'Do Social Historians need Social Capital?', *Social History*, 29:4 (Nov. 2004), 499–513.

Gaggio, Dario, 'Pyramids of Trust: Social Embeddedness and Political Culture in Two Italian Gold Jewelry Districts', *Enterprise & Society*, 7:1 (2006), 19–57.

Gaggio, Dario, *In Gold We Trust: Social Capital and Economic Change in the Italian Jewellery Towns* (Princeton and Oxford: Princeton University Press, 2007).

Galassi, Francesco L., and Lucy A. Newton, 'My Word is My Bond: Reputation as Collateral in Nineteenth-Century English Provincial Banking', http://www2.warwick.ac.uk/fac/soc/economics/research/workingpapers/publications/twerp599.pdf, accessed 20 Jan. 2010.

Games, Alison, *Migration and the Origins of the English Atlantic World* (Cambridge, MA and London: Harvard University Press, 1999).

Garber, Peter M., *Famous First Bubbles: The Fundamentals of Early Manias* (Cambridge, MA: MIT Press, 2000).

Genovese, Eugene D., *Roll, Jordan, Roll: The World the Slaves Made* (New York: Vintage Books, 1972).

Gestrich, Andreas, and Margrit Schulte Beerbühl, eds., *Cosmopolitan Networks in Commerce and Society, 1660–1914* (London: Supplement no. 2 of German Historical Institute London Bulletin, 2011).

Gilroy, Paul, *The Black Atlantic: Modernity and Double Consciousness* (Cambridge, MA: Harvard University Press, 1993).

Gould, Elijah H., 'Entangled Histories, Entangled Worlds: The English-Speaking Atlantic as a Spanish Periphery', *American Historical Review*, 112:3 (Jun. 2007), 764–86.

Granovetter, Mark S., 'The Strength of Weak Ties', *American Journal of Sociology*, 78:6 (May 1973), 1360–80.

Granovetter, Mark S., 'Economic Action and Social Structure: The Problem of Embeddedness', *American Journal of Sociology*, 91:3 (Nov. 1985), 481–510.

Granovetter, Mark S., 'Business Groups and Social Organization', in Neil J. Smelser and Richard Swedberg, *The Handbook of Economic Sociology*, 2nd edn (New York and Oxford: Princeton University Press, 2005), pp. 429–50.

Greene, Jack P., 'Society and Economy in the British Caribbean during the Seventeenth and Eighteenth Centuries', *American Historical Review*, 79:5 (1974), 1499–1517.

Greene, Jack P., 'Comparing Early Modern Worlds: Some Reflections on the Promise of a Hemispheric Perspective', *History Compass*, 1 (Aug. 2003), 1–10.

Greene, Jack P., John J. Tepaske, Edward L. Cox, Kenneth R. Maxwell and Anne Perotin-Dumon, 'The Atlantic Empires in the Eighteenth Century', *International History Review*, 6:4 (Nov. 1984), 507–69.

Greer, Allan, and Kenneth Mills, 'A Catholic Atlantic', in Jorge Cañizares-Esguerra and Erik Seeman, eds., *The Atlantic in Global History* (Upper Saddle, NJ and London: Pearson Education, 2006), pp. 3–19.

Greif, Avner, 'Reputation and Coalitions in Medieval Trade: Evidence of the Maghribi Traders', *Journal of Economic History*, 49:4 (Dec. 1989), 857–82.

Greif, Avner, *Institutions and the Path to the Modern Economy: Lessons from Medieval Trade* (Cambridge: Cambridge University Press, 2006).

Griffiths, P. J., *A Licence to Trade: The History of English Chartered Companies* (London: E. Benn, 1974).

Hagan, Maria Jacqueline, 'Social Networks, Gender and Immigrant Incorporation: Resources and Constraints', *American Sociological Review*, 63:1 (Feb. 1998), 55–67.

Haggerty, John, and Sheryllynne Haggerty, 'Visual Analytics of an Eighteenth-Century Business Network', *Enterprise & Society*, 11:1 (Mar. 2010), 1–25.

Haggerty, John, and Sheryllynne Haggerty, 'The Rise and Fall of a Metropolitan Business Network: Liverpool 1750–1810', *Explorations in Economic History*, 48:2 (2011), 189–206.

Haggerty, Sheryllynne, 'Trade and the Trans-Shipment of Knowledge in the Late Eighteenth Century', in Yrjo Kaukiainen, ed., special issue on information, communications and knowledge of *International Journal of Maritime History*, 14:2 (2002), 157–72.

Haggerty, Sheryllynne, *The British-Atlantic Trading Community 1760–1810: Men, Women, and the Distribution of Goods* (Leiden: Brill Press, 2006).

Haggerty, Sheryllynne, 'The Structure of the Philadelphia Trading Community on the Transition from Colony to State', *Business History*, 48:2 (2006), 171–92.

Haggerty, Sheryllynne, 'Liverpool, the Slave Trade and Empire', in Sheryllynne Haggerty, Anthony Webster and Nicholas J. White, eds., *The Empire in One City? Liverpool's Inconvenient Imperial Past* (Manchester: Manchester University Press, 2008), pp. 17–34.

Haggerty, Sheryllynne, 'Risk and Risk Management in the Liverpool Slave Trade', *Business History*, 51:6 (Nov. 2009), 817–34.

Haggerty, Sheryllynne, 'I "could do for the Dickmans": When Networks Don't Work', in Andreas Gestrich and Margrit Schulte Beerbühl, eds., *Cosmopolitan Networks in Commerce and Society, 1660–1914* (London: Supplement no. 2 of German Historical Institute London Bulletin, 2011), pp. 317–42.

Haggerty, Sheryllynne, '"You Promise Well and Perform as Badly": The Failure of the "implicit contract of family" in the Scottish Atlantic', *International Journal of Maritime History*, 23:2 (Dec. 2011), 1–16.

Hamilton, Douglas J., *Scotland, the Caribbean and the Atlantic World, 1750–1820* (Manchester: Manchester University Press, 2005).

Hamilton, Henry, 'The Failure of the Ayr Bank', *Economic History Review*, new ser., 8:3 (1956), 405–17.

Hamilton, Marsha L., *Social and Economic Networks in Early Massachusetts: Atlantic Connections* (Pennsylvania: Pennsylvania University Press, 2009).

Hancock, David, *Citizens of the World: London Merchants and the Integration of the British Atlantic Community, 1735–1785* (Cambridge: Cambridge University Press, 1995).

Hancock, David, 'Self-Organized Complexity and the Emergence of an Atlantic Economy, 1651–1815', in Peter Coclanis, ed., *The Atlantic Economy during the Seventeenth and Eighteenth Centuries: Organization, Operation, Practice, and Personnel* (Columbia, SC: University of South Carolina Press, 2005), pp. 30–71.

Hancock, David, 'The Trouble with Networks: Managing the Scots' Early-Modern Madeira Trade', *Business History Review*, 79, Special Edition on Networks in the Trade in Alcohol (Autumn 2005), 467–91.

Harris, Ron, 'The Bubble Act: Its Passage and its Effects on Business Organization', *Journal of Economic History*, 54:3 (Sep. 1994), 610–27.

Hatfield, April Lee, 'Dutch and New Netherland Merchants in the Seventeenth-Century English Chesapeake', in Peter A. Coclanis, ed., *The Atlantic Economy during the Seventeenth and Eighteenth Centuries: Organization, Operation, Practice, and Personnel* (Columbia, SC: University of South Carolina Press, 2005), pp. 205–28.

Heckscher, Eli F., 'Mercantilism', *Economic History Review*, 7:1 (1936–37), 44–54.

Hedges, James B., *The Browns of Providence Plantation*, 2 vols (Providence: Brown University Press, 1952, 1968).

Heylen, Freddie, and Lorenzo Pozzi, 'Crises and Human Capital Accumulation', *Canadian Journal of Economics*, 40:4 (Nov. 2007), 1261–85.

Higman, B. W., 'The Sugar Revolution', *Economic History Review*, 53:2 (2000), 213–36.

Hilgartner, Stephen 'The Social Construction of Risk Objects; Or; How to Pry Open Networks of Risk', in James F. Short Jr. and Lee Clark, eds., *Organisation, Uncertainties and Risk* (Boulder, San Francisco and London: Westview Press, 1992), pp. 39–56.

Hoppit, Julian, 'Financial Crises in Eighteenth-Century England', *Economic History Review*, new ser., 39:1 (Feb. 1986), 39–58.

Hoppit, Julian, *Risk and Failure in English Business 1700–1800* (Cambridge: Cambridge University Press, 1987).

Hoppit, Julian, 'The Myths of the South Sea Bubble', *Transactions of the Royal Historical Society*, 6th ser., 12 (2002), 141–65.

Hoppit, Julian, 'Compulsion, Compensation and Property Rights in Britain, 1688–1833', *Past and Present*, 210 (Feb. 2011), 93–128.

Horn, James, *A Land as God Made It: Jamestown and the Birth of America* (New York: Basic Books, 2005).

Horn, James, and Philip D. Morgan, 'Settlers and Slaves: European and African Migrations to Early Modern British America', in Elizabeth Mancke and Carole Shammas, eds., *The Creation of the British Atlantic World* (Baltimore and London: Johns Hopkins University Press, 2005), pp. 19–44.

Howman, Brian, 'Abolitionism in Liverpool', in David Richardson, Suzanne Schwarz and Anthony Tibbles, eds., *Liverpool and Transatlantic Slavery* (Liverpool: Liverpool University Press, 2007), pp. 277–96.

Hughes, John, *Liverpool Banks and Bankers 1760–1837* (Liverpool: Henry Young and Sons, 1906).

Humphrey, John, and Hubert Schmitz, *Trust and Economic Development*, Institute of Development Discussion Paper, 355 (Aug. 1996).

Hunt, Margaret, *The Middling Sort: Commerce, Gender, and the Family in England, 1680–1780* (Berkeley, Los Angeles and London: University of California Press, 1996).

Hyde, F. E., B. B. Parkinson, and S. Marriner, 'The Port of Liverpool and the Crisis of 1793', *Economica*, new ser., 18:72 (1951), 363–78.

Hyde, F. E., B. B. Parkinson and S. Marriner, 'The Nature and Profitability of the Liverpool Slave Trade', *Economic History Review*, new ser., 5:3 (1953), 368–77;

Inikori, Joseph, *Africans and the Industrial Revolution in England: A Study in International Trade and Economic Development* (Cambridge: Cambridge University Press, 2002).

Jacob, Margaret C., and Catharine Secretan, eds., *The Self Perception of Early Modern Capitalists* (New York: Palgrave MacMillan, 2008).

Jensen, Michael C., and William H. Meckling, 'Theory of the Firm: Managerial Behaviour and Ownership Structure', *Journal of Financial Economics*, 3 (1976), 305–60.

Johnson, Marion, 'The Atlantic Slave Trade and the Economy of West Africa', in Roger Anstey and Paul E. Hair, eds., *Liverpool, the African Slave Trade, and Abolition* (Liverpool: Historic Society of Lancashire and Cheshire, Occasional Series, Vol. 2, 1976), pp. 14–38.

Jones, J. R., 'Limitations of British Sea Power in the French Wars, 1689–1815', in Jeremy Black and Philip Woodfine, eds., *The British Royal Navy and the Use of Naval Power in the Eighteenth Century* (Leicester: Leicester University Press, 1988), pp. 33–49.

Jones, S. R. H., 'Routines, Capabilities and the Growth of the Firm: Messrs. Ross & Glendinning, Dunedin, 1862–1900', *Australian Economic History Review*, 42:1 (Mar. 2002), 34–53.

Keeney, Ralph L., 'The Role of Values and Risk Management', *Annals of the American Academy of Political and Social Science*, 545, Challenges in Risk Assessment and Risk Management (May 1996), 126–34.

Keith, Alice B., 'Relaxations in the British Restrictions on the American Trade with the British West Indies, 1783–1802', *Journal of Modern History*, 20:1 (1948), 1–18.

Kerridge, Eric, *Trade and Banking in Early-Modern England* (Manchester: Manchester University Press, 1998).

Khodyakov, Dmitry, 'Trust as a Process: A Three Dimensional Approach', *Sociology*, 41:1 (Feb. 2007), 115–32.

Kidd, Colin, *British Identities before Nationalism: Ethnicity and Nationhood in the Atlantic World, 1600–1800* (Cambridge: Cambridge University Press, 1999).

Klein, Herbert S., *The Atlantic Slave Trade* (Cambridge: Cambridge University Press, 1999).

Klein, Herbert S., and Stanley L. Engerman, 'Slave Mortality Rates on British Ships 1791–1797', in Roger Anstey and Paul E. Hair, eds., *Liverpool, the African Slave Trade, and Abolition* (Liverpool: Historic Society of Lancashire and Cheshire, Occasional Series, Vol. 2, 1976), pp. 113–25.

Klein, Herbert S., and Stanley L. Engerman, 'Long-term Trends in African Mortality in the Trans-Atlantic Slave Trade', in David Eltis and David Richardson, *Routes to Slavery: Direction, Ethnicity and Mortality in the Atlantic Slave Trade* (London and Portland, OR: Frank Cass, 1997), pp. 36–48.

Klooster, Wim., 'An Overview of Dutch Trade with the Americas', in Johannes Postma and Victor Enthoven, eds., *Riches from Atlantic Commerce: Dutch Transatlantic Trade and Shipping 1585–1817* (Leiden and Boston: Brill Press, 2003), pp. 365–83.

Klooster, Wim, *Revolutions in the Atlantic World: A Comparative History* (New York: New York University Press, 2009).

Kranton, Rachel E., and Deborah F. Minehart, 'Networks versus Vertical Integration', *Rand Journal of Economics*, 31:3 (2000), 570–601.

Krikler, Jeremy, 'The Zong and the Lord Chief Justice', *History Workshop Journal*, 64:1 (2007), 29–47.

Kumagai, Yukihisa, 'The Lobbying Activities of Provincial Mercantile and Manufacturing Interests against the Renewal of the East India Company's Charter, 1812–1813 and 1829–1833' (unpublished Ph. D. thesis: University of Glasgow, 2008).

Kupperman, Karen Ordahl, 'Errand to the Indies: Puritan Colonization from Providence Island through the Western Design', *William and Mary Quarterly*, 3rd Ser. 45:1 (1988), 70–99.

Kupperman, Karen Ordahl, *Roanoke: The Abandoned Colony*, 2nd edn (Lanham, MD and Plymouth: Rowman & Littlefield Publishers, 2007).

Kuratko, Donald K., and Richard N. Hodgetts, *Entrepreneurship: Theory, Process and Practice* (Mason, Ohio: Thomson/South Western, 2004).

Laird, Pamela Walker, *Pull: Networking and Success since Benjamin Franklin* (Cambridge, MA and London: Harvard University Press, 2006).

Lamb, D. P., 'Volume and Tonnage of the Liverpool Slave Trade 1772–1807', in Roger Anstey and Paul E. Hair, eds., *Liverpool, the African Slave Trade, and Abolition* (Liverpool: Historic Society of Lancashire and Cheshire, Occasional Series, Vol. 2, 1976), pp. 91–112.

Lambert, David, and Alan Lester, 'Imperial Spaces, Imperial Subjects', in David Lambert and Alan Lester, eds., *Colonial Lives Across the British Empire: Imperial Careering in the Long Nineteenth Century* (Cambridge: Cambridge University Press, 2006), pp. 1–31.

Lamikiz, Xabier, *Trade and Trust in the Eighteenth-Century Atlantic: Spanish Merchants and Their Overseas Networks* (Woodbridge, Suffolk and Rochester, New York: Boydell Press for the Royal Historical Society, 2010).

Lamoreaux, Naomi, 'Reframing the Past: Thoughts about Business Leadership and Decision Making under Uncertainty', *Enterprise & Society*, 2:4 (Dec. 2001), 639–59.

Lang, James, *Conquest and Commerce: Spain and England in the Americas* (New York and London: Academic Press, 1975).

Lawler, Edward J., and Yeongkoo Yoon, 'Commitment in Exchange Relations: Test of a Theory of Relational Cohesion', *American Sociological Review*, 61:1 (Feb. 1996), 89–108.

Lemire, Beverly, *The Business of Everyday Life: Gender, Practice and Social Politics in England, c.1600–1900* (Manchester: Manchester University Press, 2005).

Lenman, Bruce P., 'Colonial Wars and Imperial Instability, 1688–1793', in P. J. Marshall, ed., *The Oxford History of the British Empire: Vol. II, The Eighteenth Century* (Oxford: Oxford University Press, 1998), pp. 151–68.

Lipp, Carola, 'Kinship Networks, Local Government, and Elections in a Town in Southwest Germany, 1800–1850', *Journal of Family History*, 30 (2005), 347–65.

Littler, Dawn, 'The Earle Collection: Records of a Liverpool Family of Merchants and Shipowners', *Transactions of the Historical Society of Lancashire and Cheshire*, 146 (1997), 93–106.

Llorca-Jaña, Manuel, 'The Organisation of British Textile Exports to the River Plate and Chile: Merchant Houses in Operation, c. 1810–59', *Business History* 53:6 (2011), pp. 821–65.

Lovejoy, Paul E., and David Richardson, 'Trust, Pawnship and Atlantic History: The Institutional Foundations of the Old Calabar Slave Trade', *American Historical Review*, 104:2 (1999), 333–55.

Lovejoy, Paul E., and David Richardson, '"This Horrid Hole": Royal Authority, Commerce and Credit and Bonny, 1690–1840', *Journal of African History*, 45 (2004), 363–92.

Lovejoy, Paul E., and David Richardson, 'African Agency and the Liverpool Slave Trade', in David Richardson, Suzanne Schwarz and Anthony Tibbles, eds., *Liverpool and Transatlantic Slavery* (Liverpool: Liverpool University Press, 2007), pp. 43–65.

Luhmann, Niklas, 'Familiarity, Confidence and Trust: Problems and Alternatives', in Diego Gambetta, ed., *Trust: Making and Breaking Cooperative Relations* (New York and Oxford: Basil Blackwell Ltd, 1988), pp. 94–107.

Lupton, Deborah, *Risk* (London and New York: Routledge, 1999).

Luskey, Brian P., '"What is My Prospects?": The Contours of Mercantile Apprenticeship, Ambition, and Advancement in the Early American Economy', *Business History Review*, 78 (Winter 2004), 665–702.

Lyng, Stephen, 'Edgework: A Social Psychological Analysis of Voluntary Risk Taking', *American Journal of Sociology*, 95:4 (Jan. 1990), 851–86.

MacKenzie, John, 'The "Second City of Empire": Glasgow – Imperial Municipality', in Felix Driver and David Gilbert, eds., *Imperial Cities* (Oxford: Oxford University Press, 1999), pp. 215–37.

Mancke, Elizabeth, 'Chartered Enterprises and the Evolution of the British Atlantic World', in Elizabeth Mancke and Carole Shammas, eds., *The Creation of the British Atlantic World* (Baltimore and London: Johns Hopkins University Press, 2005), pp. 237–62.

Bruce H. Mann, 'The Transformation of Law and Economy in Early America', in Michael Grossberg and Christopher Tomlins, eds., *The Cambridge History of Law in America, Vol. I, Early America 1580–1815* (Cambridge: Cambridge University Press, 2008), pp. 365–99.

Mapp, Paul W., 'Atlantic History from Imperial, Continental, and Pacific Perspectives', *William and Mary Quarterly*, 63:4 (Oct. 2006), 713–24.

Marshall, Bill, *The French Atlantic: Travels in Culture and History* (Liverpool: Liverpool University Press, 2009).

Marzagalli, Silvia, 'The Failure of a Trans-Atlantic Alliance? Franco-American Trade, 1783–1815', *History of European Ideas*, 34 (2008), 456–64.

Mason, Keith, 'A Loyalist's Journey: James Parker's Response to the Revolutionary Crisis', *The Virginia Magazine of History and Biography*, 102:2 (Apr. 1994), 139–66.

Mathias, Peter, 'Risk, Credit and Kinship in early Modern Enterprise', in John J. McCusker and Kenneth Morgan, eds., *The Early-Modern Atlantic Economy* (Cambridge: Cambridge University Press, 2000), pp. 15–35.

Matson, Cathy, *Merchants and Empire: Trading in Colonial New York* (Baltimore and London: Johns Hopkins University Press, 1998).

Matson, Cathy, 'Introduction: The Ambiguities of Risk in the Early Republic', *Business History Review*, 78 (Winter 2004), 595–606.

Matson, Cathy, 'Accounting for War and Revolution: Philadelphia Merchants and Commercial Risk, 1774–1811', in Margaret C. Jacob and Catharine Secretan, eds., *The Self Perception of Early Modern Capitalists* (New York: Palgrave MacMillan, 2008), pp. 183–202.

Matthews, Gelein, *Caribbean Slave Revolts and the British Abolitionist Movement* (Baton Rouge: Louisiana State Press, 2006).

McCusker, John J., *Money and Exchange in Europe and America, 1600–1775: A Handbook* (London and Basingstoke: MacMillan Press, 1978).

McCusker, John J., 'The Shipowners of British America before 1775', Paper given at the International Symposium on 'The Shipowner in History' at the National Maritime Museum, UK (Sep. 1984).

McCusker, John J., 'Sources of Investment Capital in the Colonial Philadelphia Shipping Industry', in John J. McCusker, *Essays in the Economic History of the Atlantic World* (London and New York: Routledge, 1997), pp. 245–57.

McCusker, John J., 'The Demise of Distance: The Business Press and the Origins of the Information Revolution in the Early Modern Atlantic World', *American Historical Review*, 110:2 (Apr. 2005), 295–321.

McCusker, John J., and Kenneth Morgan, eds., The *Early-Modern Atlantic Economy* (Cambridge: Cambridge University Press, 2000).

McDade, Katie, 'A Particular Spirit of Enterprise': Bristol and Liverpool Slave Trade Merchants as Entrepreneurs in the Eighteenth Century (Unpublished PhD, University of Nottingham, 2011).

McGowan, Alan, *The Ship: The Century before Steam, The Development of the Sailing Ship 1700–1820* (London: Her majesty's Stationery Office for the National Maritime Museum, 1980).

McKendrick, Neil, 'George Packwood and the Commercialization of Shaving: The Art of Eighteenth-Century Advertising or "The Way to Get Money and be Happy"', in Neil McKendrick, John Brewer and J. H. Plumb, *The Birth of a Consumer Society: The Commercialization of Eighteenth-Century England* (Bloomington: Indiana University Press, 1985), pp. 146–94.

Mentz, Søren, 'The Commercial Culture of the Armenian Merchant: Diaspora and Social Behaviour', *Itinerario*, 28:1 (2004), 16–28.

Merriman, John, *A History of Modern Europe: From the Renaissance to the Age of Napoleon*, 2nd edn (New York and London: W. W. Norton and Company, 2004).

Merry, Sally Engle, 'Rethinking Gossip and Scandal', in Daniel B. Klein, ed., *Reputation: Studies in the Voluntary Elicitation of Good Conduct* (Ann Arbor: University of Michigan Press, 1997), pp. 47–74.

Milne, Graeme J., *Trade and Traders in Mid-Victorian Liverpool* (Liverpool: Liverpool University Press, 2000).

Milne, Graeme, J., 'Reputation, Information and Ethics', in W. R. Lee, ed., *Networks of Influence and Power: Business, Culture and Identity in Liverpool's Merchant Community, c.1800–1914* (Aldershot: Ashgate, forthcoming).

Mitchell, B. R., and Phyllis Deane, *Abstract of British Historical Statistics* (London: Cambridge University Press, 1962).

Molm, Linda D., Nobuyuki Takahashi and Gretchen Peterson, 'Risk and Trust in Social Exchange: An Experimental Test of a Classical Proposition', *American Journal of Sociology*, 105:5 (Mar. 2000), 1396–1427.

Moore, Mick, 'How Difficult is it to Construct Market Relations? A Commentary on Platteau', *Journal of Development Studies*, 30:3 (1994), 818–30.

Morgan, Kenneth, *Bristol and the Atlantic Trade in the Eighteenth Century* (Cambridge: Cambridge University Press, 1993).

Morgan, Kenneth, 'Business Networks in the British Export Trade to North America, 1750–1800', in John J. McCusker and Kenneth Morgan, eds., The *Early-Modern Atlantic Economy* (Cambridge: Cambridge University Press, 2000), pp. 36–62.

Morgan, Kenneth, 'Remittance Procedures in the Eighteenth-Century British Slave Trade', *Business History Review*, 79 (Winter 2005), 715–49.

Morgan, Kenneth, 'Liverpool's Dominance in the British Slave Trade, 1740–1807', in David Richardson, Suzanne Schwartz and Anthony Tibbles, eds., *Liverpool and Transatlantic Slavery* (Liverpool: Liverpool University Press, 2007), pp. 14–42.

Mui, Hoh-Cheung, and Lorna H. Mui, 'Smuggling and the British Tea Trade before 1784', *American Historical Review*, 74:1 (Oct. 1968), 44–73.

Muir, Donal E., and Eugene A. Weinstein, 'The Social Debt: An Investigation of Lower-Class and Middle-Class Norms of Social Obligation', *American Sociological Review*, 27:4 (Aug. 1962), 532–59.

Mulcahy, Matthew, '"Melancholy and Fatal Calamities": Disaster and Society in Eighteenth-Century South Carolina', in Jack P. Greene, Rosemary Brana-Shute, and Randy J. Sparks, eds., *Money, Trade, and Power: The Evolution of Colonial South Carolina's Plantation Society* (Columbia, SC: University of South Carolina Press, 2001), pp. 278–98.

Mulcahy, Matthew, 'Weathering the Storms: Hurricanes and Risk in the British Greater Caribbean', *Business History Review*, 78 (Winter 2004), 635–63.

Muldrew, Craig, 'The Culture of Reconciliation: Community and the Settlement of Economic Disputes in Early Modern England', *Historical Journal*, 39:4 (Dec. 1996), 915–42.

Muldrew, Craig, *The Economy of Obligation: The Culture of Credit and Social Relations in Early Modern England* (Basingstoke and New York: Palgrave, 1998).

Mullin, Michael, *Africa in America: Slave Acculturation and Resistance in the American South and the British Caribbean, 1736–1831* (Urbana: University of Illinois Press, 1992).

Munro, Forbes, and Tony Slaven, 'Networks and Markets in Clyde Shipping: The Donaldsons and the Hogarths 1970–1939', *Business History*, 43:2 (Apr. 2001), 19–50.

Murphy, Anne L., *The Origins of English Financial Markets: Investment and Speculation before the South Sea Bubble* (Cambridge: Cambridge University Press, 2009).

Nash, Gary B., *The Urban Crucible, The Northern Seaports and the Origins of the American Revolution*, Abridged edn (Cambridge, MA and London: Harvard University Press, 1986).

Náter, Laura, 'The Spanish Empire and Cuban Tobacco during the Seventeenth and Eighteenth Centuries', in Peter A. Coclanis, ed., *The Atlantic Economy during the Seventeenth and Eighteenth Centuries: Organization, Operation, Practice, and Personnel* (Columbia, SC: University of South Carolina Press, 2005), pp. 252–76.

Neal, F., 'Liverpool Shipping in the Early Nineteenth Century', in J. R. Harris, ed., *Liverpool and Merseyside: Essays in the Economic and Social History of the Port and its Hinterland* (London: Frank Cass & Co. Ltd, 1969), pp. 147–81.

Nenadic, Stana 'The Small Family Firm in Victorian Britain', *Business History*, 35:4 (1993), 86–114.

Newell, Margaret, E., *From Dependency to Independence: Economic Revolution in Colonial New England* (Ithaca and London: Cornell University Press, 1998).

North, Douglass, C., 'Transaction Costs in History', *Journal of European Economic History*, 14:3 (1985), 557–76.

Nottingham, Lucie, *Rathbone Brothers: From Merchant to Banker, 1742–1792* (London: Rathbone Bros PLC, 1992).

O'Brien, Patrick, 'Inseparable Connections: Trade, Economy, Fiscal State, and the Expansion of Empire, 1688–1815', in P. J. Marshall, ed., *The Oxford History of the British Empire: Vol. II, The Eighteenth Century* (Oxford: Oxford University Press, 1998), pp. 53–77.

O'Brien, Patrick, 'The Nature and Historical Evolution of an Exceptional Fiscal State and its Possible Significance for the Precocious Commercialization and Industrialization of the British Economy from Cromwell to Nelson', *Economic History Review*, 64:2 (May 2011), 408–46.

O'Neill, Onora, *A Question of Trust: The BBC Reith Lectures 2002* (Cambridge: Cambridge University Press, 2002).

O'Reilly, William, 'Genealogies of Atlantic History', *Atlantic Studies*, 1:1 (2004), 66–95.

O'Shaughnessy, Andrew J., 'The Formation of a Commercial Lobby: The West India Interest, British Colonial Policy and the American Revolution', *The Historical Journal*, 40:1 (1997) 71–95.

O'Shaughnessy, Andrew J., *An Empire Divided: The American Revolution and the British Caribbean* (Philadelphia: University of Pennsylvania Press, 2000).

Offer, Avner, 'Between the Gift and the Market: The Economy of Regard', *Economic History Review*, new ser., 50:3 (Aug. 1997), 450–76.

Ogborn, Miles, *Indian Ink: Script and Print in the Making of the English East India Company* (Chicago and London: University of Chicago Press, 2007).

Ogborn, Miles, *Global Lives: Britain and the World 1550–1800*, Cambridge Studies in Historical Geography, 41 (Cambridge: Cambridge University Press, 2008).

Ogilvie, Sheilagh. 'Guilds, Efficiency, and Social Capital: Evidence from German Proto-Industry', *Economic History Review*, new ser., 57:2 (May 2004), 286–333.

Oldfield, J. R., *Popular Politics and British Anti-Slavery: The Mobilisation of Public Opinion Against the Slave Trade 1787–1807* (Manchester and New York: Manchester University Press, 1995).

Ormrod, David, *The Rise of Commercial Empires: England and the Netherlands in the Age of Mercantilism, 1657–1770* (Cambridge: Cambridge University Press, 2003).

Ortberg, John C. Jr., Richard L. Gorsuch and Grace J. Kim, 'Changing Attitude and Moral Obligation: Their Independent Effects on Behaviour', *Journal for the Scientific Study of Religion*, 40:3 (2001), 489–96.

Pagden, Anthony, 'The Destruction of Trust and its Economic Consequences in the Case of Eighteenth-Century Naples', in Diego Gambetta, ed., *Trust: Making and Breaking Cooperative Relations* (New York and Oxford: Basil Blackwell Ltd, 1988), pp. 127–41.

Pares, Richard, 'American versus Continental Warfare, 1739–1763', *The English Historical Review*, 31:203 (Jul. 1936); 429–65.

Patterson, Orlando L., 'Slavery, Acculturation and Social Change: The Jamaican Case', *British Journal of Sociology*, 17 (1966), 151–64.

Pearce, Adrian J., *British Trade with Spanish America, 1763–1808* (Liverpool: Liverpool University Press, 2007).

Pearson, Robin, 'Moral Hazard and the Assessment of Insurance Risk in Eighteenth- and Early-Nineteenth-Century Britain', *Business History Review*, 76 (Spring 2002), 1–35.

Philip's World Atlas and Gazeteer, in Association with The Royal Geographical Society with the Institute of British Geographers, *9th edn* (London: George Philip, 2001).

Pietschmann, Horst, 'Introduction: Atlantic History – History between European History and Global History', in Horst Pietschmann, ed., *Atlantic History: History of the Atlantic System 1580–1830* (Göttingen: Vandenhoeck and Ruprecht, 2002), 11–54.

Platt, D. C. M., *Latin America and British Trade 1806–1914* (London: Adam & Charles Black, 1972).

Platteau, Jean-Phillipe, 'Behind the Market Stage Where Real Societies Exist – Part 1: The Role of Public and Private Order Institutions', *Journal of Development Studies*, 30:3 (Apr. 1994), 533–77.

Platteau, Jean-Phillipe, 'Behind the Market Stage Where Real Societies Exist – Part II: The Role of Moral Norms', *Journal of Development Studies*, 30:3 (Apr. 1994), 753–817.

Podolny, Joel M., and Karen L. Page, 'Network Forms of Organization', *Annual Review of Sociology*, 24 (1998), 57–76.

Pope, David, 'The Wealth and Social Aspirations of Liverpool's Slave Merchants of the Second Half of the Eighteenth Century', in David Richardson, Suzanne Schwartz and Anthony Tibbles, eds., *Liverpool and Transatlantic Slavery* (Liverpool: Liverpool University Press, 2007), pp. 164–226.

Popp, Andrew, 'Building the Market: John Shaw of Wolverhampton and Commercial Travelling in Early Nineteenth-Century England', *Business History*, 49:3 (May 2007), 321–47.

Portes, Alejandro, 'Social Capital: Its Origins and Applications in Modern Sociology', *Annual Review of Sociology*, 24 (1998), 1–24.

Portes, Alejandro, 'The Two Meanings of Social Capital', *Sociological Forum*, 15:1 (Mar. 2000), 1–12.

Price, Jacob M., 'The Rise of Glasgow in the Chesapeake Tobacco Trade, 1707–1775', *William and Mary Quarterly*, 3rd ser., 11:2 (Apr. 1954), 179–99.

Price, Jacob M., 'Buchanan & Simson, 1759–1763: A Different Kind of Firm Trading to the Chesapeake', *William and Mary Quarterly*, 41:1 (1983) 3–41.

Price, Jacob M., 'Directions for the Conduct of a Merchant's Counting House, 1766', *Business History*, 28:3 (1986), 134–50.

Price, Jacob M., 'The Imperial Economy, 1776–1776', in P. J. Marshall, ed., *The Oxford History of the British Empire: Vol. II, The Eighteenth Century* (Oxford: Oxford University Press, 1998), pp. 78–104.

Priest, Claire, 'Law and Commerce, 1580–1815', in Michael Grossberg and Christopher Tomlins, eds., *The Cambridge History of Law in America, Vol. I, Early America 1580–1815* (Cambridge: Cambridge University Press, 2008), pp. 400–46.

Priestley, Margaret, *West African Trade and Coast Society: A Family Study* (London: Oxford University Press, 1969).

Prior, Ann, and Maurice Kirby, 'The Society of Friends and the Family Firm', *Business History*, 35:4 (1993), 66–85.

Putnam, Robert, *Bowling Alone: The Collapse and Revival of American Community* (New York and London: Simon and Schuster paperbacks, 2000).

Rabuzzi, Daniel A., 'Eighteenth-Century Commercial Mentalities as Reflected and Projected in Business Handbooks', *Eighteenth Century Studies*, 29:2 (Winter 1995/96), 169–89.

Ragatz, Lowell J., *The Fall of the Planter Class in the British Caribbean, 1763–1833: A Study in Social and Economic History* (New York and London: Century Co., 1928).

Raub, Werner, and Jeroen Weesie, 'Reputation and Efficiency in Social Interactions: An Example of Network Effects', *American Journal of Sociology*, 96:3 (Nov. 1990), 626–54.

Rathbone, Eleanor, A., *William Rathbone: A Memoir* (London: MacMillan, 1908).

Rathbone, William, *A Memoir of the Proceedings of the Society Called Quakers, Belonging to the Monthly Meeting of Hardshaw, in Lancashire* (Liverpool: Printed by M'Creery, 1805).

Rauch, James E., 'Business and Social Networks in International Trade', *Journal of Economic Literature*, 39 (Dec. 2001), 1177–1203.

Rediker, Marcus, *The Slave Ship: A Human History* (London: John Murray, 2007).

Rediker, Marcus, 'History from Below the Waterline: Sharks and the Atlantic Slave Trade', *Atlantic Studies*, 5:2 (Aug. 2008), 285–97.

Renzulli, Linda A., Howard Aldrich and James Moody, 'Family Matters: Gender, Networks, and Entrepreneurial Outcomes', *Social Forces*, 79:2 (Dec. 2000), 523–46.

Richardson, David, 'Profits in the Liverpool Slave Trade: the Accounts of William Davenport, 1757–1784', in R. Anstey and P. E. Hair, eds., *Liverpool, the African Slave Trade, and Abolition* (Liverpool: Historic Society of Lancashire and Cheshire, Occasional Series, Vol. 2, 1976), pp. 60–90.

Richardson, David, 'West African Consumption Patterns and Their Influence on the Eighteenth-Century English Slave Trade', in Henry A. Gemery and Jan S. Hogendorn, eds., *The Uncommon Market: Essays in the Economic History of the Atlantic Slave Trade* (New York and London: Academic Press, 1979), pp. 303–30.

Richardson, David, 'Slavery and Bristol's "Golden Age"', *Slavery and Abolition*, 26:1 (2005), 35–54.

Rommelse, Gijs, 'The Role of Mercantilism in Anglo-Dutch Political Relations, 1650–74', *Economic History Review*, new ser., 63:3 (Aug. 2010), 591–611.

Rose, Mary B., 'The Family Firm in British Business, 1780–1914', in Maurice W. Kirby and Mary B. Rose, eds., *Business Enterprise in Modern Britain from the Eighteenth to the Twentieth Century* (London, 1994), pp. 61–87.

Rosenband, L. N., 'Social Capital in the Early Industrial Revolution', *Journal of Interdisciplinary History*, 29:3 (1999) 435–57.

Rupprecht, Anita, 'Excessive Memories: Slavery, Insurance and Resistance', *History Workshop Journal*, 64:1 (2007), 6–28.

Ruymbeke, Bertrand Van, 'The Huguenots of Proprietory South Carolina', in Jack P. Greene, Rosemary Brana-Shute, and Randy J. Sparks, eds., *Money, Trade, and Power: The Evolution of Colonial South Carolina's Plantation Society* (Columbia, SC: University of South Carolina Press, 2001), pp. 26–48.

Ryden, David Beck, *West Indian Slavery and British Abolition, 1783–1807* (Cambridge: Cambridge University Press, 2009).

Rydgren, Jens, 'The Power of the Past: A Contribution to a Cognitive Sociology of Ethnic Conflict', *Sociological Theory*, 25:3 (Sep. 2007), 225–44.

Safley, Thomas Max, 'Business Failure and Civil Scandal in Early Modern Europe', *Business History Review*, 83:1 (Spring 2009), 35–60.

Sainsbury, John, 'The Pro-Americans of London, 1769–1782', *William and Mary Quarterly*, 3rd ser., 35:3 (Jul. 1978), 423–54.

Sako, Mari, *Prices, Quality and Trust: Inter-Firm Relations in Britain and Japan* (Cambridge: Cambridge University Press, 1992).

Salmon, Marylynn, *Women and the Law of Property in Early America* (Chapel Hill: University of North Carolina Press, 1986).

Sanderson, F. E., 'The Liverpool Delegates and Sir William Dolben's Bill', *Transactions of the Historic Society of Lancashire and Cheshire*, 124 (1972), 57–84.

Sanderson, F. E., 'Liverpool Abolitionists', in Roger Anstey and P. E. H. Hair, eds., *Liverpool, the African Slave Trade, and Abolition* (Liverpool: Historic Society of Lancashire and Cheshire, Occasional Series, Vol. 2, 1976), pp. 196–238.

Sawyers, Larry, 'The Navigation Acts Revisited', *Economic History Review*, new ser., 45:2 (May 1992), 262–84.

Schofield, M. M., 'The Virginia Trade of the Firm of Sparling and Bolden of Liverpool 1788–99', *Transactions of the Historic Society of Lancashire and Cheshire*, 116 (1965), 117–65.

Schumpeter, Joseph A., *The Theory of Economic Development: An Inquiry into Profits, Capital, Credit Interest, and the Business Cycle*, Harvard Economic Studies, Vol. XLVI [1911] (Cambridge, MA: Harvard University Press, 1934).

Schnurmann, Claudia, 'Atlantic Trade and American Identities: The Correlations of Supranational Commerce, Political Opposition, and Colonial Regionalism', in Peter A. Coclanis, ed., The *Atlantic Economy during the Seventeenth and Eighteenth Centuries: Organization, Operation, Practice, and Personnel* (Columbia, SC: University of South Carolina Press, 2005), pp. 186–204.

Seligman, Adam B., 'Trust and Sociability: On the Limits of Confidence and Role Expectations', *American Journal of Economics and Sociology*, 57:4 (Oct. 1998), 391–404.

Shapin, Steven, *A Social History of Truth: Civility and Science in Seventeenth-Century England* (Chicago and London: University of Chicago Press, 1994).

Shapiro, Susan P., 'The Social Control of Impersonal Trust', *American Journal of Sociology*, 93:3 (Nov. 1987), 623–58.

Shearmur, Jeremy, and Daniel B. Klein, 'Good Conduct in the Great Society: Adam Smith and the Role of Reputation', in Daniel B. Klein, ed., *Reputation: Studies in the Voluntary Elicitation of Good Conduct* (Ann Arbor: University of Michigan Press, 1997), pp. 29–46.

Shepherd, James F., and Gary M. Walton, *Shipping, Trade, and the Economic Development of Colonial North America* (London and New York: Cambridge University Press, 1972).

Sheridan, Richard, 'The British Credit Crisis of 1772', *Journal of Economic History*, 20:2 (Jun. 1960), 161–86.

Sheridan, Richard B., *Sugar and Slavery: An Economic History of the British West Indies, 1623–1775* (Kingston, Jamaica: Canoe Press, 1974).

Short, James F., 'Defining, Explaining, and Managing Risk', in James F. Short Jr. and Lee Clark, eds., *Organisation, Uncertainties and Risk* (Boulder, San Francisco and London: Westview Press, 1992), pp. 3–23.

Silverstone, Scott A., *Divided Union: The Politics of War in the Early American Republic* (Ithaca and London: Cornell University Press, 2004).

Simmel, Georg, and Everett C. Hughes, 'The Sociology of Sociability', *American Journal of Sociology*, 55:3 (Nov. 1949), 254–61.

Skaggs, David Curtis, 'John Semple and the Development of the Potomac Valley, 1750–1773', *Virginia Magazine of History of Biography*, 92:3 (Jul. 1984), 282–308.

Skidmore, Mark, and Hideki Toya, 'Do Natural Disasters Promote Long-Run Growth?', *Economic Inquiry*, 40:4 (2002), 664–87.

Smail, John, 'The Culture of Credit in Eighteenth-Century Commerce', *Enterprise & Society*, 4:2 (2003), 299–325.

Smail, John, 'Coming of Age in Trade: Masculinity and Commerce in Eighteenth-Century England', in Margaret C. Jacob and Catharine Secretan, eds., *The Self Perception of Early Modern Capitalists* (New York: Palgrave MacMillan, 2008), pp. 229–52.

Smith, Alan, *The Illustrated Guide to Liverpool Herculaneum Pottery 1796–1840* (London: Barrie and Jenkins, 1970).

Smith, Simon D., *Slavery, Family, and Gentry Capitalism in the British Atlantic: The World of the Lascelles, 1648–1834* (Cambridge: Cambridge University Press, 2006).

Smith-Doerr, Laurel, and Walter W. Powell, 'Networks and Economic Life', in Neil J. Smelser and Richard Swedberg, *The Handbook of Economic Sociology*, 2nd edn (New York and Oxford: Princeton University Press, 2005), pp. 379–402.

Soltow, J. H., 'Scottish Traders in Virginia, 1750–1775', *Economic History Review*, new ser., 12:1 (1959), 83–98.

Stallings, Robert A., 'Media Discourse and the Social Construction of Risk', *Social Problems*, 37:1 (Feb. 1990), 80–95.

Starkey, David J., *British Privateering Enterprise in the Eighteenth Century*, Exeter Maritime Series No. 4 (Exeter: University of Exeter Press, 1990).

Steele, Ian K., *The English Atlantic 1675–1740: An Exploration of Communication and Community* (New York: Oxford University Press, 1986).

Stillson, Richard T., *Spreading the Word: A History of Information in the California Gold Rush* (Lincoln and London: University of Nebraska Press, 2006).

Stone, Lawrence, 'Introduction', in Lawrence Stone, ed., *An Imperial State at War: Britain From 1689–1815* (London and New York, Routledge, 1994), pp. 1–32.

Strong, Norman, and Michael Waterson, 'Principals, Agents and Information', in Roger Clarke and Tony McGuinness, eds., *The Economics of the Firm* (New York and London: Basil Blackwell Ltd., 1987), pp. 18–41.

Sylla, Richard, Robert E. Wright and David J. Cowen, 'Alexander Hamilton, Central Banker: Crisis Management during the U.S. Financial Panic of 1792', *Business History Review*, 83 (Spring 2009), 61–86.

Taylor, C. James, 'Henry Laurens', in John A. Garraty and Mark C. Carnes, eds., *American National Biography* (Oxford: Oxford University Press, 1999).

Temin, Peter, and Hans-Joachim Voth, 'Riding the South Sea Bubble', *American Economic Review*, 94:5 (Dec. 2004), 1654–68.

Thomas, Robert Paul, 'A Quantitative Approach to the Study of the Effects of British Imperial Policy in Colonial Warfare', *Journal of Economic History*, 25 (Dec. 1965), 323–43.

Thompson, Andrew, 'Empire and the State', in Sarah Stockwell, ed., *The British Empire: Themes and Perspectives* (Malden, MA and Oxford: Blackwell Publishing, 2008), pp. 39–61.

Thompson, Kenneth, *Moral Panics* (London and New York: Routledge, 1998).

Thompson, Peter, *Rum Punch and Revolution: Taverngoing and Public Life in Eighteenth-Century Philadelphia* (Philadelphia: University of Pennsylvania Press, 1999).

Thornton, John, *Africa and Africans in the Making of the Atlantic World, 1400–1800* 2nd edn (Cambridge: Cambridge University Press, 1998).

Thye, Shane R., Michael J. Lovaglia and Barry Markovsky, 'Responses to Social Exchange and Social Exclusion in Networks', *Social Forces*, 75:3 (Mar. 1997), 1031–47.

Tibbles, Anthony, 'Oil not Slaves: Liverpool and West Africa after 1807', in Anthony Tibbles, ed., *Transatlantic Slavery: Against Human Dignity* [1995] (Liverpool: Liverpool University Press, 1994), pp. 73–77.

Tierney, Kathleen, J., 'Toward a Critical Sociology of Risk', *Sociologcal Forum*, 14:2 (Jun. 1999), 215–42.

Van Tilberg, Theo, Eric Van Sonderen and Johan Ormel, 'The Measurement of Reciprocity in Ego-Centred Networks of Personal Relationships: A Comparison of Various Indices', *Social Psychology Quarterly*, 54:1 (Mar. 1991), 54–66.

Tilly, Charles, 'Transplanted Networks', in Virginia Yans-McLaughlin, ed., *Immigration Reconsidered: History, Sociology, and Politics* (New York and Oxford: Oxford University Press, 1995), pp. 79–95.

Tolles, Frederick B., *Meeting House and Counting House: The Quaker Merchants of Colonial Philadelphia 1682–1783* [1948] (New York: The Norton Library, 1963).

Tolley, Brian H., 'The American Trade of Liverpool in the Early Nineteenth Century and the War of 1812' (unpublished MA thesis, University of Liverpool: 1967).

Tolley, Brian H., 'The Liverpool Campaign Against the Orders in Council and the War of 1812', in J. R. Harris, ed., *Liverpool and Merseyside: Essays in the Economic and Social History of the Port and its Hinterland* (London: Frank Cass & Co. Ltd, 1969), pp. 98–146.

Trepp, J., 'The Liverpool Movement for Abolition', *Journal of Negro History*, 13 (1928), 265–85.

Trivellato, Francesca, *The Familiarity of Strangers: The Sephardic Diaspora, Livorno, and Cross Cultural Trade in the Early Modern Period* (New Haven and London: Yale University Press, 2009).

Tullock, Gordon, 'Adam Smith and the Prisoners' Dilemma', in Daniel B. Klein, ed., *Reputation: Studies in the Voluntary Elicitation of Good Conduct* (Ann Arbor: University of Michigan Press, 1997), pp. 21–28.

Turgeon, Laurier, 'Codfish, Consumption and Colonization: The Creation of the French Atlantic World during the Sixteenth Century', in Caroline A. Williams, ed., *Bridging the Early Modern Atlantic: People, Products and Practices on the Move* (Aldershot: Ashgate, 2009), pp. 33–56.

Tyler, John W., 'Persistence and Change within the Boston Business Community, 1775–1790', in Conrad Edick Wright and Kathryn P. Viens, eds., *Entrepreneurs: The Boston Business Community, 1700–1850* (Boston: Massachusetts Historical Society, 1997), pp. 97–119.

Uzzi, Brian, 'Embeddedness in the Making of Financial Capital: How Social Relations and Networks Benefit Firms Seeking Financing', *American Sociological Review*, 64:4 (Aug. 1999), 481–505.

Valenze, Deborah, *The Social Life of Money in the English Past* (Cambridge: Cambridge University Press, 2006).

de Vries, Jan, 'The Dutch Atlantic Economies', in Peter A. Coclanis, ed., *The Atlantic Economy during the Seventeenth and Eighteenth Centuries: Organization, Operation, Practice, and Personnel* (Columbia, SC: University of South Carolina Press, 2005), pp. 1–29.

Walsh, Lorena S., 'Liverpool's Slave Trade to the Colonial Chesapeake: Slaving on the Periphery', in David Richardson, Suzanne Schwarz and Anthony Tibbles, eds., *Liverpool and Transatlantic Slavery* (Liverpool: Liverpool University Press, 2007), pp. 98–117.

Walvin, James, *Fruits of Empire: Exotic Produce and British Taste, 1660–1800* (New York: New York University Press, 1997).

Walvin, James, *The Quakers: Money and Morals* (London: John Murray, 1997).

Walvin, James, *The Zong: A Massacre, the Law, & the End of Slavery* (New Haven and London: Yale University Press, 2011).

Warner, Sam Bass, *The Private City* (Philadelphia: University of Pennsylvania Press, 1968).

Wasserman, Stanley, and Katherine Faust, *Social Network Analysis: Methods and Applications* (Cambridge: Cambridge University Press, 1994).

Webster, Anthony, 'The Strategies and Limits of Gentlemanly Capitalism: The London East India Agency Houses, Provincial Commercial Interests, and the Evolution of British Economic Policy in South and South East Asia, 1800–1850', *Economic History Review*, new ser., 59:4 (Nov. 2006), 743–64.

Webster, Anthony, *The Richest East India Merchant: The Life and Business of John Palmer of Calcutta 1767–1836* (Woodbridge: Boydell, 2007).

Webster, Anthony, *The Twilight of the East India Company: The Evolution of*

Anglo-Asian Commerce and Politics, 1790–1860 (Woodbridge, Suffolk: Boydell Press, 2009).

Weinstein, Eugene A., William L. DeVaughan and Mary Glenn Wiley, 'Obligation and the Flow of Deference', *Sociometry*, 32:1 (Mar. 1969), 1–12.

Westerfield, Ray B., *Middlemen in English Business: Particularly Between 1660 and 1760* (New Haven, CT: Yale University Press, 1915).

Whelan, Kevin, 'The Green Atlantic: Radical Reciprocities between Ireland and America in the Long Eighteenth Century', in Kathleen Wilson, ed., *A New Imperial History: Culture, Identity and Modernity in Britain and the Empire, 1660–1840* (Cambridge: Cambridge University Press, 2004), pp. 216–38.

White, Deborah Gray, 'Yes, There is a Black Atlantic', *Itinerario*, 23:2 (1999), 127–40.

Williams, Eric, *Capitalism and Slavery* (Chapel Hill, NC: University of North Carolina Press, 1944).

Williamson, Oliver, E., 'Calculativeness, Trust and Economic Organisation', *Journal of Law and Economics*, 36:2 (1993), 453–86.

Wilson, John F., and John Singleton, 'The Manchester Industrial District, 1750–1939: Clustering, Networking and Performance', in John F. Wilson and Andrew Popp, eds., *Industrial Clusters and Regional Business Networks in England 1750–1970* (Aldershot: Ashgate, 2003), pp. 44–67, pp. 44–45.

Wilson, Richard G., *Gentleman Merchants: The Merchant Community in Leeds 1700–1830* (Manchester: Manchester University Press, 1971).

Wood, Gordon S., *The Radicalism of the American Revolution* (New York: A. A. Knopf, 1991).

Wood, Gordon S., *The American Revolution: A History* (London: Weidenfeld & Nicholson, 2003).

Woolcock, Michael, 'The Place of Social Capital in Understanding Social and Economic Outcomes', in John F. Helliwell, ed., *The Contribution of Human and Social Capital to Sustained Economic Growth and Well-Being: International Symposium Report* (Canada: OECD and Human Resources Development, 2001), pp. 65–88.

Wright, Robert E., 'Bank Ownership and Lending Patterns in New York and Pennsylvania, 1782–1831', *Business History Review*, 73:1 (Spring 1999), 40–60.

Wright, Robert E., *The First Wall Street, Chesnut Street, Philadelphia, and the Birth of American Finance* (Chicago and London: University of Chicago Press, 2005).

Zahediah, Nuala, 'The Merchants of Port Royal, Jamaica, and the Spanish Contraband Trade, 1655–1692', *William and Mary Quarterly*, 43:4 (Oct. 1986), 570–93.

Zahedieh, Nuala, 'Credit, Risk and Reputation in Late-Seventeenth-Century Colonial Trade', *Research in Maritime History*, 15, Merchant Organization and the Maritime Trade in the North Atlantic, 1660–1715, ed. Olaf Janzen (1993), 53–74.

Zahediah, Nuala, *The Capital and the Colonies: London and the Atlantic Economy* (Cambridge: Cambridge University Press, 2010).

Zucker, Lynne G., 'Production of Trust: Institutional Sources of Economic Structure, 1840–1920', *Research in Organizational Behaviour*, 8 (1986), 53–111.

Other

John Cannon, 'Jenkinson, Charles', Oxford Dictionary of National Biography online, accessed 30 Dec. 2010.

University of Greenwich/National Maritime Museum project *Sustaining the Empire: War, the Navy and the Contractor State* at http://www.nmm.ac.uk/researchers/research-areas-and-projects/sustaining-the-empire/, accessed 24 Sep. 2010.

Holberg, Tom, 'The Acts, Orders in Council, &c. Of Great Britain [on Trade], 1793–1812', http://www.napoleon-series.org/research/government/british/decrees/c_britdecrees1.html, accessed 3 Jun. 2010.

General Index

Index of Actors

283

Printed and bound by CPI Group (UK) Ltd, Croydon, CR0 4YY

16/04/2025

14658574-0001